Smart Global Value Chain

Innovation is a critical facilitator in today's fast-changing global value chain landscape. This book describes the interplay of technological breakthroughs enabling efficiency and intelligence within value chains, making them smart and sustainable. From service models and smart technologies to the application of smart global value chains across sectors, this book offers a unique insight into the transformational role of smart global value chains in bringing agility and sustainability to the global value chain ecosystem.

This book is an essential guide for academics, industry leaders, and policymakers to navigate the future where smart technologies like artificial intelligence, machine learning, blockchain, Internet of Things, and beyond reshape the global economic landscape.

Smart Global Value Chain

Future Innovations

Edited by
Adarsh Garg
Amrita Jain
Manisha Singh
Fadi Al-Turjman

CRC Press
Taylor & Francis Group
Boca Raton London New York

CRC Press is an imprint of the
Taylor & Francis Group, an **informa** business

First edition published 2025
by CRC Press
2385 NW Executive Center Drive, Suite 320, Boca Raton FL 33431

and by CRC Press
4 Park Square, Milton Park, Abingdon, Oxon, OX14 4RN

CRC Press is an imprint of Taylor & Francis Group, LLC

Library of Congress Cataloging-in-Publication Data
Names: Garg, Adarsh, author. | Jain, Amrita, author. | Singh, Manisha, author. | Al-Turjman, Fadi, author.
Title: Smart global value chain : future innovations / edited by Adarsh Garg, Amrita Jain, Manisha Singh, and Fadi Al-Turjman.
Description: First edition. | Boca Raton, FL : CRC Press, 2025. | Includes index.
Identifiers: LCCN 2024004714 (print) | LCCN 2024004715 (ebook) | ISBN 9781032609928 (hardback) | ISBN 9781032609935 (paperback) | ISBN 9781003461432 (ebook)
Subjects: LCSH: International business enterprises--Management. | Comparative management. | Economic geography. | Business logistics.
Classification: LCC HD62.4 .G36 2024 (print) | LCC HD62.4 (ebook) | DDC 658/.049--dc23/eng/20240326
LC record available at https://lccn.loc.gov/2024004714
LC ebook record available at https://lccn.loc.gov/2024004715

ISBN: 978-1-032-60992-8 (hbk)
ISBN: 978-1-032-60993-5 (pbk)
ISBN: 978-1-003-46143-2 (ebk)

DOI: 10.1201/9781003461432

Typeset in Sabon
by SPi Technologies India Pvt Ltd (Straive)

"If you really look closely, most overnight successes took a long time."

– *Steve Jobs*

Contents

About the Editors

Adarsh Garg

An acknowledged researcher and academician, Dr Adarsh Garg has 24 years of teaching, research, consultancy, and administrative experience. She received her PhD degree in information technology from GGSIP University, Delhi. She is currently working as Professor of Data Analytics and IT at GL Bajaj Institute of Management and Research (GLBIMR), Gautam Buddh Nagar, Greater Noida, and as a Visiting Professor at Delhi Technical University, Delhi. Prior to joining GLBIMR, she worked with organizations like Galgotias University, WIPRO Tech, GE, IMT Ghaziabad, and Punjabi University, Patiala. She is currently supervising eight PhDs. She has published over 70 research papers in refereed international/national journals and conference proceedings, 7 case studies, and 5 edited books, *Information Systems Development: A Software Engineering Approach*, *Environment Sustainability: A True Value of IT*, *Global Health Disaster: Predicting the Unpredictable with Emerging Technologies* (AAP, CRC, USA), *Reinventing Technological Innovations with Artificial Intelligence* (Bentham Books), *Advances in Technological Innovations in Higher Education: Theory and Practices* (CRC, Taylor & Francis). She is a member of various professional bodies, such as the Computer Society of India and ACM Computer Science Teacher's Association. She is also a member of various national and international academic and administrative committees. She is on the editorial board and is a reviewer of articles for various journals of repute. Her areas of interest include business analytics, data mining, business intelligence, Python, RapidMiner, PowerBI, MIS, e-learning, and project management.

Amrita Jain

Amrita Jain has teaching experience spanning over 11 years. She is working at GL Bajaj Institute of Management and Research, PGDM Institute, and has contributed to prestigious organizations like Galgotias University. Her academic endeavours demonstrate her dedication to lifelong learning. She has qualified University Grants Commission-National Eligibility Test for Junior Research Fellowship. Her sincere passion is to give students practical knowledge in areas like data analytics, advanced Excel, and Power BI, all of which are essential in today's business environment.

Manisha Singh

Manisha Singh is an Associate Professor at G L Bajaj Institute of Management and Research, Greater Noida, India, with over 13 years of experience teaching management students at premier Institutes in Delhi NCR. She holds a doctorate in economics from the University of Allahabad, Prayagraj, India, with specialization in development economics and related policy frameworks.

Fadi Al-Turjman

Fadi Al-Turjman received his PhD in computer science from Queen's University, Canada, in 2011. He is the associate dean for research and the founding director of the International Research Center for AI and IoT at Near East University, Nicosia, Cyprus. Prof Al-Turjman is the head of the Artificial Intelligence Engineering Department and a leading authority in the areas of smart/intelligent Internet of Things (IoT) systems, wireless, and mobile networks' architectures, protocols, deployments, and performance evaluation in Artificial Intelligence of Things (AIoT). His publication history spans over 500 SCI/E Science Citation Index Expanded publications, in addition to numerous keynotes and plenary talks at flagship venues. He has authored and edited more than 60 books about cognition, security, and wireless sensor network deployments in smart IoT environments, which have been published by well-reputed publishers such as Taylor and Francis, Elsevier, IET, and Springer. He has received several recognitions and best paper awards at top international conferences. He also received the prestigious Best Research Paper Award from Elsevier's *Computer Communications Journal* for the period 2015–2018, in addition to the Top Researcher Award for 2018 at Antalya Bilim University, Turkey, and the Lifetime Golden Award of Dr Suat Gunsel from Near East University, Cyprus, in 2022. Prof Al-Turjman has led a number of international symposiums and workshops in flagship communication society conferences. Currently, he serves as book series editor and the lead guest/associate editor for several top-tier journals, including the *IEEE Communications Surveys and Tutorials* (IF 23.9) and the Elsevier's *Sustainable Cities and Society* (IF 10.8), in addition to organizing international conferences and symposiums on the most up to date research topics in AI and IoT.

Contributors

Poorvi Agrawal
Galgotias University, Greater Noida, India

Chadi Altrjman
Department of Chemical Engineering, Waterloo University, ON, N2L 3G1, Canada

Fadi Al-Turjman
Artificial Intelligence, Software, and Information Systems Engineering Departments, AI and Robotics Institute, Near East University, Nicosia, Mersin 10, Turkey
Research Center for AI and IoT, Faculty of Engineering, University of Kyrenia, Kyrenia, Mersin 10, Turkey

Sinem Alturjman
Artificial Intelligence, Software, and Information Systems Engineering Departments, AI and Robotics Institute, Near East University, Nicosia, Mersin 10, Turkey
Research Center for AI and IoT, Faculty of Engineering, University of Kyrenia, Kyrenia, Mersin 10, Turkey

Hannah Amarachi Uchendu
University of Nigeria, Nsukka, Nigeria

Neerja Aswale
Assistant Professor Vishwakarma University, Pune, India

Balamurugan Balusamy
Associate Dean, Student Engagement, Shiv Nadar University, Greater Noida, India

Rachita Kapoor Bhasin
Assistant Professor, Asian Business School, Noida

Upesh Bhatnagar
Assistant Professor, Asian Business School, Noida

Madala Guru Brahmam
Associate Professor, School of Computer Science Engineering and Information Systems, Vellore Institute of Technology, Vellore, India

Mahima Dogra
Assistant Professor, School of Management, NIET, Greater Noida

Abhijit Ganguly
Programme Head, DBA Programme, Westford University College Sharjah, UAE

Veer P. Gangwar
Lovely Professional University, Jalandhar, India

Adarsh Garg
Professor, GL Bajaj Institute of Management and Research Greater Noida, India

Parul Garg
Assistant Professor, GL Bajaj Institute of Technology and Management, Greater Noida, India

Ankit Goel
Associate Professor (Finance), Maharaja Agrasen Institute of Management Studies, New Delhi

Veena Grover
Professor, School of Management., Noida Institute of Engineering and Technology, Greater Noida, India

Amrita Jain
Assistant Professor, GL Bajaj Institute of Management and Research Greater Noida, India

Sabiha Kılıç
Faculty of Economics and Administrative Sciences, Department of Business Administration, Hitit University, Turkey

Manjeet Kumar
Assistant Professor, GL Bajaj Institute of Technology and Management, Greater Noida, India

Ashish Manuel
Vishwakarma University, Pune, India

Kavita Mathad
GIBS Business School, Bengaluru, India

Sankar Mukherjee
GIBS Business School, Bengaluru, India

Manju Nandal
Assistant Professor, School of Management, NIET, Greater Noida

Ambrose Nnaemeka Omeje
Department of Economics, Faculty of the Social Sciences, University of Nigeria, Nsukka

Sumit Rastogi
Assistant Professor, Asian Business School, Noida

Ravinder Rena
DUT Business School, Faculty of Management Sciences, Durban University of Technology, Republic of South Africa

Channi Sachdeva
Lovely Professional University, Jalandhar, India

Divya Sahu
Assistant Professor, School of Management, NIET, Greater Noida

Ramiz Salama
Department of Computer Engineering, AI and Robotics Institute, Research Center for AI and IoT, Near East University Nicosia, Mersin 10, Turkey

Partha Sen
GIBS Business School, India

Priyanshi Sharma
Assistant Professor, Asian Business School, Noida

Tanushree Shrivastav
Assistant Professor, Asian Business School, Noida

Manisha Singh
Associate Professor, GL Bajaj Institute of Management and Research, Greater Noida, India

Vijay Anand Rajasekaran
Associate Professor, School of Computer Science Engineering & Information Systems, Vellore Institute of Technology, Vellore, India

Abbreviations

4IR	Fourth Industrial Revolution
ACC	Associate of Corporate Counsel
AGV	Automated Guided Vehicles
AI	Artificial Intelligence
AML	Anti-Money Laundering
API	Application Programming Interfaces
AR	Augmented Reality
AWS	Amazon Web Services
BC	BlockChain
CI/CD	Continuous Improvement/Continuous Deployment
Cobots	Collaborative Robotics
CRM	Customer Relationship Management
DAOs	Decentralized Autonomous Organization
DApps	Decentralized Applications
DeFI	Decentralized Finance
DEXs	Decentralized Exchanges
DISW	Digital Industries Software
FPGAs	Field Programming Gate Arrays
GCP	Google Cloud Programme
GDP	Gross Domestic Product
GPS	Global Positioning System
GPUs	Graphics Processing Units
GSCM	Global Supply Chain Management
GVC	Global Value Chain
HRM	Human Resource Management
IaaS	Infrastructure as a Service
I:CO	International Circular Solutions Provider for the Collection, Certified Sorting, Reuse, and Recycling of Clothing and Shoes
ICT	Information Communication and Technology
IDE	Integrated Development Environments
IoT	Internet of Things
IT	Information Technology
KYC	Know Your Customer

MCC	Mobile Cloud Computing
NLP	Natural Language Processing
OEE	Overall Equipment Efficiency
OEMs	Original Equipment Manufacturers
PaaS	Platform as a Service
PLI	Production Linked Incentive
R&D	Research and Development
RPA	Robotic Process Automation
SaaS	Software as a Service
SCM	Supply Chain Management
SGVCs	Smart Global Value Chains
TGCS	Total Global Citation Score
UNCTAD	United Nations Conference on Trade and Development
VMs	Virtual Machines
VPNs	Virtual Private Networks
VR	Virtual Reality
WoS	Web of Science

Preface

Global value chain (GVC) is a crucial component of the 21st-century global economy. It demonstrates how international trade and investment build global production networks that connect nations, businesses, and employees. The objective of this book is to explain the integration of technology and artificial intelligence (AI), along with the policy implications for both developed and developing economies. The developing countries becoming efficient at the assembly or manufacturing stage can create more value overall by becoming a provider of these activities that are competitive on a global scale than they can by engaging in higher value-adding activities. The entire value that the economic activities throughout the value chain can produce is what matters most in the end.

The smart global value chain (SGVC) arose as a result of increased market liberalization and international trade deregulation in recent years. Due to the rise of information and communication technologies, GVCs have transformed tremendously. They are providing more value-creating opportunities in the world. The development of digital technologies like the Internet of Things (IoT), blockchain (BC), and AI are particularly pertinent to GVCs. These innovations usher in a new era of connectivity, cooperation, and creativity, providing GVCs with tremendous growth potential.

In the next few years, the linear supply chain is all set to move to an open, digitalized ecosystem. The scope of the smart value chain is substantial, impacting almost all supply chain functions, from inventory planning to demand and supply estimations. Its correct implementation can lead to enhanced efficiency and productivity, resulting in revenue gains for companies. Smart predictive analysis and improved supply chain transparency help in streamlining production. On the customer side, there is a strong trend towards personalization, putting pressure on supply chains to become faster and more responsive. Survival in the global economy would require companies to invest in smart supply chain management sooner or later.

Smart Global Value Chain: Future Innovations is organized, largely, on the comprehensive insights on SGVCs. Various viewpoints of authors, starting from the awareness to evolution of GVC, inclusion of diverse smart technologies as inseparable parts of the value chain, innovations to mitigate the risks and sustainability of GVCs, and inter-related areas have been deliberated. The insights are based on qualitative/quantitative empirical research, and the theoretical analysis is as follows:

Chapter 1 throws light on changing trends in sustainable economy and GVC with technology transfer. It is an effort to identify the technology transmission of GVC from its central theme to increasing and decreasing trends using a complete bibliometric analysis so as to help professionals and researchers for its future implications. The chapter explores 1,740 sources from Scopus and Web of Science databases.

Chapter 2 presents the idea of SGVCs, which are powered by blockchain, IoT, AI, and big data analytics. It looks at how these technologies promote data sharing, simplify international operations, and revolutionize manufacturing. This chapter provides a forward-looking viewpoint on the dynamic interaction between digital technologies and global value chains.

Chapter 3 emphasizes value-creating practices that will provide a competitive advantage in the GVC and differentiate businesses in terms of their sustainability. The reflects innovation as the best way to achieve competitive advantage. It also discusses the concept of MetaChain and its value architecture, which combines Metaverse and Blockchain technology.

Chapter 4 discusses that the fusion of product and information flows accelerates decision-making, promoting dynamic responses to market changes. Alongside these advantages, the increased connectivity presents formidable cybersecurity challenges, necessitating robust protective measures. It emphasises the overall IoT's influence on GVCs represents a paradigm shift.

Chapter 5 examines the mutually beneficial interaction between GVCs and cutting-edge networking technologies, illuminating the substantial effects of connection and digitization on contemporary supply chains. Advanced networking technologies like the IoT, 5G, blockchain, and AI are redefining how firms function inside these chains as GVCs continue to grow and become more complicated.

Chapter 6 talks about a novel blockchain-based security model for IoT smart city networks that are QoS-aware and sustainable. The model has a number of advantages over current approaches, including reduced latency due to improved transaction processing, increased energy efficiency due to spatio-temporal trust level selection to identify energy-efficient nodes, increased throughput enabled by sidechains and lightweight smart contracts, and increased packet delivery ratio due to effective mitigation of various security threats.

Chapter 7 investigates the new service models. The service models suggested are tailored to tackle the distinct obstacles that arise from the interconnectedness of GVCs, MCC platforms, and IoT devices. The grouping of services into layers includes end-user interactions, data processing, and device management. Every layer is designed to meet the unique requirements of the IoT-GVC-MCC ecosystem, guaranteeing effective resource usage, data flow, and communication. The usefulness of the suggested service models is confirmed by a case study.

Chapter 8 explores the impact of AI-powered predictive analytics and optimization algorithms on supply chain resilience, demand forecasting, and risk assessment in GVCs. It stresses how important AI is for eliminating operational hiccups, cutting costs, and raising overall supply chain effectiveness. This chapter also examines how AI-driven insights might boost demand-supply alignment, optimize supply chain logistics, and enhance resource allocation through the use of GVCs.

Chapter 9 takes a comprehensive look at computer network operations (CNOs), recognizing their importance in GVC protection, threat detection, and incident response. Additionally, it explores the moral and legal issues related to CNOs in cyberspace. It highlights the need for a comprehensive strategy to protect digital assets and crucial infrastructure in a world that is becoming more linked and digital.

Chapter 10 looks at how AI-driven solutions make it easier to gather, analyse, and understand medical data, which improves patient care, enables predictive diagnosis, and helps allocate resources more effectively. It is investigated whether using blockchain technology will help secure health-care data throughout the entire GVC.

Chapter 11 intends to give readers a broad review of the relevant material to help them understand GVC research. It does this by focusing on some of the most important topics that have been written about in GVC literature. It tries to figure out how SGVC can change the current GVCs in those sectors to make big changes as information and communication technologies get better. This chapter has the key areas that were used to start the GVC application in sectors like agriculture, manufacturing, health care, and education. It also goes into detail about how the GVC application will help the world economy.

Chapter 12 attempts to highlight the need for manufacturers to adapt and embrace Smart GVCs to remain competitive in the modern era. It highlights the importance of digitalization, data-driven decision-making, and strategic partnerships in achieving success within Smart GVCs. It also emphasizes the significance of government policies and international cooperation in addressing the global challenges posed by this paradigm shift.

Chapter 13 explains how the emerging paradigm of decentralized finance (DeFi) offers a revolutionary alternative as a digital finance avatar. It explores DeFi's trajectory, mapping its potential implications for the future of finance. This involves a meticulous examination of emerging trends like decentralized exchanges, lending platforms, stablecoins, and liquidity mining, which are reshaping our understanding of financial instruments and services. This chapter, therefore, serves as a comprehensive guide to the nascent world of DeFi.

Chapter 14 discovers an electronic audit system that helps SCM to carry out its operations in a much more upgraded manner by using GPS signals to navigate its suppliers and can show a real-time tracking system to the manufactures. Using the past data of any supplier, the system can automatically plan its order execution process with the help of big data analytics.

Chapter 15 evaluates the decentralized banking systems that are currently in use in terms of technology maturity, taking into account factors like scalability, interoperability, and security. The development of DeFi is discussed in light of its potential to lower transaction friction, democratize access to financial services, and lessen counterparty risk.

Chapter 16 examines entrepreneurship development and small medium enterprises (SME) performance in Nigeria utilizing the latest enterprise data sourced from the World Bank for Nigeria. Indicators of product innovation, marketing innovation, process innovation, organizational methods, and distributional methods are used as proxies for entrepreneurship development. It recommends the need for more financial credit to SMEs, review of SMEs' taxation policies, elimination of infrastructural constraints, and the need for SMEs to develop specific strategies.

Chapter 17 investigates the real-time risk mitigation capabilities of AI-driven threat detection, predictive analysis, and automated incident response systems, as well as the importance of AI in preserving the confidentiality and integrity of data. It observes the use of smart contracts for automated compliance, blockchain for supply chain provenance, and safe data sharing across GVC stakeholders. It emphasizes how blockchain technology has the potential to improve traceability and lower fraud in GVCs.

The work given in the book will give some interesting insights into technology enhancements and the transformational potential of AI and blockchain technology in influencing the GVC and opening up new avenues for safe and effective international trade.

Acknowledgements

It is our pleasure to express with a deep sense of gratitude to CRC Press, Taylor & Francis Group, for providing us the opportunity to work on the project of editing this book *Smart Global Value Chain: Future Innovations*. We would like to extend our sense of gratification and contentment to complete this project. We express our thankfulness from the bottom of our hearts to all those who enabled us in both straight and unintended ways to complete the task. First of all, we would like to thank the authors who have contributed their work to this book. We acknowledge, with sincere appreciation, the compassion of various authors at their respective institutions to carry out this work. We take this exclusive opportunity to express our sincere appreciation to Ms. Gabriella Williams, editor, CRC Press, Taylor & Francis Group, for her earnest recommendations and kind patience during this project. We would like to thank our friends, faculty colleagues, and family members for the time they spared in helping us through the project. Special mention should be made of the timely help given by various reviewers during this project, though their names cannot be revealed here. The valuable suggestions they provided to the authors cannot be left unnoticed. We are enormously thankful to the reviewers for their backing during the process of evaluation. While writing, contributors have referenced several books and journals; we take this opportunity to thank all those authors and publishers. We thank the production team of CRC Press for encouraging and extending their full cooperation to complete this book. Last but not least, we are thankful to the almighty for showing us the direction.

– Editors

Chapter 1

Realization of technology transfer in the global value chain and sustainable economy

A bibliometric analysis

Adarsh Garg
GL Bajaj Institute of Management and Research, Greater Noida, India

INTRODUCTION

Although industrialization has elevated the living values of the people, it has significantly damaged the environment with ever-increasing demand and production in recent years, thus being a big challenge to the economy. This has commanded the concept of a sustainable economy, which has the ability to regenerate itself through innovative models for the entire supply chain. It is a fiscal system that tends to curtail the waste produced due to excessive production and overuse of resources (Schmitt et al., 2021), makes the most of the used material until the time it is possible to use it, and converts litter into capital. This includes a total revamp of the linear pattern of production to environmentally sustainable and innovative technology-oriented models to produce reusable and refurbished goods (Hettich & Kreutzer, 2021). The innovative way to manage the supply chain not only impacts the environment positively but also enhances economic development through the 3Rs – i.e., Reduce, Reuse, and Recycle (Domenech and Bahn-Walkowiak, 2019; Surya et al., 2020; Szalavetz, 2019). Multiple stakeholders have to work collaboratively at the global level to bring about the shift because a sustainable economy is very complex and vital to lift and prepare businesses for competitiveness globally.

A sustainable economy, due to its regeneration ability, is also known as a circular economy or vice versa, which, in fact, frees the businesses from the hurdles of limited resources and encourages the resilience to be sustainable for the overall benefit of the society (Valenzuela and Böhm, 2017; Domenech and Bahn-Walkowiak, 2019) and the environment (Garg & Singla, 2013; Haigh & Hoffman, 2011). Businesses need to explore innovative and technology-oriented ways to remain ahead of their competitors by improving their entire supply chain from manufacturing to disposal and again to regenerate from the dumps. In the process of regeneration, garbage is converted to suitable resources through a biological process so as to be used to manufacture new products. Further embracing technological techniques helps to make these new products more environmentally responsive, thus moving

DOI: 10.1201/9781003461432-1

towards a sustainable economy. For instance, the fashion industry, which is changing and progressing continuously as one of the foremost world economies, has an estimated worth of up to 3,000 billion US dollars (Fashion United, n.d.; Lockwood et al., 2010). It is rapidly adopting 5.0 cloth production technologies, along with all the latest digital accomplishments. Today, the major goal is to enhance activities that eliminate the polluting impact of industry, and the fashion industry is among such industries (Garg, A., 2023). The last decade has witnessed significant digital innovations not only in sales and retail but also in the digitalization of the whole supply chain and design in the fashion industry to revitalize it with the help of AI (Garg, 2023). A number of initiatives have been taken to reduce the environmental impact of the fashion industry so as to optimistically move towards a sustainable economy. A few apparel companies have started to take on sustainability issues independently. I:CO has worked with H&M and Levi's to collect garments and footwear for recycling and reuse. I:CO supplies the collection bins, sorts the materials so that anything that may be worn can be sold, and recycles the remainder. In addition to collecting used clothes in its stores and via mail, Patagonia also provides repair services to help its customers prolong the life of their apparel (Garg, 2023).

These examples are among many ways of utilizing the biological and technological sustainable economy. A sustainable economy includes everything from manufacturing to disposal and reuse of goods (Kazancoglu et al., 2021). Companies are increasingly realizing the technology transfer for different prospects to integrate a sustainable economy and global value chain. The purpose of the study is to observe the level of integration between the sustainable economy, technology transfer, and global value chain. The keyword co-occurrence investigation is used to explore the research clusters of the entwined three. Additionally, a bibliometric study is carried out to examine the research topic. The analysis also finds the trends in sustainability economy and technology transfer research. It is anticipated that the findings can explore the need to investigate the projected sustainability economy issues. The following section presents the available literature.

LITERATURE REVIEW

Globally, companies need to be transformed to make use of natural resources wisely to minimize waste and regulate material salvage and retrieval, keeping in view the challenges of the appropriate implementation of the 3Rs (Szalavetz, 2019). Technology has played a significant role in reusing, recycling, and reducing waste by organizations to bring about a sustainable economy. Besides working towards cost reduction, companies have outsourced logistics and production to enhance, track, and secure the global value chain, and thus the economy. The security of transactions can be enabled through AI-enabled blockchain, and a complete value chain can be driven by emerging technologies equipped with AI (Mohamed, 2018; Saurabh & Dey, 2021; Valenzuela and Böhm, 2017). This paradigm shift, however, must include more collaborative efforts among the stakeholders to make the global value chain robust, secure, and sustainable. The research themes are explored here.

Technological transfer plays a significant role in the success or failure of any organization in the Industry 4.0 era. Expansion of the industries and the global economy is driven by emerging technologies (Garg, 2023; Mishra et al., 2021). Technology transfer itself is a chain where a new technology has emerged in a place and spreads to different geographical areas for the growth of the economy globally. Technology usage practices support the economy by enhancing the 3Rs throughout the value chain. This includes raw material to manufacturing, manufacturing to usage, and usage to reduce wastage, reuse, and recycle. These practices help to combat climate and economic corrosion. Technological transmission allows organizations to use new communication with their suppliers and vendors. Technology-enabled machines are shaped to allow organizations to replace many jobs with a single machine (Durán-Romero et al., 2020; Ghatak & Garg, 2022). Also, the spreading of technology knowledge about manufacturing, resource recovery and reprocessing, and e-waste and solid waste management (Garg & Singla, 2013, 2017; Schröder et al., 2020) improves sustainability and profitability (Garg, 2022). However, a complete exploration of the existing body of knowledge on technology transfer is essential to know its connection with the value chain and sustainable economy.

Value chain networks are usually physically dispersed, causing monitoring of the supply chain to be more challenging. This may interrupt the communication among supply chain contributors (Hopkinson et al., 2020; Yiu, 2021). Global value chain extends beyond the business boundaries and business sectors (Schmitt et al., 2021), and technology transfer essentially becomes a support for the companies to manage the value chain. Technology, to an extent, guarantees the value and security of products and services. But data privacy and security need to be monitored. Organizations have started using recent advances in technology, like blockchain, to create secure digital records for the complete value chain globally. Blockchain technology ensures data security by sustaining the original form of the data (Hopkinson et al., 2020; Saurabh and Dey, 2021; Yiu, 2021). The use of technology in the form of optimized delivery routes, some electrical vehicles, and AI-enabled logistics applications enables the transformation of the supply and value chain of the organization on the global front.

A sustainable economy, generally, requires a fundamental transformation of production and resource consumption transversely in all sectors (Christopher, 2000). It reflects the aim of understanding intricate economic and social procedures, as well as seeing consumer effects (Ferasso et al., 2020). This also includes reconsidering how waste is reduced and how products are reused and recycled to sustain resource efficiency (Mohamed, 2018;

Schröder et al., 2020). Globally, the sustainable economy requires a common vision among various customers, organizations, and strategy makers because of the recent transformations for more sustainable goods and services (Merli et al., 2018). The recent body of knowledge also reflected the new considerations and observations of natural resource management (Lockwood et al., 2010; Hopkinson et al., 2020). The emerging technology innovations have contributed to a sustainable economy, and the studies are not complete but are more demonstrative (Manninen et al., 2018) and need further exploration.

PURPOSE OF STUDY

In the era of information technology, specifically in the context of Industry 4.0, there is a strong need to align organizational goals with socio-technological goals to sustain the economy and create new avenues for growth. There has been extensive research in support of this, but a link between a sustainable economy and global value chain in the past must be studied to work on the alignment (Koval et al., 2021). The present study is an effort to explore the possible interconnection between technology, global value chain, and sustainable economy through bibliometric analysis. The research aims to study the available literature on the research theme to know the trend of studies which were published between the years 2021 and 2023 by identifying some hidden patterns of research using documents, themes of documents, keywords, authors, and their affiliations. The study's goal is to recognize the development of the most frequently occurring themes and keywords in the available literature, keeping the following research questions (RQ) in mind.

RQ1: What is the document analysis outcome for the documents published between 2021 and 2023?
RQ2: What is the keywords analysis outcome for the documents published between 2021 and 2023?
RQ3: What is the keywords plus analysis outcome for the documents published between 2021 and 2023?
RQ4: What is the thematic pattern analysis outcome for the documents published between 2021 and 2023?

To answer the research questions, the methodology adopted is given as follows.

METHODOLOGY

The study evaluated the significant inter-relationship between research themes using bibliometric markers – i.e., documents, keywords, citations, and authorship and co-authorship networks (Donthu et al., 2021). The bibliometric tools – i.e., the Bibliometrix R package and VOSviewer – were used to analyse the downloaded data. Bibliometric analysis helps us to understand the evolution of a research theme by using large datasets from the existing body of knowledge (Aria & Cuccurullo, 2017). The current study evaluates the topics of sustainable economy, global value chain, and technology transfer from documents, authors, keywords, and citation perspectives, exploring future research avenues by monitoring the trends over a specific time period – i.e., from 2021 to 2023. In the current study, Scopus and Web of Science (WoS) databases were used to search the relevant documents on the keywords, such as "global value chain" OR "sustainable economy" OR "technology transfer". Three thousand four hundred seventy-eight documents met the filtering criteria and were downloaded. The downloaded data was then processed and visualized in Bibliomatrix R and VOSviewer software packages.

FINDINGS

The present study is an attempt to find out the association between the clusters of the study – i.e., technology transfer, global value chain/supply chain, and sustainable economy. The downloaded information was analysed at the document, keyword, author, citations, theme, and journal levels, as presented in the following section.

Document analysis

A bibliometric analysis is carried out on the documents downloaded based on the keywords mentioned earlier. The downloaded information of 3,478 articles from Scopus and WoS databases was uploaded to the Biblioshiny app for bibliometric analysis in the R package. The analysis gave the basic description of the articles. The summary of the downloaded documents is shown in Tables 1.1 and 1.2.

The analysis of 1,740 documents elaborated on countries of origin, citation count, authorship, and co-authorship. Table 1.1 reflects the basic description of the origin of sources based on research themes – i.e., technology transfer, global value chain, and sustainable value chain in the Scopus and WoS databases from the time period between 2021 to 2023 with

Table 1.1 Types of documents downloaded for bibliometric analysis

Document type	*Number of documents*
Review Articles	3,407
Early Access Articles	71

Source: As reported in Biblioshiny

Table 1.2 Description of documents downloaded for bibliometric analysis

Description	*Results*
Time span	2021:2023
Sources (journals, books, etc.)	1,740
Documents	3,478
Document average year in publication	1.07
Average citations per document	6.046
References	1
Document Content	
Author's keywords (DE)	10,960
Authors Data	
Authors	11,154
Authors of single-authored documents	426
Authors of multi-authored documents	10,728
Single-authored documents	442
Co-authors per document	3.86
International co-authorships %	30.51

Source: As reported in Biblioshiny

20 articles as the minimum threshold for analysis. The results of data analysis in the Biblioshiny app depicted the most relevant authors came from countries like China, the United States, the United Kingdom, Italy, India, Germany, and Australia. Spain, the Netherlands, and Canada were the top ten cited countries for article production, as shown in Figure 1.1. The citation results sketched from the author's perspective are shown in Figure 1.2, as the most globally cited documents, and the most relevant authors, their articles, and the total global citation score are depicted in Table 1.3.

3478 documents, then, outlined as the most relevant sources and ranked as per the no. of documents published with keywords of this research. The *Sustainability* journal appeared on the top of the table followed by the *Journal of Technology Transfer*, the Journal of Cleaner Production in producing maximum number of relevant documents as well as the total global citation score (Table 1.4). These three journals also appeared as top journals with respect to H-index (Table 1.5).

KEYWORDS ANALYSIS

The keywords analysis helps with visualizing the knowledge which is created by different articles published in various journals from different perspectives. It displays a three-dimensional map of various keywords which co-occurred in various articles. The analysis of co-occurrence of 314 keywords

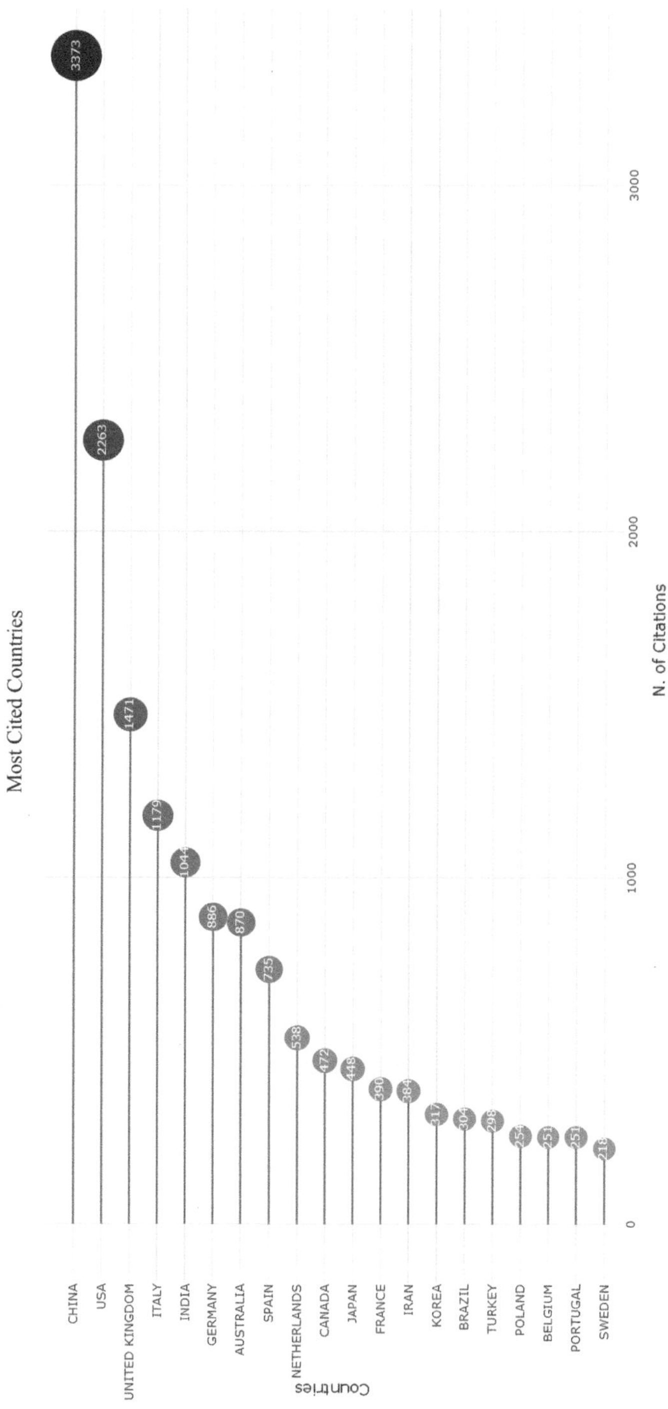

Figure 1.1 Most cited countries on analysis of downloaded documents.

Source: As reported in Biblioshiny

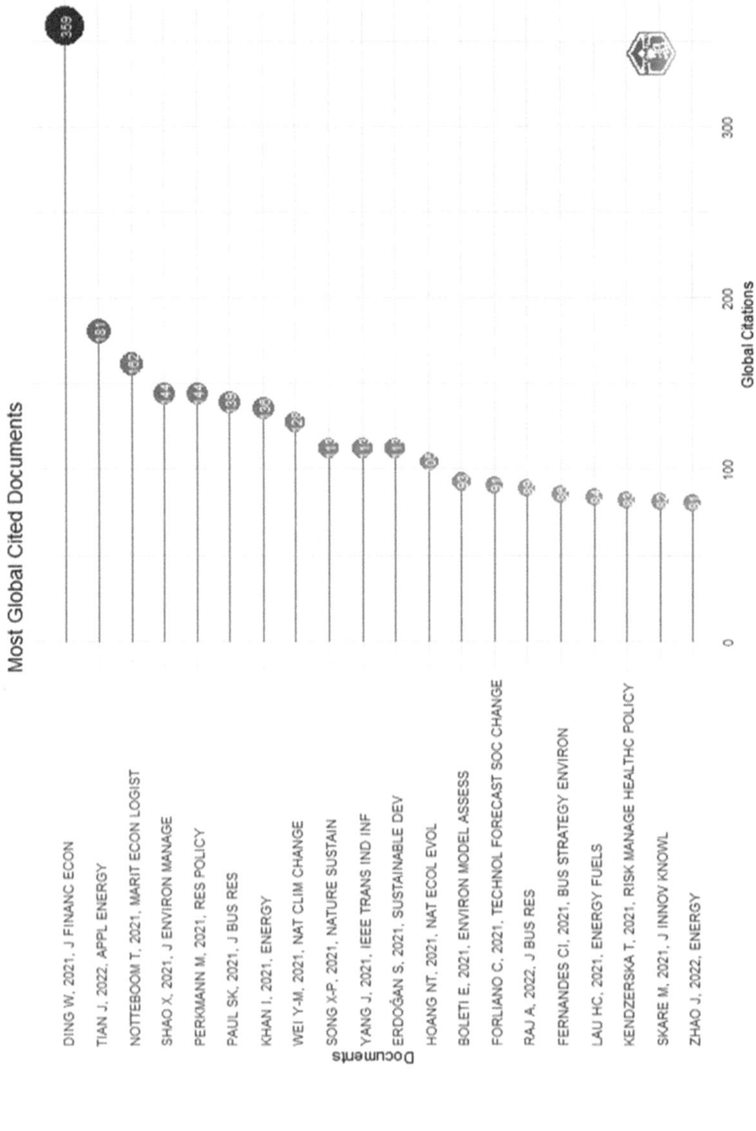

Figure 1.2 Most globally cited documents on analysis of downloaded documents.

Source: As reported in Biblioshiny

Table 1.3 Most relevant authors with number of articles published and total global citation score (TGCS)

Ranking of author	*Author*	*No. of articles*	*TGCS*
1	Wang Y	5	139
2	Kumar A	3	99
3	Liu Y	3	165
4	Li X	2	67
5	Wang H	2	75
6	Chen X	1	38
7	Chen Y	1	21
8	Li J	1	12
9	Liu X	1	29
10	Wang J	1	31
11	Wang S	1	21
12	Wang Z	1	24
13	Wu X	1	12
14	Zhang J	1	11
15	Zhang Y	1	38

Source: Compiled by author from Biblioshiny

Table 1.4 Most relevant journals with number of articles published and TGCS

			Number of documents		*TGCS*
Ranking of journal	*Journal*	*2021*	*2022*	*2023*	*TGCS*
1	*Sustainability (Switzerland)*	53	99	140	610
2	*Journal of Technology Transfer*	40	74	79	804
3	*Journal of Cleaner Production*	19	39	56	688
4	*Technological Forecasting and Social Change*	9	27	41	410
5	*Energies*	18	28	35	179
6	*Research Policy*	6	14	23	249
7	*Technology in Society*	10	19	23	167
8	*IEEE Transactions on Engineering Management*	4	15	22	109
9	*Science of the Total Environment*	9	17	20	193
10	*Sensors*	10	14	19	89

Source: Compiled by author from Biblioshiny

Table 1.5 Most relevant journals with H-index

Journal	*H-index*
Journal of Technology Transfer	17
Journal of Cleaner Production	15
Sustainability (Switzerland)	13
Technological Forecasting and Social Change	10
Research Policy	8
Science of the Total Environment	8
Energies	8
Technology in Society	8
Technovation	8
Journal of Business Research	7

Source: As reported in Biblioshiny

out of a total of 10,960 from the 3,478 articles is carried out. The resultant 314 keywords met the threshold of a minimum occurrence of at least five counts in each article. The co-occurrence linking strength calculated with other sources is reflected in Figure 1.3, with higher density keywords shown with bigger-sized words in comparison to low-density keywords, as given in Figure 1.4. Further, the strength of the link is given by the closer display of keywords portraying a high level of clustering. The technology transfer cluster is connected to other clusters of the current research represented by different colours. Figure 1.3 shows a grouping of six different clusters, including each research theme using 314 keywords, restricting the cluster size to a minimum of 35 with a resolution of 1.00. These clusters also co-occur with additional keywords, such as 'sustainability', 'knowledge transfer', and 'resilience' associated with innovations.

Figure 1.3 depicts the association between different clusters. The one cluster is centralized on technology transfer, showing studies related to technology acquisition, knowledge transfer, innovation ecosystem, and absorption capacity. The another cluster is centralized on global value chain, showing studies related to international trade, supply chain risk, globalization, and game theory. One cluster is centralized on innovations depicting studies related to 3D printing, agility, artificial intelligence, blockchain, additive manufacturing, and performance. The sustainable economy cluster has focused studies on a circular economy, sustainable development, economic growth, supply chain integration, bioeconomy, bioenergy, biofuels, and corporate social responsibility. There are two mild clusters, but important among six clusters are economic growth and knowledge transfer. A smaller cluster is centralized with studies on environmental policy, financial development, SDGs, technology innovation, and international trade. The last cluster, however, is more scattered with studies on collaboration, absorptive capacity, supply chain resilience, and supply chain risks.

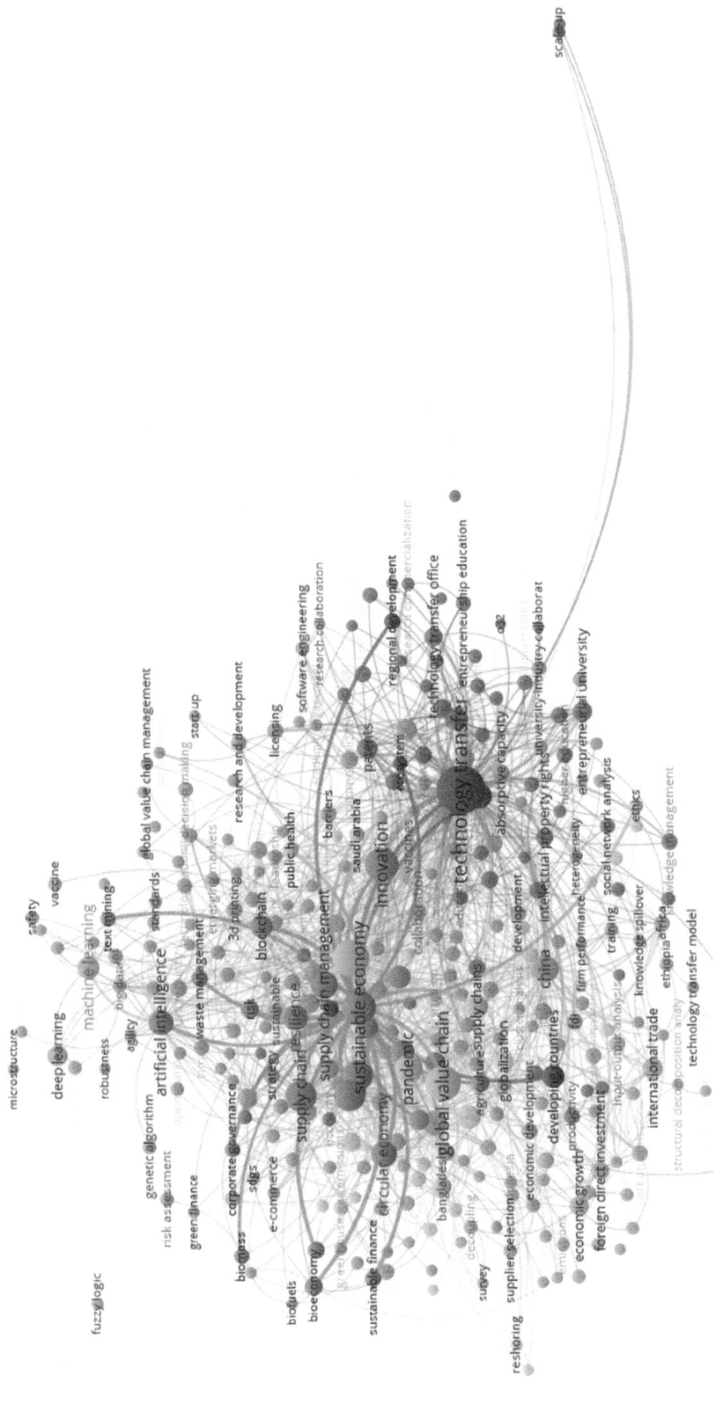

Figure 1.3 Cluster network presentation of six clusters of keywords.

Source: On analysis in VOSviewer

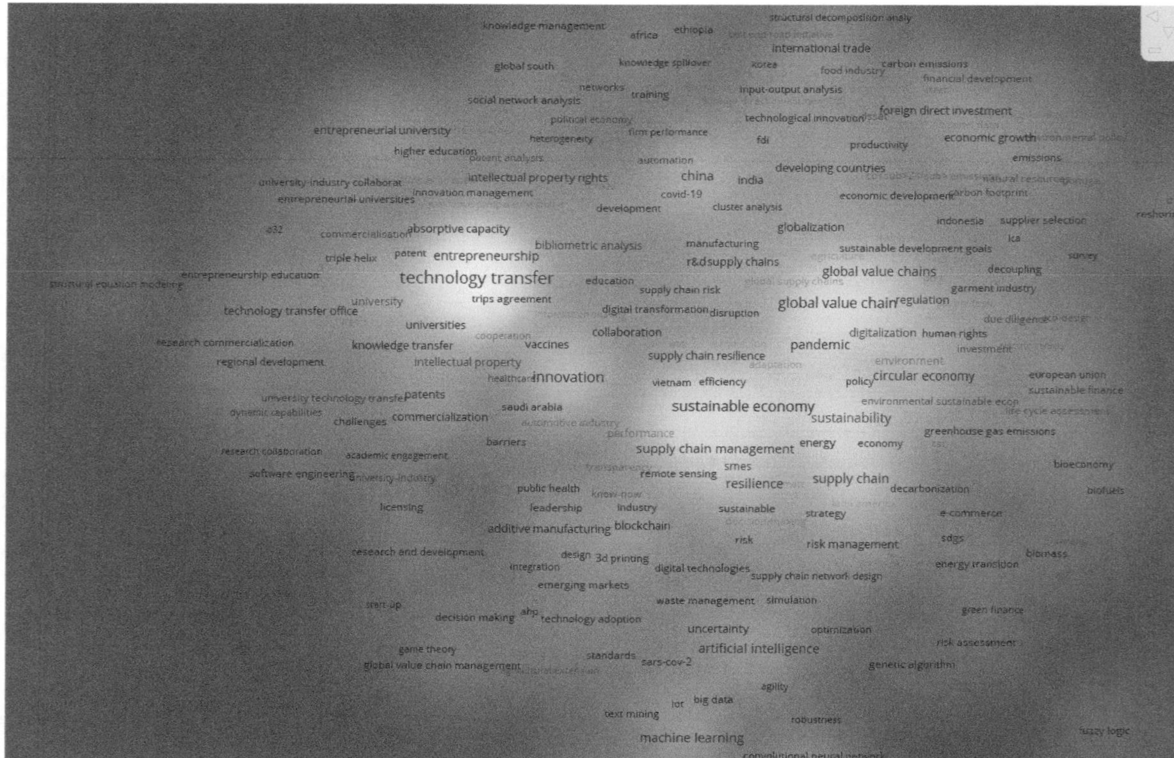

Figure 1.4 Density view presentation of keywords.

Source: On analysis in VOSviewer

The analysis of research themes – i.e., technology transfer, global value chain, and sustainable economy – has been carried out separately to explore the trend of association between different themes and possible research areas in the near future. They are given as follows.

Study of the "technology transfer" keyword

The analysis of the technology transfer keyword showed the spread to all other research themes – i.e., global value chain and sustainable economy. Further, a very strong link is observable between the technology transfer keyword and innovation, commercialization academic entrepreneurship, knowledge transfer, and academic entrepreneurship keywords, as depicted in Figure 1.5. This close proximity depicted the scope of future research in these avenues and the vast connotation of technology transfer, especially with a high-strength link with innovation and knowledge transfer, as shown in Figure 1.4–1.6.

Study of the "global value chain" keyword

The centrality of global value chain shows strong evidence of a link with other studies, such as technology transfer, innovations, sustainability, green economy, and sustainable finance, as given in Figure 1.7. This is just the reverse of the evidence of the studies with the technology transfer keyword, which may be seen as research on technogy transfer shows less focus on global value chain; however, research on global value chain emerges with a strong focus on technology transfer and innovations in global value chain.

Study of the "sustainable economy" keyword

Studies linked to the sustainable economy were spread to other clusters. Sustainable economy studies were linked to technology transfer strongly, as well as to global value chain, supply chain, artificial intelligence, bioeconomy, and blockchain (Figure 1.8). The strength of the link is depicted with the size of the cluster and the text size. The links suggested the overlapping of the studies in different clusters, also.

The analysis of Keyword Plus on 3,478 sources between 2021 and 2023 was analysed in Bibliometrix R package for the frequency of appearance of relevant words. Figure 1.9 portrays the word advances between 2021 and 2023 in all the sources. Analysis indicated technology transfer, sustainable development, supply chain, global value chain, human, and global value chain are among the frequently occurring words with technology transfer at the top. Figure 1.10 describes the word trend and its growth over a period selected in the research. It indicated the steady growth of digitization, with technology transfer studies dominating the other keywords, like sustainable economy and global value chain, which are broader. Figure 1.10 also depicts the year-wise

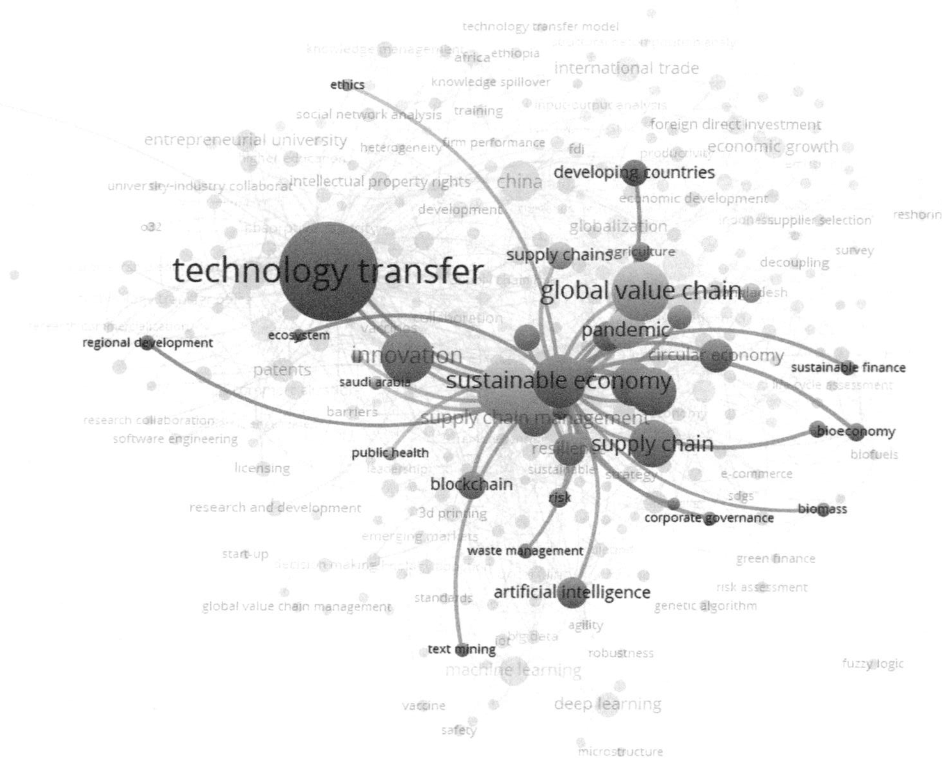

Figure 1.5 Cluster network presentation centred on the technology transfer keyword in relation to other keywords.

Source: On analysis in VOSviewer

Figure 1.6 High-strength link presentation between technology transfer, innovation, and knowledge transfer keywords.

Source: On analysis in VOSviewer

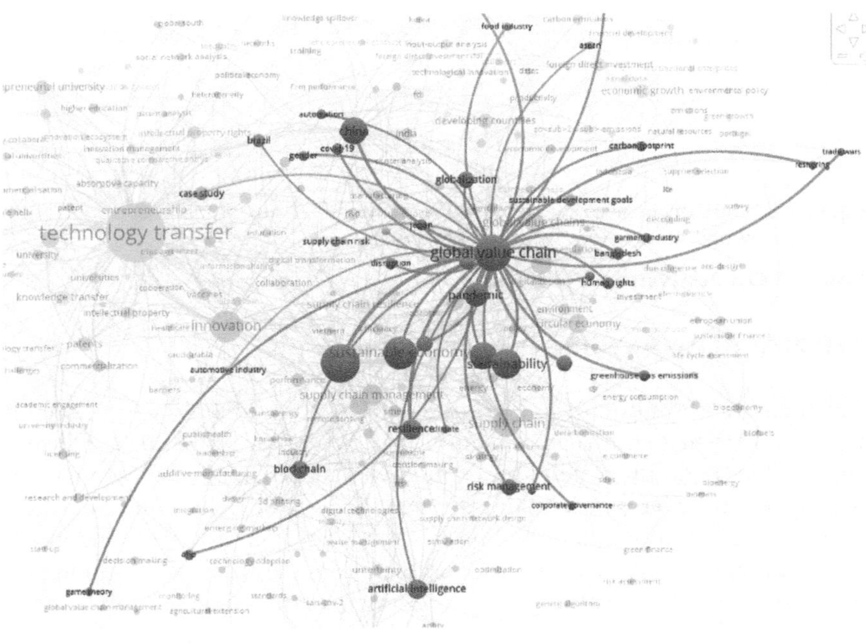

Figure 1.7 Cluster network presentation centred on the global value chain keyword in relation to other keywords.

Source: On analysis in VOSviewer

trend of the words with the latest studies focussing more on sustainable economy performance, carbon emissions, 3D printing, and social network analysis in the year 2023, in comparison to technology transfer, sustainable economy, global value chain/chains, knowledge transfer, bio-sustainable economy, and innovation management, which grew in 2021 and 2022, where global value chain and sustainable economy continued in 2023 also.

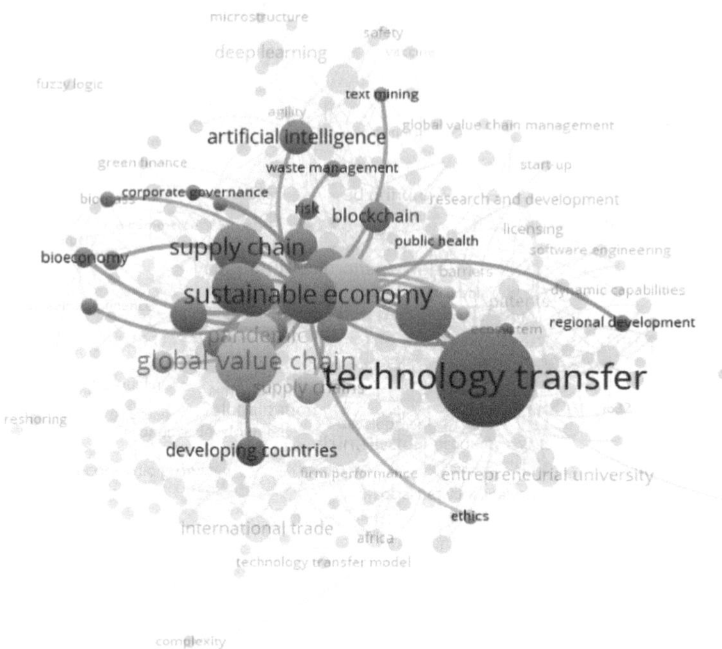

Figure 1.8 Cluster network presentation centred at sustainable economy keyword in relation to other keywords.

Source: On analysis in VOSviewer

THEMATIC ANALYSIS

The thematic evolution of Keyword Plus from 2021 to 2023 can be seen in Figure 1.11. The major themes identified between 2021 and 2022 indicated sustainable economy, sustainable economy resilience, machine learning, and technology transfer as the major studies. These studies became interdisciplinary and multidisciplinary while moving from 2021 to 2023, and global value chain, sustainable economy, and technology transfer were among the major studies. Global value chain evolution appeared to be the combination of sustainable economy resilience, Industry 4.0, and some part of sustainable economy studies while sustainable economy studies progressed from sustainable economy and economic growth studies. This was suggestive of a tendency of the researchers to explore a combination of different fields to study the growth of the global value chain.

The degree of development against the relevance quadrant for Keyword Plus is depicted in Figure 1.12. It divides the relevant studies into four quadrants relative to each other. For the top-right quadrant, the matrix indicated the studies grouped into motor themes, including technology transfer, innovations, artificial intelligence, investment, and renewable energy. This quadrant is taken as the most developed and relevant to research. Waste management

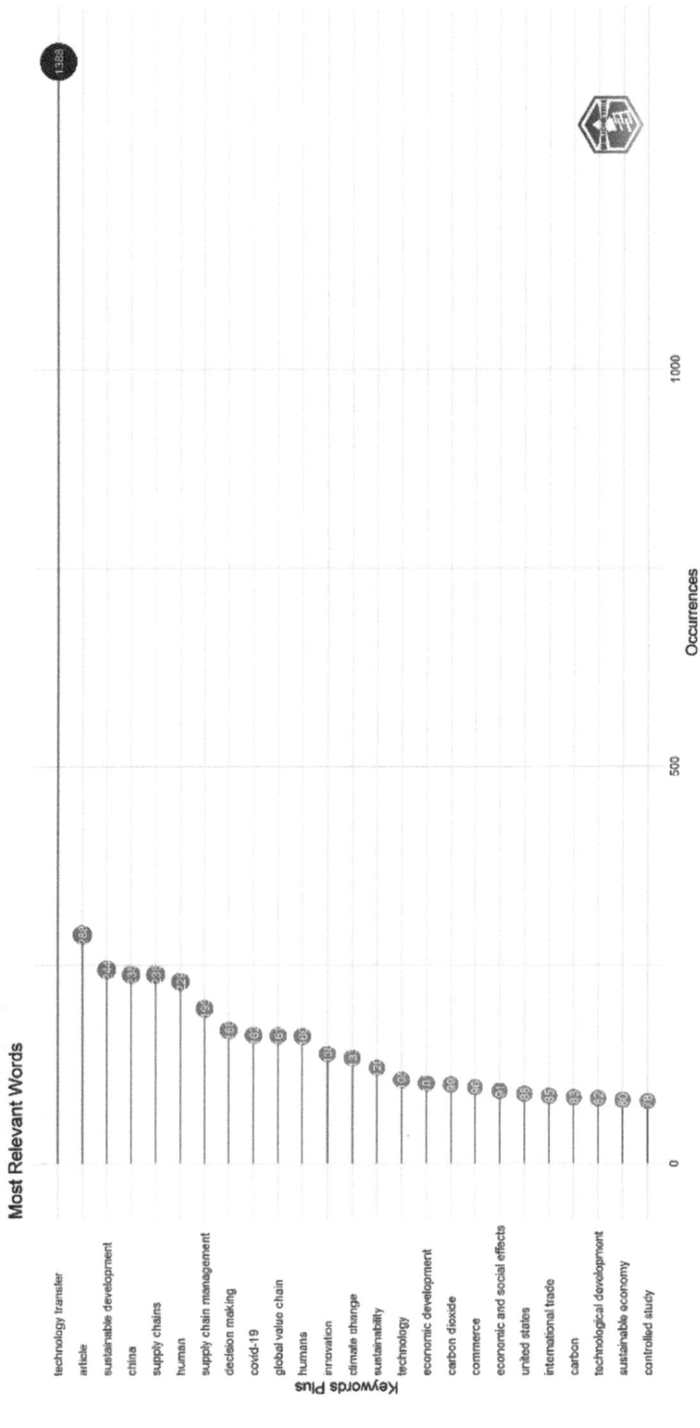

Figure 1.9 Analysis of Keyword Plus appearing in WoS.

Source: On analysis in Biblioshiny

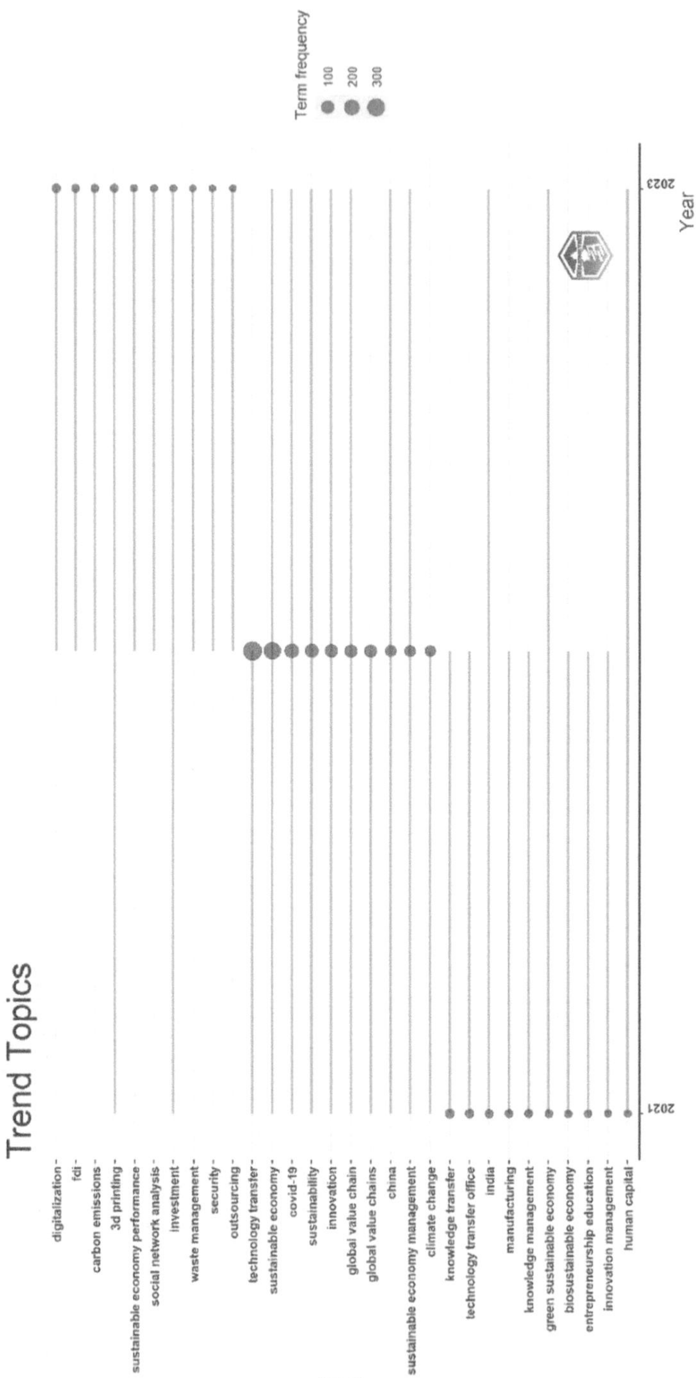

Figure 1.10 Trend analysis of keywords appearing in WoS.

Source: On analysis in Biblioshiny

Figure 1.11 Thematic evolution of Keyword Plus from 2021 to 2023.

Source: On analysis in Biblioshiny

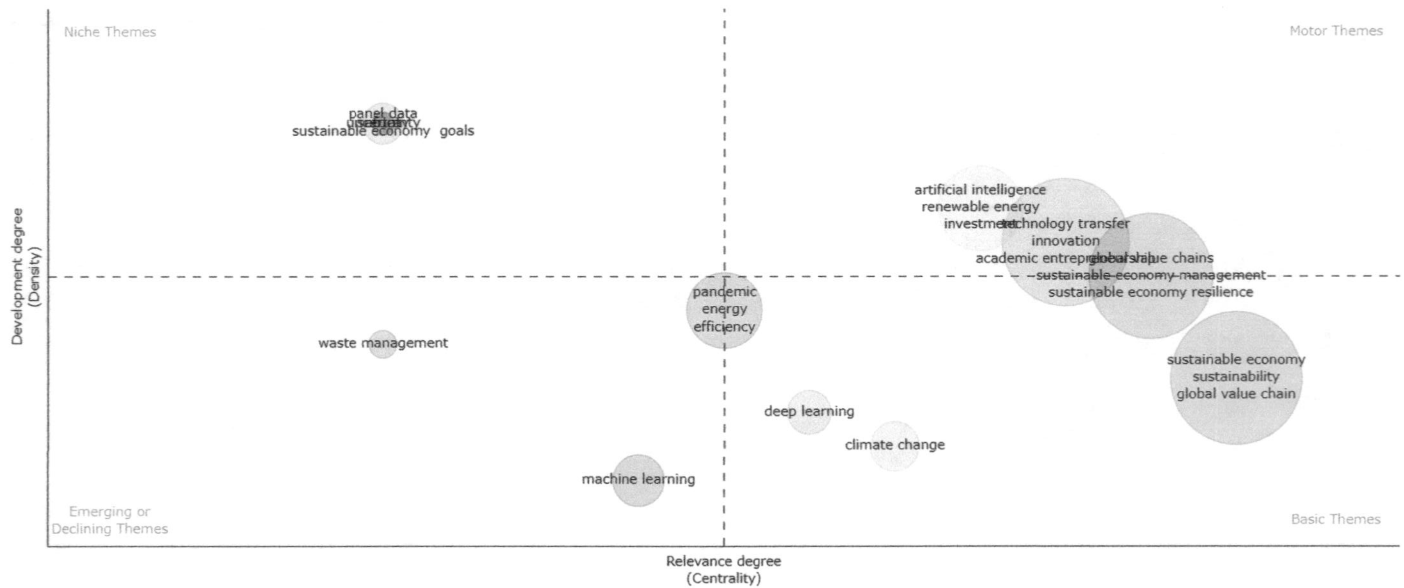

Figure 1.12 Analysis of the degree of development against the relevant quadrant for keywords.

Source: On analysis in Biblioshiny

and machine learning are grouped in the bottom-left quadrant, indicating either emerging or declining themes. They may also not be considered relevant to the researchers.

The themes grouped in the top-left quadrant – i.e., niche theme quadrant – included sustainable economy goals. The studies may be considered developed but less relevant to make niche panel data; the related studies are developed and form a niche. The major themes of sustainable economy, global value chain, technology transfer, sustainable economy management, and resilience came under basic themes, which lie between the top and bottom-right quadrants. These were the main research themes, and thematic analysis supported the development and relevance of the research themes for the existing literature.

DISCUSSION AND IMPLICATIONS

The findings of the data analysis provide a complete picture of research on technology's association with the global value chain and sustainable economy. The analysis of different clusters reveals, first, the global value chain keyword shows the spread to all other research themes of research – i.e., technology transfer and sustainable economy. The findings show the linkage between technology transfer with the global value chain and sustainable economy. The keyword co-occurrence analysis discovered the six themes. The main and largest-size cluster is centralized on technology transfer, showing studies related to technology acquisition, knowledge transfer, innovation ecosystem, and absorption capacity. The global value chain cluster, showing studies related to international trade, supply chain risk, globalization, and game theory. The innovations cluster is depicting studies related to 3D printing, agility, artificial intelligence, blockchain, additive e manufacturing, and performance. The sustainable economy cluster had focused studies on circular economy, sustainable development, economic growth, supply chain integration, bioeconomy, bioenergy, biofuels, and corporate social responsibility. The smaller cluster is centralized with studies on environmental policy, financial development, SDGs, technology innovation, and international trade. The smallest cluster, however, is more scattered with studies on collaboration, absorptive capacity, supply chain resilience, supply chain risks. The bibliometric analysis indicated the overlapping studies on research themes. The analysis revealed less focused research on technology transfer and global supply chain; however, research on global supply chain emerges with a strong focus on technology transfer and innovations in the global value chain. The findings indicated a close proximity of technology transfer with innovation and knowledge transfer depicting a scope of future research on these themes.

The analysis of Keyword Plus from 2021 to 2023 indicated technology transfer, sustainable development, supply chain, global value chain, human, and global value chain are among the frequently occurring words, with technology transfer at the top, and the trend is growing steadily. The trend shows digitization and technology transfer studies are dominating the other keywords, like sustainable economy and global value chain. This may be due to increased awareness of emerging technologies and their applications in the value chain. The bibliometric analysis further showed the thematic evolution of research between 2021 and 2022 has sustainable economy, sustainable economy resilience, machine learning, and technology transfer as the major studies which are more interdisciplinary and multidisciplinary. While moving from 2021 to 2023, global value chain, sustainable economy and technology transfer are among the major studies. The thematic analysis further identifies technology transfer, innovations, artificial intelligence, investment, and renewable energy as the most developed and relevant to research.

The findings have significant implications for thoughtful research on the global value chain in association with technology and sustainable economy. The practical implications for for future researchers include the necessity to delve into the latest growth of the value chain with technology and address sustainability economy issues to stay updated with emerging trends which are aligned with the practical challenges. The study will help researchers gain insights into the research themes to carry out future research. Practitioners gain insights into deliberate sustainable economy strategies and various initiatives.

CONCLUSION

In conclusion, this study brings valuable awareness to the recent status and the growing trends in research pertaining to the technology transfer of the global value chain and further its relationship with sustainable economy. It shows the significance of awareness of current and emerging topics in the field and the necessity for sustained research in the related topics. However, this presented research is based on a bibliometric examination of Scopus and WoS publications only, without considering the in-depth analysis of each publication. This may not have supported and explored the actual as well as important viewpoints of authors' works on the topic of research. Consequently, it is possible that the findings of this study may have weaknesses in accurately reflecting the state of research on the technology transfer of the global value chain and sustainable economy. Future studies may focus on a detailed systematic literature review, a review of the scope of research, and some qualitative analysis to realize the status of a sustainable economy and technology-enabled global value chain. Though a detailed, in-depth analysis is not available yet, the study provides valuable information on the research topics.

REFERENCES

Aria, M., & Cuccurullo, C., 2017. bibliometrix: an R-tool for comprehensive science mapping analysis. *J. Inf.* 11 (4), 959–975. https://doi.org/10.1016/j.joi.2017.08.007

Christopher, M., 2000. The agile supply chain: competing in volatile markets. *Ind. Market. Manag.* 29 (1), 37–44. https://doi.org/10.1016/S0019-8501(99)00110-8

Domenech, T., & Bahn-Walkowiak, B., 2019. Transition towards a resource efficient circular economy in Europe: policy lessons from the EU and the member states. *Ecol. Econ.*, 155, 7–19.

Donthu, N., Kumar, S., Mukherjee, D., Pandey, N., & Lim, W.M., 2021. How to conduct a bibliometric analysis: an overview and guidelines. *J. Bus. Res.* 133, 285–296.

Durán-Romero, G., López, A.M., Beliaeva, T., Ferasso, M., Garonne, C., & Jones, P., 2020. Bridging the gap between circular economy and climate change mitigation policies through eco-innovations and Quintuple Helix Model. *Technol. Forecast. Soc. Change.* 160, 120246. https://doi.org/10.1016/j.techfore.2020.120246

Fashion United, n.d. Global fashion industry statistics – International apparel. https://fashionunited.com/global-fashion-industry-statistics/

Ferasso, M., Beliaeva, T., Kraus, S., Clauss, T., & Ribeiro-Soriano, D., 2020. Circular economy business models: the state of research and avenues ahead. *Bus. Strat. Environ.* 29 (8), 3006–3024. https://doi.org/10.1002/bse.2554

Garg, A., 2022. CoReS-Respiratory Strength Predicting Framework using noninvasive technology for remote monitoring during heath disasters. *Global Healthcare Disasters: Predicting the Unpredictable with Emerging Technologies*, 109–121.

Garg, A. (Ed.), 2023. *Reinventing Technological Innovations with Artificial Intelligence*. Bentham Science Publishers.

Garg, A., & Singla, N., 2013. E-waste vis-à-vis human health and environment. *Interdiscip. Environ. Rev.* 14 (3–4), 187–193.

Garg, A., & Singla, N., 2017. Environment sustainability awareness model for IT SMEs. *Interdiscip. Environ. Rev.* 18 (1), 1–5.

Ghatak, A., & Garg, A., 2022. Power transmission project: a framework to align project success with organization goal. *Int. J. Syst. Assur. Eng. Manag.* 13 (4), 1817–1833.

Haigh, N., & Hoffman, A.J., 2011. Hybrid organizations: the next chapter in sustainable business (SSRN scholarly paper ID 2933616). *Soc. Sci. Res. Netw.* https://doi.org/10.2139/ssrn.2933616

Hettich, E., & Kreutzer, M. (2021). Strategy formation across organizational boundaries: An interorganizational process model. *Br. J. Manag.*, 32(1), 147–199.

Hopkinson, P., De Angelis, R., & Zils, M., 2020. Systemic building blocks for creating and capturing value from circular economy. *Resour. Conserv. Recycl.* 155, 104672. https://doi.org/10.1016/j.resconrec.2019.104672

Kazancoglu, I., Sagnak, M., Kumar Mangla, S., & Kazancoglu, Y., 2021. Circular economy and the policy: a framework for improving the corporate environmental management in supply chains. *Bus. Strat. Environ.* 30 (1), 590–608.

Koval, V., Mikhno, I., Udovychenko, I., Gordiichuk, Y., & Kalina, I., 2021. Sustainable natural resource management to ensure strategic environmental development. *TEM J.* 10 (3), 1022.

Lockwood, M., Davidson, J., Curtis, A., Stratford, E., & Griffith, R., 2010. Governance principles for natural resource management. *Soc. Nat. Resour.* 23 (10), 986–1001.

Manninen, K., Koskela, S., Antikainen, R., Bocken, N., Dahlbo, H., & Aminoff, A., 2018. Do circular economy business models capture intended environmental value propositions? *J. Clean. Prod.* 171, 413–422. https://doi.org/10.1016/j.jclepro.2017.10.003

Merli, R., Preziosi, M., & Acampora, A., 2018. How do scholars approach the circular economy? A systematic literature review. *J. Clean. Prod.* 178, 703–722. https://doi.org/10.1016/j.jclepro.2017.12.112

Mishra, J.L., Chiwenga, K.D., & Ali, K., 2021. Collaboration as an enabler for circular economy: a case study of a developing country. *Manag. Decis.* 59 (8), 1784–1800.

Mohamed, M., 2018. Challenges and benefits of industry 4.0: an overview. *Int. J. Supply Oper. Manag.* 5 (3), 256–265. https://doi.org/10.22034/2018.3.7

Saurabh, S., & Dey, K., 2021. Blockchain technology adoption, architecture, and sustainable agri-food supply chains. *J. Clean. Prod.* 284, 124731. https://doi.org/10.1016/j.jclepro.2020.124731

Schmidt, W., Commeh, M., Olonade, K., Schiewer, G. L., Dodoo-Arhin, D., Dauda, R., … Rogge, A. (2021). Sustainable circular value chains: from rural waste to feasible urban construction materials solutions. *Develop. Built Environ.* 6, 100047.

Schröder, P., Lemille, A., & Desmond, P., 2020. Making the circular economy work for human development. *Resour. Conserv. Recycl.* 156, 104686 https://doi.org/10.1016/j.resconrec.2020.104686

Surya, B., Syafri, S., Sahban, H., & Sakti, H.H., 2020. Natural resource conservation based on community economic empowerment: perspectives on watershed management and slum settlements in Makassar City, South Sulawesi, Indonesia. *Land* 9 (4), 104.

Szalavetz, A., 2019. Industry 4.0 and capability development in manufacturing subsidiaries. *Technol. Forecast. Soc. Change.* 145, 384–395.

Valenzuela, F., & Böhm, S., 2017. Against wasted politics: a critique of the circular economy. *Ephemera Theory Polit. Organ.* 17 (1), 23–60.

Yiu, N.C.K., 2021. Toward blockchain-enabled supply chain anti-counterfeiting and traceability. *Future Internet* 13 (4), 86. https://doi.org/10.3390/fi13040086

Chapter 2

Global value chain to smart global value chain

A synthesis of best practices

Manisha Singh and Amrita Jain
GL Bajaj Institute of Management and Research, Greater Noida, India

INTRODUCTION

Between the 1990s and 2020, there were two main stages of globalization. The 1990s to about 2008 saw a surge in integration during the first phase. Subramanian and Kessler (2013) define this as "hyper-globalization." During this time, there was a sharp decline in the price of information and communication technology (ICT), which encouraged growth of global value chains (GVCs) rapidly. The global financial crisis caused trade to collapse in the second phase, and ever since, globalization has been substantially slower (World Bank, 2020), bringing in the period of "slowbalization." Reshoring of supply chains following the global financial crisis resulted in a sudden and severe decline in GVC participation, which had recovered by 2010.

One believes $15.2 billion worth of Japanese goods and services travelling over to be enjoyed by Indians when one hears that Japan exported $15.2 billion worth of goods and services to India in 2019. However, this is not true. Certain imports, including those from Germany, India, and Vietnam, are included in some Japanese exports. Meanwhile, some of the exports that India gets are processed before being sent back out again, possibly to Canada, Singapore, or even Japan. In fact, just $14.8 billion worth of Japanese value-added was shipped to and consumed in India. These kinds of operations are indicative of GVCs.

These include breaking up the production process into multiple phases that are carried out across multiple locations. The 1990s saw an increase in this new kind of globalization as market economies extended throughout the formerly communist countries and with advances in information and communication technologies and other cutting-edge technologies. They have spared economies from having to start from zero when creating a whole value chain by allowing them to specialize in tasks (assembly, marketing, business processing) as opposed to products (automobiles, computers, appliances).

GVCs cannot be fully studied with the data found in trade statistics. This is due to the fact that flows are reported in gross terms, while value-added flows are also crucial to consider in GVC study (Figure 2.1).

DOI: 10.1201/9781003461432-2

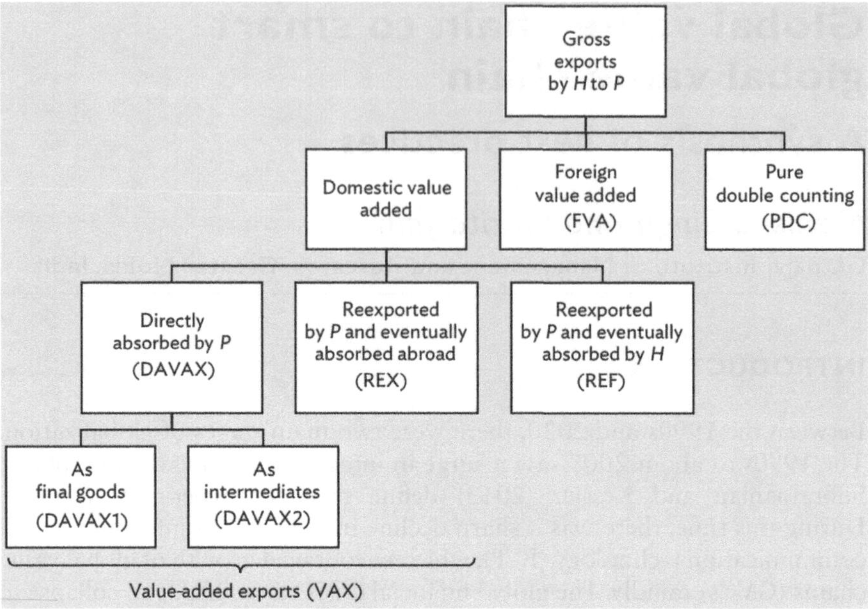

Figure 2.1 Decomposition of home's (H) gross exports to partner (P).

Source: UNCTAD

The percentage of inputs produced in other countries that make up the country's gross exports is indicated by its foreign value-added or foreign value-added as a fraction of exports. It is the portion of the nation's exports that does not raise gross domestic product (GDP).

Exports with domestic value-added are those that are produced domestically and add to the GDP. Gross exports are the total of value-added from both domestic and foreign sources. Domestic value-added can be related to other variables in the following ways:

a. It displays the contribution of trade to a nation's GDP as a percentage of GDP.
b. A country's part in global gross exports or global GDP can be compared to its share in global value-added trade as measured in terms of global shares.

Double counting arises when added value crosses a border multiple times, leading to duplicated data. The primary category, DAVAX, can be divided into items absorbed as final goods (DAVAX1) and those received as intermediate goods, subsequently completed locally and absorbed (DAVAX2). Some of the exported DVA may return as imports and be consumed, known as reflection (REF). The remaining segment constitutes value-added exports (VAX), representing DVA exports ultimately consumed abroad. VAX can be further categorized into the portion absorbed by a direct trading partner (DAVAX) and the portion reexported before final consumption (REX).

Recent developments in trade statistics seek to uncover instances of double counting in gross trade data and illustrate the points in global production chains where value is generated. The following diagram presents a simplified illustration of value-added trade (Figure 2.2).

According to the UNCTAD EORA database, there is a clear indication that the percentage of global participation in GVCs has been on the rise over the years. The ascendancy of GVCs appears to have coincided with the ICT revolution. Foster and Graham (2016) undertook an effort to comprehend how companies in the tea industry connect themselves to GVCs. A noteworthy discovery from their on-site research is the essential role played by digital infrastructure in the integration of firms into production networks. In an extension of their research, Foster et al. (2017) broadened their focus to a larger sample of firms in East Africa, qualitatively exploring the effects of enhanced internet connectivity on firms involved in GVCs. Interestingly, they highlight that despite the evident benefits to firms in GVCs, arising from increased internet connectivity and greater adoption, there are still noteworthy consequences (Figure 2.3).

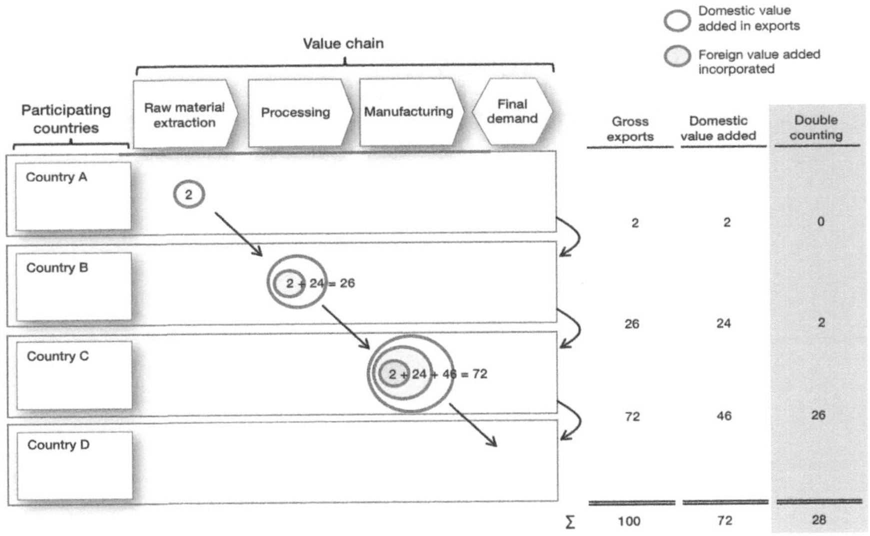

Figure 2.2 Value-added trade: how it works.

Source: World Investment Report 2013: Global Value Chains: Investment and Trade for Development

Figure 2.3 Global trends in GVC participation (1990–2018).

Source: UNCTAD EORA Database

Over 40% of the world's trade goods, exceeding $9 trillion in 2021 (Figure 2.4) comprise intermediate products. Recent data on the global export of intermediate goods, encompassing parts and components used in final product production, serves as a gauge for supply chain activity. Despite a 2020 dip, intermediate goods exports have consistently risen in 2021, surpassing pre-COVID-19 levels in 2019.

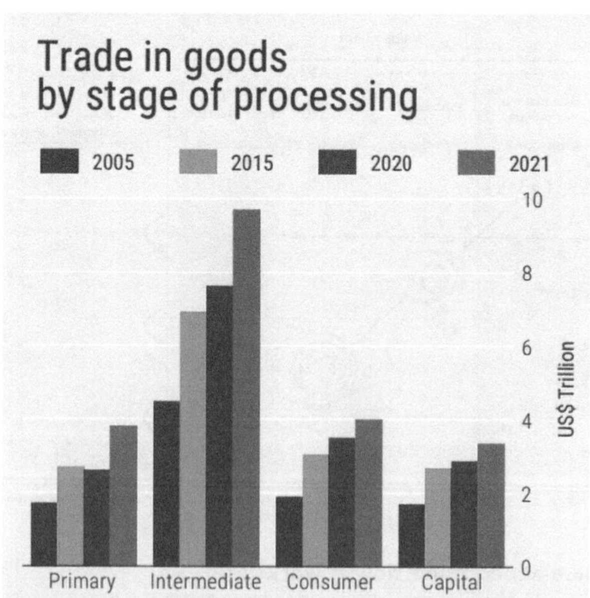

Figure 2.4 Values of world trade in goods by stage of processing.

Source: UNCTAD (2023)

Most of the research on GVCs focuses on the manufacturing sector, where production processes are broken down into numerous discrete steps, resulting in increased trade of parts and components; there are dimensions of GVCs that extend beyond manufacturing. Notably, the generation of value-added and employment in GVCs is becoming less dependent on manufacturing production. Value chains serve as an effective mechanism for companies to leverage their brands, patents, and other intellectual property. In an extreme scenario, this leads to "factory-less" production, where firms designing and marketing manufactured products do not own any part of the production process. A significant aspect of contemporary GVCs involves innovator countries exporting the services of their intellectual property in exchange for manufactured goods (Figure 2.5).

This chapter explores the impact of embracing emerging technologies on the development of intelligent GVCs. As we enter the 21st century, a transformative wave driven by advanced technologies is reshaping the conventional landscape of global trade. This shift has given rise to smart global value chains (SGVCs), representing a significant change in how businesses operate on a global scale. This transformation is not merely a conceptual idea; it is a tangible reality that fundamentally alters the way industries collaborate and innovate. The collaborative model of SGVCs streamlines processes, reduces costs, and facilitates the smooth flow of products across the globe.

The advent of SGVCs marks a digital renaissance in the domain of global commerce. These intelligent chains harness technologies such as the Internet of Things (IoT), artificial intelligence (AI), big data analytics, and blockchain to revolutionize the manufacturing landscape. Envision a world where

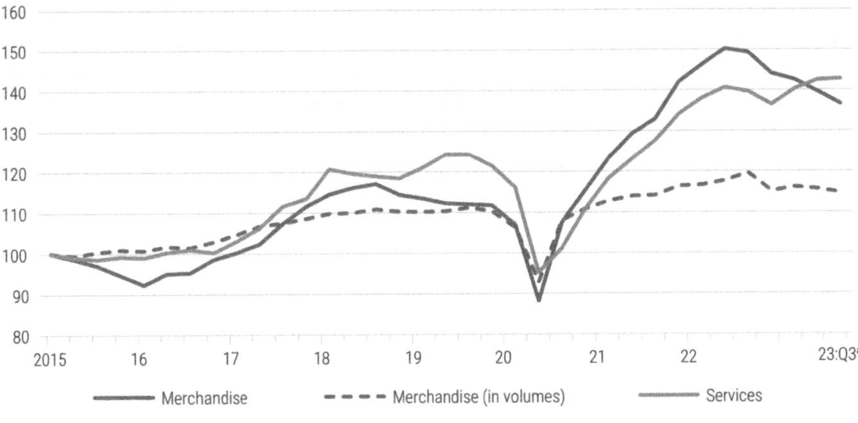

Figure 2.5 Global trade merchandise is declining while services appear more resilient.

Source: UNCTAD (2023)

machines, products, and packaging incorporate sensors, fostering a continuous exchange of real-time data. This interconnected system ensures meticulous monitoring and optimization of each production step, resulting in increased productivity and minimized delays.

EMERGING TECHNOLOGIES: GVC TO SGVC

Digital emerging technologies play a crucial role in transforming and optimizing GVCs, which are the series of activities involved in the production and distribution of goods and services on a global scale. Big data analytics can be used to analyse vast amounts of data from different stages of the supply chain. This enhances visibility, allowing companies to make more informed decisions and respond quickly to changes or disruptions. Blockchain can provide an immutable and transparent ledger that allows participants in the value chain to trace the origin and journey of products. This is particularly valuable in industries where provenance and authenticity are crucial, such as food and pharmaceuticals. IoT devices can be embedded in physical assets to monitor their status and location in real time. This helps in optimizing logistics, predicting maintenance needs, and reducing downtime, ultimately improving efficiency in the value chain. AI and machine learning (ML) algorithms can analyse historical data to predict demand more accurately, help companies optimize inventory levels, and reduce the risk of stockouts or overstock situations. AI can predict equipment failures and maintenance needs, reducing downtime and preventing disruptions in the production process. 3D printing allows for more flexible and localized production. This is especially beneficial for companies looking to customize products to meet specific market demands or reduce shipping costs by producing closer to the point of consumption. Augmented reality (AR) and virtual reality (VR) technologies can be used for training employees and technicians remotely, reducing the need for physical presence. They can also assist in remote maintenance and troubleshooting. Automation and robotics can improve labour efficiency, particularly in repetitive and labour-intensive tasks. This can result in cost savings and improved overall productivity. As digital technologies become more integral to value chains, ensuring the security of data and intellectual property is crucial. Cybersecurity measures help protect sensitive information from unauthorized access and cyber threats. Digital twin technology creates a virtual replica of physical assets, allowing for simulation and optimization of processes. This helps in identifying bottlenecks, improving efficiency, and testing changes before implementation. By leveraging these digital emerging technologies, companies can streamline their operations, enhance collaboration across the value chain, reduce costs, improve product quality, and respond more effectively to the dynamic challenges of the global marketplace.

THE IMPACT OF DIGITAL TECHNOLOGIES ON GVCS

Digital technologies, such as IoT and AI, have the potential to boost the involvement of small and medium-sized enterprises (SMEs) from developing nations in GVCs. By overcoming geographical distances and reducing trade-related costs, these technologies facilitate participation. AI optimizes shipping routes, and Industry 4.0 can decentralize advanced activities, offering opportunities in peripheral locations. For instance, Cloud Factory conducts higher-end tasks at its US headquarters while outsourcing lower-end activities to subsidiaries in Nepal and Kenya, providing employment opportunities.

Blockchain enhances transparency in value chains by reducing information asymmetries and tracking inventories. It improves the speed and cost-effectiveness of goods delivery, fostering trust and enabling consumers to consider social and environmental sustainability. SMEs benefit by accessing digital marketplaces securely and engaging with other value chain firms. Beyond the food industry, blockchain finds applications in preventing fraud in diamond origins and addressing counterfeit products in the pharmaceutical industry. It also disintermediates financial processes, making trading more efficient, particularly advantageous for small firms with limited access to traditional financial services (UNCTAD, 2021b).

Across Industries and Companies, smart GVCs have been used to respond effectively to market demands and maximize efficiency. A few case studies provide rich insights into the way this has been done.

Schneider electric

Schneider Electric, a French multinational specializing in digital automation and energy management, offers ingenious solutions for manufacturing. Their estimates show potential energy cost reductions between 10% and 30%, and maintenance cost reductions spanning 30% to 50%. One of their innovative solutions, EcoStruxure, implements Industrial Internet of Things (IIoT) across their global supply chain. These Smart Factories have gained recognition from the World Economic Forum for spearheading advancements in smart manufacturing. Among them, the factories in Lexington, United States, and Le Vaudreuil, France, stand out as Sustainability Lighthouses, two of just six globally acknowledged. Additionally, sites in Batam, Indonesia; Hyderabad, India; and Wuxi, China, are designated as Advanced 4th Industrial Revolution (4IR) Lighthouses. Meanwhile, facilities in Wuhan, China, and Monterrey, Mexico, are acknowledged as developing 4IR Lighthouses.

EcoStruxure Power: EcoStruxure Power represents an IoT-powered architecture and platform designed to digitalize and streamline low and medium-voltage electrical distribution systems. This system furnishes actionable data crucial for making informed decisions, ensuring the safety of individuals, safeguarding assets, optimizing operational efficiency and business continuity, and upholding regulatory compliance.

Ecostruxure Building: From initial design to seamless integration and eventual commissioning, EcoStruxure Building streamlines engineering processes, offering top-notch efficiency for a client's building. Paired with their asset and energy performance services, they facilitate lifelong efficiency for a client's building, ensuring the productivity and comfort of its occupants.

Ecostruxure Machine: Attain business excellence through intelligent machine solutions. EcoStruxure Machine integrates essential technologies for product connectivity and on-site edge control, leveraging cloud-based technologies to deliver analytics and digital services.

EcoStruxure Plant: EcoStruxure Plant empowers the scalable development and management of interconnected systems, integrating top-notch cybersecurity measures at every level to ensure secure and measurable enhancements in operational profitability.

These offerings are provided by AVEVA, a company formed through the merger of AVEVA and Schneider Electric's industrial software business, creating a premier engineering and industrial software entity.

EcoStruxure Grid: EcoStruxure Grid enhances the client's grid's efficiency for sustainable networks, seamlessly facilitating local production and integration at the grid edge while bridging the gap between demand and supply.

Ecostruxure™ IT: In our interconnected world, safeguarding critical information and data has become paramount. It's crucial to ensure that the client's data centre's physical infrastructure remains adaptable, swiftly accommodating future demands fuelled by IoT and expansion-whether in the cloud or at the edge, while steadfastly maintaining both availability and operational efficiency without compromise.

EcoStruxure™ Augmented Operator Advisor (AOA): The AOA, a tailor-made application, provides real-time information at the customer's fingertips, available whenever and wherever needed. It grants immediate access to on-site data diagnosis, user manuals, instructions, diagrams, and more. This significantly enhances operational efficiency through AR, allowing operators to overlay current data and virtual objects onto machinery or plants.

Benefits:

- Enhanced operational and maintenance efficiency
- Reduced time and cost associated with operations and maintenance
- Minimized operator errors during maintenance activities
- Streamlined support and simplified information delivery

IoT Monitoring and System Alert: This cloud-connected monitoring and control system is designed for plants and machinery. It identifies issues that generate predictive maintenance alerts, enabling service personnel to be dispatched promptly to address problems before they escalate into failures.

Benefits:

Machine Andon: Alerts management, maintenance teams, and other personnel instantly about quality or process-related problems.

Quality Statistical Process Control (SPC): Monitors process behaviour systematically to identify and resolve production issues effectively.

Predictive Maintenance: Proactively addresses and prevents equipment failure before it happens or promptly upon detection.

Additive manufacturing

Additive manufacturing through 3D printing technology has revolutionized prototyping capabilities for new products. It facilitates the creation of a wider array of prototypes, maintenance spare parts, jigs, fixtures, and customized assemblies in various shapes and designs, empowering the production of tailored end products.

Benefits

The quality of parts can match that of the originals; maintenance spare parts are available more quickly; prototypes receive faster feedback. It offers a more economical alternative for specific imported spare parts and jigs.

Results

Schneider Electric introduced the EcoStruxure Resource Advisor, an energy and sustainability management platform utilized by Whirlpool to monitor and track data across their global facilities. With guidance from Schneider experts, data collection has become consistent and precise, and Whirlpool's staff is proficient in using the EcoStruxure Resource Advisor. Remarkably, three plants in Brazil have accomplished the zero-waste-to-landfill objective two years ahead of schedule, aligning with their 2020 ambition for zero waste.

Improved parallel robots performance and efficiency for Siasun

Utilizing Schneider Electric's advanced PacDrive 3 motion control platform, Siasun has elevated the performance of its single and multiple parallel robots. This enhancement translates to heightened efficiency and cost savings for both Siasun and its clientele, leading to greater parallel robot performance and up to 30% increase in efficiency with IoT EcoStruxure™.

Walmart Canada

Walmart Canada's innovative application of blockchain technology addressed a longstanding issue in logistics – payment disputes with its numerous third-party freight carriers. The implementation of a blockchain network not only resolved payment discrepancies but also significantly enhanced operational efficiencies. The success of this endeavour presents valuable insights for companies aiming to deploy blockchain networks to streamline business processes.

Engage key stakeholders

Involving Bison Transport, a major truck fleet operator in North America, provided crucial insights into the challenges faced by carriers. Collaboration with logistics partners ensures solutions benefit all involved parties, not just the primary company.

Assess private versus public blockchain

Understanding the differences between private and public blockchain networks is critical. While a public blockchain allows unrestricted participation and transparency, a private network offers controlled access and governance. Choosing the suitable type depends on the specific business needs, considering factors like privacy requirements and the extent of network openness.

Establish consensus on business rules and calculations

Agreement on business rules and calculations is paramount. In a blockchain-enabled system, alignment of formulas and rules among participating entities is crucial. For Walmart and its carriers, this entailed harmonizing diverse data sets and defining agreed-upon formulas used by the blockchain to compute invoices in real time, incorporating variables like fuel rates and contract terms.

Integrate checks and balances

Incorporating automated checks within the blockchain system is essential for error prevention and performance enhancement. For instance, real-time comparison of carrier-reported data with IoT-derived metrics identifies discrepancies promptly, fostering a self-improving system. These checks extend beyond payments, streamlining financial services and enabling efficient working capital management.

Complement legacy IT systems

Rather than replacing existing legacy systems, blockchain solutions should complement and integrate with these systems, leveraging their unique strengths and valuable data. The ability of blockchain to coexist with legacy systems is one of its key advantages.

Walmart Canada's blockchain initiative not only aimed to resolve disputes and optimize resources but also unearthed valuable insights leading to substantial operational enhancements. The technology facilitated enhanced supply chain visibility, allowing for route optimization based on safety, time, fuel consumption, and load factors. Moreover, it enabled improved coordination of deliveries by sharing real-time truck arrival data with distribution centres and stores.

Alibaba

Alibaba Cloud, in collaboration with DAMO Academy and Cainiao, offers a cutting-edge smart logistics solution driven by data intelligence and AI. This comprehensive solution streamlines warehouse operations, accelerates location-based services, and enhances dispatch efficiency through AI-powered tools.

Enterprise smart warehouse

Cainiao specializes in creating, constructing, and managing large-scale automated warehouses. Utilizing smart hardware like automated guided vehicles (AGVs), this solution automates daily warehouse tasks and integrates order, warehouse, transportation, and billing management. It ensures synchronized data flow across the logistics chain, facilitating real-time monitoring via customizable dashboards. This capability enables precise forecasting, production planning, and swift troubleshooting to mitigate potential risks.

Intelligent address recognition

This service leverages Natural Language Processing (NLP) technology to process addresses with high accuracy. It corrects, completes, normalizes, structures, and labels addresses in multiple languages, providing standardized and recognizable addresses. Additionally, it simplifies and optimizes address recognition through features like address autocomplete, associated address searching, geocoding, reverse geocoding, and geofencing. These functionalities expedite location-based services.

AI-based dispatch

The EasyDispatch solution centralizes real-time dispatch services, significantly enhancing logistics efficiency and performance. Dispatch algorithms, based on industry best practices from Cainiao, deliver optimal results within predefined business constraints. Leveraging Alibaba Cloud's robust cloud-native and ML platforms, users can replicate service dispatch systems periodically or develop ML models seamlessly without the need for extensive coding.

Altogether, these features ensure logistics operations remain on schedule, resilient, and aligned with the dynamic demands of customers, showcasing the power of data intelligence and AI in revolutionizing the logistics landscape.

Flex

Flex has received the esteemed 2023 Value Champion Award from the Associate of Corporate Counsel (ACC) for its pioneering use of an AI-driven contract review tool. This accolade, a first-time inclusion for Flex in this ranking, underscores the company's dedication to reshaping the industry through innovation. The company, known for its focus on harnessing AI-driven tools across various enterprise functions, particularly within manufacturing operations, embarked on a transformative journey led by its Global Procurement and Supply Chain legal team. Initially employing AI to streamline non-disclosure agreement reviews, Flex expanded the tool's application to optimize supply chain contract evaluations. The result: a process that once took days is now completed in a mere five minutes, liberating valuable time and accelerating responsiveness to business demands.

Iringo Csifo-Nagy, lead attorney for Flex Global Procurement and Supply Chain, highlighted the need for change as complex supply chain agreements averaged an eight-day turnaround time while contract volumes were on the rise. Seeking to eliminate repetitive manual tasks, the company collaborated with the DocJuris team to develop a comprehensive AI-driven contract review solution.

This ground-breaking innovation establishes a new standard in contract review and approval, presenting a cost-effective and time-efficient approach that sets a benchmark for businesses worldwide. Flex's commitment to freeing its workforce from mundane tasks and enabling focus on more impactful endeavours positions it as a trailblazer in the industry.

Siemens AG

Siemens Digital Logistics offers cloud-based solutions serving as the digital backbone for seamless collaboration across enterprises in the logistics realm. We establish a framework that harmonizes processes, ensuring seamless synchronization regardless of businesses' existing in-house systems and solutions. Its control tower provides supply chain management and real-time monitoring capabilities, allowing proactive measures to prevent unforeseen alterations or disruptions in shipping processes. As part of Digital Industries Software (DISW), they stay attuned to industry trends, delivering software and consulting solutions vital for mastering logistics. Their offerings encompass empowering data for informed decision-making and industry-proven software tools enabling efficient supply chain planning, control, and security. Whether the requirement is a comprehensive system or individual modules, their scalable portfolio caters to businesses' unique needs and those of their customers. Partnering with a global leader like Siemens provides businesses with a technological edge. Harnessing the power of their digital twin, businesses can plan and optimize processes by simulating various events or scenarios affecting their supply chain. The digital twin replicates businesses' network configuration, granting them a level of transparency and accuracy akin to foresight into future events. This capability empowers strategic, tactical, and operational decision-making, akin to peering into a crystal ball. Leveraging these tools enables cost optimization and the mitigation of production bottlenecks, transforming a business's supply chain into an intelligent value chain. This comprehensive approach empowers businesses to streamline operations and drive efficiency in their logistics ecosystem.

CONCLUSION

The evolution from a traditional GVC to an SGVC has been made possible through transformative technologies and best practices. The integration of cutting-edge technologies, data-driven intelligence, and collaborative ecosystems has paved the way for exceptional efficiency and resilience. As industries adopt the era of smart GVCs, this synthesis serves as an insightful guide illuminating the way forward. It highlights the importance of continuous evolution to create intelligent value chains that effectively respond to the demands of a dynamic world. The case studies of five global firms illustrate how they have successfully used smart GVCs to maximize efficiency and create sustainable solutions leading to competitive advantage. Indian companies like Reliance, Tata Consultancy Services (TCS), Mahindra Group and Infosys, Wipro, and Tech Mahindra have successfully integrated advanced technologies and innovative practices into their operations. In terms of policy support, the Indian Government's Production Linked Incentive (PLI) initiatives, spanning 14 categories and involving an anticipated capital expenditure of ₹4 lakh crore over the next five years, aim to integrate India into global supply chains. In the fiscal year 2022, an investment of ₹47,500 crores was made under the PLI schemes, surpassing the designated target for the year by 106%. As a result of the PLI schemes, production and sales totalling ₹3.85 lakh crore have been achieved, contributing to the generation of 3.0 lakh jobs.

REFERENCES

Foster, C., & Graham, M. (2016). Reconsidering the Role of the Digital in Global Production Networks. *Global Networks – A Journal of Transnational Affairs*, *17*(1), 68–88. https://doi.org/10.1111/glob.12142

Foster, C., Graham, M., Mann, L., Waema, T. M., & Friederici, N. (2017). Digital Control in Value Chains: Challenges of connectivity for East African Firms. *Economic Geography*, *94*(1), 68–86. https://doi.org/10.1080/00130095.2017.1350104

Subramanian, A., & Kessler, M. (2013). The Hyperglobalization of Trade and its Future. *Social Science Research Network*. https://doi.org/10.2139/ssrn.2297994

UNCTAD (2021b). *Harnessing Blockchains for Sustainable Developments: Prospect and Challenges*. UNCTAD: Geneva.

UNCTAD(2023).https://unctad.org/publication/trade-and-development-report-2023

World Development Report (2020). *Trading for Development in the Age of Global Value Chains*. World Bank. https://www.worldbank.org/en/publication/

https://hbr.org/2022/01/how-walmart-canada-uses-blockchain-to-solve-supply-chain-challenges

https://www.alibabacloud.com/solutions/supply-chain/smart-logistics#J_5458742970

https://flex.com/resources/flex-recognized-for-groundbreaking-use-of-new-ai-driven-tool#:~:text=Flex%20has%20been%20recognized%20as,AI%2Ddriven%20contract%20review%20tool

https://siemens-digital-logistics.com/home-en

Chapter 3

Smart future innovations in the global value chain

Sabiha Kılıç
Hitit University, Corum, Turkey

INTRODUCTION

The value chain (VC) is a production model that explains how added value emerges in the process from the idea stage of services and products to design, production, and reaching the final consumer (Kaplinsky and Morris, 2001). Global value chains (GVC) were formed as a result of VCs taking place in different countries rather than in a single country. The GVC has developed with the increase in trade between countries as a result of developments in the fields of economics, politics, industry, transportation, logistics, and information and communication technologies (ICT). Before globalization, each stage of the VC was carried out in a single country. After globalization, countries specializing in different stages of production traded with each other to realize the final product within the scope of the theory of comparative advantage, which led to the development of the production model based on the GVC system. In this production model, the aim is to reduce costs and increase quality in production, marketing, and sales activities to create higher added value (Hummels, Ishii, and Yi, 2001). For this purpose, businesses take part in the GVC.

The main purpose of businesses in the GVC is to earn high income from their economic activities (Daniels, Radebaugh, and Sullivan, 2007). So much so that they need income for their sustainability and the continuation of their activities. In today's digital age, the survival of businesses depends on their ability to adapt to the evolving dynamic structure of the market. In the globalizing world, limited resources have made it necessary for each business to specialize in areas suitable for their core competencies. Specialization enables businesses to have a competitive advantage over other businesses in the GVC. Competitive advantage may be possible by having different basic capabilities from other businesses with similar resources as the business. Another way to achieve competitive advantage is innovation capacity (Becerra, 2008).

Innovation includes the production of new products, the application of new production methods, new forms of organization, the opening of new markets, and the acquisition of new sources of raw materials (Schumpeter,

DOI: 10.1201/9781003461432-3

1934, 1983). Innovation in the digital age requires continuity for businesses to maintain their competitive advantage. Therefore, when determining corporate strategies, emphasis should be placed on adapting to innovation. Dynamic market structures, constantly changing consumer needs, an increasing number of competitors entering the market, and developments in information technologies shape the changes and new trends in the global economy. Thus, these new trends paved the way for the evolution of convergence and the development of a new business environment, "covergenomic". Covergenomics are new business models that emerge from the combination of different types of technology. Products such as biotechnology, nanotechnology, e-commerce, digital banking, smartphones, hybrid cars, and unmanned vehicles are some of the final products developed as a result of covergenomics business models (Lee and Olson, 2010).

Covergenomics business models, which include strategic innovations, are important for the sustainability and success of businesses in the age of convergence. Therefore, in the study, the topics of GVC, innovation, smart future, convergence evolution, and strategic innovations are examined in detail.

THE GLOBAL VALUE CHAIN CONCEPT

Globalization dynamics, easier transportation, and developments in the communication sector have been effective in the development of the GVC. In addition, the elimination of regulatory obstacles to cross-border trade and thus the development of international trade has been the driving force in the development of the GVC (Gibbon and Ponte, 2008) In the GVC process, value is created by using different production factors such as labour force, raw materials, materials and technology in the production of valuable products and services and their delivery to end users (Norman and Ramizerz, 1993). A business's competitiveness, strategic choices, and resources determine the added value it provides to the GVC (Ireland, Hitt, and Vaidyanath, 2002). Therefore, businesses need to restructure their actions and resources to adapt to innovations in process and product technologies and thus maintain their competitive advantage (Porter, 1991). As a result, it can be stated that GVC structures are not static but dynamic and constantly evolving (Gibbon and Ponte, 2008). Economic activities performed by a business can be classified under two groups. The first group of activities includes activities related to the production of goods and services and their marketing for delivery to buyers.

The second group of activities is supporting activities. These activities provide input and infrastructure for businesses to carry out their primary activities. Supportive activities can be grouped under four headings: technology development, infrastructure, human resources management, and procurement (Porter, 1985). The VC provides a systematic analysis of cost-creating behaviours and value-producing activities to determine the cost position and value-creation potential of enterprises (Porter, 1991; Stabell and Fjeldstad, 1998; Daniels, Radebaugh, and Sullivan, 2007). In this sense, the operational efficiency of a business refers to its VC, and the unit of analysis in this VC represents the business (Porter, 1991; Stabell and Fjeldstad, 1998). In the GVC, the value chain refers to the industry itself, and the unit of analysis in this VC represents the industry (Kogut, 1985; Gibbon and Ponte, 2008). The concept of value creation is examined in detail in the following section.

VALUE CREATION AND CAPTURE

The positioning of high-value-added activities of a business depends on which activities and technologies the business should focus on, its relatively superior capabilities, and its strategic preferences regarding competitive advantages (Kogut, 1985; Porter, 1991). Businesses can succeed in creating value according to their resources and production capacities, depending on their areas of expertise and level of differentiation (Daniels, Radebaugh, and Sullivan, 2007). For businesses to generate high income and maintain their competitive advantage, they need to organize, structure, and coordinate value-added activities across borders. However, the process has become increasingly complex and challenging due to the separation of ownership and fragmentation of the production process (Gereffi, Humphrey, and Sturgeon, 2005).

One of the most important approaches that enables businesses in the GVC to achieve their value creation and retention goals is GVC governance (Dyer and Singh, 1998). GVC governance has five basic management model approaches: hierarchy, market relations, fixed, relational, and modular. Governance topology covers the characteristics of the industrial structure with VC processes, on the one hand, and the relationships between suppliers and businesses in the market, on the other hand (Gereffi, Humphrey, and Sturgeon, 2005). This governance topology covers both the relationships between the leading companies in the market and their suppliers and the characteristics of the VC processes and industrial structure (Gibbon and Ponte, 2008). Three key factors determine how the GVC will be managed. These can be listed as the capabilities of the suppliers, the coding of the information, and the complexity of the transactions. The GVC process is a dynamic process that is constantly renewed as the relationships between buyer and supplier businesses and changes in the product features and capabilities of suppliers restructure value-added activities. It is important to manage the process because of the capabilities of the suppliers, the codability of the information, and the complexity of the transactions. The GVC is a type of network in which the businesses in the chain work in cooperation with their suppliers to create value for their consumers and to ensure a fair share of the value produced. The GVC process is a dynamic process that is constantly renewed as the relationships between buyer and supplier businesses and changes in the product features and capabilities of suppliers restructure value-added activities. The capabilities of the suppliers, the coding of the information, and the complexity of the transactions are important in managing the process (Gereffi, Humphrey, and Sturgeon, 2005). Three key factors determine how the GVC will be managed. These can be listed as the capabilities of the suppliers, the coding of the information, and the complexity of the transactions (Porter, 1991; Gereffi, Humphrey, and Sturgeon, 2005). In this process, collaborative assets, complementary resources, knowledge sharing, capabilities, and effective governance are determinants of value creation and retention (Dyer and Singh, 1998). Innovation capacity and resource specificity of enterprises are the most important conditions for them to provide high returns (Becerra, 2008).

In the GVC, the most effective method of managing relationships between businesses is contracting and monitoring. To maintain higher profits from lower costs and value-creation initiatives, there are six elements to avoid. These are time pressure, cost of inventory, causal uncertainty, indivisibility of resources, complexity of the corporate social environment, and scarcity of complementary partners (Dyer and Singh, 1998).

The ability of businesses to collaborate with similar businesses allows them to seize opportunities to create value in the GVC (von Raesfeld and Roos, 2008). Three paradoxes are defined regarding how businesses can improve their collaboration capabilities. These can be listed as follows (Hakansson and Ford, 2002):

- Opportunities and limitations: A business's ability to seize current opportunities in the GVC depends on its interactions, agreements, goals, and actions with other businesses in the network.
- Influence or being affected: It concerns whether a business is affected or affected by network relationships in the GVC. This depends on the company's relationships with other businesses in the network, similar business choices, and the results of its strategic decisions and activities carried out simultaneously with other businesses.
- Controlling or being controlled: Whether businesses control or are controlled by businesses in the network in the GVC depends on the specificity of their resources and resource dependency on other businesses.

To achieve high returns and value in the network in which they operate, businesses need to harmonize their goals and objectives, strategies, and corporate structures with the network structure. In addition, other necessary conditions include being able to choose their partners correctly, adapting to the dynamic network structure, and having effective network governance (Lavie, 2006; Becerra, 2008). When the GVC literature is examined, it can be said that there are studies suggesting that businesses operating in the chain can earn high incomes by providing effective collaborations with the right partners and managing these collaborations effectively. Businesses can directly reach other businesses in the network with the right strategies and proactively adapt to the dynamic nature of the network.

Thus, they can achieve their goals of creating and retaining value through effective governance (Dyer and Singh, 1998). In this case, the following hypotheses can be stated:

- A business's ability to create value across the GVC depends on its ability to engage with the right businesses.
- A business's ability to capture value from innovation across the GVC depends on its ability to improve network governance.
- Collaborations across a business's GVC depend on their ability to generate and secure high returns.

Owners of supply sources and consumers are the two parties that create value for themselves, and opportunities to create value depend on environmental dynamics. So much so that environmental uncertainty due to industry structure, unstable market demand, environmental shock possibilities, and environmental generosity, which are among the environmental dynamics, offer opportunities for value creation (Sirmon, Hitt, and Ireland, 2007). According to Becerra (2008), three main factors increase income for businesses. These include resource specificity, business-based innovation, and value uncertainty (Becerra, 2008). Value uncertainty is caused by uncertainty about the value potential of resources, the difference between the expectation and perception of return, information asymmetry, luck, or exploratory entrepreneurship. Resource specificity results from the heterogeneity of resources across industries, and businesses have unique assets that generate high revenues (Oliver, 1998; Becerra, 2008). Business-level innovation refers to the firm's ability to recombine or restructure resources in new ways to gain a competitive advantage (Becerra, 2008).

In short, the constantly changing environmental conditions and the dynamics of the industry provide an opportunity for businesses to develop different ways of combining and using resources and generating revenue by innovating. Value is the benefit derived from the use of products and services. Perception of value, on the other hand, can be expressed by what consumers or users give up to purchase these products and services (Al-Mudimigh, Zairi, and Ahmed, 2004).

The ultimate goal of a business in the GVC is to generate high returns from its economic activities (Daniels, Radebaugh, and Sullivan, 2007). This can be achieved by providing a competitive advantage over other businesses in the GVC. Competitive advantage is the difference in value created by using more effective management strategies or by innovating compared to other companies with similar resources (Porter, 1991; Becerra, 2008).

Knowledge-intensive businesses generate revenue by organizing and structuring the necessary resources through their ability to solve problems. The returns of such enterprises are not obtained by the production of goods. Thanks to their tangible and intangible skills and abilities, they generate returns by producing solutions to their consumers' problems (Woiceshyn and Falkenberg, 2008).

CORPORATE VALUE CREATION

Creating value is one of the most fundamental purposes of institutions. What is expressed as the value may be increasing the level of social welfare, ensuring social justice, financial issues, psychological problems, etc. Every institution, including government, private, or non-profit institutions, has unique VC architectures. Five key innovation areas can be created through innovation in these value chain architectures (Gupta and Govindarajan, 2004; Chui, Löffler, and Roberts, 2010; Lee and Olson, 2010; Kavadias, Ladas and Loch, 2016; Lenovo, 2019):

- Utilitarian, hedonistic, or experiential consumer value
- New products and services
- Redefining the consumer base
- New business models with advanced ICT
- Designing the value architecture to ensure high efficiency from beginning to end

Each institution has its own unique mission, vision, purpose, target and strategic plans suitable for them. The common goal of all institutions' work is to increase the effectiveness of the aforementioned areas of value creation. For this reason, institutions need to rank their value-creation areas according to their importance levels to increase their performance (Govindarajan, 2016). Among the five areas of value creation listed earlier, the areas of developing new business models, redefining the consumer base, and redesigning the value chain architecture have been areas where many new developments have occurred due to globalization, digitalization, and technology combining different types of technology (Lee and Olson, 2010).

Consumer value can be associated with the concepts of speed, customization, good quality and reasonable price. However, these values represent only market entry requirements. These alone cannot provide a sustainable competitive advantage. Today, consumers want to participate in the production process, have hedonistic experiences, and capture sharing and learning opportunities. These demands go beyond utilitarian values. Therefore, businesses have to develop goods, services, and business models that will create new consumer value. For example, "do it yourself" has become a new area of interest for consumers, especially in food, tourism, clothing, and jewellery (von Hippel, Ogawa, and De Long, 2011).

Today, there are significant changes in the consumer base of businesses. New types of consumer bases include regular consumers who shop in-store, consumers who shop only online, and consumers who shop via e-commerce. Additionally, there are markets with low competition for newly developed goods or services, called the blue ocean market. These markets feature business models created using different types of technology. E-commerce has become widespread all over the world. Cloud computing, open source software, and information technology-supported new sharing economy-based services such as Uber, Zipcar, and Airbnb are widely used (Sundararajan, 2016).

Massive open online courses (MOOCs), surgical robotics (Social, Location, and Mobile Services (SoLoMo)), and Instagram are goods and services that create new business opportunities that combine different types of technology that are being used shortly. Such goods and services will continue to increase and be used in the smart future (Heinemann and Gaiser, 2015).

SMART FUTURE

There are different interpretations of different views on the concept of "smart". According to one view, the concept of "smart" requires the proactive implementation of innovative ideas to achieve the imagined future. Therefore, it is necessary to be goal-oriented and willing (Smart Future Initiative, 2016).

There are big differences between wanting a smart future and creating it. So much so that it requires the ability to foresee scenarios that include possible challenges regarding the imagined smart future (Canton, 2015).

The smart future includes open-access digital connections, Internet of Things (IoT), artificial intelligence (AI), smart sensors, and cloud computing technologies (Bhaskar et al., 2023). In this sense, it can be said that the smart future can make people's lives freer, more prosperous, and more comfortable. In the modern social order, people may have to deal with many problems and difficulties. In the smart societies of the future, people will be able to find solutions to these problems in cooperation with other people using existing technology and information (Lee and Trimi, 2018). There are needs needed to create such a future, and detailed information about these needs is examined in the following section.

NEEDS OF THE SMART FUTURE

Although a smart future is the goal of many countries, businesses, organizations, and even individuals today, just wanting it is not enough. A smart future also requires many needs. These needs can be listed as follows:

- Smart people: The smart future requires well-educated and well-equipped people. The global environment has become dynamic as a result of rapid developments in the field of information technologies.

Some researchers claim that 90% of the world's knowledge has been created in the last decade (Kim, Trimi, and Chung, 2014). For this reason, there is a need for individuals who can think analytically and make important predictions for the future using big data.

- Smart leadership: In a global and dynamic world, it is not enough for leaders to simply have charismatic personalities who make tough decisions. They also have to be good communicators. They should also have the ability to co-create the mission, vision, and goals shared by the employees within a common mind and discipline (Kramer and Pfitzer, 2016; Ramaswammy and Ozcan, 2014). Advanced technologies are not always successful in creating prosperous societies. Therefore, smart leaders need to be able to convince and motivate their societies to create the smart societies of the future (Schumpeter, 1934). Technological applications do not always create new employment areas. On the contrary, in sectors with advanced technologies, many jobs are performed by machines and robots. This leads to automation and thus to unemployment of many people around the world (Frey and Osborne, 2013). For this reason, smart leadership involves creating business lines that meet the requirements of the age, instead of many business lines that have been eliminated by increasing automation as a result of advances in ICT.
- Smart governments: In the century we live in, governments are no longer institutions that merely manage their people and carry out the necessary controls. So much so that the masses have turned into smart people thanks to advanced ICT. For this reason, smart governments should be in a structure that adopts the understanding of accountability, rule of law, transparency, and social justice and ensures the creation of a safe country with the joint participation of their citizens. In this sense, smart governments are structures with sustainable economic growth and stability, and reliable and consistent discipline (Lenovo, 2019).
- Smart infrastructure: Smart future includes effective management of issues such as public safety, smart infrastructure (water, environment, waste, etc.) systems, smart electricity distribution network, and security of ICT. Smart infrastructure systems required for smart cities require the use of applications such as closed-circuit TV, the IoT, cloud computing systems, smart sensors, and advanced analytics (Chui, Löffler, and Roberts, 2010). The "Smart City Forum" was developed to develop smart infrastructures. On this platform, applications that can be developed and implemented to develop and manage smart city infrastructures are shared (Hamblen, 2016).
- Smart industries: The digital age requires making predictable decisions about the digital evolution process while meeting the demands and needs of today's consumers (Rogers, 2016). The developments in the service sector require commercial enterprises to make their products

high added value by packaging them with unique services that will provide a competitive advantage. Besides all these, the new digital age and the new business models that emerge with it reveal new initiatives with high levels of efficiency in consumer services. Instagram, WhatsApp, and Airbnb are some of the examples of these new initiatives. These new initiatives have significant advantages in terms of collaboration, low cost, speed, and accessibility. In addition, such new ventures benefit from technology-intensive business models such as mobile applications, social commerce, and smart corporate systems (Lee, 2015).

- Smart health and education systems: The most important changes in the smart future will occur in two areas. These areas are education and health (Garg, 2022). Today, smart devices that read magnetic resonance imaging (fMRI) and X-rays and technologies equipped with new and intelligent systems such as e-pulse are used, and it is stated that many new technologies that will replace human resources will be developed in the future. MOOCs, for example, are already prevalent in education worldwide. Such intelligent systems will have profound effects and consequences at the economic, social, and individual levels.
- Smart homes and automobiles: In the hierarchy of needs, the first two needs that are in the first place and arouse the desire of people are a comfortable and affordable house and a car. In the smart future, with the support of advanced ICT, smart homes and cars will also become widespread. Many smart infrastructure systems and devices (IoT, AI, unmanned vehicles, etc.) are used in the development of smart home and smart car systems, and it is estimated that their usage levels will increase in the future. For example, in smart home systems, home security systems, lighting, and heating systems can be controlled by mobile devices, and the contents of the refrigerator can be managed thanks to IoT technology. For example, Apple, Tesla, and Google, which are among the world brands, are carrying out many projects together on unmanned cars. It can be said that such developments and innovations will improve people's quality of life (Lenovo, 2019).

Rapid globalization and technological developments reveal new market forces. So much so that it has become a living in a dynamic and fluid global community. In such an environment, innovation has become one of the most important requirements for the sustainability of businesses (Lee and Trimi, 2018). Thanks to the ongoing innovation efforts throughout human history, people have been able to continue their lives and live a quality life. Developments in agriculture, industry, ICT, and innovations developed or created aim to create higher added value (Lee, Olson, and Trimi, 2012). Innovation aims to create higher consumer value, provide a competitive advantage for businesses, and increase the quality of life of people. But its ultimate goal is to design a better future. The concept of innovation is generally used synonymously with the concept of change (Tushman and O'Reilly, 1997). Change refers to changing something from its current state to another state, and it can be caused by natural phenomena, unique designs, or the collaborative efforts of individuals (Lee and Olson, 2010). Innovation, on the other hand, is a broader concept that includes the concept of change. The development process of the innovation is described in detail in the following section.

DEVELOPMENT STAGES OF INNOVATION

The development stages of innovation consist of four stages. These are known as Innovation 1.0, 2.0, 3.0, and 4.0 (Lee and Olson, 2010). Innovation 1.0 is a closed innovation in which innovations are carried out within the enterprise. So many of the new ideas are developed in in-house research and development (R&D) (Lee, Olson, and Trimi, 2012). Innovation 1.0 innovations have been implemented by many market-leading businesses in the past. For example, revolutionary technologies such as information theory, the C programming language, radio astronomy, the UNIX operating system, transistors, and laser, which were the most successful products of their time, were invented and developed in Bell Laboratories. NASA develops its unique core capabilities within its R&D department. Innovation 2.0 is an innovation based on collaboration with other organizations and businesses in the VC. (Tapscott, 2006). Most of the world's brands, such as Boeing, Zara, Mattel, Apple, and Dell are innovating in the Innovation 2.0 phase. Innovation 3.0 is defined as open innovation. In this innovation stage, businesses look for innovation sources inside and outside the organization (Chesbrough, 2003). It expresses the common mind and the use of common resources (Afuah and Tucci, 2013). In this innovation phase, innovation intermediaries defined as "knowledge intermediaries" are used. The most well-known information brokers include Inno Centive, Your Encore, Yet2.com, and Nine Sigma. Although open innovation has many advantages, it also has challenges (Lee, Olson, and Trimi, 2012). Innovation 4.0 is defined as collaborative innovation. It has an innovation ecosystem. In this ecosystem, the ideas of the enterprises are evaluated and/or combined. Innovations at this stage are developed together with the in-house R&D department, the use of open source, collaborating organizations, and consumers. The development and implementation of innovation plans are also carried out together. Thus, innovations are produced jointly (Lee, Olson, and Trimi, 2012; Gobble, 2014; Ramaswammy and Ozcan, 2014; Govindarajan, 2016). The best-known strengths of collaborative innovation are (Porter and Kramer, 2011; Kim, Trimi, and Chung, 2014; Kramer and Pfitzer, 2016):

- There is a continuous stream of information.
- It provides the creation of big data.

- It creates an innovation culture.
- It designs a convergence filter that is difficult to imitate.

Nike and Samsung are two of the best-known brands to have joint innovation programmes.

THE INNOVATION LIFECYCLE

In the digital age, the life cycle of the core capabilities of organizations is short. For example, Kodak, Nokia, Blackberry, Shap, Wang Computer, and K-Mart are the brands whose deaths we have witnessed have failed to adapt to the digital age and develop innovation. For this reason, it is stated that innovations should have a continuous activity process to provide a sustainable competitive advantage, not a one-off. The shape of the innovation lifecycle is the S-curve (Christensen, 1992). The curve is shown in Figure 3.1.

The starting point of the curve is the stage at which an innovation is cultivated, and the necessary resources are allocated. At this stage, many new ideas, patents, or inventions may not even make it to the application stage. Others, even with the necessary management support and resources, may not be in demand in the market and thus have a short lifecycle. In contrast, the marginal rate of return (MRR) (cash cows) of some innovations in detergents, medicinal products, and similar consumer products can lead to a long lifecycle. The MRR increases rapidly until the innovation is harvested, but after that point, it declines as it reaches the inflection point. The S-curve declines rapidly after this point. In this case, businesses either cease their

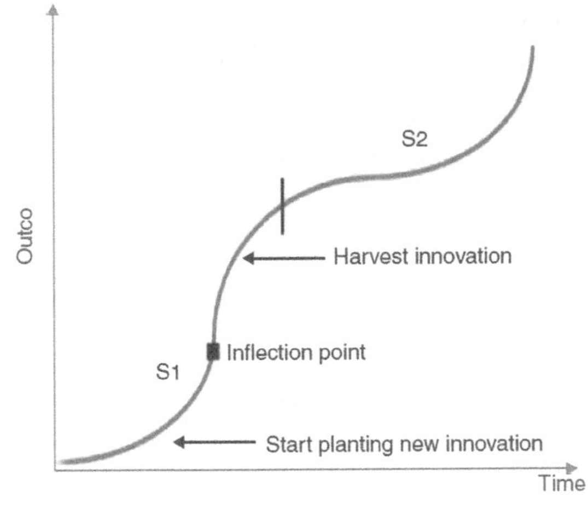

Figure 3.1 S-curve: innovation lifecycle.

(Lee and Trimi, 2018)

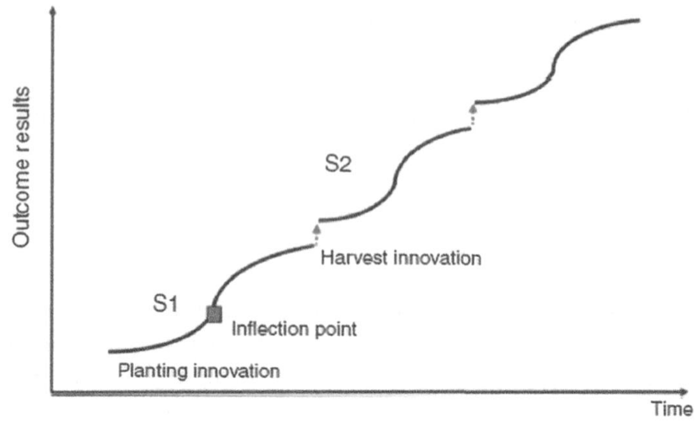

Figure 3.2 S-curves: continuous innovation.

(Lee and Trimi, 2018)

efforts to harvest innovation or an innovative rival business may initiate a new S-curve, as seen in Figure 3.1. This is known as the continuous innovation curve and can be seen in Figure 3.2.

Figure 3.2 shows the continuous innovation of S-curves. This curve is the innovative product curve of flexible, agile, and versatile high-performance enterprises (O'Reilly and Tushman, 2013). These businesses create dynamic capabilities in line with the market environment as their innovation strategies change rapidly. Therefore, they try to adapt between radical and constantly changing innovations. (Teece, 2014). Therefore, they manage their continuous innovation S-curves with proactive strategies. In addition, these businesses initiate new S-curves over the top of the S-curves by using new technologies and business ideas that combine different technologies, as seen in Figure 3.2. Businesses need to plan the sustainability of their continuous innovation S-curves. That's why they make strategic innovations. The following section provides detailed information on the convergence era and the evolution of strategic innovations.

CONVERGENCE AGE AND STRATEGIC INNOVATIONS

The global economy is shaped by the rapid changes and new trends that are experienced today. On the other hand, these new trends paved the way for the evolution of convergence and thus the development of a new business environment, "covergenomic". Covergenomics are new business models that emerge from the merging of different types of technology and are called convergence economies. In the field of convergence, there are many topics ranging from organizational factors, technologies, industry, and biological artificial systems. In convergence economies, strategic innovations are needed to create new values in the VC (Lee and Olson, 2010). Strategic innovation will be discussed further in the following sections. The evolution of convergence is explained in detail in the following section.

EVOLUTION OF CONVERGENCE

Convergence is a combination of data processing and word processing. It involves combining different types of technology. Convergence has emerged as a result of human creativity and adaptability. Humans can learn and creatively transfer a great deal of practical knowledge. Convergence can be as complex as biotechnology, which is the combination of biology and information technology, or as simple as the pencil sharpener, which is a combination of an eraser and a pencil sharpener. Today, there is a wave of convergence in which societies, institutions, businesses and individuals change the way and process of working. Convergence evolution offers new opportunities in different ways to create new value in the traditional business world. Table 3.1 presents the six stages of convergence evolution (Lee and Olson, 2010).

Phase 1: PPC – part and product convergence

Part-product convergence has improved over a long period. Clock radios, for example, are a combination of two mature products. It is the convergence of mobile phones, iPods, internet access, cameras, and even telecommunication functions. The Braun Oral-B electric toothbrush is also a combination of battery and electronics technology. More recently, Apple and Nike brands have combined iPod and gym equipment to enable exercisers to have more fun during their workouts. These two brands have recently brought to market an important example of convergence with the combination of the iPod Nano and Nike running shoes. Nike running shoes, equipped with wireless

Table 3.1 Evolution of convergence (Anonymous, 2006)

	Level of convergence	*Purpose*
Phase 1	Part and Product Convergence	Product Innovation
Phase 2	Functional Convergence	Process Innovation
Phase 3	Enterprise Convergence	Enterprise Value Chain Efficiency
Phase 4	Technology Convergence	New Technology. Product Innovation
Phase 5	Industry Convergence	New Industries. Customer Value Innovation
Phase 6	Bio-artificial Systems	Ubiquitous Innovation

systems that can communicate with iPod Nano, have been developed to monitor the heart rate, running speed, and distance covered by the athletes while they are running and also listening to music. LCD technology, on the other hand, is another example of convergence that contributes to the development of education and training abilities, as well as to playing more realistic video games, as well as to experience better quality movies on long journeys (Anonymous, 2007).

Phase 2: FC – functional convergence

Business process reengineering was an innovative approach adopted in the 1990s to determine the best way to do things. In these years, business processes were being redesigned to perform the work in the best possible way. Thus, innovation in production processes has enabled value chains to be more efficient and leaner. This approach, known as functional convergence, has been implemented by many brands. Dell PC, for example, has removed wholesalers and retailers from its VC to enable faster delivery of PCs to consumers. McDonalds has played a role in making the fast food industry an important part of the world economy, especially in the United States. McDonald's has developed a functional business model that brings mass production to the food industry. In this business model, the service process is designed to be ready for use in a short time, with low-cost labour and a limited set of products within the framework of meticulous instructions. The preparation process of McDonald's hamburgers is a good example of functional convergence, which led to a major revolution in food distribution in the United States (Anonymous, 2006).

Phase 3: OC – organizational convergence

In the digital economy and e-global era, businesses collaborate with other businesses to enrich their value chains. Strategic alliances and joint ventures with supplier organizations, assembly parts manufacturers, distributors, and even competing businesses are the best examples of organizational convergence. Brands like Walmart, Dell, and Nike need to have strong collaborative functions in their supply chains. Business networks are new business models where each business partner brings its core talent to the VC. These business models are used to provide competitive advantage and to maintain competitive advantage (Bacon and Leung, 2007; Ghatak and Garg, 2022). For this purpose, cooperative assemblies are formed, and supply chains are created all over the world that allow participants to benefit from their fields of expertise (Stock and Boyer, 2009; Chandra and Kumar, 2000). For example, Nike only carries out brand management activities, while its products are manufactured by contract manufacturing businesses around the world.

Phase 4: TC – technology convergence

Revolutionary developments have been experienced in the field of technology convergence in the period after the 1980s. During this period, different types of technologies were brought together to create new goods, services, processes, and technologies (Bacon and Leung, 2007; Ghatak and Garg, 2022). AI, ICT, engineering and nanotechnology are the areas where the best-known examples of technological convergence are seen. The most widely used technology for technology convergence is LCDs. LCD screens have replaced instrument screens in automobiles. By converging LCD screen technology with computer technology, it is ensured that text and graphics are reflected from a small screen. As a result of the convergence of agricultural and chemical engineering in the pharmaceutical industry, many new drugs have been introduced to the market through biotechnology. So much so that these drugs can significantly treat genetic structure diseases. Neurotechnology has emerged as a result of the convergence of biology with computer science. In the field of neuroscience, studies are carried out on the neocortex to better understand how brain diseases and psychiatric disorders can be treated and to explain how learning and memory work. As a result of the convergence of biology with engineering, new products and services with important functions, such as fMRI and positron emission tomography (PET) scanning, have emerged (Talbot, 2005).

Phrase 5: IC – industry convergence

Industry convergence is two or more competing or cooperating industries coming together to create a new industry. For example, iTunes is the convergence of the IT and music industries. Walt Disney is a convergence of the entertainment, film, hotel, and golf industries. Industry convergence can be classified into three groups. These can be listed as functional convergence, complementary convergence, and institutional convergence. Functional convergence is when products from different sectors perform the same function or functions. TVs becoming smart TVs is a good example of functional convergence as a combination of personal computers and the television industry. Complementary convergence is the purchase of multiple products and services from different industries in a single location. Taking travel and accommodation services from the same place can be given as an example. Just as travel agencies sell both flight tickets and hotel rooms in their holiday packages. Institutional convergence is when the products of the two industries are interconnected. Complementary convergence is focused on the product under development, while institutional convergence is focused on organizational structure. For example, as a result of the convergence of the banking sector and the mortgage sector, both check deposit services and mortgage loans can be offered to consumers. Convergence in the energy sector gives some oil industry firms the freedom to develop oil alongside hybrid fuels. The digital convergence that emerged as a result of the convergence of information technologies and publishing has laid the groundwork for digital publishing products and services. Digital publishing combines editorial work, TV, radio, print, and web services to serve all media (Lee and Trimi, 2018).

Phase 6: CBA – convergence of biology and artificial systems

The convergence of biological and artificial systems is the highest level of convergence. It represents the cutting edge of product development, where ideas from previous levels of convergence are transformed into radically new methods and products. Ubiquitous life (u-life) is the management and control of human life by technology-system combination. So much so that miniaturization, visualization, manipulation, and evaluation are changing people's lifestyles Garg (2023). There are many areas where miniaturization is applied. For example, thanks to the developments in the field of chip technology and the ever-smaller size of the chips, the production of more miniature electronic devices has become possible. Miniaturization has also made revolutionary contributions to health care through gene and molecular biology. Significant advances have been made in the field of visualization thanks to molecular technology. X-ray crystallography provides resolution down to the size of a water molecule. Atomic force microscopy enables the detection of variances in atoms by converting scanning surfaces into images. Manipulation (processing) expands the knowledge gained through visualization. NanoManipulator combines virtual reality and haptic feedback. This allows operators to process the material at the nanoscale. It also allows students in medical education to experience the sensation of a needle sticking into the spinal cord. Evaluation is to gain value from technology. The genome project is a technology developed as a result of the use of hybrid technologies such as biotechnology and information technologies. Table 3.2 contains some examples of product and service convergences.

Table 3.2 Examples of best product and service convergence (Lee and Olson, 2010)

	Phase	*Manufacturing*	*Service*
1	Product Convergence	Mobile phones (phones, access to information, camera, games) Coffee (soy milk, decaf, diet, frappuccino)	Jazzercise (jazz sport)
2	Functional Convergence	Lean manufacturing Enterprise Resouce Planning System	McDonald's hamburgers (Fast service, consistent quality, fun for kids)

(Continued)

Table 3.2 (Continued)

	Phase	*Manufacturing*	*Service*
3	Organizational Convergence	Steel (from mass production to mini-factories)	Banks
4	Technological Convergence	Hybrid Cars	Mobile phones
5	Industrial Convergence	Starbucks Political ads	e-Bay
6	Convergence of bio-artifical systems	Medical tests (from X-rays to MRIs)	Chinese Medicine

The following section provides detailed information on the age of convergence that reshaped the VC and the strategic innovations in this age.

CONVERGENCE REVOLUTION AND STRATEGIC INNOVATIONS

The convergence revolution, which has changed traditional management approaches, offers new opportunities to create value. Traditional management approaches aim to strengthen and optimize the core competencies of businesses. Some of the best-known traditional management approaches are cost leadership, global strategy, consumer-centric management, focus, differentiation, continuous improvement, and benchmarking. Traditional management approaches strive to increase efficiency in the VC. However, these approaches alone contribute to a limited extent for businesses to explore the blue oceans (Kim and Mauborgne, 2005).

With the age of convergence, businesses are no longer isolated and independent entities. Rather, they are members of a large and open GVC for strategic alliances and joint ventures. Convergence technologies have required businesses to pursue not only economies of scale and scope but also economies of expertise and cooperation (Gupta and Govindarajan, 2004). In the age of convergence, strategic innovations are the reconceptualization of how an organization creates value in different ways. At this point, the innovation activities that organizations will implement to create value according to the level and purpose of the innovations they will carry out for strategic innovations can be examined under three headings. These are process innovation, consumer value innovation, and consumer base innovation. These innovations are briefly discussed next (Lee and Trimi, 2018):

- Process innovation: It involves increasing efficiency by redesigning the VC architecture from one end to the other. For this purpose, it receives support from supply, transformation, distribution channel innovations, and supply innovation. It consists of just-in-time manufacturing, outsourcing, and innovations for electronic markets. Transformation innovation. It includes innovations in areas such as lean manufacturing, additive manufacturing, modular manufacturing, batching, sorting, and repackaging. Distribution channel innovation encompasses innovations for direct distribution, direct marketing through the demand chain, and outsourcing.

- Consumer value innovation: It involves recreating and enriching consumer value. For this purpose, quality, speed, sensory marketing, and mass customization tools are used. So much so that businesses need to be fast enough to provide instant responses to the needs of today's consumers, perform mass customization to meet consumer expectations fully or even beyond, and seek new types of convergence that will also meet the emotional needs of consumers such as a sense of security, hope, beauty, and grace. Although high quality and low cost are necessary criteria for market entry, they are not sufficient to create consumer value.
- Innovation of the consumer base: A consumer is an end user of a product or service. However, in today's e-global economy, people who do not consume the product are also considered consumers. Therefore, global consumers, e-consumers, consumer communities, and potential consumers are also included in the consumer base. Therefore, businesses should look for ways to create new demands and develop new markets in the blue ocean, thanks to the new types of convergence they will develop using the convergence of technology and new methods.

The VC for process, consumer value, and consumer base innovations is summarized in Figure 3.3.

Apart from these, strategic innovations can also be classified according to the type of approach used. The first type of innovation is the optimal innovation achieved through continuous improvement and development of existing core competencies using the Kaizen approach. The second type of innovation is a revolutionary innovation in which new frontiers are

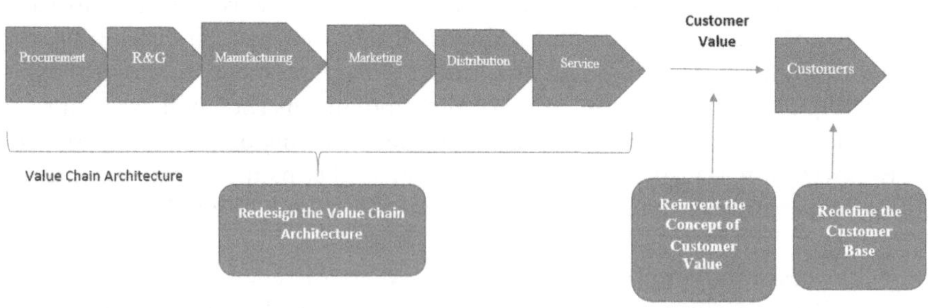

Figure 3.3 The VC and innovation areas.

(Lee and Olson, 2010)

discovered to create the core capabilities of the enterprise. The third type of innovation is the combination of the first two types of innovation. It is a convergence-based innovation that expresses the combination of different types of technology. The optimum balance between benefit and discovery for any organization is achieved by factors such as the type of industry in which it operates, the size of the business, its age, management approach, vision, product lines, and DNA of the organization. The areas of strategic innovation classifications are shown in Figure 3.4.

Strategic innovation is necessary for businesses to be sustainable and successful in the age of convergence. Strategic innovations have many successful examples. For example, airline companies that want to create consumer value by reducing their costs in the airline industry have redefined their VCs by redefining their criteria. Thanks to fleet standardization, they have reduced their maintenance costs. They reduced operating costs by using cabin crews for inter-flight aircraft cleaning. They have obtained a price advantage by using small and low-tax airports (Thamara, 2007). Advanced technological innovations can be utilized in airline innovations. For example, the use of biometrics with the joint venture of Singapore Airlines and the Singapore Civil Aviation Authority provides a fully automated, seamless consumer experience travel (Kaplinsky and Morris, 2001).

In air transportation, biometrics is used for check-in. It ensures that security checks and immigration permits are issued before immigration. However, the main purpose is not just security. It is also to integrate processes for high service quality. This strategic innovation enables reducing the error rate, increasing the security level, increasing the level of consumer service, effective use of self-service technologies and simplifying processes (Lee and Trimi, 2018).

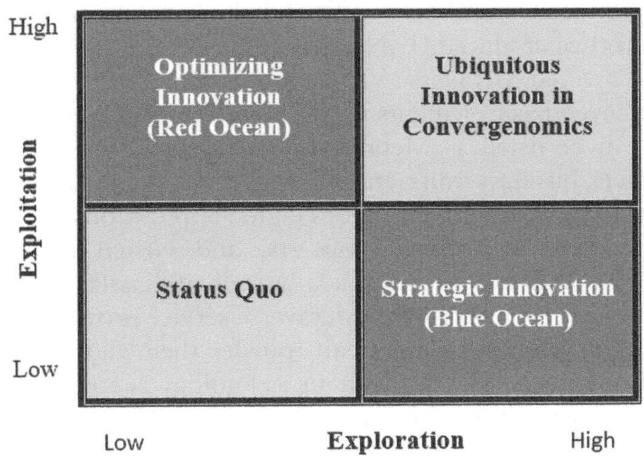

Figure 3.4 Strategic innovation classification.

(Lee and Olson, 2010)

Another sector where strategic innovations are heavily used is banking. The banking sector serves a mature market in a competitive market environment. The sector establishes collaborations with the automobile industry for automobile loans and with insurance and consulting firms for financial advice. It uses web technologies for internet banking, which represents an evolutionary process in product/service innovation. It uses ATM technology as a process innovation to increase productivity and reduce staffing. It gains a competitive advantage by providing superior consumer value and creating new demand through corporate system technology. Consumer relationship management is an important tool in creating consumer value (Tapscott, Ticoll, and Lowy, 2000).

Increasing developments in the field of digital technology and the Metaverse applications that have started to be discussed again have created a new environment for strategic innovations. One of these strategic innovations is MetaChain, suitable for the age of convergence, which brings together the Metaverse universe and blockchain technology. The following section contains detailed information about the VC architecture with the MetaChain concept.

METACHAIN VALUE CHAIN

MetaChain is a next-generation VC that automates the complex interaction process between Metaverse Users-MU and Metaverse Service Producer-MSP. Smart contracts are used to manage transactions in the MetaChain system. MetaChain uses blockchain technology to protect digital assets and ensure the data integrity of Metaverse applications. In addition to its immutability and transparency features, blockchain technology ensures the protection of digital assets in the Metaverse universe, thanks to asymmetric key and digital signature technologies, and also protects the privacy of users in the system (Lee et al., 2021; Nguyen et al., 2022). Figure 3.5 shows the blockchain-powered Metaverse VC Architecture.

There are seven basic elements in the MetaChain VC, as shown in Figure 3.5. These can be listed as Metaverse service providers, Metaverse users, smart contracts, business transactions, blockchain, digital assets, and blocks. MSP is a service provider that provides digital applications and services such as virtual conferences, virtual concerts, and virtual reality games to Metaverse users. Metaverse users each have digital assets in the Metaverse system. Metaverse users must pay Metaverse service providers to access services in the VC. Metaverse users can transfer their digital assets to other Metaverse users in the VC. Blockchain technology is a platform that plays an intermediary role in the safe execution of all these transactions. All digital assets of Metaverse users and interactions that occur in the Metaverse value chain are recorded on the blockchain. Thus, all processes in the VC are automated. For example, the Metaverse Service Provider publishes its smart contract containing the fees and conditions for the services it offers. The

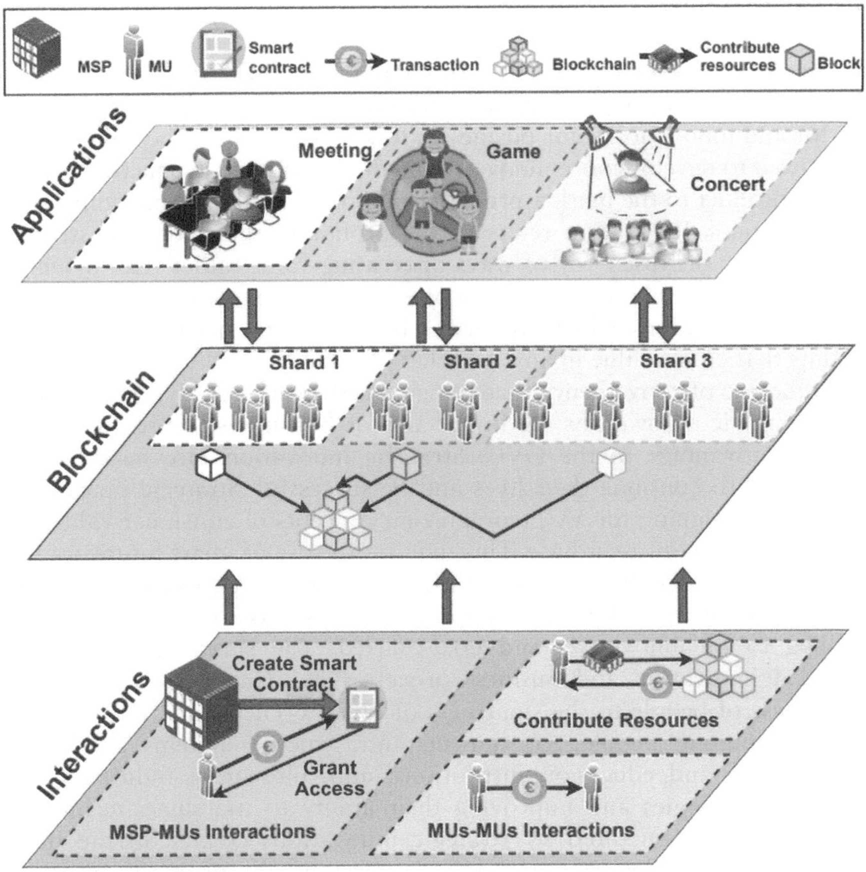

Figure 3.5 MetaChain VC.

(Nguyen et al., 2022)

Metaverse user makes the payment for the service requested by the terms of this agreement. After the payment process is completed, a confirmation message is sent to the relevant parties by the smart contract. This message is used as the access key in the MetaChain VC (Luu et al., 2016).

The blockchain also represents a database where digital asset transfers of Metaverse users are recorded. Digital assets of Metaverse users in the MetaChain VC can be transferred or exchanged seamlessly through the blockchain. For example, if a Metaverse user who has a virtual concert ticket has decided not to go to the concert, he can resell this ticket to another Metaverse user in the MetaChain VC. The MetaChain VC enables such exchanges to be made securely and transparently, thanks to smart contracts and blockchain technology (Zamani, Movahedi, and Raykova, 2018).

CONCLUSION

Technological developments, the growth of the world economy, the increase in international trade, and digitalization have begun to highlight the value factor and innovations. For businesses to keep up with the new digital age, they need to develop more innovative methods from the production process of the product to the market presentation process and even including after-sales services. Innovation refers to the profitable application of strategic creativity or the discovery of ways of creating value rather than inventing the undiscovered. Thus, innovation offers a system of transforming creative ideas and inventions, which are formed in line with the needs of the age, into results that create value in any field that affects life.

In the age of convergence that brings together different types of technology, strategic innovations are important for businesses to provide a competitive advantage in the GVC. Strategic innovations are necessary for businesses to continue their lives and be successful. Strategic innovations include redesigning the VC, reorganizing concepts of consumer value, and redefining the consumer base. This requires the use of smart future applications in GVC design. The smart future requires being proactive in implementing innovative ideas. It is important for businesses to be goal-oriented, willing to be innovative, and goal-centred. The smart future includes detailed innovation and business processes in many subjects, from the smartness of people to the smartness of objects. The smart future encompasses equipping people, governments, infrastructure systems, administrators, health and education institutions, and, ultimately, industries with smart technologies and improving their ability to use smart technology. Thus GVCs restructured by strategic innovations created in the future world dominated by smart technologies offer significant opportunities for businesses, individuals, and countries.

The study contains detailed information on the above-mentioned issues and is a resource for students, academic staff, professionals, and businesses working on the GVC.

REFERENCES

Afuah, A. and Tucci, C. L. (2013). Value capture and crowdsourcing. *Academy of Management Review*. 38(3), 457–460. doi: 10.5465/amr.2012.0423

Al-Mudimigh, A. S., Zairi, M. and Ahmed, A. M. (2004). Extending the concept of the supply chain: the effective management of value chains. *International Journal of Production Economics*. 87(3), 309–320. doi: 10.1016/j.ijpe.2003.08.004

Anonymous. (2006). Storage insurance. *Health Management Technology*. 27(10), 58–66.

Anonymous. (2007). Displays to keep an eye on. *The Economist*, 4–6.

Bacon, D. and Leung, D. (2007). Toward a world with quantum computers. *Communications of the ACM*. 50(9), 55–59. doi: 10.1145/1284621.1284648

Becerra, M. (2008). A resource-based view analysis of the conditions for the emergence of profits. *Journal of Business*. 34(6), 1110–1126. doi: 10.1177/0149206308324323

Bhaskar, A., Yadav, P., Singh, S. P., Kumar, V., Srivastava, S. (2023). "Role of Artificial Intelligence in Healthcare Management" (Chapter 3) into A. Garg, R. V. E. Balas, P. Ojha and P. K. Srivasta (Eds.) *Reinventing Technological Innovations with Artifical Intelligence*. Singapore: Bentham Science Publishers.

Canton, J. (2015). *Future Smart: Managing The Game-Changing Trends That Will Transform Your World*. Boston: Da Capo Press.

Chandra, C. and Kumar, S. (2000). Supply chain management in theory and practice: a fad or a fundamental change? *Industry Management & Data Systems*. 100(3), 100–113. Retrieved from https://www.icesi.edu.co/blogs/logisticamiercoles141/files/2014/02/supply-cahin-in-theory-and-practice.pdf

Chesbrough, H. (2003). *Open Innovation: The New Imperative for Creating and Profiting from Technology*. Boston: Harvard Business School Press.

Christensen, C. M. (1992). Exploring the limits of the technology S-curve. *Production and Operations Management*. 1(4), 334–357. doi: 10.1111/j.1937-5956.1992.tb00001.x

Chui, M., Löffler, M. and Roberts, R. (2010). *The Internet of Things*. McKinsey, Quarterly. Retrieved from https://www.mckinsey.com/industries/technology-media-and-telecommunications/our-insights/the-internet-of-things#/

Daniels, J. D., Radebaugh, L. H. and Sullivan, D. P. (2007). *International Business: Environments and Operations, Upper Saddle River*. New Jersey: Pearson Education, Inc.

Dyer, J. H. and Singh, H. (1998). The relational view: cooperative strategy and sources of inter-organizational competitive advantage. *Academy of Management Review*. 23(4), 660–679. doi: 10.2307/259056

Frey, C. B. and Osborne, M. A. (2013). *The Future of Employment: How Susceptible Are Jobs to Computerisation?* Oxford, UK: Oxford Martin School.

Garg, A. (2022). *CoReS-Respiratory Strength Predicting Framework Using Noninvasive Technology for Remote Monitoring During Heath Disasters*. Global Healthcare Disasters: Predicting the Unpredictable with Emerging Technologies, 109–121.

Garg, A. (Ed.). (2023). *Reinventing Technological Innovations with Artificial Intelligence*. Bentham Science Publishers.

Gereffi, G., Humphrey, J. and Sturgeon, T. (2005). The governance of the global value chain. *Review of International Political Economy*. 12(1), 78–104. doi: 10.1080/09692290500049805

Ghatak, A. and Garg, A. (2022). Power transmission project: a framework to align project success with organization goal. *International Journal of System Assurance Engineering and Management*. 13(4), 1817–1833.

Gibbon, P. and Ponte, S. (2008). Global value chains: from governance to governmentality? *Economy and Society*. 37(3), 365–392. doi: 10.1080/03085140802172680

Gobble, M. M. (2014). Charting the innovation ecosystem. *Research and Technology Management*. 57(4), 55–57. doi: 10.5437/08956308X5704005

Govindarajan, V. (2016). *The Three Box Solution: A Strategy For Leading Innovation*. Boston: Harvard Business Review Press.

Gupta, A. K. and Govindarajan, V. (2004). *Global Strategy and Organization*. Hoboken, NJ: John Wiley & Sons.

Hakansson, H. and Ford, D. (2002). How should companies interact in business networks? *Journal of Business Research*. 55(2), 133–139. doi: 10.1016/S0148-2963(00)00148-X

Hamblen, M. (2016). In Atlanta, smart city plans aim for safety. *Computerworld*. 1, 1–6. Retrieved from https://www.computerworld.com/article/3028610/in-atlanta-smart-city-plans-aim-for-safety.html

Heinemann, G. and Gaiser, C. (2015). *Always on and Always in Touch: The New Buying Behaviors*. Berlin: Springer.

Hummels, D., Ishii, J. and Yi, K. M. (2001). The nature and growth of vertical specialization in world trade. *Journal of International Economics*. 54(1), 75–96. doi: 10.1016/S0022-1996(00)00093-3

Ireland, R. D., Hitt, M. A. and Vaidyanath, D. (2002). Alliance management as a source of competitive advantage. *Journal of Management*. 28(3), 413–446. doi: 10.1177/014920630202800308

Kaplinsky, R. and Morris, M. (2001). *A Handbook for Value Chain Research*. IDRC, January. 1–109. Retrieved from https://www.researchgate.net/publication/42791981_A_Handbook_for_Value_Chain_Research

Kavadias, S., Ladas, K. and Loch, C. (2016). The transformative business model: how to tell if you have one. *Harvard Business Review*. 94(10), 90–98. Retrieved from https://hbr.org/2016/10/the-transformative-business-model

Kim, G. H., Trimi, S. and Chung, J. H. (2014). Big data applications in the government sector. *Communications of the ACM*. 57(3), 78–85. doi: 10.1145/2500873

Kim, W. C. and Mauborgne, R. (2005). *Blue Ocean Strategy*. Cambridge, MA: Harvard Business School Press.

Kogut, B. (1985). Designing global strategies: comparative and competitive value-added chains. *Sloan Management Review*. 26(4), 15–28. doi: 10.1002/tie.5060280105

Kramer, M. R. and Pfitzer, M. W. (2016). The ecosystem of shared value. *Harvard Business Review*. 94(10), 81–89. Retrieved from https://hbr.org/2016/10/the-ecosystem-of-shared-value

Lavie, D. (2006). Capability reconfiguration: an analysis of incumbent responses to technological change. *Academy of Management Review*. 31(1), 153–174. doi: 10.5465/amr.2006.19379629

Lee, L. H., Braud, T., Zhou, P., Wang, L., Xu, D., Lin, Z., Kumar, A., Bermejo, C. and Hui, P. (2021). All one needs to know about Metaverse: a complete survey on technological singularity, virtual ecosystem, and research agenda. *Journal of Latex Class Files*. 14(8), 1–66. doi: 10.13140/RG.2.2.11200.05124/8

Lee, S. and Olson, D. (2010). *Convergenomics: Strategic Innovation in the Convergence Era*. Surrey, UK: Gower Publishing.

Lee, S., Olson, D. L. and Trimi, S. (2012). Co-innovation: convergenomics, collaboration, and co-creation for organizational values. *Management Decision*. 50(5), 817–831. doi: 10.1108/00251741211227528

Lee, S. M. (2015). The age of quality innovation. *International Journal of Quality Innovation*. 1(1), 1–9. doi: 10.1186/s40887-015-0002-x

Lee, S. M. and Trimi, S. (2018). Innovation for creating a smart future. *Journal of Innovation & Knowledge*. 13(1), 1–8. doi: 10.1016/j.jik.2016.11.001

Lenovo. (2019). *The Internet of Things: Becoming a Practical Reality*. Retrieved from https://news.lenovo.com/the-internet-of-things-becoming-a-practical-reality/

Luu, L., Chu, D., Olickel, H., Saxena, P. and Hobor, A. (2016). Making smart contracts smarter. In *Proceedings of the ACM SIGSAC Conference on Computer and Communications Security*. Vienna, Austria, October, 254–269.

Nguyen, C. T., Hoang, D. T., Nguyen, D. N. and Dutkiewicz, E. (2022). MetaChain: a novel blockchain-based framework for metaverse applications. In *IEEE 95th Vehicular Technology Conference (VTC2022-Spring)*. doi: 10.1109/VTC2022-Spring54318.2022.9860983

Norman, R. and Ramizerz, R. (1993). From value chain to value constellation: design interactive strategy. *Harvard Business Review*. 71(4), 65–77. Art No: 10127040.

O'Reilly, C. A. and Tushman, M. L. (2013). Organizational ambidexterity: the past, present, and future. *Academy of Management Perspectives*. 27(4), 324–338. Retrieved from https://www.jstor.org/stable/i40156742

Oliver, C. (1998). Sustainable competitive advantage: combing institutional and resource-based view. *Strategic Management Journal*. 18(9), 697–713. doi:10.1002/(SICI)1097-0266(199710)18:9<697::AID-SMJ909>3.0.CO;2-C

Porter, M. E. (1985). *Competitive Advantages: Creating and Sustaining Superior Performance*. New York, NY: The Free Press.

Porter, M. E. (1991). Towards a dynamic theory of strategy. *Strategic Management Journal*. 12, 95–117. doi: 10.1002/smj.4250121008

Porter, M. E. and Kramer, M. R. (2011). Creating shared value. *Harvard Business Review*. 89(1), 62–77. Retrieved from https://hbr.org/2011/01/the-big-idea-creating-shared-value

Ramaswammy, V. and Ozcan, K. (2014). *The Co-Creation Paradigm*. Stanford, CA: Stanford University Press.

Rogers, D. L. (2016). *The Digital Transformation Playbook*. New York: Columbia University Press.

Schumpeter, J. A. (1934). *Capitalism, Socialism, and Democracy*. London: Routledge.

Schumpeter, J. A. (1983) American institutions and economic progress. *Journal of Institutional and Theoretical Economics*. 139(2), 191–196. Retrieved from https://www.jstor.org/stable/40750589

Sirmon, D. G., Hitt, M. A. and Ireland, R. D. (2007). Managing firm resources in dynamic environments to create value: looking inside the black box. *Academy of Management Review*. 32(1), 273–292. doi: 10.5465/amr.2007.23466005

Smart Future Initiative. (2016). Website. Retrieved from http://smart-future.net/1.html

Stabell, C. B. and Fjeldstad, O. D. (1998). Configuring value for competitive advantage: on chains, shops, and networks. *Strategic Management Journal*. 19(5), 413–437. Retrieved from http://www.jstor.org/stable/3094221

Stock, J. R. and Boyer, S. L. (2009). Developing a consensus definition of supply chain management: a qualitative study. *International Journal of Physical Distribution & Logistics Management*. 39(8), 690–711. doi: 10.1108/09600030910996323

Sundararajan, A. (2016). *The Sharing Economy*. Boston: MIT Press.

Talbot, D. (2005). IBM: the computer brain. *Technology Review*. September, 52.

Tapscott, D. (2006). *Wikinomics: How Mass Collaboration Changes Everything*. NewYork: Portfolio.

Tapscott, D., Ticoll, D. and Lowy, A. (2000). *Digital Capital: Harnessing the Power of Business Webs*. Boston, MA: Harvard Business School Press.

Teece, D. J. (2014). The foundation of enterprise performance: dynamic and ordinary capabilities in an (economic) theory of firms. *Academy of Management Perspectives*. 28(4), 328–352. Retrieved from https://www.jstor.org/stable/43822373

Thamara, T. (2007). Strategic banking innovation. *ABA Bank Marketing*. 39(4), 4–5.

Tushman, M. L. and O'Reilly, C. A. (1997). *Winning through Innovation: A Practical Guide to Leading Organizational Change and Renewal*. Boston: Harvard Business School Press.

von Hippel, E., Ogawa, S. and De Long, J. P. J. (2011). The age of the consumer-innovator. *MIT Sloan Management Review*. 53(1), 27–35. Retrieved from https://www.researchgate.net/publication/265097170_The_Age_of_the_Consumer-Innovator#fullTextFileContent

von Raesfeld, A. and Roos, K. (2008). How should a small company interact in its business network to sustain its exchange effectiveness? *Small Companies and Exchange Effectiveness*. 17(4), 271–280. Retrieved from https://www.zbw.eu/econis-archiv/bitstream/11159/54798/1/EBP084304634_0.pdf

Woiceshyn, J. and Falkenberg, L. (2008). Value creation in knowledge-based firms: aligning problems and resources. *Academy of Management Perspective*. 22(2), 85–99, doi: 10.5465/amp.2008.32739761

Zamani, M., Movahedi, M. and Raykova, M. (2018). Rapidchain: scaling blockchain via full sharding. In *Proceedings of the 2018 ACM SIGSAC Conference on Computer and Communications Security*. Toronto, Canada, October, 15–19, 931–948.

Chapter 4

The game-changing role of the Internet of Things (IoT) in the global value chain (GVC) in India

Poorvi Agrawal
Galgotias University, Greater Noida, India

Kavita Mathad
GIBS Business School, India

Partha Sen
ESGlytics, India

Sankar Mukherjee
GIBS Business School, India

INTRODUCTION

A global value chain (GVC) is a complicated, linked structure that depicts the processes involved in producing and delivering a good or service worldwide. It entails a network of specialized jobs and activities distributed across many different nations, and all contribute to the development, transformation, and delivery of a finished product to consumers. This strategy enables businesses to use a variety of benefits and skills available worldwide, maximizing production effectiveness, cutting costs, and encouraging global cooperation in today's linked economy.

Technology is pivotal in optimizing and streamlining the GVC. From advanced supply chain management systems that enhance coordination and reduce operational costs to integrating Internet of Things (IoT) devices for real-time tracking and monitoring of products and machinery, technology facilitates seamless communication and collaboration among stakeholders across various stages of production, distribution, and delivery (Ghatak & Garg, 2022).

Additionally, data analytics and artificial intelligence (AI) help analyze vast amounts of information to make informed decisions, predict demand, and optimize resource allocation, ultimately enhancing efficiency and competitiveness within the GVC. Overall, technology acts as a catalyst for transforming traditional value chains into agile, data-driven, and globally connected ecosystems.

DOI: 10.1201/9781003461432-4

GVC's long history dates back to ancient trade networks that linked far-flung areas. However, the current idea of GVCs started to take shape in the latter half of the 20th century. Thanks to developments in communication and transportation technology, international commerce and investment significantly increased after World War II. Globalization and liberalization policies encouraged the splintering of manufacturing processes across several nations in the 1980s and 1990s.

Companies began to distribute different production stages throughout the globe to save costs and get access to specialized talent. The digital revolution and advances in logistics further expedited this trend, allowing for a more intricate and integrated global industrial network.

Although the idea of networked devices dates back further, the IoT has roots in the late 20th century. While employed at "The Massachusetts Institute of Technology (MIT)" in the late 1990s, Kevin Ashton coined the Internet of Things. IoT's core concept is linking everyday objects and equipment to the Internet so they may communicate and gather data for various uses. Sensors and devices were employed in early IoT applications in industrial and commercial settings to monitor and improve operations. However, in the early years of the 21st century, IoT's broad acceptance and disruptive potential started to take shape. A seamless connection was made possible by improvements in communication technology, the miniaturization of sensors, and the expanding accessibility of the Internet.

Globally, the manufacturing industry is progressively utilizing the IoT potential to transform operations and boost competitiveness. By incorporating IoT technology into every manufacturing process step, GVC is essential to this change. Real-time monitoring, preventive maintenance, and data-driven decision-making are made possible by IoT devices that come with sensors and connections. This network of interconnected devices and systems allows manufacturers to increase production efficiency, decrease downtime, enhance product quality, and simplify supply chain operations. GVC enables the seamless integration of IoT-enabled solutions across multiple industrial value chain stages, from raw material procurement through distribution, encouraging a more responsive, adaptable, and sustainable manufacturing environment.

INVENTIONS OF IoT IN THE WORLD AS TECHNOLOGY

The IoT has ushered in several ground-breaking discoveries that have changed the face of technology. Smart thermostats, invented by Nest and powered by the IoT, revolutionized household energy management by enabling consumers to optimize heating and cooling systems for energy efficiency (Garg, 2023). Fitbit's wearable fitness trackers, which demonstrate the promise of IoT in health monitoring, make it easy for people to measure their vital signs and physical activity. Uber and other GPS-enabled IoT services have revolutionized mobility in the transportation industry, improving the comfort and effectiveness of travel.

Industrial IoT applications such as remote asset monitoring and predictive maintenance, which have improved operational efficiency across numerous industries, also demonstrate the immense potential of IoT to drive automation, data-driven decision-making, and, ultimately, a more connected and efficient world.

APPLICATIONS OF IoT IN LOGISTICS AND SUPPLY CHAIN MANAGEMENT

Real-time tracking and monitoring capabilities brought about by IoT have significantly influenced logistics and supply chain management. Precision tracking of shipments is made possible by sensors and GPS technology integrated into trucks, containers, and items. This information details the location, temperature, humidity, and shipment handling conditions. This enables effective inventory management, timely equipment maintenance, and optimized route planning. Predictive analytics and demand forecasting powered by IoT improve decision-making even more, ensuring that things arrive at their destinations quickly and in the best possible condition. Additionally, IoT-enabled automated inventory systems reduce waste, minimize losses, and automate reordering procedures, saving costs and enhancing operational effectiveness across the logistics and supply chain ecosystems (Garg & Singla, 2017, 2013).

LITERATURE REVIEW

The idea of the IoT originally surfaced in the late 1990s and has been around for about 20 years. The phrase was created by British scientist Kevin Ashton in the context of the GVC while working on a research project at MIT's Auto-ID center to investigate ways to boost operational efficiency by linking RFID information technology (IT) to the Internet (de Vass, Shee, & Miah, 2021; Garg, 2023). While there is disagreement over the definition of an industrial revolution, it is generally agreed that three significant technical shifts influenced how products were produced throughout history. That is the development of water and steam-powered factories, the invention of electrically powered tools that allowed for mass production, and the incorporation of information and communication technology (ICT) into manufacturing (Ghatak & Garg, 2022).

The advent of a new set of digital (and intelligent) technologies has lately received attention from governments, businesses, and academics as one of the leading forces behind the fourth industrial revolution (4IR) wave, also known as Industry 4.0 (Brynjolfsson & McAfee, 2014).

GVC analysis has gained popularity over the past ten years as an approach to researching global economic governance. Sociologists and geographers often use it to analyze the global structure of varied sectors, including apparel, electronics, and tropical commodities, and increased interest in the GVC method from anthropologists, historians, and economists (Gibbon et al., 2008). There is currently no agreed-upon definition of the IoT. However, it generally refers to integrating physical objects that talk to one another through the Internet to accomplish a specific goal (Borgia, 2014). Additionally, IoT may make GVC more appealing by more effectively controlling the distribution of goods and services and promoting the alteration of crucial procedures and punctual schedules (Mital et al., 2018). The value chain must be integrated if the company's success is to increase. This may be done through reducing expenses, improving responsiveness, improving service levels, and simplifying decision-making. The core components of value chain integration are communication, collaboration, and agility (Guo et al., 2012).

Each item may become visible through IoT in the GVC, creating a transparent value chain. Every object in the value chain's position and characteristics might be known at any moment (Nagy et al., 2018). The manufacturing industry has undergone a radical transition thanks to the IoT, which has transformed conventional procedures and ushered in a new era of intelligent production. IoT provides in-the-moment data gathering and analysis by integrating connections, actuators, and sensors into machinery, tools, and goods. With this data-driven strategy, manufacturers may optimize processes, boost production, and increase efficiency. IoT makes predictive maintenance possible, allowing machines to identify potential problems before they result in expensive failures, reducing downtime and maintenance costs. Furthermore, the IoT improves supply chain management by offering insightful data on inventory levels, demand trends, and logistics, resulting in efficient operations.

IoT promotes automation, agility, and innovation in the manufacturing sector by providing a seamless connection between devices and systems, ultimately leading to higher competitiveness and sustainable practices.

GVCs have significantly influenced the manufacturing industry, making it an interconnected and integrated ecosystem. In GVCs, production processes are dispersed throughout several nations, with each country specializing in phases of the value chain. Utilizing the comparative advantages of distinct locations, firms may use this labor division to increase productivity and cut costs. Based on labor costs, experience, and infrastructure variables, businesses can produce components in one nation, manufacture raw materials in another, and assemble the finished product in a third. GVCs make it possible for manufacturing to be more adaptable and quick-response, allowing for a speedier response to changes in the market and fluctuations in demand.

The manufacturing sector has seen a radical transformation due to the IoT, which is revolutionizing operations and ushering in the age of intelligent manufacturing. IoT integrates sensors, actuators, and linked devices throughout the production environment, enabling real-time data gathering and analysis. Predictive maintenance, overall productivity, and operational efficiency are all improved by this data-driven strategy. Manufacturers may save money, minimize downtime, and maximize resources by using remote monitoring to track equipment performance, identify abnormalities, and forecast maintenance requirements. Moreover, IoT makes integrating algorithms for machine learning (ML) and AI easier, enabling automated and intelligent decision-making. Data moves seamlessly across the manufacturing line, giving valuable insights into operations that support quality optimization and continual development.

The industrial sector's GVCs are expected to expand and change significantly in the upcoming years. GVCs are anticipated to grow in size and complexity as technology improvements quicken and globalization continues to deepen. This rise will be primarily attributed to the digitalization of industrial processes and the incorporation of cutting-edge technologies like automation, AI, and the IoT. With these technologies, manufacturing operations across several geographic areas will be seamlessly coordinated and integrated, allowing manufacturers to maximize productivity, save costs, and optimize efficiency (Garg, 2023).

Furthermore, trade liberalization and the creation of trade agreements are expected to accelerate the growth of GVCs further by enabling the flow of information, products, and services across borders. The division and dispersion of manufacturing operations over several locations will remain essential for businesses looking to take advantage of cost benefits, access specialized knowledge, and diversify supply chain risks. This will cause cross-border alliances and collaborations to flourish, developing a highly interconnected and interdependent industrial environment.

GVCs will also be reshaped in response to the continuous emphasis on sustainability and environmental issues, promoting the advancement of more environmentally friendly and sustainable manufacturing techniques. GVCs will adjust to manage disruptions by stressing risk management and business continuity plans as supply chains get more agile and resilient. In summary, trade dynamics, sustainability imperatives, technical improvements, and the continuous pursuit of efficiency and competitiveness are all expected to fuel the expansion of GVCs in the manufacturing sector.

GVC importance: GVCs dominate global trade, with over two-thirds of world trade occurring through these chains. They have evolved, with multi-stakeholders, specialization, and the service trade becoming crucial characteristics.

Influence on the economy: GVCs influence a nation's competitiveness, economic growth, labor markets, and trade costs. They shape economic landscapes significantly and play pivotal roles in determining trade dynamics.

Measurement: GVCs can be measured at macro (country or regional) and micro (firm-level) scales. While macro studies offer insights into value-added in trade and price correlations, micro studies delve deeper into firm-level decisions and productivity. Despite differences, there is an expectation that both dimensions will merge in understanding.

Governance: GVC governance revolves around value-added distribution across the chain. Different models, from market to hierarchical, dictate how value is distributed among participants. Governance is pivotal in upgrading value chains in various aspects, be it products, processes, or functions.

China's challenges: While participation in GVCs has advanced China's industrial sector and augmented its trade interests, it has faced considerable challenges. The low-end position in GVCs has made China vulnerable to economic strategies such as anti-dumping practices by countries like the United States. This low-end positioning risks "low-end lock-up," where China might find it challenging to move to high-value chain segments.

GVC IN DEVELOPING COUNTRIES

While GVCs offer developing countries a platform to integrate into the global economy, the benefits are only sometimes evenly distributed. Strategic policies, investments in skills and technology, and a focus on sustainable development are crucial to ensure that participation in GVCs translates to broad-based economic and social benefits. GVCs have revolutionized production and trade in the modern global economy. Participating in GVCs has become a primary strategy for economic integration, industrialization, and export-led growth for many developing countries. However, while undeniable benefits exist, several concerns are also associated with developing countries' heavy reliance on GVCs. Here is a breakdown of how developing countries might lose more than they gain:

- **Low-value-added activities**: Many developing countries need help in the lower-value-added segments of GVCs, such as raw material extraction or simple assembly tasks. This means they capture only a tiny fraction of the product's value while contributing to production. Over time, reliance on low-value-added activities can limit a country's ability to generate higher incomes for its population. It could perpetuate a cycle of low-value production and low incomes.
- **Dependence on multinational companies (MNCs)**: GVCs are often dominated by large multinational corporations. These MNCs can exert significant power over supplier firms in developing countries, constantly pressuring them to reduce costs, leading to low wages and

poor working conditions. MNCs need to be more committed to long-term development in host countries. If production costs rise or other factors change, they can quickly relocate to a different country, leaving the former dependent country with potential unemployment and economic downturns.

- **Vulnerability to external shocks**: A heavy reliance on GVCs can make countries more susceptible to global economic downturns, trade disputes, or disruptions in the supply chain. For instance, if consumer demand in a developed country declines, it can directly impact production and exports in the developing country. Furthermore, external factors like natural disasters or geopolitical events in one part of the chain can have a ripple effect, causing disruptions in countries even if they aren't directly affected.
- **Technological stagnation**: Developing countries might miss technological learning and innovation opportunities by focusing mainly on a narrow part of the production process. Without exposure to the entire product lifecycle from design and innovation to marketing and after-sales service – they might struggle to build indigenous capabilities.
- **Erosion of domestic industries**: With an emphasis on being a part of the GVC, some domestic industries outside the chain might need help. This could be due to a lack of attention investment or because they cannot compete with imported intermediate goods' prices and quality.
- **Environmental and social concerns**: GVC participation can sometimes exacerbate environmental degradation, especially in mining, agriculture, or mass manufacturing sectors, where regulations might be lax. Similarly, the push for low-cost production might compromise labor rights, leading to poor working conditions, inadequate safety measures, and suppressed wages.
- **Trade balance concerns**: As noted in your provided data, higher GVC participation only sometimes leads to an improved balance of payments. This is because countries might need to import many intermediate goods to participate in the GVC, which can offset export earnings.

Developing countries in comparison with developed countries

GVCs represent various countries' intricate web of production processes to produce a finished good or service. They epitomize globalization at its most complex, where components of a single product might cross multiple borders before reaching a consumer. While GVCs present opportunities for countries at all stages of development, the distribution of benefits remains skewed in favor of advanced economies. Asian countries, despite their impressive growth and increasing participation, still face challenges in accessing the higher value-added segments of GVCs. The dynamics of

GVCs underscore the need for strategic investments in intangible assets, innovation, and capacity-building to ensure a more equitable distribution of benefits.

- **Position in the GVC**: Advanced countries: These nations, especially the United States and those in the European Union, primarily occupy the upstream parts of GVCs. This means they are often involved in research and development (R&D), design, branding, and other high-value-added activities. Their position allows them to extract higher portions of the value from the finished product.
- **Asian countries**: While advanced Asian countries like Japan dominate the upstream segments, many Asian countries (like China, Vietnam, and the Philippines) are more enmeshed downstream. These involve assembly, low-tech manufacturing, and other lower-value-added activities. However, countries like China are trying to move upstream, particularly in the technology sector.
- **Dependence on GVCs**: Advanced countries: Their superior technological prowess and ownership of intangible assets mean that while they benefit significantly from GVCs, they are not necessarily dependent on them. They maintain control over crucial parts of the GVC, especially in regulation, intellectual property rights (IPR), innovation, financing, and marketing.
- **Asian countries**: Many countries, especially the fast-growing ones, have become deeply integrated into GVCs. Their economic growth has become intertwined with their GVC participation. However, this has also increased dependence, especially on advanced economies.
- **Benefits and drawbacks**: Advanced countries have leveraged GVCs to their advantage, garnering a more significant portion of the value added due to their upstream activities and intangible assets. This domination in the regulatory, IPR, and innovation fronts ensures they remain positioned to dictate terms and capture more value.
- **Asian countries**: Despite their active participation, not all benefits are passed on to these nations. They often need help to move up the technology ladder swiftly or tap into higher value-added segments of the GVC. This can lead to trade imbalances and over-reliance on sectors or partners.

Advanced countries will likely continue to use their technological and intangible asset advantage to maintain dominance in GVCs. They will also play a significant role in setting the game's rules, especially in IPR, standards, and regulations. These nations will strive to move up the value chain. While some, like China, are making significant strides in technology and innovation, others must invest heavily in intangible assets to reduce dependence and capture more value (Amador & Cabral, 2016). The rise of the IoT has led to an increase in physical products being embedded with sensors that can capture, process, and communicate data. While consumer applications like connected household devices have garnered much attention, the potential for business-to-business applications is profound. These applications include real-time data provision for preventive maintenance, inventory monitoring, and product usage assessment. IoT will facilitate deeper data integration between firms, suppliers, and customers, diminishing the role of intermediaries.

One significant shift with the IoT is merging product flows with information flows. Instead of separately monitoring these flows, IoT links products with unique identifiers, providing information about their origin, use, and destination. This integration will enhance production and distribution efficiency, especially in cross-border GVCs. Such efficiencies may lead to reduced transaction costs related to international production, encouraging a more intricate international division of labor.

Drawing parallels to past technological advances like the telephone and telegraph, the IoT may also influence the expansion of firm sizes, as better communication tools have historically done.

However, there are challenges. The very connectivity that IoT offers also introduces heightened cybersecurity risks. As businesses connect with millions of sensors and devices, each becomes a potential cyberattack vulnerability. The interconnected nature of these systems offers operational efficiency and increases exposure to cyber threats.

METHODOLOGY

Secondary data is the foundation of this literature-based integrated model study on the IoT and the GVC. We concentrated on published journal papers and ignored books, following other literature studies on GVC and IoT. This was because, in most cases, book writers also published academic articles that included many of the stated results. We also did not have book chapters since they were often less widely available digitally and underwent a less stringent review procedure than journal articles. In addition to IB, general management, supply chain management, operations management, and a particular set of social science journals that published GVC research – economic geography, economic sociology, regional and development studies, and international political economy – we also carried out a multidisciplinary literature search. This broad breadth should encompass the majority of necessary GVC investigations that are published in scholarly publications. The top publications in each field were included, encouraging researchers to submit their finest GVC findings.

We searched for publications published in the last 30 years for each journal. As the introduction discusses, this period was marked by the fast development and greater sophistication of GVC research. The four search phrases we used were the "global value chain," the "Internet of Things," and "risk mitigation." We selected conceptual papers that focused on GVCs and how they affect IoT applications, as well as empirical research – qualitative or quantitative – that included at least one search term as a relevant variable. Articles that used any of the four phrases as a control variable or were only sporadically quoted were disqualified.

Furthermore, the studies that made the shortlist focused on the business or network level rather than other analytical units like global organizations, sectors, or geographic areas.

We used extra criteria to reduce this substantial body of research to a proportional number of articles because social science journals include several hundred publications on GVCs. We have established three more screening criteria for empirical publications. First, we incorporated more current studies that were released after 2005. Our second focus was the publications that closely matched IB academics' study interests. Thirdly, we ensured that our chosen studies included GVC and IoT with industry coverage, research methods, and empirical locations in developed and developing nations. We also made sure that our selection covered a reasonable mix of authors from different disciplines, institutions, and geographical locations.

FINDINGS

This study shows how IoT can strengthen GVC and value-creating networks. Therefore, the findings of this study provide a wealth of knowledge about the impact of IoT on GVC and how using this technology can increase value chain performance. Also, the study serves as a basis for incorporating global chain and IoT technologies through GVC. It is a primary source for future research to understand further the business benefits of global chain and IoT system integration. This study also provides information on the challenges of IoT on GVT. Integrating the IoT into GVCs offers immense opportunities for businesses to optimize operations and deliver enhanced value to customers. While challenges exist, the benefits of real-time connectivity and data-driven decision-making outweigh the drawbacks. As the IoT continues to evolve, it will likely reshape the dynamics of GVCs, paving the way for a more interconnected and efficient global economy.

India is a significant player in the global economy with its unique strengths and challenges

Diversifying trade partners: India is strengthening its trade relations with ASEAN, Africa, and the Middle East. The nation also plays a vital role in initiatives like the Quad, which can provide avenues for trade diversification.

Investing in domestic innovation: India's IT industry is robust, and there is a burgeoning startup ecosystem, particularly in tech, biotech, and pharmaceuticals. However, R&D investment as a percentage of gross domestic product is lower compared to China.

Promoting Domestic consumption: India has a vast domestic market, and the middle class is expanding. However, the nation also faces challenges like income inequality and rural-urban disparities.

Strengthening regional supply chains: India has been working on regional initiatives like the South Asian Association for Regional Cooperation (SAARC) and BIMSTEC. However, regional tensions, especially with Pakistan, can sometimes be a barrier.

Policy reforms and business environment: India has been working on improving its "Ease of Doing Business" ranking and has implemented reforms like the Goods and Services Tax (GST). However, bureaucratic red tape can still be an obstacle for businesses.

Alternative technological pathways: India enjoys unrestrictive technological access from the West but is also keen on promoting indigenous technologies, which is evident in sectors like space research and digital platforms.

Human capital investment: India has a vast pool of engineering talent, and the IT sector is a testament to this. However, the country needs help in improving the quality and consistency of primary and secondary education.

Financial and digital integration: India's digital transformation is notable, especially in fintech with platforms like UPI. The country is also working on promoting the international use of the rupee.

Environmental and sustainable manufacturing: India is adopting sustainable practices, especially in renewable energy like solar power. However, challenges like air and water pollution need significant attention.

IMPORTANCE OF IoT ON GVC

The IoT is transforming GVCs at an unprecedented pace. Its integration into GVCs profoundly impacts how businesses operate, from product design and manufacturing to logistics and customer service.

- **Enhanced visibility and transparency**: IoT devices can track products and materials in real-time as they move through the value chain. This gives businesses unprecedented visibility into their operations, enabling them to quickly identify and address bottlenecks and inefficiencies. It also enhances transparency for consumers, who can now track the provenance of products and ensure they meet their ethical and sustainability standards.
- **Optimized decision-making**: The data generated by IoT devices can be used to optimize decision-making at all levels of the value chain. For example, manufacturers can use IoT data to optimize production schedules and reduce inventory costs. Retailers can use IoT data to forecast demand and ensure that the right products are in the right

place at the right time. Furthermore, logistics providers can use IoT data to optimize routes and delivery times.
- **New business models and opportunities**: The IoT enables the development of new business models and opportunities. For example, companies can now offer product-as-a-service (PaaS) models, where customers pay for the use of a product rather than owning it outright. This can help businesses reduce costs and generate recurring revenue streams. The IoT also enables new data-driven services, such as predictive maintenance and personalized marketing.

Overall, the IoT is having a transformative impact on GVCs. It enhances visibility and transparency, optimizes decision-making, and enables new business models and opportunities. However, it is essential to note that some challenges are associated with adopting IoT in GVCs, such as cybersecurity risks, interoperability issues, and data overload.

Integrating the IoT into GVCs marks a paradigm shift in how businesses function globally. This confluence of technology and commerce offers unprecedented advantages but also introduces unique challenges.

Positive impacts

Enhanced real-time monitoring: IoT provides real-time data access, enabling businesses to make swift decisions about maintenance, inventory control, and product functionality. This leads to more proactive management and superior efficiency.

- **Streamlined data flows**: The continuous data streams from products enable firms to reduce discrepancies and inefficiencies, ensuring that product and information flows are synchronized.
- **Reduced transaction costs**: IoT can reduce the costs linked to international production. Enhanced transparency and real-time data sharing streamline the global supply chain by cutting down intermediaries and expediting decision-making.
- **Increased integration**: IoT bridges the gap between firms, suppliers, and consumers. This fosters better collaboration, timely problem resolution, and a more unified value chain.
- **Enhanced production and distribution efficiency**: Integrating products and information flows through IoT can significantly improve global production and distribution methods.

Challenges and concerns

- **Cybersecurity risks**: The proliferation of connected devices heightens the risk of cyberattacks. Each device becomes a potential vulnerability, making the entire chain susceptible to data breaches and operational interruptions.

- **Interoperability issues:** With diverse companies adopting varied standards and technologies, ensuring smooth communication and integration between systems becomes challenging.
- **Data overload:** IoT devices generate vast amounts of data. Businesses require advanced systems and skills to parse this data for actionable insights.
- **Privacy concerns:** The extensive data sharing inherent in IoT systems can raise privacy and data ownership issues, potentially leading to disputes and regulatory hurdles.
- **Reliability and dependence:** A heavy reliance on IoT systems can be precarious in the event of technical failures or system breaches. Businesses must have redundant systems and contingency plans in place.

CONCLUSION

The dynamics of GVCs are complex, involving a delicate balance of economic, political, and logistical factors. As a significant player in the world economy, China has to strategically navigate its position in GVCs to maximize benefits and minimize vulnerabilities. Its journey offers insights for other nations aiming to leverage GVCs for economic growth and development. Integrating emerging technologies has fundamentally reshaped GVCs and the broader world economy. In this new landscape, data assumes paramount importance, citizen-consumers appear as pivotal actors, and businesses must strategically harness digital tools for operational efficiency, value creation, and competitive differentiation. While the advent of IoT presents significant opportunities for GVCs to become more efficient and integrated, it also brings forth challenges that need careful navigation. Firms must balance leveraging the benefits of IoT and mitigating the associated risks. While IoT offers significant advantages in reshaping and optimizing GVCs, it also presents specific challenges that businesses must address. Balancing the benefits with the inherent risks and challenges will be vital to harnessing the full potential of IoT in GVCs.

REFERENCES

Amador, J., & Cabral, S. (2016). Global value chains: A survey of drivers and measures. *Journal of Economic Surveys*, 30(2), 278–301.

Borgia, E. (2014). The Internet of Things vision: Key features, applications, and open issues. *Computer Communications*, 54, 1–31.

Brynjolfsson, E., & McAfee, A. (2014). *The second Machine Age: Work, progress, and prosperity in a time of brilliant technologies*. WW Norton & Company.

De Vass, T., Shee, H., & Miah, S. J. (2021). IoT in supply chain management: A narrative on retail sector sustainability. *International Journal of Logistics Research and Applications*, 24(6), 1–20.

Garg, A. (Ed.). (2023). *Reinventing technological innovations with artificial intelligence*. Bentham Science Publishers.

Garg, A., & Singla, N. (2013). E-waste vis-à-vis human health and environment. *Interdisciplinary Environmental Review*, 14(3–4), 187–193.

Garg, A., & Singla, N. (2017). Environment sustainability awareness model for IT SMEs. *Interdisciplinary Environmental Review*, 18(1), 1–5.

Ghatak, A., & Garg, A. (2022). Power transmission project: A framework to align project success with organization goal. *International Journal of System Assurance Engineering and Management*, 13(4), 1817–1833.

Gibbon, P., Bair, J., & Ponte, S. (2008). Governing global value chains: An introduction. *Economy and Society*, 37(3), 315–338.

Guo, B., Yu, Z., Zhou, X., & Zhang, D. (2012). Opportunistic IoT: Exploring the social side of the Internet of Things. In *Proceedings of the 2012 IEEE 16th International Conference on Computer-Supported Cooperative Work in Design (CSCWD)*.

Mital, M., Chang, V., Choudhary, P., Papa, A., & Pani, A. K. (2018). Adoption of Internet of things in India: A test of competing models using a structured equation modeling approach. *Technological Forecasting and Social Change*, 136, 339–346.

Nagy, J., Olah, J., Erdei, E., Mate, D., & Popp, J. (2018). The role and Impact of Industry 4.0 and the internet of things on the business strategy of the value chain -the case of Hungary. *Sustainability*, 10(10), 3491.

Chapter 5

An overview of advanced networking technologies and the global value chain

Ramiz Salama

Artificial Intelligence, Software, and Information Systems Engineering Departments, Research Center for AI and IoT, AI and Robotics Institute, Near East University, Nicosia, Mersin 10, Turkey

Fadi Al-Turjman

Artificial Intelligence, Software, and Information Systems Engineering Departments, Research Center for AI and IoT, AI and Robotics Institute, Near East University, Nicosia, Mersin 10, Turkey

INTRODUCTION

The term "smart networking" refers to the practice of leveraging digital resources to facilitate more productive interpersonal interactions. Building and maintaining professional relationships and accomplishing individual and organizational objectives require the use of a wide range of online platforms and applications, such as social media, messaging apps, and collaboration software. Smart networking is crucial for achievement in today's digital age, be it in one's personal life or one's professional life. It is becoming increasingly necessary for individuals to be able to network and create relationships effectively online due to the growth of online platforms and the rising reliance on technology for communication. Connecting with more people from various backgrounds is a major advantage of intelligent networking. Individuals can find others all around the world who share their interests, ambitions, and beliefs by utilizing social media and other internet channels. This can pave the way for fruitful professional interactions and the development of novel avenues for collaboration and creativity.

Smart networking is more than just making connections; it also requires sharing knowledge and experiences. One's own development, as well as that of one's professional and personal networks, might benefit from the exchange of information and ideas. To be sure, networking is about making connections and sharing knowledge, but that's only part of being a savvy networker. Also essential is a calculated approach to making and maintaining interpersonal connections. Being considerate of one's own reputation and brand, as well as the aims and requirements of the people one is interacting with, is essential. Connecting with others and working together effectively also

DOI: 10.1201/9781003461432-5

requires taking the initiative to do so. The very definition of "smart networking" is subject to change as new computing platforms and associated tools enter the market. Virtual and augmented reality may play a more significant part in networking and communication in the future [1–5]. In sum, knowing how to network effectively is a must in today's competitive digital world. People's personal and professional development, as well as their ability to interact with and influence others, can benefit greatly from their judicious use of digital tools for networking and communication.

Machine learning and artificial intelligence (AI) facilitators have started to be part of our daily lives and have significant effects on the rapid developments of the Internet of Things. One of the leading attempts in this field is the AI learning facilitator Prof. DUX [6]. It is a novel AI facilitator that aims at personalizing the education process for learners and providing the fastest and best quality of education in numerous fields.

THE PURPOSE OF NETWORKING AND BEYOND

1. The purpose of networking is to build relationships and contacts that can lead to career and personal advancement chances.
2. Benefits may include the chance to work with like-minded people, learn about new fields, and make connections that can help you succeed in your career.
3. Combining social skills like communication and connection building with technical abilities like knowing how to use digital tools and platforms to meet new people is essential for successful networking. Individuals can maintain their competitive edge and move closer to their career and personal goals by working to enhance and refine these talents over time.
4. Networking's benefits extend beyond the individual, though, and can have a significant effect on the world at large. Positive social change can be brought about when individuals and groups work together to tackle societal problems.

BENEFITS OF NETWORKING AND BEYOND

Networking is the process of making and keeping professional connections to move personal and business goals forward. It means making connections with other people, sharing information and ideas, and working together to make things better for everyone. In the digital age we live in now, networking has grown to include online platforms and tools like social media and messaging apps. Networking is good for both individuals and organizations in many ways. Some of the most important advantages of networking are:

1. ***Access to new opportunities***: Networking can lead to new chances to work together and come up with new ideas, as well as to the formation of helpful and valuable professional relationships. These connections can give you access to resources, information, and opportunities that might not be easy to get anywhere else.
2. ***Personal and professional growth***: When people share their ideas and knowledge with each other, they can learn from and inspire each other. This can help them grow as people and as professionals.
   Networking can also give people access to resources and information that can help them keep up with changes in their field.
3. ***Better communication and social skills***: Networking requires you to be able to talk to people and build relationships, which can help you become more confident and improve your social skills. These skills can help you both in your personal life and at work.
4. ***More visibility and credibility***: By establishing yourself as a thought leader and expert in your field, networking can help you get more visibility and credibility. This can help a person get new job opportunities and move up in their career.
5. ***Positive effects on society***: People and organizations can work together to solve problems and make positive changes in society if they build relationships and work with others.

In the digital age we live in now, networking is an important skill for success. By using technology and digital tools to connect and communicate with others in a smart and effective way, people and organizations can find new opportunities, grow personally and professionally, improve their communication and social skills, gain more visibility and credibility, and have a positive effect on society [7–10]. As technology changes, so will the idea of networking, giving people and groups more ways to connect, work together, and reach their goals.

DIFFERENT KINDS OF NETWORKING

There are many kinds of networking, and each has its own benefits and ways of working.

1. *Networking in person*: This type of networking involves meeting people in person and talking to them, such as at industry events, conferences, and meetings. In-person networking can be more personal and intimate, which can help people make connections that are deeper and more meaningful. It can also work better in some jobs and industries, like sales, where building relationships and trust is important.
2. *Online networking*: To connect with people far away, you can use digital platforms and tools like social media, messaging apps, and collaboration software. Online networking is easy and lets people connect

with a bigger, more diverse group of people, no matter where they live. It can also be more efficient and save money because people can talk to each other without having to travel.

3. *Professional networking organizations*: These are groups or associations whose main goal is to connect people who work in the same industry or profession. These groups often hold events and meetings to help their members network and give those resources and support. Joining a professional networking group can give you access to a specific and relevant group of people. This can be especially helpful for people who want to move up in their careers in a certain field.
4. *Informal networking*: With informal networking, you build relationships and connections with other people in a more casual and natural way, such as through social events, hobbies, and activities outside of work. Informal networking can be a more relaxed and fun way to get to know people, and it can lead to important personal and professional relationships.
5. *Networking through social media*: Sites like LinkedIn and Twitter have become popular ways to meet new people and make connections. People can connect with others in their field or industry and share information and ideas through these platforms. Social media networking can be a good way to make new friends and show that you are an expert in your field.

In the digital age we live in now, networking is an important skill for success. There are many kinds of networking, and each has its own benefits and ways of working. By using the right kind of networking, people and organizations can find new opportunities, grow personally and professionally, improve their communication and social skills, get more attention and credibility, and do good things for society. As technology changes, so will the idea of networking, giving people and groups more ways to connect, work together, and reach their goals [11–15].

THE 3 P's OF NETWORKING

The 3 P's of networking are presence, professionalism, and persistence, which are the three most important parts of networking [16–17].

1. *Presence*: In networking, being present and engaged in the moment, whether in person or online, is what presence means. This means being open to new ideas and opportunities and making an effort to listen and take part in conversations.
2. *Professionalism*: Being professional is a key part of networking because it shows what kind of brand and reputation you have. This means dressing and acting in a professional way, being respectful and kind to others, and being ready and knowledgeable about one's field or industry.

3. *Be persistent*: It takes time and work to build and keep professional relationships, so you need to be persistent when networking. This means keeping in touch with other people and going out of your way to find and make connections and opportunities to work together.

By focusing on the 3 P's of networking, people can connect with others, talk to them, and build valuable professional relationships that can help them grow and succeed in their personal and professional lives.

FOUR IMPORTANT STEPS TO MAKING NETWORKING WORK WELL

Exchanging information and ideas and working together to make things better for both sides. There are four important steps to making networking work well:

1. *Figure out what you want*: The first step in networking is to figure out what you want. This will help you figure out what kind of networking is best for your needs and how to go about it. It will also guide your networking efforts.
2. *Build your network*: The next step is to build your network by connecting with people who have similar interests, goals, and values. This can be done in person, online, through professional networking groups, or informally by talking to people. Instead of just making a lot of contacts, it's important to focus on building strong relationships.
3. *Get involved and talk to people*: Once you've built your network, it's important to get involved and talk to people in a meaningful way. This means being open to new ideas and opportunities and making an effort to listen and take part in conversations. It's also important to actively look for and make connections and opportunities to work together.
4. *Keep and grow your network*: Networking is an ongoing process, and to keep and grow your network, you have to keep working at it. This means keeping in touch with people, following up with them, and actively looking for new ways to connect and work together.

By doing these four important things, people can build and keep professional relationships that can help them grow and succeed in their personal and professional lives.

SEVERAL THINGS THAT MAKE UP A NETWORK

A network is a group of people or groups that are linked together through relationships, communication, and the sharing of resources and information

[17–25]. There are several things that make up a network, such as the following:

1. *Interdependence*: Networks are made up of people who depend on each other. This means that what one person does and how it turns out can affect what other people do and how it turns out.
2. *Connectivity*: Networks are linked through relationships, communication, and the sharing of resources and information. These connections can be in person or online, and they can be personal relationships, connections on social media, or business ties.
3. *Diversity*: Networks are usually made up of people or groups with different backgrounds, experiences, and points of view. This can lead to a wider range of ideas and resources and make it easier for people to work together and come up with new ideas.
4. *Trust*: Trust is an important part of a network because it lets people depend on and help each other. The success of a network depends on people being able to talk to each other and work together.
5. *Influence*: The actions and decisions of one network member can affect the actions and decisions of other network members. This effect can be good or bad, and it can cause ideas, behaviours, and resources to spread through the network.
6. *Emergence*: Networks are dynamic and can change and grow over time, allowing new patterns and relationships to appear. This can happen because of what members do and decide, as well as because of things like technological progress and market conditions.
7. *Resilience*: Networks are often resilient, which means they can handle problems and get back to normal after they happen. This resilience can be boosted by how different and connected the network is, as well as by how much its members trust and help each other.

Overall, networks are made up of things like interdependence, connectedness, diversity, trust, influence, emergence, and resilience. These traits describe what a network is and how it works, and they can have a big effect on the success and outcomes of its members.

SOME TIPS FOR BUILDING STRONG NETWORKING SKILLS

To network well, you need both social skills, like being able to talk to people and build relationships, and technical skills, like being able to use digital tools and platforms to connect with others [26–31]. Here are some tips for building strong networking skills:

1. *Write down your goals and objectives*: The first step to getting good at networking is to write down your goals and objectives. This will help you figure out what kind of networking is best for your needs and how to go about it. It will also guide your networking efforts.
2. *Build your network*: The next step is to build your network by connecting with people who have similar interests, goals, and values. This can be done in person, online, through professional networking groups, or informally by talking to people. Instead of just making a lot of contacts, it's important to focus on building strong relationships.
3. *Get involved and talk to people*: Once you've built your network, it's important to get involved and talk to people in a meaningful way. This means being open to new ideas and opportunities and trying to listen and take part in conversations. It's also important to actively look for and make connections and opportunities to work together.
4. *Work on your communication skills*: To network well, you need to be able to talk to people. This includes being able to listen and speak well, as well as write emails and messages that are clear and to the point. Practice these skills by talking to other people often and asking them for feedback on how you talk to them.
5. *Build your personal brand*: Your personal brand is how you present yourself to others. It shows what you stand for, what you're good at, and what you've been through. Creating a strong personal brand can help you stand out and become known as an expert in your field.
6. *Stay up to date*: If you want to stay competitive and important, you need to know what's going on in your industry. This can be done by always learning new things and staying in touch with people in your field.

By using these tips and always working to improve your networking skills, you can connect with others, talk to them, and build valuable professional relationships that can help you grow and succeed in both your personal and professional life.

HOW TO DEVELOP YOUR NETWORKING AND BEYOND

Having a positive and proactive attitude can help with networking and help people connect and talk to each other more effectively. Some of the most important traits of a mind that is good for networking are as follows:

1. *Confidence*: Confidence is an important part of networking because it helps people talk about their skills and experiences and build relationships with other people.

2. *Openness*: It's important to be open to new ideas and opportunities when networking because it lets people try out new connections and work together.
3. *Empathy*: To build strong relationships and connections, you need to be able to understand and connect with other people. Empathy helps people see things from the other person's point of view and understand their needs. It can also help people communicate and work together better.
4. *Proactive*: This is important for networking because it means looking for and making connections and opportunities to work together. This can be done by reaching out to people, going to events and meetings, and keeping in touch with the people in one's network.
5. *Gratitude*: Showing gratitude and appreciation for the connections and opportunities you have can help you network because it can build good relationships and encourage others to keep helping you and staying in touch.

Overall, it can be helpful to have a confident, open, empathetic, proactive, and grateful attitude when networking. This can help people connect and communicate with others and build valuable professional relationships.

WHAT IS A SYNONYM FOR NETWORKING?

Connecting is another word for "networking." "Networking" can also be called "linking", "interconnecting", "interfacing", or "building relationships". Networking is the process of making and keeping professional or social connections, usually to share information, resources, or opportunities.

EXTENT OF PAST WORK OF NETWORKING AND BEYOND

Networking has been around for centuries and has changed a lot over time, so there has been a lot of work done on it in the past. In the past, networking often involved face-to-face interactions, such as going to professional conferences or social events or making connections through personal or professional relationships. In recent years, however, the internet and social media have greatly expanded the reach and potential of networking, making it possible for people to connect with others from different places and cultures. Networking happens today in a lot of different ways, like through social media, professional networking sites, and online communities. It can also include virtual events like webinars and video conferences, which let people connect and share ideas in real time without having to be in the same room. Networking can include building relationships with organizations and institutions as well as with other people. This can be done by joining industry groups or professional associations or by working on projects or initiatives with other businesses or organizations. Overall, the work done in networking in the past has been very large and included a wide range of activities and ways to make and keep connections with other people. As technology changes and new ways to connect come about, networking will continue to grow and change, as will the ways it can be done.

MATERIALS AND METHODS OF NETWORKING AND BEYOND

Networking means getting to know people and keeping in touch with them so you can share information, resources, and opportunities. Networking can be done in a lot of different ways and with a lot of different tools, depending on the goals and situation of the person or organization. People often network in person at things like conferences, trade shows, and networking mixers. People can meet and connect with others in their industry or field of interest at these events. This can be a good way to build relationships and find out about new opportunities. Networking can also happen online, through social media, professional networking sites, or online communities, in addition to in-person events. People can connect with others from far away through these virtual channels. They are especially useful for building connections with people or groups in different parts of the world. Business cards, email, and other forms of digital communication, like video conferencing or instant messaging, are other things that can be used for networking. Networking can also mean using tools or resources, like shared document folders or project management software, to help people work together and talk to each other. Overall, the materials and methods used in networking are varied and can be changed to fit the goals and needs of the person or group. Networking is often done with a mix of different tools and methods, and it can include both in-person and online meetings.

THE RESULTS OF NETWORKING AND WHAT COMES NEXT

Networking can have big effects on both the individual and the organization. On a personal level, networking can help you find new jobs, move up in your career, and get access to useful resources and information. By getting to know people in their industry or field of interest, people can find out about new job openings, make useful connections and referrals, and get advice and help as they move up in their careers. Networking can also help businesses in several ways. By building relationships with other businesses or organizations, an organization can gain access to new markets and customers, work together on projects or initiatives, and share resources and expertise. Networking can also help organizations stay up to date on industry trends and changes, and it can open valuable research and development opportunities. In addition to these obvious benefits, networking can also have more subtle and long-term effects. By making connections with others and sharing information and ideas, people and groups can learn more, see things from different points of view, and understand their field or industry better. This can help people make better decisions, solve problems better, think of new ideas, and be more creative. Overall, networking can have a lot of different effects that can be big for both people and businesses. By making and keeping connections with others, people and organizations can find out about new opportunities, get access to useful resources and expertise, and encourage collaboration and new ideas.

CONCLUSION

In conclusion, networking is an important and valuable part of professional and personal growth, and it can have a big effect on both individuals and businesses. By making and keeping connections with others, people and organizations can find out about new opportunities, get access to useful resources and expertise, and encourage collaboration and new ideas. There has been a lot of work done in networking in the past, and it has changed a lot as technology has gotten better. Networking happens today in a lot of different ways, such as in-person events, social media, professional networking sites, and online communities. Networking is often done with a mix of different tools and methods, and it can include both in-person and online meetings. Networking can have big and far-reaching effects. It can lead to new job opportunities, career advancement, access to valuable resources and information, and better ability to make decisions and solve problems. As technology changes and new ways to connect come out, networking will continue to grow and change.

REFERENCES

[1] Salama, R., Al-Turjman, F., & Culmone, R. (2023, March). AI-Powered Drone to Address Smart City Security Issues. In *International Conference on Advanced Information Networking and Applications* (pp. 292–300). Cham: Springer International Publishing.

[2] Salama, R., & Al-Turjman, F. (2023). Cyber-Security Countermeasures and Vulnerabilities to Prevent Social-Engineering Attacks. In *Artificial Intelligence of Health-Enabled Spaces* (pp. 133–144). CRC Press.

[3] Salama, R., Al-Turjman, F., Altrjman, C., & Bordoloi, D. (2023, April). The Ways in Which Artificial Intelligence Improves Several Facets of Cyber Security – A Survey. In *2023 International Conference on Computational Intelligence, Communication Technology and Networking (CICTN)* (pp. 825–829). IEEE.

[4] Salama, R., Al-Turjman, F., Bhatla, S., & Mishra, D. (2023, April). Mobile Edge Fog, Blockchain Networking and Computing – A Survey. In *2023 International Conference on Computational Intelligence, Communication Technology and Networking (CICTN)* (pp. 808–811). IEEE.

[5] Salama, R., Al-Turjman, F., Chaudhary, P., & Banda, L. (2023, April). Future Communication Technology Using Huge Millimeter Waves—An Overview. In *2023 International Conference on Computational Intelligence, Communication Technology and Networking (CICTN)* (pp. 785–790). IEEE.

[6] Prof.DUX available online: https://dux.aiiot.website/

[7] Salama, R., Al-Turjman, F., Chaudhary, P., & Yadav, S. P. (2023, April). Benefits of Internet of Things (IoT) Applications in Health Care – An Overview. In *2023 International Conference on Computational Intelligence, Communication Technology and Networking (CICTN)* (pp. 778–784). IEEE.

[8] Salama, R., Al-Turjman, F., Altrjman, C., & Gupta, R. (2023, April). Machine Learning in Sustainable Development – An Overview. In *2023 International Conference on Computational Intelligence, Communication Technology and Networking (CICTN)* (pp. 806–807). IEEE.

[9] Salama, R., Al-Turjman, F., Aeri, M., & Yadav, S. P. (2023, April). Intelligent Hardware Solutions for COVID-19 and Alike Diagnosis – A Survey. In *2023 International Conference on Computational Intelligence, Communication Technology and Networking (CICTN)* (pp. 796–800). IEEE.

[10] Salama, R., Al-Turjman, F., Bhatla, S., & Gautam, D. (2023, April). Network Security, Trust & Privacy in a Wiredwireless Environments – An Overview. In *2023 International Conference on Computational Intelligence, Communication Technology and Networking (CICTN)* (pp. 812–816). IEEE.

[11] Salama, R., Al-Turjman, F., Altrjman, C., Kumar, S., & Chaudhary, P. (2023, April). A Comprehensive Survey of Blockchain-Powered Cybersecurity – A Survey. In *2023 International Conference on Computational Intelligence, Communication Technology and Networking (CICTN)* (pp. 774–777). IEEE.

[12] Salama, R., Al-Turjman, F., Bordoloi, D., & Yadav, S. P. (2023, April). Wireless Sensor Networks and Green Networking for 6G communication – An Overview. In *2023 International Conference on Computational Intelligence, Communication Technology and Networking (CICTN)* (pp. 830–834). IEEE.

[13] Salama, R., Al-Turjman, F., Bhatia, S., & Yadav, S. P. (2023, April). Social Engineering Attack Types and Prevention Techniques – A Survey. In *2023 International Conference on Computational Intelligence, Communication Technology and Networking (CICTN)* (pp. 817–820). IEEE.

[14] Salama, R., Altrjman, C., & Al-Turjman, F. (2023). Smart Grid Applications and Blockchain Technology in the AI Era. *NEU Journal for Artificial Intelligence and Internet of Things*, 1(1), 59–63.

[15] Salama, R., Alturjman, S., & Al-Turjman, F. (2023). Internet of Things and AI in Smart Grid Applications. *NEU Journal for Artificial Intelligence and Internet of Things*, 1(1), 44–58.

[16] Salama, R., Altrjman, C., & Al-Turjman, F. (2023). A Survey of Machine Learning (ML) in Sustainable Systems. *NEU Journal for Artificial Intelligence and Internet of Things*, 2(3), (pp 1-8).

[17] Salama, R., Altrjman, C., & Al-Turjman, F. (2023). A Survey of Machine Learning Methods for Network Planning. *NEU Journal for Artificial Intelligence and Internet of Things*, 2(3), (pp 1-11).

[18] Salama, R., Altrjman, C., & Al-Turjman, F. (2023). A Survey of the Architectures and Protocols for Wireless Sensor Networks and Wireless Multimedia Sensor Networks. *NEU Journal for Artificial Intelligence and Internet of Things*, 2(3), (pp 1-11).

[19] Al-Turjman, F., Salama, R., & Altrjman, C. (2023). Overview of IoT Solutions for Sustainable Transportation Systems. *NEU Journal for Artificial Intelligence and Internet of Things*, 2(3), (pp 1-18).

[20] Salama, R., Altrjman, C., & Al-Turjman, F. (2023). An Overview of the Internet of Things (IoT) and Machine to Machine (M2M) Communications. *NEU Journal for Artificial Intelligence and Internet of Things*, 2(3), (pp 1-19).

[21] Salama, R., Al-Turjman, F., Altrjman, C., & Bordoloi, D. (2023, April). The Use of Machine Learning (ML) in Sustainable Systems – An Overview. In *2023 International Conference on Computational Intelligence, Communication Technology and Networking (CICTN)* (pp. 821–824). IEEE.

[22] Al-Turjman, F., & Salama, R. (2021). Cyber Security in Mobile Social Networks. In *Security in IoT Social Networks* (pp. 55–81). Academic Press.

[23] Ghatak, A., & Garg, A. (2022). Power Transmission Project: A Framework to Align Project Success with Organization Goal. *International Journal of System Assurance Engineering and Management*, 13(4), 1817–1833.

[24] Garg, A., & Singla, N. (2017). Environment Sustainability Awareness Model for IT SMEs. *Interdisciplinary Environmental Review*, 18(1), 1–5.

[25] Garg, A., & Singla, N. (2013). E-Waste vis-à-vis Human Health and Environment. *Interdisciplinary Environmental Review*, 14(3–4), 187–193.

[26] Garg, A. (Ed.). (2023). *Reinventing Technological Innovations with Artificial Intelligence*. Bentham Science Publishers.

[27] Garg, A. (2022). *CoReS-Respiratory Strength Predicting Framework Using Noninvasive Technology for Remote Monitoring During Heath Disasters.* Global Healthcare Disasters: Predicting the Unpredictable with Emerging Technologies, 109–121.

[28] Al-Turjman, F., & Salama, R. (2021). Security in Social Networks. In *Security in IoT Social Networks* (pp. 1–27). Academic Press.

[29] Salama, R., & Al-Turjman, F. (2022, August). AI in Blockchain towards Realizing Cyber Security. In *2022 International Conference on Artificial Intelligence in Everything (AIE)* (pp. 471–475). IEEE.

[30] Al-Turjman, F., & Salama, R. (2020). An Overview about the Cyberattacks in Grid and Like Systems. *Smart Grid in IoT-Enabled Spaces*, 233–247.

[31] Garg, A., & Ghatak, A. (2020). An Empirical Study on Power Evacuation Projects' Performance: A Strategic Layout in the Indian Context. *Asia-Pacific Journal of Management Research and Innovation*, 16(1), 31–42.

Chapter 6

BSMQSC

Design of an efficient blockchain-based security model for QoS-aware sustainable IoT smart city networks

Vijay Anand Rajasekaran
Vellore Institute of Technology, Vellore, India

Veena Grover
Noida Institute of Engineering & Technology, Greater Noida, India

Madala Guru Brahmam
Vellore Institute of Technology, Vellore, India

Balamurugan Balusamy
Shiv Nadar University, Delhi, India

INTRODUCTION

As a result of the proliferation of Internet of Things (IoT) devices within the context of smart city networks, our interactions with urban environments have been fundamentally altered. These networks enable the seamless integration of a variety of smart devices and sensors in order to optimize resource management, enhance public services, and enhance quality of life. The rapid expansion of IoT networks, however, presents a number of significant challenges, especially in terms of security, scalability, and sustainability. Given the number of interconnected devices and the sensitivity of the data they generate, IoT-based smart city networks must provide robust security to deter malicious actors [1–3]. Traditional security measures are insufficient to address the unique characteristics and requirements of these networks, necessitating innovative solutions that can successfully protect confidential data, prevent unauthorized access, and mitigate multiple attack vectors. Scalability is an urgent issue in IoT networks, as traditional centralized architectures struggle to manage the rising data volume and expanding number of devices. In addition, the resource-intensive nature of blockchain technology, which is widely regarded as a potential solution for security and trust in IoT networks, creates issues with scalability and transaction throughput. To circumvent these restrictions and permit the seamless

DOI: 10.1201/9781003461432-6

expansion and integration of IoT devices, novel solutions are required. As IoT devices proliferate and have a greater environmental impact, sustainability is a crucial aspect of the development of smart cities. The long-term viability of smart city networks depends on maximizing resource utilization and increasing energy efficiency without compromising security or performance. In this chapter, we propose a novel blockchain-based security model designed specifically for QoS-aware networks of sustainable IoT smart cities. Our model employs innovative techniques such as smart contracts with Q Learning and trust-based consensus mechanisms to address the aforementioned issues. Using a combination of smart contracts and Q Learning, our model enables the development of sidechains within the blockchain infrastructure. Sidechains provide a scalable solution by enabling the execution of thin and application-specific smart contracts that are tailored to the needs of various IoT devices and applications. This strategy effectively addresses the scalability issues of the blockchain and enables the rapid processing of IoT transactions. In addition, our model selects network miner nodes using a trust-based consensus mechanism process. We ensure that only trustworthy and secure nodes participate in the consensus process by evaluating the nodes' reputation and reliability levels. This increases the network's overall security by reducing the likelihood of malicious nodes undermining the block chain's integrity levels [4–6]. This is done via the use of Blockchain-Assisted Secure Smart Home Network using Gradient Based Optimizer with Hybrid Deep Learning (BSSHN-GBOHDL) operations. The proposed blockchain-based security model has several advantages over existing methods. First, it reduces transaction delay by processing IoT transactions as efficiently as possible, thereby enhancing network responsiveness in smart cities. Second, it improves energy efficiency by enabling the identification and utilization of energy-efficient nodes through spatio-temporal selection of trust levels. Third, it satisfies the growing needs of IoT networks by enabling a higher transaction throughput via sidechains and lightweight smart contracts. Lastly, it improves packet delivery ratio by successfully mitigating a variety of security risks, including Man-in-the-Middle, Sybil, Masquerading, Spoofing, and Finney attacks. Our proposed model has numerous potential applications in smart city networks based on the IoT. By ensuring secure and effective communication between smart metres, power grids, and energy management systems, our model enables accurate monitoring, billing, and load balancing in the smart grid domain, for example. Our model enables secure and reliable communication in intelligent transportation systems, thereby facilitating applications such as traffic management, autonomous driving, and vehicle-to-vehicle coordination. Our model also enhances the security and dependability of IoT environmental monitoring devices, allowing for the collection and analysis of real-time data for pollution control, waste management, and resource optimization. This chapter concludes with the introduction of a novel QoS-aware, blockchain-based IoT smart city security model. Combining smart contracts with Q Learning and trust-based consensus mechanisms addresses issues of security, scalability, and sustainability. Our model is a promising option for ensuring the efficiency and security of IoT-based smart city networks due to its advantages, which include reduced delay, improved energy efficiency, increased throughput, and a higher packet delivery ratio. In the following sections of this chapter, the specifics of our proposed model, its application, evaluation, and potential impact on the development of smart cities will be discussed in greater depth.

MOTIVATION AND OBJECTIVES

Motivation

Due to their rapid expansion, IoT-based smart city networks have encountered numerous challenges in terms of sustainability, scalability, and security. These obstacles motivate our efforts to develop a cutting-edge blockchain-based security model for QoS-aware, sustainable IoT smart city networks. This section describes the major contributions of our proposed model and the primary motivations for our research. In smart city networks, IoT devices handle sensitive data and perform essential functions, making them prime targets for cyberattacks. Frequently, traditional security measures are insufficient to defend against evolving threats such as Sybil attacks, Man-in-the-Middle attacks, masquerading, spoofing, and Finney attacks. These security concerns must be addressed for IoT networks to maintain the availability, integrity, and confidentiality of data. Limitations on scalability: The centralized architectures commonly used in IoT networks are incapable of handling the growing data volume and number of interconnected devices. Blockchain technology has demonstrated promise in addressing security and trust issues despite its resource-intensive nature. For the seamless operation of smart city networks, it is necessary to find scalable solutions to accommodate the growing IoT ecosystem. As IoT networks expand, there are growing concerns regarding the associated energy consumption and environmental impact. Vital is the development of sustainable solutions that optimize energy efficiency, reduce waste, and reduce the carbon footprint of smart city networks [7, 8]. The long-term viability of these networks is contingent upon striking a balance between sustainability, performance, and security.

Contributions

In our proposed model, a blockchain-based security framework specifically designed for QoS-aware, durable IoT smart city networks is introduced. Using the blockchain's decentralized nature, we improve the security and integrity of IoT transactions while addressing scalability and sustainability concerns.

Smart contracts with Q Learning: To circumvent blockchain technology's scalability issues, we use smart contracts powered by Q Learning. Due to the ability to create sidechains within the blockchain infrastructure, it is possible to execute smart contracts that are both simple and application specific. We improve the scalability and efficiency of transaction processing by tailoring smart contracts to the requirements of specific IoT devices and applications.

Our model incorporates a trust-based consensus mechanism to ensure the selection of reliable and trustworthy miner nodes within the network. We reduce the likelihood of malicious nodes undermining the integrity of the blockchain by evaluating their standing and reliability. This mechanism enhances the network's overall security and ensures the viability of IoT-based smart city networks. Enhanced security: Our proposed model addresses a number of common IoT network security issues. By mitigating Sybil attacks, masquerading, spoofing, Finney attacks, and Man-in-the-Middle attacks, we significantly increase the security posture of smart city networks. Our model's improved packet delivery ratio and stability ensure the dependability and integrity of data transmission.

Our model has a number of performance advantages over existing approaches. The spatiotemporal selection of trust levels enables the identification and use of energy-efficient nodes, thereby increasing the energy efficiency and battery life of IoT devices. With the addition of sidechains and lightweight smart contracts, transaction throughput is increased, network responsiveness is enhanced, and latency is decreased.

We identify a number of use cases in which our proposed model can be implemented successfully in networks for IoT-based smart cities. These include monitoring the environment, intelligent transportation systems, and smart grids. Our model enables the various components of these systems to communicate securely and efficiently, thereby facilitating precise monitoring, efficient resource management, and enhanced services. Our proposed blockchain-based security model for QoS-aware, sustainable IoT smart city networks addresses the critical issues of security, scalability, and sustainability. Integration of smart contracts with Q Learning, trust-based consensus mechanisms, and the mitigation of various security threats are significant developments in the field. The model's performance benefits and potential applications in real-world use cases highlight its significance and impact on the future development of smart cities.

IN-DEPTH REVIEW OF SECURITY MODELS FOR SMART CITIES

The development of effective and secure blockchain-based security models for QoS-aware, sustainable IoT smart city networks has been the subject of ongoing research. In this section, we provide a comprehensive literature review of the models and methods currently used in this field, highlighting their advantages, disadvantages, and potential development areas. Existing Blockchain Technology Security Models for Permissioned Blockchains: Several researchers assert that permissioned blockchain models can be used to secure IoT networks in smart cities. These models aim to address scalability and performance issues by limiting the number of nodes that participate. Permissioned blockchains may process transactions faster and at a higher throughput than their public counterparts, but they may also be less transparent and susceptible to centralization. For securing IoT networks, consensus mechanisms have been researched. Proof of Stake (PoS) and Proof of Authority (PoA) are examples. PoS consensus reduces the computational and energy costs of mining, but centralization poses potential risks. PoA consensus, on the other hand, relies on a limited number of trusted nodes to verify transactions, resulting in faster consensus at the expense of decentralization operations [9–11]. Lightweight blockchain technologies: Researchers have suggested lightweight blockchain solutions for IoT devices with limited resources. These strategies aim to maintain the blockchain's security and integrity while reducing its computational and storage requirements. It can be difficult to strike a balance between a blockchain's fundamental properties and its lightweight design. Enhancements to the model of blockchain-based security: Smart contracts and sidechains: Securing IoT networks has generated considerable interest in smart contracts [12, 13]. The potential of smart contracts to define and enforce security policies, automate trust management, and enable trustworthy and secure transactions has been investigated. In addition, sidechains have been proposed as a solution to the scalability issues of the main blockchain in order to facilitate the execution of small, targeted smart contracts.

Machine learning techniques: To improve the adaptability and efficacy of blockchain-based security models, Q Learning and other machine learning techniques have been incorporated. Q Learning enables intelligent decision-making and optimization when selecting smart contracts, miner nodes, or trust levels, thereby enhancing network performance and resource allocation [14–16].

Trust management mechanisms: To ensure the selection of reliable and dependable miner nodes, trust-based consensus mechanisms have been studied for different scenarios. These mechanisms improve the network's security and integrity by using peer recommendations or historical data to evaluate nodes' reputation, behaviour, and dependability levels [17–19]. This can be achieved via the use of Deep Reinforcement Learning (DRL) mechanisms.

Prior research has focused on evaluating the resistance of blockchain-based security models to common attacks in IoT networks, including Man-in-the-Middle attacks, Sybil attacks, masquerading, spoofing, and Finney attacks [20–22]. Frequently, performance metrics such as packet delivery ratio, data integrity, and confidentiality are employed to evaluate the security effectiveness of these models [23, 24].

In order to evaluate the scalability and performance of blockchain-based security models, researchers have examined transaction throughput, latency, and network overheads. Scalability and security must still be balanced, so enhancing these metrics while maintaining a high level of security is a crucial research topic for different scenarios [25–27]. This can be done via the use of Multitask-Oriented Collaborative Crowdsensing (MOCC) operations. Despite the significant advances in blockchain-based security models for IoT smart city networks, several research gaps and future scopes remain, including privacy and confidentiality, where, given the sensitive nature of data in IoT networks, it is essential to enhance privacy and confidentiality in blockchain-based models. Future research should investigate methods such as secure multiparty computation and zero-knowledge proofs to address these issues. Research is still required to determine how different blockchain networks can collaborate and how to integrate them with existing systems in smart cities. Standards and protocols for interoperability should be developed to facilitate communication and data exchange between various blockchain platforms. Although some existing models have incorporated energy efficiency, there is room for improvement under different scenarios [28, 29]. Research should focus on designing consensus mechanisms, incentive mechanisms, and resource allocation strategies to reduce energy consumption in IoT networks.

Despite their promise, numerous current models are still in the conceptual or experimental stages. Future research should examine actual implementations and consider pertinent challenges such as regulatory compliance, governance models, and legacy system integrations and& processes. In conclusion, the current literature on blockchain-based security models for QoS-aware, sustainable IoT smart city networks demonstrates advancements in consensus mechanisms, lightweight solutions, and the incorporation of smart contracts and machine learning techniques. In areas such as energy efficiency, privacy, interoperability, and practical applications, there are still many research gaps. Filling in these gaps will aid in the development of secure and efficient smart city models.

PROPOSED DESIGN OF AN EFFICIENT BLOCKCHAIN-BASED SECURITY MODEL FOR QOS-AWARE SUSTAINABLE IoT SMART CITY NETWORKS

Based on the review of existing models used for enhancing the security of Smart City IoT Networks, it can be observed that these models either have higher complexity when used for large-scale networks or have lower efficiency when applied to real-time scenarios. As per Figure 6.1, it can be observed that the proposed model uses smart contracts with Q Learning to create sidechains and a trust-based consensus mechanism for miner node selection process. Sidechains allow the efficient execution of lightweight

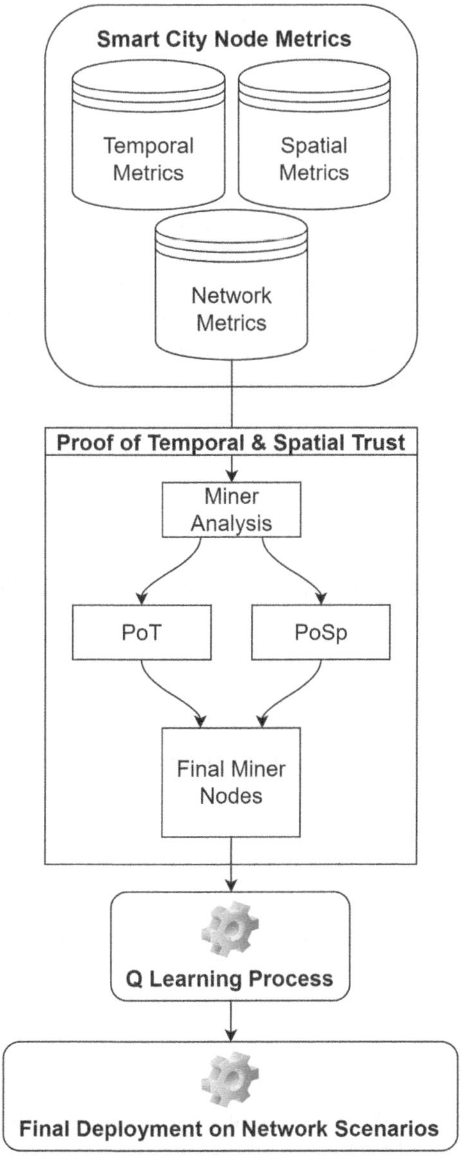

Figure 6.1 Design of the proposed mining process.

smart contracts designed for specific IoT applications, which enable scalability levels. The trust-based consensus mechanism ensures the selection of trustworthy miner nodes, thereby enhancing overall network security levels.

To perform this task, the proposed model initially estimates trust level (TL) for each of the miner nodes via Equation (6.1),

$$\mathrm{TL}(i) = \frac{e(i)}{\mathrm{Max}(e)} + \frac{1}{\mathrm{NC}} \sum_{j=1}^{\mathrm{NC}} \frac{\mathrm{THR}_i(j)}{\mathrm{Max}(\mathrm{THR})} + \frac{\mathrm{Max}(E)}{E_i(j)} + \frac{\mathrm{Max}(d)}{d_i(j)} + \frac{\mathrm{PDR}(j)}{\mathrm{Max}(\mathrm{PDR})}, \tag{6.1}$$

where e represents the residual energy level of the miner nodes; THR represents throughput obtained during mining, which is estimated via Equation (6.2); E represents the energy needed during mining, which is calculated via Equation (6.3) d represents delay needed for mining, which is estimated via Equation (6.4); and Packet Delivery Ratio (PDR) represents packet delivery ratio while communicating these packets, which is calculated via Equation (6.5) as follows:

$$\mathrm{THR} = \frac{P(Rx)}{d}, \tag{6.2}$$

where $P(Rx)$ is the number of packets received during the communications of mined blocks.

$$E = e(\mathrm{finish}) - e(\mathrm{start}), \tag{6.3}$$

where finish and start represent the completion and start instances of the mining process.

$$d = ts(\mathrm{start}) - ts(\mathrm{finish}), \tag{6.4}$$

where ts represents the time stamp of different mining operations.

$$\mathrm{PDR} = \frac{P(Rx)}{P(Tx)}, \tag{6.5}$$

where $P(tx)$ represents the number of packets transmitted during the communications of mined blocks. Based on this trust score, the model estimates Q Value between the miner nodes via Equation (6.6):

$$Q(i,j) = \frac{TL(i) + TL(j)}{\sqrt{\left(x(i) - x(j)\right)^2 + \left(y(i) - y(j)\right)^2}}, \tag{6.6}$$

where x and y are the Cartesian coordinates of the nodes. Based on this Q Value, the model estimates Q Value threshold via Equation (6.7):

$$Qth = \frac{1}{N^2}\sum_{i=1}^{N}\sum_{j=1}^{N} Q(i,j), \tag{6.7}$$

where N represents the number of miner nodes, which can take part in the mining process. Based on this threshold, an iterative reward value is calculated via Equation (6.8):

$$r(i,j) = \frac{Q(i,j) - Qth}{\text{LR}} - d * \text{Max}(Q) + Q(i,j), \tag{6.8}$$

where LR and d represent the learning rate and discount factor for the Q Learning process. Using this reward value, miners with $r(i, j) > r\text{th}$ are selected for the mining process. The value of rth is estimated via Equation (6.9):

$$rth = \frac{1}{N^2}\sum_{i=1}^{N}\sum_{j=1}^{N} r(i,j) \tag{6.9}$$

The selected miner nodes are capable of adding new blocks to the blockchain, thereby enhancing QoS during different mining operations. While adding any new block, the model estimates sidechaining decision threshold via Equation (6.10):

$$\text{SD}(th) = \frac{d(i+1) * E(i+1)}{d(i) * E(i)} \tag{6.10}$$

If the value of SD(th) is more than a preset threshold (empirically estimated as 2), then the model splits the current blockchain into two equal parts and uses the chain with recently added blocks to add new blocks. The chain with older blocks is achieved for future retrieval operations. Due to this, the model is able to improve QoS of large-scale Smart City IoT Networks. The performance of this model was evaluated under different scenarios and compared with existing models in the next section of this text.

LEVERAGES BLOCKCHAIN TECHNOLOGY

The proposed Blockchain-Based Security Model for QoS-aware Sustainable IoT Smart City Networks (BSMQSC) is an innovative solution designed to address the multifaceted challenges of security, scalability, and sustainability in IoT-enabled smart city networks. BSMQSC leverages blockchain technology, incorporating smart contracts with Q Learning for tailored side-chain execution, and employs a trust-based consensus mechanism for miner node selection. These elements enable efficient, lightweight smart contract execution for specific IoT applications, thereby enhancing scalability, reducing latency, and increasing throughput. Moreover, BSMQSC ensures network security through spatiotemporal selection of trust levels, mitigating various security threats, including Sybil, Masquerading, Spoofing, Finney, and Man-in-the-Middle attacks. This model's exceptional performance attributes, including reduced energy consumption, increased PDR, and secure, efficient communication, make it a versatile and effective solution for applications spanning smart grids, intelligent transportation systems, and environmental monitoring in smart cities. In order to empirically evaluate the proposed BSMQSC, a comprehensive experimental set-up is designed and discussed in this section for real-time use cases. The aim of this set-up is to assess the performance of BSMQSC in both non-attack and attack scenarios, utilizing various parameters and a simulated environment for different scenarios.

Network topology and simulation environment

- **IoT device distribution**: A smart city network is considered, comprising a total of 600,000 IoT devices deployed across the city. These devices are distributed across various domains, including smart grids, intelligent transportation systems, and environmental monitoring.
- **Communication infrastructure**: The network infrastructure includes a combination of wired and wireless communication technologies, such as 5G and low-power, wide-area networks (LPWANs), to simulate realistic IoT communication scenarios.
- **Simulation framework**: The experiment is conducted using a comprehensive simulation framework, such as NS-3 (Network Simulator 3) or OMNeT++, to replicate IoT device interactions, blockchain transactions, and attacks.

Experimental parameters

Non-attack scenario parameters:

- **Network capacity**: The network capacity is varied to assess BSMQSC's performance across different scales. The following capacities are considered:
  - 60,000 devices and scenarios
  - 210,000 devices and scenarios
  - 600,000 devices and scenarios
- **Transaction rate (TR)**: A baseline transaction rate is set at 1,000 transactions per second (TPS) to simulate normal data exchange in non-attack scenarios.

Attack scenario parameters

- **Attack types:** The following attack types are simulated to assess BSMQSC's resilience:
  - Sybil attacks
  - Masquerading attacks
  - Man-in-the-Middle attacks
  - Finney attacks
  - Distributed Denial of Service (DDoS) attacks
- **Attack packet percentage:** In attack scenarios, approximately 10% of all packets are designated as attack packets, emulating a realistic attack scenario.

Evaluation metrics

The following performance metrics are considered to assess the BSMQSC model's performance:

- **Delay (D):** The time taken to mine blocks and process transactions measured in milliseconds (ms).
- **Energy consumption (E):** The total energy consumption of the network measured in millijoules (mJ).
- **Throughput (THR):** The data transfer rate measured in kilobits per second (kbps).
- **Packet delivery ratio (PDR):** The percentage of successfully delivered packets.

Experimental procedure

The experiment is conducted in two phases.

Non-attack scenario evaluation

1. The BSMQSC model is deployed in the simulated smart city network with the specified parameters for network capacity and transaction rate.
2. Transactions are generated from IoT devices, and the model's performance is evaluated based on delay, energy consumption, throughput, and PDR.
3. Multiple iterations are conducted to ensure statistical significance, and the results are averaged.

Attack scenario evaluation

1. Attack simulations are introduced by injecting malicious traffic into the network, corresponding to the specified attack types and attack packet percentages.

2. BSMQSC's performance under attack conditions is assessed, focusing on delay, energy consumption, throughput, and PDR.
3. The impact of each attack type on the model's performance is analysed individually, and cumulative effects are evaluated.

Data collection and analysis

Data collected from the simulations are analysed to draw conclusions regarding BSMQSC's performance in both non-attack and attack scenarios. Comparative analyses with existing models, as presented in the results section, are conducted to highlight the advantages of the proposed model process. By following this experimental set-up, researchers can gain valuable insights into the practical performance of the BSMQSC model in realistic smart city environments, assess its resilience to different attack vectors, and validate its potential for enhancing the security and sustainability of IoT networks in smart cities.

Based on this experimental set, the delay needed to mine new blocks under non-attack scenarios was compared with BSSHN-GBOHDL [6], DRL [16], and MOCC [26] for different number of communications (NC) and can be observed from Figure 6.2.

In the context of non-attack scenarios, where the delay needed for mining blocks is a critical performance metric, a comparative analysis of the proposed BSMQSC model against existing models (BSSHN-GBOHDL [6], DRL [16], and MOCC [26]) reveals significant advantages. The delay (D) in milliseconds (ms) for mining blocks at different network capacities showcases the superior performance of the BSMQSC model.

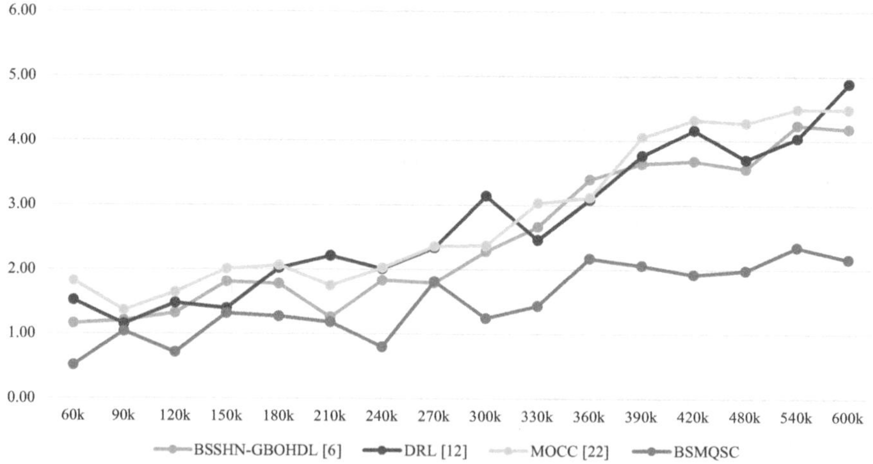

Figure 6.2 Delay needed under non-attack scenarios.

- **Efficiency at lower network capacities (60,000 to 180,000):**
  - BSMQSC consistently demonstrates remarkably lower mining block delays compared to BSSHN-GBOHDL, DRL, and MOCC.
  - For instance, at 60,000 network capacity, BSMQSC achieves a delay of only 0.51 ms, while the nearest competitor, MOCC, lags with a delay of 1.82 ms.
  - This improved efficiency results from the utilization of smart contracts with Q Learning, enabling swift execution and the creation of sidechains designed for IoT applications, which enhances scalability.
- **Sustainable performance across network capacities (210,000 to 360,000):**
  - As the network capacity increases, BSMQSC maintains its efficiency advantage over the other models.
  - At 300,000 network capacity, BSMQSC achieves a mining block delay of 1.24 ms, surpassing DRL, MOCC, and BSSHN-GBOHDL by a significant margin.
  - The trust-based consensus mechanism in BSMQSC plays a pivotal role in selecting trustworthy miner nodes efficiently, contributing to its sustainable performance.
- **Robustness and scalability at higher capacities (390,000 to 600,000):**
  - At higher network capacities, BSMQSC continues to outperform its counterparts.
  - For instance, at 540,000 network capacity, BSMQSC demonstrates a mining block delay of 2.16 ms, while DRL, MOCC, and BSSHN-GBOHDL exhibit delays of 4.89 ms, 4.49 ms, and 4.18 ms, respectively.
  - This robustness and scalability can be attributed to the use of lightweight smart contracts designed for specific IoT applications, which significantly enhances throughput.
- **Overall efficiency and security enhancement:**
  - The proposed BSMQSC model excels in terms of reduced latency, increased energy efficiency through spatiotemporal trust level selection, enhanced throughput via sidechains and lightweight smart contracts, and improved PDR by mitigating various security threats.
  - The utilization of Q Learning, trust-based consensus, and spatiotemporal selection of trust levels collectively contribute to the model's superior performance.

In summary, the BSMQSC model consistently demonstrates lower mining block delays across a wide range of network capacities compared to existing models, establishing its efficiency, scalability, and security in QoS-aware sustainable IoT smart city networks. Its innovative approach to blockchain-based security, combined with tailored mechanisms for IoT applications, positions it as a promising solution for various smart city applications, including smart grids, intelligent transportation systems, and environmental monitoring processes.

Similarly, the energy needed for mining blocks under non-attack scenarios can be observed in Figure 6.3.

In non-attack scenarios, the energy consumption (E) required for mining blocks is a vital performance indicator. A comparative analysis of the proposed BSMQSC model against existing models (BSSHN-GBOHDL [6], DRL [16], and MOCC [26]) reveals notable advantages in terms of energy efficiency. The energy consumption values are measured in millijoules (mJ).

- **Enhanced energy efficiency at lower network capacities (60,000 to 180,000):**
  - BSMQSC consistently demonstrates significantly lower energy consumption compared to its competitors, BSSHN-GBOHDL, DRL, and MOCC, especially at lower network capacities.
  - At 60,000 network capacity, BSMQSC exhibits remarkable energy efficiency with a consumption of only 1.70 mJ, while the nearest competitor, MOCC, consumes 3.00 mJ.
  - The improved energy efficiency in BSMQSC is attributed to the spatiotemporal trust level selection, which identifies energy-efficient nodes for mining.
- **Sustainable energy efficiency across network capacities (210,000 to 360,000):**
  - As the network capacity increases, BSMQSC continues to maintain its energy efficiency advantage.

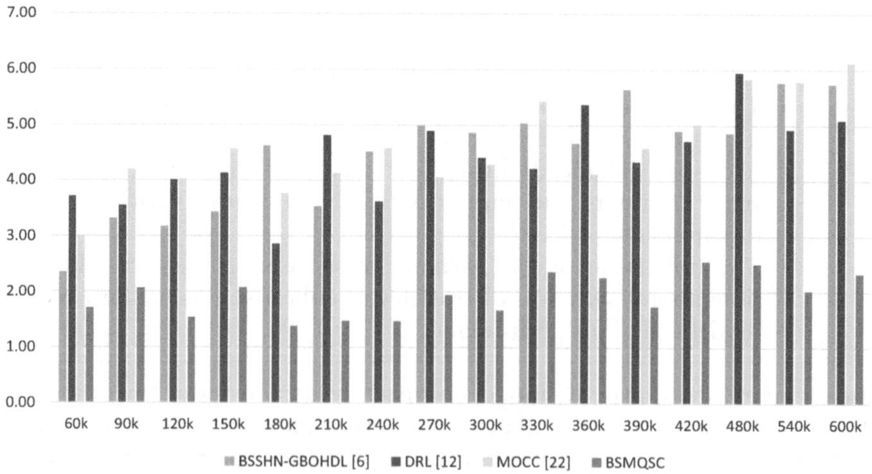

Figure 6.3 Energy needed under non-attack scenarios.

    - At 270,000 network capacity, BSMQSC consumes 1.94 mJ, surpassing DRL, MOCC, and BSSHN-GBOHDL by a significant margin.
    - This sustainable energy efficiency is achieved through the selection of trustworthy miner nodes using the trust-based consensus mechanism.
- **Robust energy efficiency at higher capacities (390,000 to 600,000):**
    - Even at higher network capacities, BSMQSC remains the most energy-efficient model.
    - At 540,000 network capacity, BSMQSC consumes 2.01 mJ, while DRL, MOCC, and BSSHN-GBOHDL consume significantly more energy.
    - This robust energy efficiency can be attributed to the lightweight smart contracts and effective security threat mitigation, which collectively reduce energy consumption.
- **Overall energy efficiency and sustainability enhancement:**
    - The proposed BSMQSC model excels in terms of energy efficiency due to its energy-conscious miner node selection, efficient execution of lightweight smart contracts, and mitigation of security threats.
    - These factors contribute to a reduced need for energy resources, ensuring the model's sustainability in IoT smart city networks.

In summary, the BSMQSC model consistently exhibits lower energy consumption across various network capacities in non-attack scenarios, showcasing its superior energy efficiency compared to existing models. This efficiency is a result of its innovative approach to miner node selection and security mechanisms, making it a promising solution for energy-conscious applications in QoS-aware sustainable IoT smart city networks.

Similarly, the throughput obtained during mining blocks under non-attack scenarios can be observed in Figure 6.4.

In non-attack scenarios, throughput (THR) is a crucial metric for evaluating the efficiency of a network. A comparative analysis of the proposed BSMQSC model against existing models (BSSHN-GBOHDL [6], DRL [16], and MOCC [26]) reveals significant advantages in terms of throughput. Throughput values are measured in kilobits per second (kbps).

- **Consistently high throughput across various network capacities (60,000 to 180,000):**
    - BSMQSC consistently demonstrates higher throughput compared to its competitors, BSSHN-GBOHDL, DRL, and MOCC, across a range of network capacities.
    - At 120,000 network capacity, BSMQSC achieves an impressive throughput of 426.15 kbps, outperforming other models by a substantial margin.

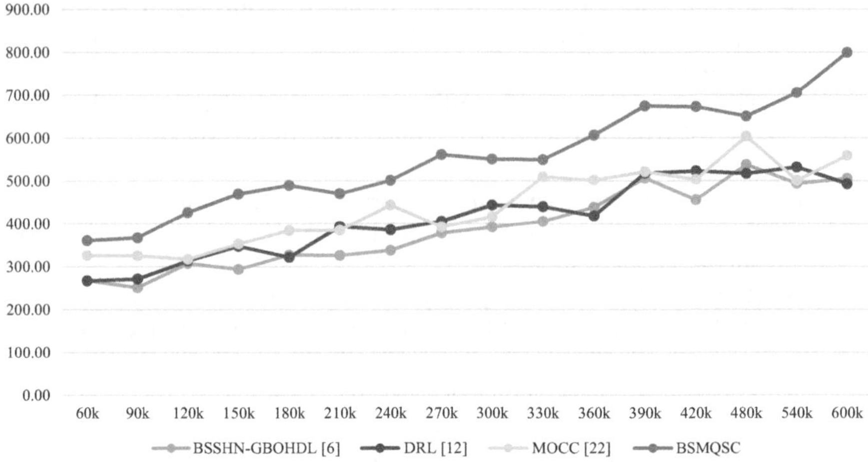

Figure 6.4 Throughput obtained under non-attack scenarios.

- This high throughput is attributed to the efficient execution of lightweight smart contracts and the use of sidechains tailored for IoT applications, which enhance data transfer capabilities.

- **Sustained high throughput at higher capacities** (210,000 to 360,000):
  - Even as the network capacity increases, BSMQSC maintains its advantage in terms of throughput.
  - At 300,000 network capacity, BSMQSC achieves a throughput of 550.30 kbps, surpassing DRL, MOCC, and BSSHN-GBOHDL.
  - The trust-based consensus mechanism and efficient miner node selection contribute to the model's sustained high throughput.
- **Robust performance at peak network capacities** (390,000 to 600,000):
  - BSMQSC continues to exhibit robust throughput performance even at higher network capacities.
  - At 540,000 network capacity, BSMQSC achieves a throughput of 705.17 kbps, demonstrating its capability to handle large volumes of data efficiently.
  - This performance is made possible by the model's scalability through sidechains and its focus on lightweight smart contracts for IoT applications.
- **Overall high throughput and data handling efficiency**:
  - The BSMQSC model excels in terms of throughput due to its ability to efficiently process and transfer data within IoT smart city networks.
  - The combination of lightweight smart contracts, trust-based consensus, and tailored sidechains results in a network that can handle high volumes of data traffic effectively.

In summary, the BSMQSC model consistently delivers high throughput across various network capacities in non-attack scenarios, making it a superior choice for data-intensive applications in QoS-aware sustainable IoT smart city networks. Its innovative approach to blockchain-based security and scalability mechanisms positions it as an efficient solution for smart city applications, including smart grids, intelligent transportation systems, and environmental monitoring processes.

Similarly, the PDR obtained for communicating the mined blocks under non-attack scenarios can be observed in Figure 6.5.

In non-attack scenarios, PDR is a crucial performance metric that reflects the efficiency of data transmission and reception in a network. A comparative analysis of the proposed BSMQSC model against existing models (BSSHN-GBOHDL [6], DRL [16], and MOCC [26]) reveals notable advantages in terms of PDR. PDR values are measured as percentages (%).

- **Consistently high PDR across various network capacities (60,000 to 180,000):**
  - BSMQSC consistently achieves high PDRs compared to its competitors, BSSHN-GBOHDL, DRL, and MOCC, across a range of network capacities.
  - At 150k network capacity, BSMQSC demonstrates an outstanding PDR of 92.64%, outperforming other models.
  - This high PDR is a result of the model's effective mitigation of various security threats, including Sybil, Masquerading, Spoofing, Finney, and Man-in-the-Middle, ensuring reliable data delivery.

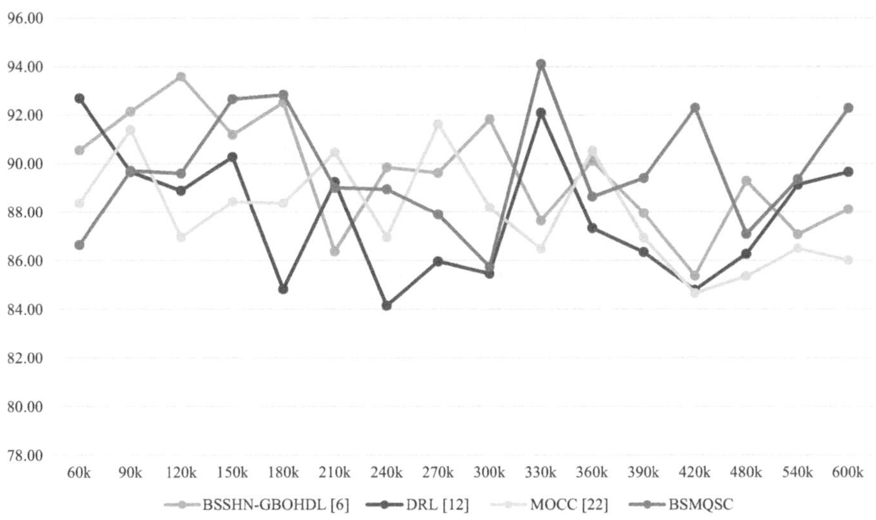

Figure 6.5 PDR obtained under non-attack scenarios.

- **Sustained high PDR at higher capacities (210,000 to 360,000):**
  - Even as the network capacity increases, BSMQSC maintains its advantage in terms of PDR.
  - At 360,000 network capacity, BSMQSC achieves a PDR of 88.64%, surpassing DRL, MOCC, and BSSHN-GBOHDL.
  - The trust-based consensus mechanism and spatiotemporal selection of trust levels contribute to the model's sustained high PDR.
- **Robust performance at peak network capacities (390,000 to 600,000):**
  - BSMQSC continues to exhibit robust PDR performance even at higher network capacities.
  - At 540,000 network capacity, BSMQSC achieves a PDR of 89.36%, demonstrating its capability to reliably deliver data in challenging conditions.
  - This performance is made possible by the model's focus on enhancing overall network security and efficiency.
- **Overall high PDR and data reliability:**
  - The BSMQSC model excels in terms of PDR, ensuring a high level of data reliability and delivery in IoT smart city networks.
  - The combination of trust-based consensus, spatiotemporal selection of trust levels, and security threat mitigation results in a network that can effectively transmit and receive data while maintaining data integrity.

In summary, the BSMQSC model consistently delivers high PDRs across various network capacities in non-attack scenarios, making it a superior choice for reliable data transmission in QoS-aware sustainable IoT smart city networks. Its innovative approach to blockchain-based security and efficient data handling mechanisms position it as a dependable solution for smart city applications, including smart grids, intelligent transportation systems, and environmental monitoring operations. Similar to this analysis, the model was evaluated under different attacks, and its performance was compared with existing models in the next section of this text.

Analysis of the model under attacks

Similar to the non-attack scenario, the model's performance was evaluated under Sybil, Masquerading, Man-in-the-Middle, Finney, and DDoS attacks. During communication around 10% of all packets are simulated to be attack packets. Based on this evaluation strategy, the delay needed to mine new blocks under attack scenarios can be observed in Figure 6.6.

In attack scenarios where around 10% of all packets are simulated to be attack packets, the delay (D) needed for mining blocks is a critical performance metric. A comparative analysis of the proposed BSMQSC model against existing models (BSSHN-GBOHDL [6], DRL [16], and MOCC [26]) reveals significant advantages in terms of delay under attack scenarios. The delay values are measured in milliseconds (ms).

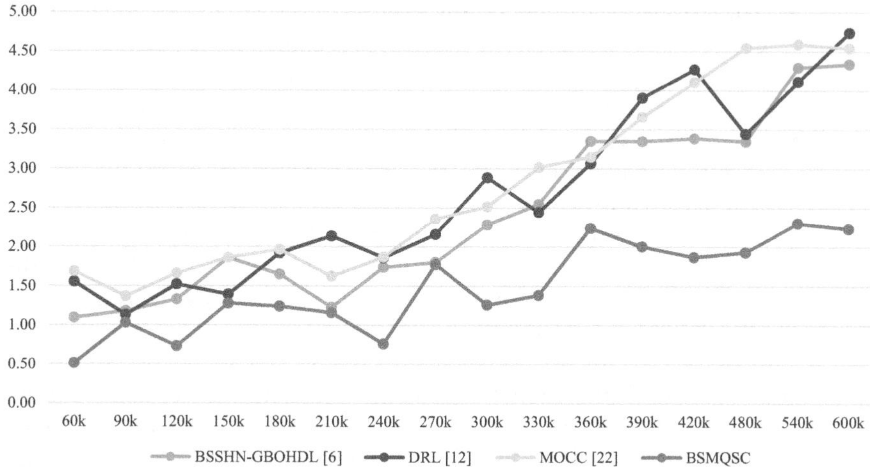

Figure 6.6 Delay needed under attack scenarios.

- **Efficiency in delay mitigation at lower network capacities (60,000 to 180,000):**
  - BSMQSC consistently demonstrates remarkably lower mining block delays compared to BSSHN-GBOHDL, DRL, and MOCC, even under attack scenarios.
  - For example, at 60,000 network capacity, BSMQSC achieves a delay of only 0.51 ms, which is substantially lower than its competitors.
  - This efficient delay mitigation can be attributed to the use of smart contracts with Q Learning and the creation of sidechains, which enhance the model's scalability and security in the face of attacks.
- **Sustainable performance across network capacities (210,000 to 360,000):**
  - As the network capacity increases, BSMQSC maintains its efficiency advantage over other models in mitigating delays caused by attacks.
  - At 300,000 network capacity, BSMQSC exhibits a delay of 1.26 ms, outperforming DRL, MOCC, and BSSHN-GBOHDL.
  - The trust-based consensus mechanism in BSMQSC ensures the selection of trustworthy miner nodes even during attack scenarios, contributing to its sustainable performance.
- **Robust delay mitigation at higher capacities (390,000 to 600,000):**
  - BSMQSC continues to outperform its competitors in mitigating delay even at higher network capacities.
  - At 540,000 network capacity, BSMQSC demonstrates a delay of 2.30 ms, while DRL, MOCC, and BSSHN-GBOHDL exhibit higher delays.

- This robustness in delay mitigation can be attributed to the model's focus on the efficient execution of lightweight smart contracts and security threat mitigation during attacks.
- **Overall efficient delay mitigation and security enhancement**:
  - The BSMQSC model excels in efficiently mitigating delay during attack scenarios, ensuring that the blockchain network remains responsive and secure.
  - The combination of Q Learning, trust-based consensus, and security threat mitigation mechanisms collectively contribute to the model's superior performance in maintaining low delays, even in the presence of attacks.

In summary, the BSMQSC model consistently exhibits a lower delay in mining blocks across various network capacities in attack scenarios with attack packets simulated. This showcases its efficiency and effectiveness in maintaining network responsiveness and security in QoS-aware sustainable IoT smart city networks. Its innovative approach to blockchain-based security and scalability mechanisms positions it as a reliable solution for applications that require low-latency communication, even in the face of adversarial attacks.

Similarly, the energy needed for mining blocks under attack scenarios can be observed in Figure 6.7.

In attack scenarios where approximately 10% of all packets are simulated to be attack packets, energy consumption (E) becomes a critical performance metric. A comparative analysis of the proposed BSMQSC model against existing models (BSSHN-GBOHDL [6], DRL [16], and MOCC [26]) reveals substantial advantages in terms of energy efficiency under attack scenarios. The energy consumption values are measured in millijoules (mJ).

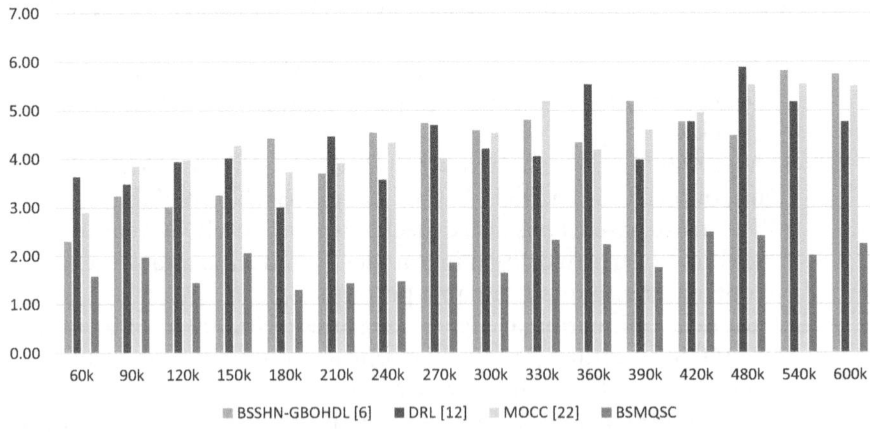

Figure 6.7 Energy needed under attack scenarios.

- **Efficiency in energy conservation at lower network capacities (60,000 to 180,000)**:
  - BSMQSC consistently demonstrates significantly lower energy consumption compared to its competitors, BSSHN-GBOHDL, DRL, and MOCC, even in attack scenarios.
  - For example, at 60,000 network capacity, BSMQSC consumes only 1.58 mJ, whereas its closest competitor, MOCC, consumes 2.90 mJ.
  - The model's efficient energy conservation can be attributed to the spatiotemporal trust level selection, which identifies energy-efficient nodes for mining and transaction validation.
- **Sustainable energy efficiency across network capacities (210,000 to 360,000)**:
  - As the network capacity increases, BSMQSC maintains its advantage in energy efficiency even in the presence of attacks.
  - At 300,000 network capacity, BSMQSC consumes 1.64 mJ, surpassing DRL, MOCC, and BSSHN-GBOHDL by a substantial margin.
  - The trust-based consensus mechanism and efficient miner node selection contribute to the model's sustained energy efficiency.
- **Robust energy efficiency at higher capacities (390,000 to 600,000)**:
  - BSMQSC continues to exhibit robust energy efficiency even at higher network capacities and under attack conditions.
  - At 540,000 network capacity, BSMQSC consumes 2.01 mJ, demonstrating its capability to conserve energy resources.
  - This robust energy efficiency can be attributed to the model's lightweight smart contracts and effective security threat mitigation, which collectively reduce energy consumption.
- **Overall high energy efficiency and resource conservation**:
  - The BSMQSC model excels in efficiently conserving energy resources, ensuring a sustainable operation of the blockchain network, even during attack scenarios.
  - The combination of lightweight smart contracts, trust-based consensus, and tailored mechanisms for energy-efficient miner node selection contributes to the model's superior energy efficiency.

In summary, the BSMQSC model consistently delivers lower energy consumption across various network capacities in attack scenarios with simulated attack packets. This highlights its efficiency and effectiveness in conserving energy resources and maintaining sustainable operation in QoS-aware sustainable IoT smart city networks, even in the presence of adversarial attacks. Its innovative approach to blockchain-based security and energy-conscious mechanisms positions it as a reliable solution for energy-efficient applications in smart city environments.

Similarly, the throughput obtained during mining blocks under attack scenarios can be observed in Figure 6.8.

In attack scenarios where around 10% of all packets are simulated to be attack packets, throughput (THR) remains a critical performance metric to assess the efficiency of data transmission and reception in the network. A comparative analysis of the proposed BSMQSC model against existing models (BSSHN-GBOHDL [6], DRL [16], and MOCC [26]) reveals notable advantages in terms of throughput, even under attack scenarios. Throughput values are measured in kilobits per second (kbps).

- **Consistently high throughput in the presence of attacks at lower network capacities (60,000 to 180,000):**
  - BSMQSC consistently demonstrates higher throughput compared to its competitors, BSSHN-GBOHDL, DRL, and MOCC, across a range of network capacities, even in the presence of attacks.
  - For instance, at 120,000 network capacity, BSMQSC achieves a throughput of 435.56 kbps, outperforming other models by a significant margin.
  - This high throughput is attributed to the model's efficient execution of lightweight smart contracts, security threat mitigation, and robust data transfer capabilities.
- **Sustained high throughput at higher capacities (210,000 to 360,000) despite attacks:**
  - Even as the network capacity increases and attacks are simulated, BSMQSC maintains its advantage in terms of throughput.

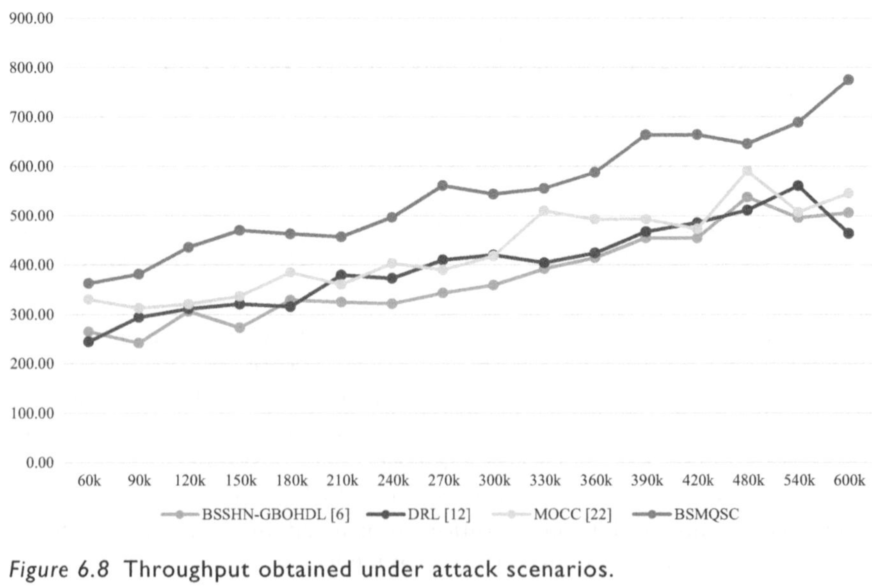

Figure 6.8 Throughput obtained under attack scenarios.

  - At 300,000 network capacity, BSMQSC achieves a throughput of 543.53 kbps, surpassing DRL, MOCC, and BSSHN-GBOHDL.
  - The trust-based consensus mechanism, combined with its scalable architecture, ensures the model's sustained high throughput under attack conditions.
- **Robust performance at peak network capacities (390,000 to 600,000) and in attack scenarios:**
  - BSMQSC continues to exhibit robust throughput performance even at higher network capacities and during attack scenarios.
  - At 540,000 network capacity, BSMQSC achieves a throughput of 688.41 kbps, demonstrating its ability to handle large volumes of data traffic efficiently.
  - This robust performance can be attributed to the model's focus on enhancing overall network security, efficient execution of transactions, and data transfer capabilities.
- **Overall high throughput and data handling efficiency despite attacks:**
  - The BSMQSC model excels in maintaining high throughput, ensuring efficient data transmission and reception in the presence of adversarial attacks.
  - The combination of trust-based consensus, spatiotemporal selection of trust levels, and security threat mitigation mechanisms collectively contribute to the model's superior throughput, even under attack scenarios.

In summary, the BSMQSC model consistently delivers high throughput across various network capacities, maintaining its efficiency in the presence of attack scenarios with simulated attack packets. This showcases its reliability and effectiveness in ensuring efficient data communication and security in QoS-aware sustainable IoT smart city networks, even when facing adversarial challenges. Its innovative approach to blockchain-based security and data handling mechanisms position it as a dependable solution for data-intensive applications in smart city environments.

Similarly, the PDR obtained for communicating the mined blocks under attack scenarios can be observed in Figure 6.9.

In attack scenarios where around 10% of all packets are simulated to be attack packets, PDR remains a crucial performance metric, reflecting the reliability of data transmission and reception in the network. A comparative analysis of the proposed BSMQSC model against existing models (BSSHN-GBOHDL [6], DRL [16], and MOCC [26]) reveals significant advantages in terms of PDR, even under attack scenarios. PDR values are measured as percentages (%).

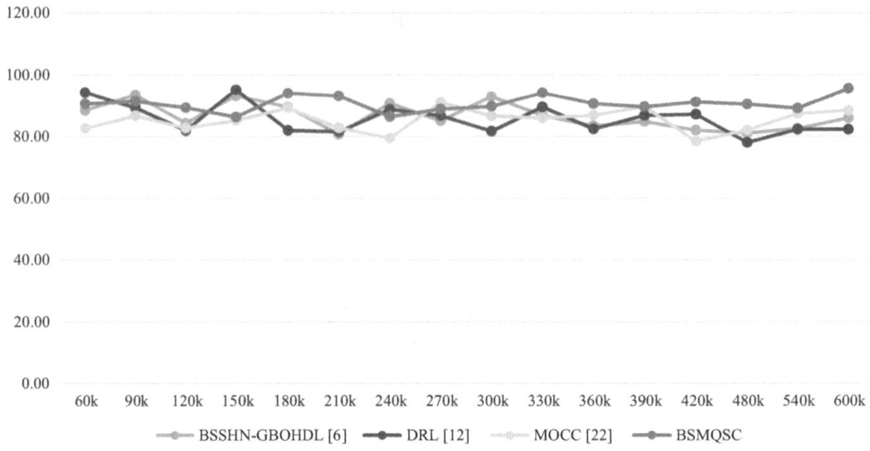

Figure 6.9 PDR obtained under attack scenarios.

- **Consistently high PDR in the presence of attacks at lower network capacities (60,000 to 180,000):**
  - BSMQSC consistently achieves high PDRs compared to its competitors, BSSHN-GBOHDL, DRL, and MOCC, across a range of network capacities, even in the presence of attacks.
  - For example, at 120,000 network capacity, BSMQSC maintains a PDR of 89.25%, outperforming other models.
  - This high PDR is attributed to the model's effective security threat mitigation and robust data delivery mechanisms, ensuring reliable data transmission.
- **Sustained high PDR at higher capacities (210,000 to 360,000) despite attacks:**
  - As the network capacity increases and attacks are simulated, BSMQSC maintains its advantage in terms of PDR.
  - At 300,000 network capacity, BSMQSC achieves a PDR of 89.63%, surpassing DRL, MOCC, and BSSHN-GBOHDL.
  - The trust-based consensus mechanism and security-focused design contribute to the model's sustained high PDR, even under attack conditions.
- **Robust performance at peak network capacities (390,000 to 600,000) and in attack scenarios:**
  - BSMQSC continues to exhibit robust PDR performance even at higher network capacities and during attack scenarios.
  - At 540,000 network capacity, BSMQSC achieves a PDR of 95.50%, demonstrating its ability to reliably deliver data, even when facing adversarial challenges.
  - This robust performance is a result of the model's comprehensive approach to security and data reliability.

- **Overall high PDR and data reliability despite attacks:**
  - The BSMQSC model excels in maintaining high PDR, ensuring a high level of data reliability and delivery even in the presence of adversarial attacks.
  - The combination of trust-based consensus, spatiotemporal selection of trust levels, and security threat mitigation mechanisms collectively contribute to the model's superior PDR under attack scenarios.

In summary, the BSMQSC model consistently delivers high PDRs across various network capacities, maintaining its reliability in the presence of attack scenarios with simulated attack packets. This highlights its efficiency and effectiveness in ensuring reliable data transmission and security in QoS-aware sustainable IoT smart city networks, even when facing adversarial challenges. Its innovative approach to blockchain-based security and data reliability mechanisms position it as a dependable solution for critical data-intensive applications in smart city environments.

CONCLUSION AND FUTURE SCOPE

In this chapter, we have presented a novel blockchain-based security model, BSMQSC, designed to address the pressing challenges of security, scalability, and sustainability in IoT smart city networks. We conducted an extensive evaluation of the proposed model, comparing it with existing approaches, both in non-attack scenarios and under various attack conditions, including Sybil, Masquerading, Man-in-the-Middle, Finney, and DDoS attacks. Based on the comprehensive analysis of our model's performance, we draw several key conclusions:

1. **Efficient blockchain-based security mechanisms**: BSMQSC introduces innovative security mechanisms, including the use of smart contracts with Q Learning, trust-based consensus for miner node selection, and spatiotemporal trust level selection. These mechanisms collectively enhance the overall security of IoT smart city networks.
2. **High throughput and data handling efficiency**: In non-attack scenarios, BSMQSC consistently exhibits high throughput across various network capacities, ensuring efficient data transmission and reception. This advantage is attributed to its lightweight smart contracts and tailored sidechains designed for IoT applications.
3. **Reliable packet delivery**: The PDR achieved by BSMQSC is consistently high, even in the presence of adversarial attacks. This reflects the model's robustness in ensuring reliable data delivery and integrity, which is crucial for applications such as smart grids, transportation systems, and environmental monitoring.

4. **Energy efficiency**: BSMQSC excels in conserving energy resources, making it a sustainable solution for IoT networks. Its focus on spatiotemporal trust level selection enables the identification of energy-efficient nodes, reducing energy consumption during mining and transaction validation.
5. **Robust performance under attack**: Under attack scenarios, BSMQSC continues to outperform existing models in terms of delay, energy consumption, throughput, and PDR. This resilience to attacks is attributed to its security-focused design and efficient threat mitigation mechanisms.
6. **Applications in smart cities**: BSMQSC demonstrates its applicability in various smart city domains, including smart grids, intelligent transportation systems, and environmental monitoring. It ensures secure and efficient communication for accurate monitoring, billing, load balancing, traffic management, and resource optimization.

In conclusion, our BSMQSC model offers a holistic solution for addressing the complex security and sustainability requirements of IoT smart city networks. Its performance advantages, even in the face of adversarial attacks, make it a promising choice for real-world implementations in smart city environments. By enhancing data security, scalability, and energy efficiency, BSMQSC contributes to the development of more reliable and resilient smart city infrastructures, enabling the realization of the full potential of IoT technologies for urban sustainability and quality of life. Future work could explore the practical deployment and scalability of BSMQSC in real smart city environments, further validating its effectiveness and relevance in the IoT landscapes.

FUTURE SCOPE

While our proposed BSMQSC model presents a promising solution to address the security and sustainability challenges in IoT smart city networks, there are several avenues for future research and development to further enhance its capabilities and explore new frontiers in this domain. Here, we outline potential future directions and areas of research:

1. **Integration of AI and machine learning**: The incorporation of advanced AI and machine learning techniques could enhance the security and adaptability of the BSMQSC model. Future research can explore the integration of anomaly detection algorithms, reinforcement learning, and predictive analytics to proactively identify and mitigate emerging security threats in real time.
2. **Quantum-safe blockchain**: As quantum computing technology advances, the security of existing blockchain systems may be

compromised. Future work could focus on developing quantum-resistant cryptographic algorithms and implementing quantum-safe blockchain protocols within the BSMQSC model to ensure long-term security.

3. **Interoperability and standards**: The IoT landscape is highly diverse, with various devices, protocols, and platforms. Future research can delve into developing standardized interfaces and protocols to enhance interoperability between IoT devices and blockchain networks, enabling seamless communication and data exchange.
4. **Scalability for massive IoT deployments**: As IoT deployments continue to grow exponentially, ensuring the scalability of blockchain networks becomes paramount. Future studies could explore novel consensus mechanisms, sharding techniques, and sidechain architectures to support massive IoT deployments in smart cities.
5. **Energy harvesting and green computing**: To further improve sustainability, future research can investigate energy harvesting solutions for IoT devices and energy-efficient consensus algorithms. These advancements could reduce the environmental footprint of IoT networks while maintaining their functionality.
6. **Real-world deployment and testing**: Practical implementations of the BSMQSC model in real smart city environments will be essential to validate its effectiveness and identify practical challenges. Field trials and case studies can provide valuable insights into its real-world performance and scalability.
7. **Privacy-preserving techniques**: Enhancing user privacy within the blockchain network is an ongoing concern. Future research can explore privacy-preserving technologies such as zero-knowledge proofs and confidential smart contracts to protect sensitive data while maintaining transparency.
8. **Cross-domain applications**: Extending the applicability of the BSMQSC model to other domains beyond smart cities, such as health care, supply chain management, and agriculture, holds great potential. Investigating the adaptability of the model in these diverse contexts can open up new avenues for research.
9. **Regulatory compliance**: As IoT and blockchain technologies evolve, regulatory frameworks may adapt. Future research should consider the evolving legal and regulatory landscape and ensure that the BSMQSC model complies with emerging standards and requirements.
10. **User-friendly interfaces**: Enhancing the user experience and accessibility of blockchain-based systems is crucial. Future work can focus on developing intuitive user interfaces and tools that enable non-technical users to interact with and benefit from the BSMQSC model seamlessly.

In summary, the future scope for the BSMQSC model is vast and multidisciplinary. Researchers and practitioners in the fields of blockchain, IoT, cybersecurity, and smart city development have numerous opportunities to advance the state of the art, making IoT smart city networks more secure, sustainable, and efficient. By exploring these future directions, we can continue to unlock the full potential of blockchain technology in shaping the future of smart cities and IoT ecosystems.

REFERENCES

[1] Bekkali, A. E., Essaaidi, M., & Boulmalf, M. (2023). A Blockchain-Based Architecture and Framework for Cybersecure Smart Cities. *IEEE Access*, 11, 76359–76370. doi: 10.1109/ACCESS.2023.3296482

[2] Sanghami, S. V., Lee, J. J., & Hu, Q. (2022). Machine-Learning-Enhanced Blockchain Consensus With Transaction Prioritization for Smart Cities. *IEEE Internet of Things Journal*, 10(8), 6661–6672.

[3] Zhang, L., Cheng, L., Alsokhiry, F., & Mohamed, M. A. (2022). A Novel Stochastic Blockchain-Based Energy Management in Smart Cities Using V2S and V2G. *IEEE Transactions on Intelligent Transportation Systems*, 24(1), 915–922.

[4] Kuru, K. (2023). MetaOmniCity: Towards Urban Metaverse Cyberspaces Using Immersive Smart City Digital Twins. *IEEE Access*, 11, 1–26.

[5] Pervez, Z., Khan, Z., Ghafoor, A., & Soomro, K. (2023). SIGNED: Smart cIty diGital twiN vErifiable Data Framework. *IEEE Access*, 11, 29430–29446.

[6] Almuqren, L., Mahmood, K., Aljameel, S. S., Salama, A. S., Mohammed, G. P., & Alneil, A. A. (2023). Blockchain Assisted Secure Smart Home Network Using Gradient Based Optimizer with Hybrid Deep Learning Model. *IEEE Access*, 11, 86999–87008.

[7] Garg, A., & Singla, N. (2017). Environment Sustainability Awareness Model for IT SMEs. *Interdisciplinary Environmental Review*, 18(1), 1–5.

[8] Garg, A., & Singla, N. (2013). E-Waste vis-à-vis Human Health and Environment. *Interdisciplinary Environmental Review*, 14(3–4), 187–193.

[9] Rani, S., Babbar, H., Srivastava, G., Gadekallu, T. R., & Dhiman, G. (2022). Security Framework for Internet-of-Things-Based Software-Defined Networks Using Blockchain. *IEEE Internet of Things Journal*, 10(7), 6074–6081.

[10] Lin, Y., Hu, W., Chen, X., Li, S., & Wang, F. Y. (2023). City 5.0: Towards Spatial Symbiotic Intelligence via DAOs and Parallel Systems. *IEEE Transactions on Intelligent Vehicles*, 8(7), 3767–3770.

[11] Gao, J., Asamoah, K. O., Xia, Q., Sifah, E. B., Amankona, O. I., & Xia, H. (2023). A Blockchain Peer-to-Peer Energy Trading System for Microgrids. *IEEE Transactions on Smart Grid*, 14(5), 3944–3960.

[12] Garg, A. (Ed.). (2023). *Reinventing Technological Innovations with Artificial Intelligence*. Bentham Science Publishers. 10.2174/97898151657911230101

[13] Garg, A. (2022). *CoReS-Respiratory Strength Predicting Framework Using Noninvasive Technology for Remote Monitoring During Heath Disasters*. Global Healthcare Disasters: Predicting the Unpredictable with Emerging Technologies, 109–121.

[14] Rahman, M. A., Hossain, M. S., Showail, A. J., Alrajeh, N. A., & Ghoneim, A. (2021). AI-Enabled IIoT for Live Smart City Event Monitoring. *IEEE Internet of Things Journal*, 10(4), 2872–2880.

[15] Kalapaaking, A. P., Khalil, I., & Atiquzzaman, M. (2023). Smart Policy Control for Securing Federated Learning Management System. *IEEE Transactions on Network and Service Management*, 20(2), 1600–1611.
[16] He, D., Wu, R., Li, X., Chan, S., & Guizani, M. (2023). Detection of Vulnerabilities of Blockchain Smart Contracts. *IEEE Internet of Things Journal*, 10(14), 12178–12185.
[17] Malik, V., Mittal, R., Mavaluru, D., Narapureddy, B. R., Goyal, S. B., Martin, R. J., … & Mittal, A. (2023). Building a Secure Platform for Digital Governance Interoperability and Data Exchange Using Blockchain and Deep Learning-Based Frameworks. *IEEE Access*, 11, 70110–70131.
[18] Rahmadika, S., Astillo, P. V., Choudhary, G., Duguma, D. G., Sharma, V., & You, I. (2022). Blockchain-Based Privacy Preservation Scheme for Misbehavior Detection in Lightweight IoMT Devices. *IEEE Journal of Biomedical and Health Informatics*, 27(2), 710–721.
[19] Ye, X., Li, M., Si, P., Yang, R., Wang, Z., & Zhang, Y. (2022). Collaborative and Intelligent Resource Optimization for Computing and Caching in IoV with Blockchain and MEC Using A3C Approach. *IEEE Transactions on Vehicular Technology*, 72(2), 1449–1463.
[20] Mallick, S. R., Lenka, R. K., Goswami, V., Sharma, S., Dalai, A. K., Das, H., & Barik, R. K. (2023). BCGeo: Blockchain-Assisted Geospatial Web Service for Smart Healthcare System. *IEEE Access*, 11, 58610–58623.
[21] Said, D. (2022). A Survey on Information Communication Technologies in Modern Demand Side Management for Smart Grids: Challenges, Solutions, and Opportunities. *IEEE Engineering Management Review*, 51(1), 76–107.
[22] Deebak, B. D., Memon, F. H., Khowaja, S. A., Dev, K., Wang, W., Qureshi, N. M. F., & Su, C. (2022). A Lightweight Blockchain-Based Remote Mutual Authentication for AI-Empowered IoT Sustainable Computing Systems. *IEEE Internet of Things Journal*, 10(8), 6652–6660.
[23] Rana, S. K., Rana, A. K., Rana, S. K., Sharma, V., Lilhore, U. K., Khalaf, O. I., & Galletta, A. (2023). Decentralized Model to Protect Digital Evidence via Smart Contracts Using Layer 2 Polygon Blockchain. *IEEE Access*, 11, 83289–83300.
[24] Zhou, Y., Cao, Z., Dong, X., & Zhou, J. (2022). BLDSS: A Blockchain-Based Lightweight Searchable Data Sharing Scheme in Vehicular Social Networks. *IEEE Internet of Things Journal*, 10(9), 7974–7992.
[25] Anglés-Tafalla, C., Viejo, A., Castellà-Roca, J., Mut-Puigserver, M., & Payeras-Capellà, M. M. (2022). Security and Privacy in a Blockchain-Powered Access Control System for Low Emission Zones. *IEEE Transactions on Intelligent Transportation Systems*, 24(1), 580–595.
[26] Li, M., Ma, M., Wang, L., Yang, B., Wang, T., & Sun, J. (2022). Multi-Task-Oriented Collaborative Crowdsensing Based on Reinforcement Learning and Blockchain for Intelligent Transportation System. *IEEE Transactions on Industrial Informatics*, 19(9), 9503–9514.
[27] Guo, Y., Zhang, C., Wang, C., & Jia, X. (2022). Towards Public Verifiable and Forward-Privacy Encrypted Search by Using Blockchain. *IEEE Transactions on Dependable and Secure Computing*, 20(3), 2111–2126.
[28] Haritha, T., & Anitha, A. (2023). Asymmetric Consortium Blockchain and Homomorphically Polynomial-Based PIR for Secured Smart Parking Systems. *Computers, Materials & Continua*, 75(2), 3923–3939.

[29] Wu, J., Zhou, P., Chen, Q., Xu, Z., Ding, X., & Hao, J. (2021). Blockchain-Based Privacy-Aware Contextual Online Learning for Collaborative Edge-Cloud-Enabled Nursing System in Internet of Things. *IEEE Internet of Things Journal*, 10(8), 6703–6717.

Chapter 7

Service models for Internet of Things, global value chains, and mobile cloud computing

Ramiz Salama
Artificial Intelligence, Software, and Information Systems Engineering Departments, Research Center for AI and IoT, AI and Robotics Institute, Near East University, Nicosia, Mersin 10, Turkey

Sinem Alturjman
Near East University Nicosia, Mersin, Turkey
University of Kyrenia, Mersin, Turkey

Chadi Altrjman
Waterloo University, Waterloo, Canada

Fadi Al-Turjman
Software, and Information Systems Engineering Departments, Research Center for AI and IoT, AI and Robotics Institute, Near East University, Nicosia, Mersin 10, Turkey

INTRODUCTION

Mobile cloud computing (MCC) and the Internet of Things (IoT) have emerged as two transformative technologies that are reshaping the digital landscape. The widespread adoption of mobile devices and the proliferation of connected devices have created new opportunities and challenges for delivering efficient and scalable services in these domains. To address these challenges, service models tailored specifically for MCC and IoT applications have been developed.

The aim of this research is to explore and analyse the service models for MCC and IoT, with a focus on their characteristics, benefits, and use cases. By understanding these service models, we can better comprehend how they enable the deployment, management, and scalability of MCC and IoT applications. The first part of the research will provide an overview of service models and their significance in the context of MCC and IoT. Service models act as an abstraction layer between service providers and consumers, defining the roles, responsibilities, and interactions between the two parties. Understanding the

DOI: 10.1201/9781003461432-7

different service models is crucial for selecting the most appropriate approach based on the specific requirements of MCC and IoT applications. Two common service models for MCC and IoT will be examined in detail: Infrastructure as a Service (IaaS) and Platform as a Service (PaaS). IaaS offers virtualized computing resources such as virtual machines, storage, and networking infrastructure, providing a foundation for hosting MCC and IoT applications. PaaS, on the other hand, provides a higher level of abstraction by offering a platform for application development and deployment, simplifying the development process and allowing developers to focus on the application logic [1–5].

Through a comprehensive literature review and analysis of existing studies and real-world use cases, this research aims to provide valuable insights into the benefits and challenges associated with different service models for MCC and IoT. By synthesizing the findings, we can offer guidance to developers, organizations, and researchers on selecting the appropriate service model based on their specific needs. The outcomes of this research will not only contribute to the understanding of service models for MCC and IoT but also provide a foundation for future advancements and innovations in this rapidly evolving field. By leveraging the right service model, we can unlock the full potential of MCC and IoT, paving the way for a more connected and intelligent future.

THE IMPORTANCE OF THE INTERNET OF THINGS AND MOBILE CLOUD COMPUTING

MCC and the IoT have significant implications in the digital landscape, shaping the way we interact with technology and transforming various industries [6–10].

Mobile cloud computing

MCC combines the power of mobile devices and cloud computing to deliver enhanced capabilities and services to mobile users. It enables mobile devices, such as smartphones and tablets, to offload computational tasks, store data, and access cloud-based applications and resources. The significance of MCC lies in its ability to overcome the limitations of mobile devices, such as limited processing power, storage capacity, and battery life. By leveraging cloud resources, MCC offers scalability, flexibility, and cost-effectiveness, allowing users to access a wide range of applications and services without being constrained by the limitations of their mobile devices.

Internet of Things

The IoT refers to the network of interconnected devices embedded with sensors, software, and connectivity capabilities. These devices, ranging from everyday objects to industrial machinery, collect and exchange data, enabling automation, monitoring, and control of physical systems. The significance of IoT lies in its potential to revolutionize various industries, including health care, transportation, manufacturing, and agriculture. By connecting devices and harnessing data-driven insights, IoT enables improved efficiency, productivity, and decision-making. It paves the way for smart cities, intelligent homes, and transformative applications that enhance our quality of life and drive innovation.

The significance of both MCC and IoT is further amplified when they converge. MCC provides the necessary infrastructure and services to support the massive data processing, storage, and connectivity requirements of IoT applications. Together, MCC and IoT create a powerful ecosystem where mobile devices, cloud resources, and interconnected devices collaborate to deliver intelligent, data-driven solutions.

Overall, the significance of MCC and IoT lies in their potential to enhance user experiences, enable innovative applications, optimize processes, and drive digital transformation across industries. They open up new opportunities for businesses, improve operational efficiencies, and empower individuals with access to powerful computing capabilities and real-time insights.

HOW DO SERVICE MODELS WORK?

Service models, also known as cloud service models or cloud computing service models, refer to the categories or classifications that define the level of abstraction and responsibility between service providers and consumers in cloud computing. These models outline the roles, responsibilities, and interactions of each party involved in delivering and consuming cloud services.

Service models define the scope of services provided by the cloud provider and the level of control and management retained by the service consumer. They help establish clear boundaries and expectations for both parties, enabling efficient resource utilization, scalability, and flexibility [11–14].

There are several commonly recognized service models in cloud computing:

Infrastructure as a Service:
IaaS is the most basic service model where the cloud provider offers virtualized computing resources over the internet. It includes virtual machines, storage, networks, and other fundamental infrastructure components. The consumer has control over the operating systems, applications, and some network settings, while the cloud provider manages the underlying physical infrastructure.

Platform as a Service:
PaaS provides a higher level of abstraction by offering a platform on top of which developers can build, deploy, and manage applications. It includes the underlying infrastructure, development tools, programming languages, and pre-built components. The consumer focuses on

developing and managing the applications, while the cloud provider handles the underlying infrastructure and platform maintenance.

Software as a Service:
SaaS is a service model where the cloud provider delivers complete software applications over the internet. The consumer accesses and uses the software through web browsers or dedicated interfaces without worrying about infrastructure, installation, or maintenance. The cloud provider manages the entire software stack, including infrastructure, platform, and application.

These service models provide varying degrees of control, flexibility, and management responsibilities for both the cloud provider and the consumer. The choice of service model depends on factors such as application requirements, development complexity, resource management needs, and cost considerations.

It's important to note that service models are not mutually exclusive, and hybrid models can exist where combinations of these models are used to meet specific requirements or create more customized solutions.

SERVICE MODELS GIVE CONSUMERS AND SERVICE PROVIDERS A LEVEL OF ABSTRACTION AND ACCOUNTABILITY

Yes, that's correct. Service models in cloud computing provide a level of abstraction and responsibility between service providers (cloud vendors) and consumers (users or organizations utilizing cloud services). These models define the boundaries and responsibilities of each party, establishing clear roles and interactions.

By defining the level of abstraction, service models determine the extent to which the consumer has control and visibility over the underlying infrastructure, platform, or software. This abstraction allows users to focus on their specific needs and tasks without having to manage the complexities of the underlying technology stack.

Similarly, service models assign different responsibilities to the service provider and the consumer. The provider takes on responsibilities related to managing and maintaining the infrastructure, platform, or software, ensuring its availability, scalability, security, and performance. Meanwhile, the consumer is responsible for utilizing the provided services, configuring and managing their applications or workloads, and often paying for the consumed resources [15–20].

This division of responsibilities allows service providers to specialize in delivering reliable and scalable cloud services while consumers focus on their core business or application development without the burden of managing and maintaining underlying infrastructure or software.

Overall, service models play a crucial role in defining the relationship and responsibilities between service providers and consumers in cloud computing, enabling efficient and effective utilization of cloud resources while abstracting complexities and streamlining service delivery.

OVERVIEW OF THE IAAS AND PAAS COMMON SERVICE MODELS FOR MCC AND IoT

IaaS and PaaS are two common service models that are widely used in MCC and the IoT.

Here's an overview of each service model:

Infrastructure as a Service:
IaaS provides virtualized computing resources over the internet. It offers a scalable and flexible infrastructure that includes virtual machines (VMs), storage, networking, and other fundamental components required to support MCC and IoT applications.

In the context of MCC and IoT, IaaS allows organizations to deploy and manage their applications on virtualized infrastructure without the need for upfront investment in physical hardware. It offers benefits such as on-demand resource provisioning, scalability, and cost-effectiveness. Users have control over the operating systems, applications, and configurations running on the VMs, while the cloud provider manages the underlying physical infrastructure [21].

IaaS is particularly useful in scenarios where organizations need to deploy and scale their mobile or IoT applications quickly without worrying about the complexities of hardware provisioning and maintenance.

Platform as a Service:
PaaS provides a platform on top of which developers can build, deploy, and manage applications. It includes the underlying infrastructure, development tools, runtime environments, and often pre-built components or services.

In the context of MCC and IoT, PaaS abstracts the complexities of infrastructure and provides developers with a ready-to-use platform for application development and deployment. It enables developers to focus on writing the application logic without dealing with the underlying infrastructure configuration and management.

PaaS offers features such as scalability, automatic scaling, and integration with other services, allowing developers to quickly build and deploy mobile and IoT applications. It simplifies the development process by providing development frameworks, libraries, and tools specific to MCC and IoT requirements.

PaaS is beneficial when organizations want to accelerate the development and deployment of their mobile or IoT applications, leveraging pre-built components and services provided by the platform [22].

Both IaaS and PaaS are valuable service models in MCC and IoT, catering to different needs and requirements. While IaaS provides infrastructure-level control and flexibility, PaaS offers higher-level abstractions and simplified development environments.

Explanation of IaaS in the context of MCC and IoT

In the context of MCC and the IoT, IaaS provides a crucial foundation for deploying and managing applications. Let's explore the explanation of IaaS in this context:

Virtualized computing resources: IaaS offers virtualized computing resources over the internet. This includes VMs, storage, networking infrastructure, and other essential components needed to support MCC and IoT applications. These resources are provisioned on-demand, allowing organizations to scale their infrastructure based on their requirements.

Scalability and flexibility: IaaS provides scalability, allowing organizations to quickly scale up or down their infrastructure resources as needed. This is particularly important in MCC and IoT scenarios where the demand for resources can fluctuate based on factors such as the number of connected devices, data processing requirements, or user load. IaaS ensures that organizations can easily accommodate these variations in resource needs.

Offloading computation: MCC and IoT applications often require significant computational power, which can strain the limited resources of mobile devices and edge devices. With IaaS, organizations can offload computationally intensive tasks to the cloud infrastructure, leveraging its robust processing capabilities. This offloading helps enhance the performance and responsiveness of mobile and IoT applications.

Cost-effectiveness: IaaS offers cost-effectiveness in MCC and IoT deployments. Organizations can avoid the upfront capital expenditures associated with purchasing and maintaining physical hardware. Instead, they can leverage the pay-as-you-go pricing model, where they pay only for the resources they consume. This allows for cost optimization and efficient resource utilization.

Management and maintenance: With IaaS, the cloud provider takes care of the underlying physical infrastructure, including server maintenance, networking, and hardware upgrades. This relieves organizations from the burden of infrastructure management, allowing them to focus on developing and deploying their MCC and IoT applications.

API access and control: IaaS providers typically offer application programming interfaces (APIs) that enable organizations to programmatically manage and control their infrastructure resources. This level of control allows for automation, efficient resource allocation, and integration with other systems or services.

Overall, IaaS in the context of MCC and IoT provides a flexible, scalable, and cost-effective infrastructure foundation for deploying and managing applications. It enables organizations to leverage virtualized resources, offload computation, and focus on developing innovative mobile and IoT solutions without the complexities of infrastructure management.

VIRTUALIZED COMPUTING RESOURCES ARE PROVIDED BY CLOUD PROVIDERS

In the context of IaaS in MCC and the IoT, the cloud provider offers virtualized computing resources to users or organizations. These virtualized resources typically include the following:

Virtual machines: IaaS providers offer virtual machine instances that allow users to run their applications and software. These VMs simulate physical hardware, providing processing power, memory, and storage capabilities. Users can configure and manage these VMs based on their application requirements.

Storage: IaaS providers offer virtualized storage resources, such as block storage or object storage, which users can utilize to store their data and files. These storage resources can be accessed and managed remotely over the internet. Users can scale their storage capacity as needed without worrying about the physical hardware infrastructure.

Networking infrastructure: IaaS providers also provide virtualized networking resources, such as virtual networks, subnets, load balancers, and firewalls. These resources enable users to establish secure network connectivity for their applications and control the flow of data between different components or services within their MCC and IoT deployments.

Other infrastructure components: Depending on the specific IaaS provider and their offerings, additional virtualized computing resources may be available. These can include components such as virtualized routers, switches, or specialized hardware accelerators, which are useful for certain MCC and IoT use cases.

By offering virtualized computing resources, IaaS providers abstract the underlying physical infrastructure and provide a flexible and scalable environment for users to deploy their applications. Users can request and provision these resources on-demand, allowing them to scale their infrastructure as needed without the constraints of physical hardware limitations. This flexibility is particularly beneficial in MCC and IoT scenarios where resource demands can vary based on factors such as user load, data processing requirements, or the number of connected devices. Additionally, the virtualized nature of these resources enables users to configure and manage them remotely through management interfaces or APIs provided by the IaaS provider. Users have control over their virtualized resources, allowing them to customize and optimize their environment to suit their specific MCC and IoT application requirements. Overall, the cloud provider's offering of virtualized computing resources in the IaaS model empowers organizations to leverage scalable and flexible infrastructure without the burden of managing physical hardware, enabling them to focus on building and deploying their MCC and IoT applications efficiently.

Examples: VMs, storage, and networking infrastructure

Examples of virtualized computing resources offered by IaaS providers in the context of MCC and the IoT include the following:

Virtual machines: IaaS providers offer VM instances that mimic physical servers. Users can deploy and manage these VMs to run their applications and software. Examples of popular VM offerings include Amazon EC2, Microsoft Azure Virtual Machines, and Google Compute Engine.

Storage: IaaS providers provide virtualized storage resources for users to store and manage their data. This can include block storage, object storage, or file storage. Examples of IaaS storage services include Amazon S3, Microsoft Azure Blob Storage, and Google Cloud Storage.

Networking infrastructure: IaaS providers offer virtualized networking resources to establish and manage network connectivity for MCC and IoT applications. This can include virtual networks, subnets, load balancers, firewalls, and virtual private networks (VPNs). Examples of IaaS networking services include Amazon VPC, Microsoft Azure Virtual Network, and Google VPC.

Other infrastructure components: Some IaaS providers offer additional virtualized infrastructure components tailored for specific MCC and IoT use cases. For instance, specialized hardware accelerators like graphics processing units (GPUs) or field-programmable gate arrays (FPGAs) may be available for applications that require intensive computational capabilities. Providers like Amazon Web Services (AWS) and Google Cloud Platform (GCP) offer these specialized resources as part of their IaaS offerings.

These examples demonstrate the breadth of virtualized computing resources available through IaaS providers. Users can leverage these resources to build, deploy, and manage their MCC and IoT applications effectively, scaling resources as needed and abstracting away the complexities of physical infrastructure management. The choice of specific services and providers depends on factors such as performance requirements, pricing models, geographic availability, and integration capabilities with other cloud services.

Benefits: scalability, flexibility, cost-effectiveness

The use of IaaS in MCC and the IoT brings several benefits, including scalability, flexibility, and cost-effectiveness. Let's explore each of these benefits:

Scalability: IaaS enables users to scale their computing resources on demand. This scalability is essential in MCC and IoT scenarios, where resource requirements can vary based on factors such as user demand, data processing needs, or the number of connected devices. With IaaS, users can easily increase or decrease their infrastructure capacity to match the workload, ensuring optimal performance and resource utilization.

Flexibility: IaaS provides users with a high level of flexibility in managing their infrastructure. Users have control over configuring and customizing their virtualized resources, including VMs, storage, and networking. This flexibility allows users to tailor their infrastructure to meet specific MCC and IoT application requirements. They can choose the operating systems, software, and configurations that best suit their needs, enabling efficient development and deployment processes.

Cost-effectiveness: IaaS offers cost-effectiveness in MCC and IoT deployments. Users can avoid upfront capital investments in physical hardware infrastructure, reducing the need for hardware procurement, maintenance, and upgrades. Instead, they pay for the cloud resources they consume on a pay-as-you-go basis. This cost model allows users to align their infrastructure costs with actual resource usage, optimizing spending and eliminating the need to provision excess capacity. Additionally, IaaS eliminates the operational costs associated with managing and maintaining physical infrastructure, further reducing overall expenses.

Resource efficiency: IaaS enables efficient resource utilization. Users can provision resources precisely when and where they are needed, avoiding underutilization or overprovisioning of hardware. The ability to scale resources up or down dynamically allows for efficient allocation of computing power, storage, and networking capabilities. This efficiency leads to cost savings and better overall resource utilization in MCC and IoT environments.

Rapid deployment: IaaS facilitates rapid deployment of MCC and IoT applications. With virtualized resources readily available, users can quickly provision the necessary infrastructure components and start deploying their applications without the delays associated with procuring and configuring physical hardware. This agility and speed to market are crucial in dynamic MCC and IoT landscapes, where time-to-market can be a competitive advantage.

By leveraging the scalability, flexibility, and cost-effectiveness of IaaS, organizations can effectively manage their infrastructure needs in MCC and IoT deployments. They can scale resources, customize configurations, optimize costs, and rapidly deploy applications, ultimately enabling efficient and agile operations in the mobile and IoT domains.

Platform as a Service:

PaaS is a cloud computing service model that provides a platform for developing, deploying, and managing applications without the complexity of infrastructure management. In PaaS, the cloud provider offers a complete development and runtime environment that includes the underlying infrastructure, operating systems, programming languages, libraries, and pre-built components.

The following are some crucial features and advantages of Platform as a Service:

Development environment: PaaS provides a development environment that simplifies the application development process. It typically includes development tools, integrated development environments (IDEs), and frameworks specific to the supported programming languages and technologies. This environment offers a streamlined approach, allowing developers to focus on writing application code rather than managing infrastructure configurations.

Deployment and management: PaaS platforms handle the deployment and management of applications. They provide automated deployment mechanisms, load balancing, and scalability features. Developers can easily deploy their applications to the PaaS platform with just a few clicks or commands without the need to worry about the underlying infrastructure setup or management.

Scalability and elasticity: PaaS platforms are designed to scale applications automatically based on demand. They can handle varying workloads and traffic spikes by automatically provisioning and deallocating resources. This scalability and elasticity feature enables applications to scale seamlessly without the need for manual intervention, ensuring optimal performance and user experience.

Pre-built components and services: PaaS often includes pre-built components and services that developers can leverage to enhance their applications. These can include databases, messaging queues, authentication systems, caching mechanisms, and more. By incorporating these pre-built services, developers can accelerate application development, reduce coding efforts, and leverage the expertise of the PaaS provider.

Integration capabilities: PaaS platforms offer integration capabilities with other cloud services and third-party APIs. This allows developers to integrate their applications with other services or systems, such as data storage, analytics, machine learning, or IoT platforms. PaaS simplifies the integration process by providing standardized APIs, libraries, and connectors, making it easier to build robust and interconnected applications.

Cost-efficiency: PaaS follows a pay-as-you-go model, where users pay for the resources and services they consume. This eliminates the need for upfront infrastructure investments and reduces operational costs. PaaS providers handle the infrastructure management, maintenance, and updates, freeing organizations from the associated costs and complexities.

PaaS is particularly beneficial for organizations and developers who want to focus on application development, innovation, and time-to-market. It abstracts the complexities of infrastructure management and provides a comprehensive platform for building, deploying, and managing applications in a streamlined and cost-effective manner.

Use cases for IaaS and PaaS in MCC and IoT

Both IaaS and PaaS offer valuable solutions for MCC and the IoT. Here are some use cases for IaaS and PaaS in MCC and IoT environments:

IaaS use cases

Elastic scaling: IaaS enables organizations to scale their infrastructure resources dynamically based on demand. In MCC and IoT, where resource needs can fluctuate rapidly, IaaS allows for the seamless addition or removal of VMs, storage, and networking resources to accommodate varying workloads.

Data processing and analytics: IaaS provides the computational power needed for data processing and analytics in MCC and IoT scenarios. Organizations can leverage IaaS to offload computationally intensive tasks, such as real-time data analysis, machine learning algorithms, or complex simulations, to the cloud infrastructure, enabling efficient and scalable data processing.

Storage and data management: IaaS offers scalable and reliable storage solutions, allowing organizations to store and manage large volumes of data generated by mobile devices or IoT sensors. IaaS providers provide storage options, such as object storage or block storage, that can handle the diverse data requirements of MCC and IoT applications.

Disaster recovery and business continuity: IaaS can be leveraged for disaster recovery and business continuity planning in MCC and IoT deployments. By utilizing IaaS, organizations can replicate their infrastructure and data to geographically diverse cloud regions, ensuring data redundancy and enabling swift recovery in case of a disaster or service interruption.

PaaS use cases

Rapid application development: PaaS simplifies the application development process in MCC and IoT. Developers can leverage PaaS platforms to quickly develop, test, and deploy applications without having to manage the underlying infrastructure. PaaS provides ready-to-use development frameworks, libraries, and tools tailored to MCC and IoT requirements, enabling rapid prototyping and time-to-market advantages.

IoT application enablement: PaaS platforms offer specialized tools and services for IoT application development. These platforms provide capabilities such as device management, data ingestion, real-time analytics, and integration with IoT protocols. Developers can utilize PaaS to build scalable and secure IoT applications, enabling efficient data collection, analysis, and control of connected devices.

Microservices and API management: PaaS facilitates the development and deployment of microservices architectures in MCC and IoT. With PaaS, organizations can break down complex applications into smaller, decoupled services and manage them independently. PaaS platforms often include API management capabilities, allowing developers to expose and manage APIs for integrating with other services or devices.

Collaboration and DevOps: PaaS platforms promote collaboration and streamline the DevOps process. Developers, testers, and operations teams can work together in a shared development environment, collaborating on application code, tracking changes, and managing deployments. PaaS platforms often integrate with version control systems, continuous integration/continuous deployment (CI/CD) pipelines, and monitoring tools, enabling efficient collaboration and automation.

These use cases demonstrate how IaaS and PaaS can effectively support MCC and IoT initiatives by providing scalable infrastructure, simplifying application development, facilitating data processing and analytics, and enabling collaboration and agility in the development lifecycle. The choice between IaaS and PaaS depends on factors such as the level of control, customization, and development requirements specific to each use case.

Our daily lives have begun to incorporate machine learning and artificial intelligence (AI) technology, which has had a tremendous impact on the IoT's explosive growth. Prof. DUX, an AI learning facilitator, is one of the pioneers in this field [18].

CONSIDERATIONS FOR CHOOSING SERVICE MODELS

When choosing service models for MCC and the IoT, several considerations should be taken into account. Here are some important factors to consider:

Scalability requirements: Consider the scalability requirements of your application or solution. If your application requires dynamic scaling of resources based on fluctuating demand or the number of connected devices, IaaS may be more suitable. On the other hand, if you need a platform with built-in scalability features and automatic resource allocation, PaaS might be a better choice.

Application development needs: Evaluate the development needs of your application. If you have specific requirements or need fine-grained control over the infrastructure, IaaS provides more flexibility. However, if you aim for rapid application development, prefer a streamlined development environment, and want to focus on coding rather than infrastructure management, PaaS can accelerate your development process.

Resource management: Consider the level of control and responsibility you want to have over resource management. With IaaS, you have more control over VMs, storage, and networking configurations. This level of control allows you to customize the infrastructure according to your specific requirements. PaaS, on the other hand, abstracts the infrastructure management, allowing you to focus solely on the application development and deployment without worrying about the underlying infrastructure.

Cost and budget: Evaluate your cost considerations and budget constraints. IaaS follows a pay-as-you-go model, allowing you to pay for the resources you consume. This can be cost-effective if you have fluctuating resource needs or if you want full control over resource allocation. PaaS often provides a more predictable cost structure, as you pay for the platform and services bundled together. Consider your budget and choose the service model that aligns with your financial requirements.

Expertise and support: Assess your team's expertise and the level of support you require. IaaS typically requires more technical expertise and operational management from your team, as you are responsible for configuring and maintaining the infrastructure components. PaaS platforms often provide support and managed services, reducing the operational burden on your team. Consider the level of support you need and choose the service model that matches your team's expertise and resource availability.

Integration and Ecosystem: Evaluate the integration capabilities and the ecosystem surrounding the service models. Consider the compatibility of the service models with other cloud services, third-party APIs, and tools that you may need to integrate with. Assess the availability of pre-built components, libraries, and services specific to MCC and IoT, as they can greatly facilitate your development and deployment processes.

By carefully considering these factors, you can choose the service models (IaaS, PaaS, or a combination) that best align with your specific requirements, development approach, scalability needs, cost considerations, and the expertise of your team.

CONCLUSION

In conclusion, service models such as IaaS and PaaS play a crucial role in enabling MCC and IoT applications. They provide organizations with the necessary infrastructure, development environments, and tools to build, deploy, and manage their MCC and IoT solutions effectively. IaaS offers virtualized computing resources such as VMs, storage, and networking infrastructure. It provides scalability, flexibility, and cost-effectiveness by allowing organizations to scale resources on demand, customize infrastructure configurations, and pay only for the resources they consume. IaaS is beneficial for scenarios that require dynamic scaling, data processing, storage management, and disaster recovery.

On the other hand, PaaS provides a complete development and runtime environment, including underlying infrastructure, programming languages, frameworks, and pre-built components. PaaS simplifies application development, accelerates time-to-market, and offers scalability and integration capabilities. It is particularly useful for rapid application development, IoT application enablement, microservices architectures, and collaboration within development teams. When choosing between IaaS and PaaS, organizations should consider factors such as scalability requirements, application development needs, resource management preferences, cost considerations, expertise and support availability, and integration capabilities. By carefully evaluating these considerations, organizations can select the appropriate service models that align with their specific requirements and enable them to leverage the benefits of MCC and IoT effectively.

Overall, service models like IaaS and PaaS empower organizations to harness the capabilities of cloud computing, drive innovation, and realize the potential of MCC and IoT. They provide the foundation for scalable, flexible, and cost-effective solutions, allowing organizations to focus on their core applications and services while leveraging the power of the cloud. With the right choice of service models, organizations can unlock the full potential of MCC and IoT in delivering transformative and efficient solutions in various industries and domains.

REFERENCES

[1] Alwarafy, A., Al-Thelaya, K. A., Abdallah, M., Schneider, J., & Hamdi, M. (2020). A survey on security and privacy issues in edge-computing-assisted Internet of Things. *IEEE Internet of Things Journal*, 8(6), 4004–4022.

[2] Maple, C. (2017). Security and privacy in the Internet of Things. *Journal of Cyber Policy*, 2(2), 155–184.

[3] Pishdar, M., Ghasemzadeh, F., Antucheviciene, J., & Saparauskas, J. (2018). Internet of Things and its challenges in supply chain management: A rough strength-relation analysis method, 21 2, 208–222.

[4] Haddud, A., DeSouza, A., Khare, A., & Lee, H. (2017). Examining potential benefits and challenges associated with the Internet of Things integration in supply chains. *Journal of Manufacturing Technology Management*, 28(8), 1055–1085.
[5] Yadav, S., Garg, D., & Luthra, S. (2020). Analysing challenges for Internet of Things adoption in agriculture supply chain management. *International Journal of Industrial and Systems Engineering*, 36(1), 73–97.
[6] Ahlmeyer, M., & Chircu, A. M. (2016). Securing the Internet of Things: A review. *Issues in information Systems*, 17(4).
[7] Singh, G. K., & Dadhich, M. (2023, May). Supply chain management growth with the adoption of Blockchain Technology (BoT) and Internet of Things (IoT). In *2023 3rd International Conference on Advance Computing and Innovative Technologies in Engineering (ICACITE)* (pp. 321–325). IEEE.
[8] Dang, L. M., Piran, M. J., Han, D., Min, K., & Moon, H. (2019). A survey on Internet of Things and cloud computing for healthcare. *Electronics*, 8(7), 768.
[9] Strange, R., & Zucchella, A. (2017). Industry 4.0, global value chains and international business. *Multinational Business Review*, 25(3), 174–184.
[10] Baziyad, H., Kayvanfar, V., & Kinra, A. (2022). The Internet of Things—An emerging paradigm to support the digitalization of future supply chains. In *The Digital Supply Chain* (pp. 61–76). Elsevier.
[11] Zhang, H., Nakamura, T., & Sakurai, K. (2019, August). Security and trust issues on digital supply chain. In *2019 IEEE Intl Conf on Dependable, Autonomic and Secure Computing, Intl Conf on Pervasive Intelligence and Computing, Intl Conf on Cloud and Big Data Computing, Intl Conf on Cyber Science and Technology Congress (DASC/PiCom/CBDCom/CyberSciTech)* (pp. 338–343). IEEE.
[12] Gnimpieba, Z. D. R., Nait-Sidi-Moh, A., Durand, D., & Fortin, J. (2015). Using Internet of Things technologies for a collaborative supply chain: Application to tracking of pallets and containers. *Procedia Computer Science*, 56, 550–557.
[13] Baziyad, H., Kayvanfar, V., & Kinra, A. (2022). The Internet of Things—An emerging paradigm to support the digitalization of future supply chains. In *The Digital Supply Chain* (pp. 61–76). Elsevier.
[14] Hasan, R., Hossain, M. M., & Khan, R. (2015, March). Aura: An IoT based cloud infrastructure for localized mobile computation outsourcing. In *2015 3rd IEEE International Conference on Mobile Cloud Computing, Services, and Engineering* (pp. 183–188). IEEE.
[15] Tewari, A., & Gupta, B. B. (2020). Security, privacy and trust of different layers in Internet-of-Things (IoTs) framework. *Future Generation Computer Systems*, 108, 909–920.
[16] Chalapathi, G. S. S., Chamola, V., Vaish, A., & Buyya, R. (2021). Industrial Internet of Things (IIoT) applications of edge and fog computing: A review and future directions. In *Fog/Edge Computing for Security, Privacy, and Applications* (pp. 293–325).
[17] Mollah, M. B., Azad, M. A. K., & Vasilakos, A. (2017). Security and privacy challenges in mobile cloud computing: Survey and way ahead. *Journal of Network and Computer Applications*, 84, 38–54.
[18] Garg, A. (Ed.). (2023). *Reinventing Technological Innovations with Artificial Intelligence*. Bentham Science Publishers.

[19] Prof. DUX available online: https://dux.aiiot.website/
[20] Al-Turjman, F. (2023). Enhancing higher education through Prof. DUX: A practical approach to personalized AI assisted learning. *NEU Journal for Artificial Intelligence and Internet of Things*, 1(2).
[21] Garg, A., & Goyal, D. P. (Eds.). (2022). *Global healthcare disasters: Predicting the unpredictable with emerging technologies*. CRC Press.
[22] Al-Turjman, F. (2023). Familiarizing teachers/learners with AI-assisted learning and evaluation implementations–Prof. DUX a use case. *NEU Journal for Artificial Intelligence and Internet of Things*, 2(4), pp 1-2.

Chapter 8

Overview of the global value chain and the effectiveness of artificial intelligence (AI) techniques in reducing cybersecurity risks

Ramiz Salama

Artificial Intelligence, Software, and Information Systems Engineering Departments, Research Center for AI and IoT, AI and Robotics Institute, Near East University, Nicosia, Mersin10, Turkey

Fadi Al-Turjman

Artificial Intelligence, Software, and Information Systems Engineering Departments, Research Center for AI and IoT, AI and Robotics Institute, Near East University, Nicosia, Mersin10, Turkey

INTRODUCTION

Security systems must adjust as the digital environment, threats, and players change over time to guarantee that they offer flexible and ongoing protection. Contrarily, there are certain differences between traditional reality and cyber reality. It is challenging for security frameworks to adjust to new threats because of their rigidity and lack of flexibility. In fact, adaptation mechanisms are probably going to be ineffective and delayed even when there is human involvement. With its flexible and adaptable system behaviour, artificial intelligence (AI) solutions can assist in addressing some of the drawbacks of current cybersecurity tools. AI has significantly improved cybersecurity, but there are some real concerns left. Some people think there really is an existential threat from AI to mankind. Researchers and lawyers have questioned the moral reasonability of self-governing AI substances in addition to voicing concerns about the growing role that they are playing in cyberspace. By concentrating on how the human brain works as well as how people learn, make decisions, and work to solve a problem, intelligent software and systems can be created (Figure 8.1).

Intelligent machines are those that possess intelligence and can execute jobs that ordinarily require intelligent individuals to do them. Human specialists' knowledge is incorporated into the decision-making process in a variety of ways, including conducting medical diagnoses and drawing conclusions from knowledge to reach a decision. AI has both positive and negative implications for cybersecurity. AI's negative implications include the possibility for attacks to intensify more quickly and with greater damage. AI

DOI: 10.1201/9781003461432-8

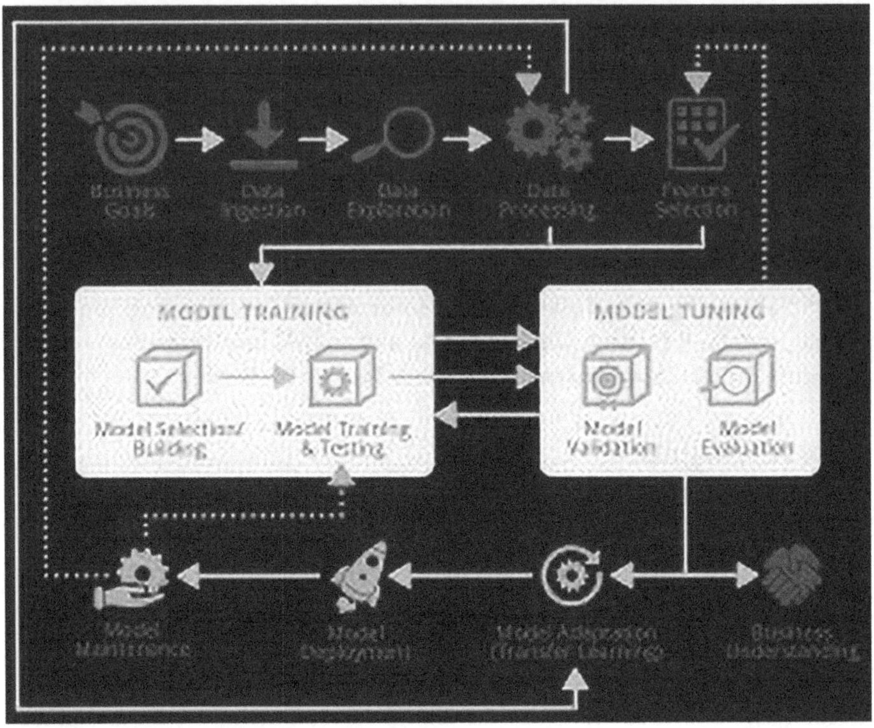

Figure 8.1 AI approaches and procedures.

improves defences and promotes cyberspace security, which are both beneficial for cybersecurity. Cyber threats grow as technology progresses, prompting the creation of new defences. This raises the possibility of facilities being physically harmed and suffering a loss of millions of dollars. Companies are more subject to cyberattacks as a result of a rising reliance on digital technology, which can contain sensitive data including financial and personal information. As a result, it is considered the most urgent issue in the contemporary environment because it not only exposes sensitive information but also causes financial harm. Hacking, denial-of-service assaults, spyware infections, and other cyberattacks of various kinds might all have an impact on everyone in the nation. Cyberattacks have negative psychological repercussions, such as stress and anxiety (Figure 8.2).

In the current climate, preserving the computer system from potential threats has become a significant and urgent issue that involves preventing cyberattacks. The US Federal Bureau of Investigations describes a political attack by subnational groups as a "cyberattack" if it results in violence against non-combatants. Security professionals may be able to identify signs of a cyber threat with the help of AI. As a result of AI, machine learning is being used more and more for malware analysis and network anomaly detection. In light of the literature, this study examines the efficacy of AI

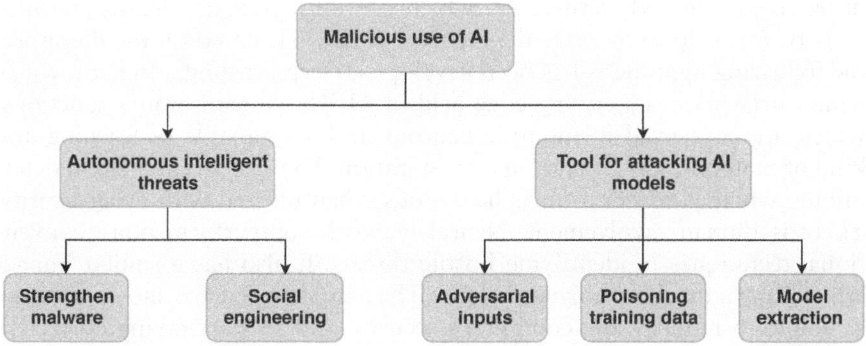

Figure 8.2 Harmful application of AI.

methods in lowering the risks connected with cybersecurity. With this study, I hope to highlight both the inadequacies of traditional security methods and the current state of the art in using AI approaches to cybersecurity. Aside from that, by analysing AI's present status, addressing present issues, and outlining a future route, this work distils the risks and worries connected with this breakthrough. Along with the enormous potential for AI in cybersecurity, its application has legitimized vulnerabilities and worries [1–5]. Since neither people nor AI has demonstrated general effectiveness in this field, a comprehensive view of associations' cyber environments that integrates both with human expertise is necessary to advance the development of cybersecurity. In this manner, socially mindful utilization of AI techniques will be needed to further mitigate related risks and concerns. Since cyberattacks are a major concern in this research, determining the role of AI in countering them is the primary goal of the study. As a result of the study, IT professionals are more aware of the importance of AI technologies when it comes to preventing cyberattacks.

Machine learning and AI facilitators have started to be part of our daily lives and have significant effects on the rapid developments of the Internet of Things (IoT). One of the leading attempts in this field is the AI learning facilitator, Prof. DUX [6]. It is a novel AI facilitator that aims at personalizing the education process for learners and providing the fastest and best quality of education in numerous fields.

REVIEW OF THE LITERATURE

In recent years, many researchers have been investigating AI-based strategies for increasing cybersecurity. Cybersecurity includes human behaviour, systems, and processes. AI has been shown to be a useful tool for assessing massive amounts of data. According to a related study, AI is rapidly being utilized to help consumers fight crime and find solutions online. AI is largely used to recognize viruses, create solutions, and put those solutions into practice in order to prevent cybercrime. AI, which can anticipate or identify harmful activity, can help to increase the security of the IoT. Based on the literature, the following hypothesis has been developed. Deep learning, often known as neural networks, is a cutting-edge field of AI. The human brain's functions, which are connected to multiple neurons and are capable of learning any kind of material, served as its main inspiration. The system can help in determining whether or not a file is hazardous when utilized with cybersecurity. There is human involvement. Neural networks outperform more conventional techniques in identifying hostile threats. It also has a similar impact when using a machine learning system. The neural network is shown to make it simple to monitor the computer's security and to start taking corrective action. The most popular AI technology, the expert system, is used to recognize queries that clients or software presents. Expert systems come in a range of shapes and sizes, from compact units to hybrid systems that are employed in diagnostics. Additionally, the system is employed to offer cyber defence security [7–10]. Similar to this, a study discovered that expert systems use input data to determine threats and weaknesses in e-commerce transactions. The following expert system hypothesis was created in this manner.

THE IDEAL FRAMEWORK

The researcher has chosen to use primary data in a quantitative research approach for the subsequent full investigation. The study's objective was to assess how well AI approaches reduced the risks associated with cybersecurity. The data was gathered from experts in the IT sector who have in-depth knowledge of cutting-edge practices, such as AI technology and cybersecurity challenges. The sample size for this study was 468 because a larger sample size improves the study's accuracy, dependability, and authenticity. This research can serve as a starting point for other researchers who want

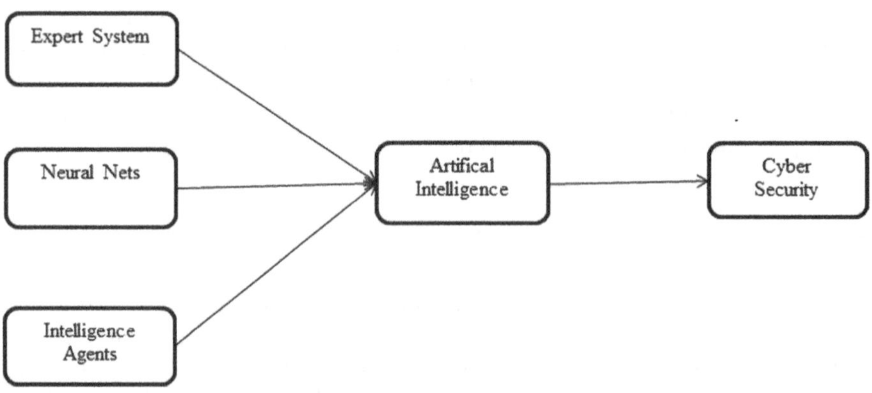

Figure 8.3 Conceptual framework.

to conduct research on a connected topic. However, a smaller sample size is always problematic and does not guarantee the reliability of the results (Figure 8.3).

AI TECHNIQUE APPLICATIONS

This section covered various AI strategies that can be used to defend against cyberattacks. As we all know, we are moving toward a day when we will deal with machines that are more intelligent than us. Threats and assaults evolve along with technology; thus, we must include AI techniques in our security systems to thwart them [11–15].

Utilizing intelligent

In order to prepare and carry out suitable responses in the event of unforeseen circumstances, intelligent agents are self-contained computer systems that communicate with one another to share knowledge and participate in one another's actions. Intelligent agent technology is suitable for thwarting cyberattacks due to its synergistic nature, mobility, and adaptability in the environments they are carried in. Intelligent agents are employed to protect against distributed denial-of-service attacks. After a number of legal and commercial issues are resolved, it should be possible to establish a basic (portable) level of cyber-police that consists of intelligent agents. Infrastructure must be set up to facilitate the mobility and communication of the cyber agent, but it must be out of enemy reach. For the whole operational image of cyberspace, a multi-agent tool is necessary. For instance, hybrid multi-agent techniques and neural network-based intrusion detection have already been described. This research shows an agent-based distributed intrusion detection.

Use of neural networks

The artificial neuron, which is said to be one of the most important components of neural nets, is where the history of neural nets begins after Frank Rosenblatt's development of the perceptron in 1957. Perceptions can learn and take on fascinating tasks by participating in small groups. Numerous synthetic neurons can be found in neural nets. Neural nets offer the advantage of learning and decision-making being greatly parallelized.

They can be recognized by how quickly they move about. They are used, among other things, for pattern recognition, organizing, and the choice of assault response. They can aid with the installation of either software or hardware. Neural networks are used in intrusion detection and prevention. The use of them in forensic investigations, malware classification, spam recognition, zombie detection, and computer worm identification are all advised.

Neural nets are well-known in the field of cybersecurity due to their quick processing speeds when implemented in hardware or as a graphic processor component. Numerous significant advancements in neural net technology have been noted, such as 3G neural nets, which more accurately replicate real neurons and provide a wide range of application possibilities. With the help of Field Programmable Gate Arrays (FPGA), substantial advancements have been made that have made it possible to quickly enhance and modify neural networks in response to evolving threats.

Application of expert systems

The most often used AI technique is, as we all know, the expert system. It is a piece of software that facilitates the search for solutions to issues raised by users or other software. Direct application as decision support in industries including banking, diagnostics, and the internet. Expert systems can be small diagnostic systems or complex hybrid systems that can tackle a wide range of problems. This system is especially robust and big. A knowledge base that contains expert knowledge about a certain application area is a component of an expert system. It also has an inference engine for drawing conclusions about the best course of action based on information already known and new details about the scenario. The knowledge base and inference engine in the expert system shell are empty, and knowledge must be loaded before it can be used. Expert system shells can be expanded with programmes for client participation, as well as other programmes that could be utilized as components of hybrid expert systems. Expert system shells must be supported by software for including knowledge in the knowledge base. An expert system is used to organize security in cyber defence. It helps in choosing safety measures and offers suggestions for making the best use of scarce resources. Expert systems are frequently used in intrusion detection. Information about network intrusions must be detected by the expert system using its knowledge base, rule sets, and other characteristics. A database that comprises an associated knowledge base is used to capture various network intrusion behaviour features, which are then stored as a web application component. Real-time data packets can't pass until the rule set does. The application infrastructure collects these rule sets from the database and stores them.

APPLICATIONS OF LEARNING

In machine learning, new skills, and improved methods to assemble existing information are combined with computational strategies for acquiring new knowledge. Learning problems vary in complexity, ranging from straightforward parametric learning to intricate symbolic learning, as in the case of learning concepts or even behaviour, grammars, and functions. Both supervised and unsupervised learning are viable options. Unsupervised learning is especially useful when there is a lot of data. This is evident in cyber protection, where huge amounts of log data can be collected. The idea of data mining originated from unsupervised learning in AI. Unsupervised learning, and more specifically the learning of self-organizing maps (SOM), can be advantageous for neural networks. One kind of learning approach is the execution of parallel learning algorithms on parallel hardware. These learning mechanisms are represented using neural networks and genetic algorithms. For instance, threat detection systems envisioned in this research path have used fuzzy logic and genetic algorithms. Computer programs that use AI employ a variety of learning strategies to develop their skills and gain knowledge through experience. The learning process is classified as either supervised or unsupervised, depending on whether the system has access to the testing data categories. Reinforcement learning can be incorporated into new learning processes and algorithms as a more concluding strategy.

Supervised learning

The computer is given sample data pairs of inputs and desired outputs with the aim of learning a general function that connects the inputs to the outputs and further identifies the unidentified outputs of the future inputs. The deep neural network (DNN) is trained online, and following convergence, it is prepared to recognize and infer new inputs.

Unsupervised learning

The SOM is trained using unsupervised learning techniques. Because of this, SOM produces a low-dimensional (usually two-dimensional) linearized generative model space of labelled data by feeding the training dataset into a neural network.

Unsupervised learning, when no classifications are supplied to the technical process of learning, requires composition in the method's generator to be identified on its own.

Reinforcement learning

This approach is predicated on an agreed-upon manner of learning between the agent and the dynamic environment. The machine interacts with a dynamic environment without the agent merely telling it whether or not it has accomplished its goals. When an agent completes a specific task, his state will reflect that and can either reward or penalize him. The agent will choose the proper course of action based on this result. The machine learns the dynamic environment by initializing via activity and prize procedure (Figure 8.4).

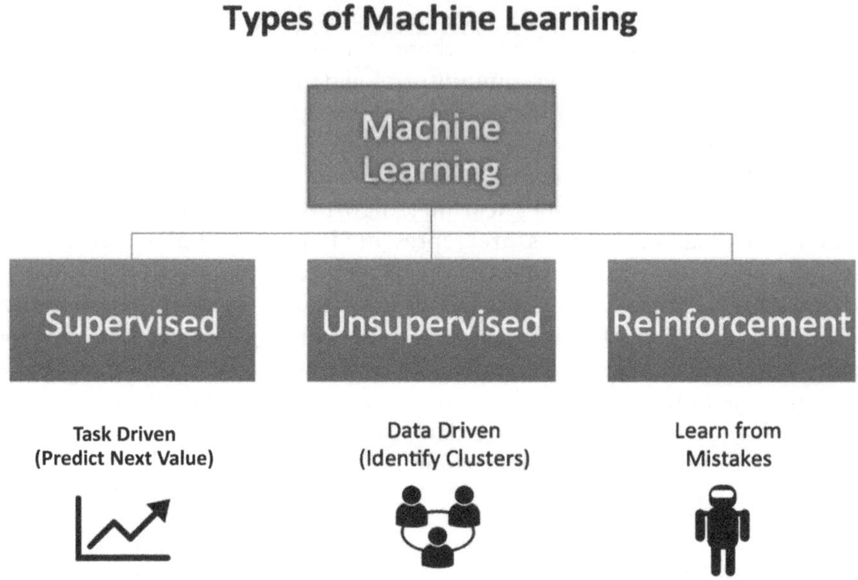

Figure 8.4 AI learning techniques.

AI CHALLENGES IN THE IoT

Although machine learning technologies are years ahead of their time, when the IoT and AI are coupled, both technologies face difficult problems [16–20] (Figure 8.5).

Some of these challenges are as follows:

1. **Data privacy and security**
   We must maintain the security of the data because AI and IoT collect vast amounts of sensitive and significant data. Large numbers of people worldwide generate data, but there is a chance that the information they have gathered could be compromised.
2. **Computational complexities**
   Linking all of those devices can be challenging because they are connected through IoT networks that utilize numerous other different technologies.
3. **Scarcity of data**
   Major firms face the dilemma of employing local knowledge to produce software for the global sector that could potentially result in discrimination due to unethical uses of consumer data gathered.
4. **Lack of self-assurance**
   Businesses worry about the security of their data and lack confidence in their ability to safeguard network applications and the veracity of the information produced because the IoT is a new, emerging technology.

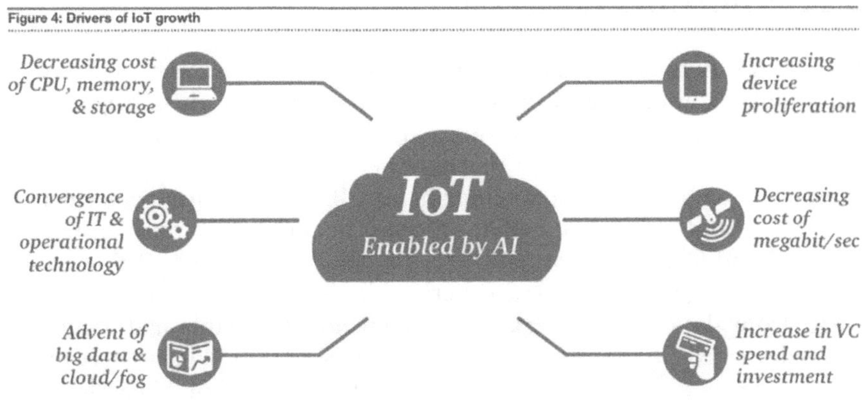

Figure 8.5 IoT enabled by AI.

5. **Cloud attacks**
   The fast growth of malicious computer viruses has brought unwanted attention to cloud computing technology. The server must host an enormous volume of data, which leads to an exponential increase in risk factors.

FUTURE ISSUES CONSIDERATION

Understanding the difference between short-term objectives and long-term perspectives is crucial for predicting future development, extension, and application of AI techniques in cyberattack prevention. There are numerous modern difficulties involving cyberattacks that call for more sophisticated solutions, and many AI techniques are helpful in preventing cyberattacks. It is possible to imagine decision-making using entirely new standards of knowledge. These standards incorporate a modular and hierarchical knowledge architecture in decision-making software. Expert systems are currently employed in a wide range of applications, although occasionally, their presence in an application or other pieces of software, such as planning software for security initiatives, is disguised [21–27]. If massive knowledge bases are created in the future, expert systems will be utilized more frequently. The creation of enormous modular information libraries and substantial financial expenditure are both necessary for this purpose's knowledge acquisition. Additional development is necessary for expert system innovation, including the use of hierarchical knowledge bases and flexible expert system tools.

DISCUSSION AND ANALYSIS

The study's findings demonstrated that AI has become one of the most important resources for businesses looking to improve their performance in terms of cybersecurity. Every firm should prioritize ensuring cybersecurity because there is a chance that internet hackers may target significant amounts of data and individual information. Because of the advancement of technology and expanding globalization, firms now store their customers' personal and financial information in the cloud. As a result of this greater reliance on digital technology, cyberattacks have become more frequent. Apart from the expert system, every independent variable had a substantial and positive connection, according to the study's findings. There are no noteworthy findings despite the fact that the majority of researchers disagree that expert systems are essential.

APPLICATION OF AI TECHNIQUES AND THEIR ADVANTAGES

Table 8.1 provides a summary of how AI approaches are used and their benefits

Table 8.1 AI methods and their application

AI techniques	*Usage*
Application of Intelligent Agent	• Proactive • Agent communication language • Reactive • Defence against distributed denial-of-service (DDoS) attack • Mobility
Application of Neural Nets	• For intrusion detection and prevention system • Very high speed of operation • For denial-of-service (DoS) attack detection • For forensics investigation • Warm detection
Application of Expert System	• For decision support • For network intrusion detection • Knowledge base • Inference engine
Application of Learning	• Machine learning • Supervised and unsupervised learning • Reinforcement learning • Malware detection, intrusion detection • SOM

CONCLUSION

One of the most intriguing developments in the information age and cybersecurity is AI. New tactics, algorithms, technologies, and companies offering AI-based services are continuously evolving in the context of the global security show. This helps to improve security execution and better protect systems from a wide range of sophisticated cyberattacks since these frameworks are more adaptable, agile, and resilient than conventional cybersecurity solutions. The most encouraging and productive AI technology today uses deep learning techniques. It has been shown that neural networks and intelligence agents have a substantial impact on AI. The increasing data security required by technological innovations' increased data storage is essential. Although AI has significantly changed the cybersecurity industry, the supporting frameworks are still unable to properly adapt and react to state changes. Additionally, a thorough understanding of a company's online environment is crucial.

REFERENCES

[1] Salama, R., Al-Turjman, F., Bhatla, S., & Mishra, D. (2023, April). Mobile Edge Fog, Blockchain Networking and Computing – A Survey. In *2023 International Conference on Computational Intelligence, Communication Technology and Networking (CICTN)* (pp. 808–811). IEEE.

[2] Salama, R., Al-Turjman, F., Chaudhary, P., & Banda, L. (2023, April). Future Communication Technology Using Huge Millimeter Waves—An Overview. In *2023 International Conference on Computational Intelligence, Communication Technology and Networking (CICTN)* (pp. 785–790). IEEE.

[3] Salama, R., Al-Turjman, F., Aeri, M., & Yadav, S. P. (2023, April). Internet of Intelligent Things (IoT)–An Overview. In *2023 International Conference on Computational Intelligence, Communication Technology and Networking (CICTN)* (pp. 801–805). IEEE.

[4] Salama, R., Al-Turjman, F., Chaudhary, P., & Yadav, S. P. (2023, April). Benefits of Internet of Things (IoT) Applications in Health care – An Overview. In *2023 International Conference on Computational Intelligence, Communication Technology and Networking (CICTN)* (pp. 778–784). IEEE.

[5] Salama, R., Al-Turjman, F., Altrjman, C., & Gupta, R. (2023, April). Machine Learning in Sustainable Development – An Overview. In *2023 International Conference on Computational Intelligence, Communication Technology and Networking (CICTN)* (pp. 806–807). IEEE.

[6] Prof. DUX available online: https://dux.aiiot.website/

[7] Salama, R., Al-Turjman, F., Bhatla, S., & Gautam, D. (2023, April). Network Security, Trust & Privacy in a Wiredwireless Environments–An Overview. In *2023 International Conference on Computational Intelligence, Communication Technology and Networking (CICTN)* (pp. 812–816). IEEE.

[8] Salama, R., Al-Turjman, F., Altrjman, C., Kumar, S., & Chaudhary, P. (2023, April). A Comprehensive Survey of Blockchain-Powered Cybersecurity

– A survey. In *2023 International Conference on Computational Intelligence, Communication Technology and Networking (CICTN)* (pp. 774–777). IEEE.

[9] Salama, R., Al-Turjman, F., Bordoloi, D., & Yadav, S. P. (2023, April). Wireless Sensor Networks and Green Networking for 6G communication – An Overview. In *2023 International Conference on Computational Intelligence, Communication Technology and Networking (CICTN)* (pp. 830–834). IEEE.

[10] Salama, R., Al-Turjman, F., Bhatia, S., & Yadav, S. P. (2023, April). Social Engineering Attack Types and Prevention Techniques – A Survey. In *2023 International Conference on Computational Intelligence, Communication Technology and Networking (CICTN)* (pp. 817–820). IEEE.

[11] Salama, R., Altrjman, C., & Al-Turjman, F. (2023). Smart Grid Applications and Blockchain Technology in the AI Era. *NEU Journal for Artificial Intelligence and Internet of Things*, 1(1), 59–63.

[12] Salama, R., Alturjman, S., & Al-Turjman, F. (2023). Internet of Things and AI in Smart Grid Applications. *NEU Journal for Artificial Intelligence and Internet of Things*, 1(1), 44–58.

[13] Salama, R., Altrjman, C., & Al-Turjman, F. (2023). A Survey of Machine Learning (ML) in Sustainable Systems. *NEU Journal for Artificial Intelligence and Internet of Things*, 2(3).

[14] Salama, R., Altrjman, C., & Al-Turjman, F. (2023). A Survey of Machine Learning Methods for Network Planning. *NEU Journal for Artificial Intelligence and Internet of Things*, 2(3).

[15] Salama, R., Altrjman, C., & Al-Turjman, F. (2023). A Survey of the Architectures and Protocols for Wireless Sensor Networks and Wireless Multimedia Sensor Networks. *NEU Journal for Artificial Intelligence and Internet of Things*, 2(3).

[16] Al-Turjman, F., Salama, R., & Altrjman, C. (2023). Overview of IoT Solutions for Sustainable Transportation Systems. *NEU Journal for Artificial Intelligence and Internet of Things*, 2(3).

[17] Salama, R., Altrjman, C., & Al-Turjman, F. (2023). An overview of the Internet of Things (IoT) and Machine to Machine (M2M) Communications. *NEU Journal for Artificial Intelligence and Internet of Things*, 2(3).

[18] Salama, R., Al-Turjman, F., Altrjman, C., & Bordoloi, D. (2023, April). The Use of Machine Learning (ML) in Sustainable Systems – An Overview. In *2023 International Conference on Computational Intelligence, Communication Technology and Networking (CICTN)* (pp. 821–824). IEEE.

[19] Al-Turjman, F., & Salama, R. (2021). Cyber Security in Mobile Social Networks. In *Security in IoT Social Networks* (pp. 55–81). Academic Press.

[20] Al-Turjman, F., & Salama, R. (2021). Security in Social Networks. In *Security in IoT Social Networks* (pp. 1–27). Academic Press.

[21] Salama, R., & Al-Turjman, F. (2022, August). AI in Blockchain towards Realizing Cyber Security. In *2022 International Conference on Artificial Intelligence in Everything (AIE)* (pp. 471–475). IEEE.

[22] Al-Turjman, F., & Salama, R. (2020). An Overview about the Cyberattacks in Grid and Like Systems. *Smart Grid in IoT-Enabled Spaces*, 233–247.

[23] Salama, R., Al-Turjman, F., & Culmone, R. (2023, March). AI-Powered Drone to Address Smart City Security Issues. In *International Conference on Advanced Information Networking and Applications* (pp. 292–300). Springer International Publishing.

[24] Salama, R., & Al-Turjman, F. (2023). Cyber-Security Countermeasures and Vulnerabilities to Prevent Social-Engineering Attacks. In *Artificial Intelligence of Health-Enabled Spaces* (pp. 133–144). CRC Press.
[25] Salama, R., Al-Turjman, F., Altrjman, C., & Bordoloi, D. (2023, April). The Ways in Which Artificial Intelligence Improves Several Facets of Cyber Security – A Survey. In *2023 International Conference on Computational Intelligence, Communication Technology and Networking (CICTN)* (pp. 825–829). IEEE.
[26] Kataria, A., Khan, F., & Garg, A. (2021). Comparative Analysis on Penetration of ATM Transactions between Public Sector Banks in India. *Turkish Online Journal of Qualitative Inquiry*, 12(10).
[27] Rathi, R., Garg, R., Kataria, A., & Chhikara, R. (2022). Evolution of luxury marketing landscape: a bibliometric analysis and future directions. *Journal of Brand Management*, 29(3), 241–257.

Chapter 9

Blockchain technology, computer network operations, and global value chains together make up "cybersecurity"

Ramiz Salama
Artificial Intelligence, Software, and Information Systems Engineering Departments, Research Center for AI and IoT, AI and Robotics Institute, Near East University, Nicosia, Mersin10, Turkey

Fadi Al-Turjman
Artificial Intelligence, Software, and Information Systems Engineering Departments, Research Center for AI and IoT, AI and Robotics Institute, Near East University, Nicosia, Mersin10, Turkey

INTRODUCTION

In today's digital age, computer networks play a vital role in our daily lives, enabling seamless communication, information sharing, and transactions. However, the increasing reliance on computer networks has also exposed individuals and organizations to various cyber threats and security breaches. Cybersecurity has emerged as a critical concern, demanding innovative approaches to protect sensitive information, maintain data integrity, and ensure the resilience of computer networks.

The traditional methods of cybersecurity, such as intrusion detection systems, firewalls, and encryption, have been shown to be ineffective in dealing with the constantly changing nature of cyber threats. Cybersecurity methods need to change paradigms since attackers always come up with new ways to exploit flaws and get around traditional security measures. Blockchain technology has arisen in this context as a viable way to improve the security and dependability of computer network operations.

Blockchain is a decentralized and distributed ledger system that first gained notoriety as the technology underpinning cryptocurrencies like Bitcoin. It functions as a peer-to-peer network where transactions are transparently, irrevocably, and impenetrably recorded. Together with cryptographic methods and consensus algorithms, the decentralized nature of blockchain creates a strong framework for protecting digital assets and data.

Specifically, the study article's focus is on computer network operations as it relates to the potential of blockchain technology in the field of cybersecurity. We'll look into the foundational ideas of blockchain, its

 DOI: 10.1201/9781003461432-9

underpinning mechanisms, and how it might be used to solve cybersecurity problems. We will also go over the advantages and disadvantages of using blockchain technology in computer network operations, taking into account elements like scalability, legal compliance, privacy issues, and performance constraints [1–8].

By analysing existing literature, case studies, and real-world implementation examples, this chapter intends to shed light on the various ways in which blockchain technology can enhance cybersecurity in computer network operations. We will examine its potential to improve data integrity, provide immutable audit trails, protect against distributed denial of service (DDoS) attacks, facilitate secure identity management, enable threat intelligence sharing, and enhance incident response and recovery processes.

We will also point out the issues that must be resolved if blockchain technology is to be fully utilized in the context of cybersecurity. Scalability, regulatory and compliance issues, system integration, governance frameworks, and privacy and confidentiality issues are a few of these obstacles. Researchers and practitioners can concentrate on creating strategies and solutions to leverage the advantages of blockchain technology while minimizing potential risks by being aware of these difficulties. In conclusion, this chapter aims to provide insights into the intersection of cybersecurity and blockchain technology, focusing on computer network operations. By exploring the potential applications, benefits, and challenges of integrating blockchain technology, we seek to contribute to the ongoing efforts to develop innovative cybersecurity solutions that can effectively protect computer networks from emerging threats

Machine learning and artificial intelligence (AI) facilitators have started to be a part of our daily lives and have significant effects on the rapid developments of the Internet of Things. One of the leading attempts in this field is the AI learning facilitator, Prof. DUX [1]. It is a novel AI facilitator that aims at personalizing the education process for learners and providing the fastest and best quality of education in numerous fields.

CYBERSECURITY IN COMPUTER NETWORK OPERATIONS

Overview of cybersecurity

Cybersecurity encompasses a wide range of technologies, practices, and processes aimed at safeguarding digital assets and mitigating the risks associated with cyber threats. Cybersecurity measures are crucial in computer network operations to ensure the confidentiality, integrity, and availability of information and services [9–15].

Common cyber threats

Computer network operations face a multitude of cyber threats, including the following:

a) ***Malware***: Malicious software such as viruses, worms, Trojans, ransomware, and spyware, which are designed to compromise systems and steal sensitive information.
b) ***Phishing***: Deceptive methods that pose as reliable institutions in order to deceive people into disclosing their personal information, like passwords or credit card numbers.
c) ***Denial of service (DoS) and DDoS attacks***: Attempts to overwhelm a network or system with excessive traffic, rendering it unavailable to legitimate users.
d) ***Data breaches***: Unauthorized access and exfiltration of sensitive data, often resulting in financial loss, reputational damage, and legal consequences.
e) ***Insider threats***: Actions or negligence by individuals with authorized access to systems who intentionally or unintentionally cause harm to the organization's network or data.
f) ***Social engineering***: Manipulation techniques that exploit human psychology to deceive individuals into divulging sensitive information or performing unauthorized actions.

Traditional approaches to cybersecurity

Traditional cybersecurity measures include the following:

a) *Firewalls*: Devices for network security that keep track of and regulate incoming and outgoing traffic in accordance with predefined security rules.
b) *Intrusion detection systems (IDS) and intrusion prevention systems (IPS)*: Technologies that detect and block unauthorized access attempts or malicious activities within a network.
c) *Antivirus software*: Programmes designed to detect, prevent, and remove malware infections.
d) *Encryption*: The procedure of codifying data to prevent unauthorized access.
e) *Access control mechanisms*: User authentication, authorization, and privilege management systems to control user access to network resources.
f) *Security awareness and training*: Educating users about best practices, potential threats, and proper handling of sensitive information.

Limitations of traditional approaches

While traditional cybersecurity measures provide a level of protection, they have limitations in dealing with sophisticated cyber threats:

a) *Centralization*: Traditional approaches often rely on centralized control points, making them vulnerable to single points of failure and potential exploitation by attackers.
b) *Lack of transparency*: It can be challenging to verify the integrity and authenticity of security controls and data within a centralized system.
c) *Inability to handle evolving threats*: Traditional approaches may struggle to adapt to emerging threats due to their static nature and the time required to update and patch vulnerabilities.
d) *Trust dependencies*: Traditional systems rely on trust in centralized authorities, which can be compromised, leading to potential security breaches.
e) *Limited incident response capabilities*: Traditional approaches may have limited visibility and effectiveness in rapidly detecting, responding to, and recovering from cyber incidents.

To address these limitations and enhance the security of computer network operations, there is a growing interest in exploring innovative technologies such as blockchain. The next sections will delve into the potential applications of blockchain technology in cybersecurity and computer network operations.

INTRODUCTION TO BLOCKCHAIN TECHNOLOGY

Definition and principles of blockchain

Blockchain is a distributed ledger system that allows for safe transaction recording and verification across a network of computers, often known as nodes. It offers an open, unchangeable, and untouchable record of all transactions or data kept on the blockchain [16–20]. The fundamental ideas behind blockchain include the following:

a) *Decentralization*: Blockchain operates on a peer-to-peer network where multiple nodes participate in the validation and maintenance of the ledger. This decentralization eliminates the need for a central authority, making the system more resilient and resistant to single points of failure or malicious attacks.
b) *Transparency*: All transactions recorded on the blockchain are visible to all participants in the network. This transparency fosters trust and accountability, as it allows network participants to independently verify the integrity and accuracy of the recorded data.

c) *Immutability*: Once a transaction is recorded on the blockchain, it becomes virtually impossible to alter or delete it. Each transaction is linked to previous transactions through cryptographic hashing, creating a chain of blocks that ensures the integrity and immutability of the entire transaction history.
d) *Security through cryptography*: Blockchain employs cryptographic algorithms to secure transactions and data. Each transaction is digitally signed, ensuring the authenticity and integrity of the information. Additionally, cryptographic hash functions are used to generate unique identifiers for each block, creating a secure and tamper-evident structure.

Blockchain architecture and components

The architecture of a blockchain typically consists of the following components:

a) *Blocks*: A block is a data structure that contains a batch of transactions. It includes a header containing metadata such as a time stamp, a unique identifier (hash), and a reference to the previous block. The transactions within a block are bundled together and secured through cryptographic hashes.
b) *Chain of blocks*: Blocks are linked together in a sequential manner, forming a chain. Each block contains a reference to the previous block, creating a chronological record of all transactions.
c) *Distributed network*: Blockchain operates on a distributed network of nodes that collectively participate in the validation, verification, and maintenance of the blockchain. Each node stores a copy of the entire blockchain, ensuring redundancy and fault tolerance.
d) *Consensus mechanisms*: Consensus mechanisms are protocols or methods that allow network nodes to concur on the legitimacy of transactions and come to a consensus on the blockchain's current state. Proof of Work (PoW), Proof of Stake (PoS), and Practical Byzantine Fault Tolerance (PBFT) are three common consensus procedures.

Cryptography and consensus mechanisms

Cryptography plays a vital role in securing blockchain transactions and ensuring data integrity. [21–23]. Some commonly used cryptographic techniques in blockchain include the following:

a) *Public-key cryptography*: Public-key cryptography utilizes a pair of cryptographic keys: a public key for encryption and a corresponding private key for decryption. This asymmetric encryption enables secure communication and ensures the authenticity and integrity of transactions.

b) *Hash functions*: Hash functions are one-way mathematical algorithms that transform input data into fixed-length hash values. The resulting hash is unique to the input data, making it suitable for verifying the integrity of transactions and blocks.
c) *Consensus mechanisms*: Consensus mechanisms are fundamental to the operation of a blockchain network. They enable nodes to agree on the validity and ordering of transactions without relying on a central authority. Different consensus mechanisms have varying requirements, security characteristics, and energy efficiency considerations.

Smart contracts in blockchain

Smart contracts are frequently incorporated into blockchain technology. Smart contracts are agreements that automatically carry out their conditions after being encoded into blockchain code. When certain circumstances are met, these contracts automatically carry out predetermined actions or transactions. With the transparency, immutability, and automation that smart contracts offer, intermediaries are unnecessary, lowering the risk of fraud or legal problems.

COMPUTER NETWORK OPERATIONS AND BLOCKCHAIN TECHNOLOGY "CYBERSECURITY"

Blockchain technology in cybersecurity

Blockchain technology offers several potential applications for enhancing cybersecurity in computer network operations. By leveraging its core principles of decentralization, transparency, immutability, and security through cryptography, blockchain can address various security challenges [24–26]. The following sections explore some key areas where blockchain can contribute to cybersecurity.

Enhancing data integrity and trust

Data integrity is crucial in ensuring the accuracy and reliability of information. Blockchain's immutable nature makes it an ideal solution for maintaining data integrity. By recording transactions or data on the blockchain, organizations can create an auditable trail that cannot be altered or tampered with. This feature is particularly useful in mitigating the risks of data manipulation and unauthorized modifications.

Additionally, blockchain's transparent and decentralized nature instils trust among network participants. With the ability to independently verify transactions and access the entire transaction history, organizations can have increased confidence in the integrity of data within their computer network operations.

Immutable audit trails and transparency

Blockchain's transparent and auditable nature enables the creation of immutable audit trails. Every transaction recorded on the blockchain leaves a permanent and time-stamped record, providing a reliable source of information for forensic analysis, investigations, and compliance purposes. This feature enhances accountability and enables organizations to track and trace any suspicious activities within their computer network operations.

Furthermore, the transparency of blockchain can foster a collaborative approach to security. Participants within a blockchain network can share information about potential threats, attacks, or vulnerabilities, facilitating a more proactive and collective response to cybersecurity incidents.

Distributed denial of service protection

DDoS attacks pose a significant threat to computer networks, aiming to disrupt services by overwhelming them with excessive traffic. Blockchain can provide enhanced DDoS protection by leveraging its decentralized nature.

In a blockchain-based network, the distribution of data across multiple nodes reduces the reliance on a single point of failure, making it harder for attackers to launch successful DDoS attacks. Additionally, blockchain's consensus mechanisms can facilitate the detection and mitigation of DDoS attacks by enabling nodes to collaborate and identify malicious traffic patterns.

Identity management and access control

Access control and identity management inside computer network operations can be improved by blockchain technology. Attacks aimed at centralized databases and user credentials are possible against traditional centralized systems for user authentication and access control.

Organizations can improve user identity security and privacy by incorporating blockchain-based identity management systems. Blockchain makes it possible to build decentralized identification systems that provide users more control over their personal data and the ability to share it with certain trustworthy parties. As a result, the dangers of centralized identity databases are diminished, and the effects of identity theft and illegal access are lessened.

Threat intelligence sharing

Collaboration and sharing of threat intelligence play a crucial role in detecting and mitigating cyber threats. Blockchain can facilitate secure and decentralized threat intelligence sharing among organizations.

By utilizing blockchain-based platforms, organizations can securely share threat intelligence data, such as indicators of compromise (IoCs) and attack signatures, without compromising the confidentiality of the shared information. Blockchain's transparency ensures the verifiability and authenticity of the shared threat intelligence, enhancing the overall effectiveness of threat detection and response mechanisms.

Incident response and recovery

Blockchain technology can also enhance incident response and recovery processes within computer network operations. The decentralized and immutable nature of blockchain ensures that critical incident data, such as time stamps, log entries, and forensic evidence, remains tamper-proof and preserved for investigation.

Furthermore, smart contracts deployed on the blockchain can automate incident response actions, such as triggering alerts, isolating affected systems, or initiating recovery procedures. This automation reduces the time required for incident response and enables a more efficient and coordinated approach to mitigating the impact of cyber incidents.

By leveraging blockchain technology in these various aspects of cybersecurity, organizations can strengthen their computer network operations and better.

Protect against evolving cyber threats. However, it is essential to consider the challenges and limitations associated with blockchain implementation, such as scalability, regulatory compliance, privacy concerns, and integration with existing systems. Addressing these challenges is crucial for the successful adoption and effective utilization of blockchain technology in cybersecurity.

RESULTS AND DISCUSSION

Challenges and opportunities in implementing blockchain technology for cybersecurity

Challenges

Scalability

One of the primary challenges in implementing blockchain technology for cybersecurity is scalability. Traditional blockchain networks, such as Bitcoin and Ethereum, face limitations in terms of transaction throughput and network latency. As cybersecurity operations generate a significant volume of transactions, it is crucial to ensure that blockchain networks can handle the scale and speed required for real-time security operations.

Regulatory compliance

Blockchain implementation in cybersecurity must adhere to regulatory requirements and compliance frameworks, such as data privacy laws (e.g., General Data Protection Regulation (GDPR)) and industry-specific regulations (e.g., Health Insurance Portability and Accountability (HIPAA) for health care). However, the decentralized and transparent nature of blockchain can conflict with certain privacy regulations, necessitating careful design and implementation approaches to ensure compliance while maintaining the benefits of blockchain technology.

Integration with existing systems

Integrating blockchain technology with existing computer network operations and security infrastructure can be complex. Organizations often have legacy systems and processes that need to coexist with blockchain solutions. Ensuring smooth integration and interoperability between blockchain and traditional systems requires careful planning, compatibility assessment, and potential system upgrades or modifications.

Governance and consensus

Blockchain networks rely on consensus mechanisms to validate transactions and maintain the integrity of the ledger. However, determining the appropriate consensus mechanism and establishing effective governance models for cybersecurity operations can be challenging. Consensus mechanisms should balance security, performance, energy efficiency, and specific requirements of cybersecurity applications.

Privacy and confidentiality

While blockchain provides transparency and immutability, it can pose challenges regarding privacy and confidentiality in cybersecurity. Not all information within a computer network operation can be made publicly accessible on the blockchain. Ensuring the privacy of sensitive data while maintaining the benefits of blockchain technology requires techniques such as zero-knowledge proofs, private or permissioned blockchains, or off-chain storage solutions.

Opportunities

Decentralization and resilience

Blockchain's decentralized nature enhances the resilience of cybersecurity operations. By eliminating single points of failure, distributing data across multiple nodes, and using consensus mechanisms, blockchain-based systems can withstand attacks and maintain the availability of critical security services even in the face of disruptions or malicious activities.

Immutable audit trails and forensic analysis

The immutability of blockchain records allows for reliable audit trials and forensic analysis in cybersecurity investigations. The ability to trace and verify the integrity of transactions or events recorded on the blockchain enables efficient incident response, root cause analysis, and evidence gathering, enhancing the effectiveness of cybersecurity operations.

Trust and transparency

Blockchain's transparency and ability to verify the integrity of data foster trust among participants in cybersecurity operations. The shared and auditable nature of blockchain can enable collaboration, information sharing, and collective defence against cyber threats. It enhances trust between entities, reduces the reliance on intermediaries, and facilitates the exchange of verified threat intelligence.

Smart contracts for automation

Smart contracts in blockchain technology can automate cybersecurity processes, such as incident response, threat detection, or access control. By leveraging self-executing code on the blockchain, organizations can streamline and enforce security protocols, reduce human error, and enable faster response times to cyber incidents.

Data integrity and tamper-proof storage

Blockchain's tamper-proof and immutable nature ensures the integrity of critical security data, such as certificates, digital identities, or vulnerability information. Storing such data on the blockchain can mitigate the risks of unauthorized modifications, tampering, or data breaches, thereby enhancing the overall security posture of computer network operations.

CASE STUDIES AND IMPLEMENTATION EXAMPLES

Guardtime and cybersecurity for Estonian government systems

Guardtime, a blockchain technology company, collaborated with the Estonian government to enhance cybersecurity in their digital infrastructure. The Estonian government implemented Guardtime's Keyless Signature Infrastructure (KSI) blockchain technology to secure various systems, including government databases and healthcare records. KSI creates a tamper-proof and auditable trail of data integrity, enabling the detection of unauthorized modifications or data breaches. By leveraging blockchain,

Estonia has established a robust cybersecurity framework, ensuring the integrity and trustworthiness of critical government systems.

REMME and decentralized authentication

REMME, a blockchain-based cybersecurity company, focuses on passwordless authentication solutions. Their blockchain-powered platform replaces traditional passwords with public-key cryptography, enabling secure and decentralized authentication. REMME's solution eliminates the risks associated with password-based attacks, such as credential theft or brute-force attacks. By using blockchain technology, REMME provides a more secure and user-friendly authentication process, improving cybersecurity for various applications, including enterprise systems and IoT devices.

IBM and food supply chain security

The blockchain-based IBM Food Trust technology improves the security and transparency of the food supply chain. IBM enables stakeholders, such as farmers, suppliers, distributors, and retailers, to track and verify the source, quality, and safety of food goods by utilizing blockchain technology. Blockchain's immutability and transparency protect the accuracy of supply chain data, lowering the likelihood of food fraud, product tampering, or contamination. IBM's Food Trust is an example of how blockchain technology can be used outside of the realms of conventional cybersecurity to enhance the security and reliability of crucial supply chains.

Microsoft Azure Blockchain and Azure Sentinel

Microsoft Azure Blockchain offers a range of blockchain services and solutions for various industries, including cybersecurity. Azure Sentinel, Microsoft's cloud-native security information and event management (SIEM) solution, incorporates blockchain technology to enhance the security of digital assets and protect against data tampering or unauthorized modifications. By leveraging blockchain's immutability, Azure Sentinel provides secure and tamper-proof log and event storage, ensuring the integrity of cybersecurity event data and enabling effective incident response and forensic analysis.

Cisco and blockchain-based threat intelligence

Cisco, a leading networking and cybersecurity company, explores the application of blockchain in threat intelligence sharing. By leveraging blockchain technology, Cisco aims to create a secure and decentralized platform for sharing threat intelligence data among organizations. The blockchain-based platform ensures the authenticity, verifiability, and privacy of shared threat intelligence, enabling faster detection and response to emerging cyber threats. Cisco's initiative showcases how blockchain can enhance collaborative cybersecurity efforts and create a more resilient defence against evolving threats.

These case studies and implementation examples demonstrate the diverse applications of blockchain technology in cybersecurity. From securing government systems and improving authentication processes to enhancing supply chain security and enabling secure threat intelligence sharing, blockchain technology offers innovative solutions to address critical cybersecurity challenges. As the technology continues to evolve, more organizations are expected to leverage blockchain to strengthen their cybersecurity posture and protect against emerging threats.

FUTURE DIRECTIONS

Blockchain technology holds immense potential for shaping the future of cybersecurity in computer network operations. As the technology continues to evolve, several future directions can be explored.

Interoperability and integration

Efforts should be made to enhance interoperability between different blockchain platforms and existing cybersecurity systems. This would enable seamless integration and facilitate the exchange of information and services between blockchain networks and traditional security infrastructure.

Privacy-enhancing techniques

Further research and development are needed to address privacy concerns in blockchain-based cybersecurity solutions. Techniques such as zero-knowledge proofs, homomorphic encryption, and privacy-focused consensus mechanisms can be explored to strike a balance between transparency and privacy in cybersecurity operations.

Scalability and performance improvements

Innovations to address scalability limitations of blockchain networks are crucial for real-time cybersecurity operations. Solutions such as sharding, off-chain transactions, and layer-2 scaling techniques can be leveraged to enhance transaction throughput and reduce network latency.

Hybrid approaches

Hybrid models that combine the strengths of both blockchain and traditional cybersecurity systems can be explored. Integrating blockchain technology with existing security frameworks can provide enhanced security, transparency, and auditability while leveraging the efficiency and scalability of traditional systems.

Standardization and regulatory frameworks

Establishing industry standards and regulatory frameworks specific to blockchain-based cybersecurity would provide clarity and guidance for organizations. It would also foster trust and adoption of blockchain technology by ensuring compliance with legal and regulatory requirements.

CONCLUSION

In conclusion, blockchain technology offers potential solutions to computer network operations' cybersecurity concerns. Blockchain can improve data integrity, enable secure authentication, facilitate the exchange of threat intelligence, and automate cybersecurity procedures by utilizing its key concepts of decentralization, transparency, immutability, and security through cryptography.

However, implementing blockchain technology for cybersecurity also comes with challenges, such as scalability, regulatory compliance, integration, governance, and privacy. Overcoming these challenges requires collaborative efforts from industry leaders, researchers, and policymakers to develop scalable and interoperable solutions that meet regulatory requirements while preserving the benefits of blockchain.

Through successful implementation and continued research, blockchain technology has the potential to revolutionize cybersecurity practices, enhance trust, and improve the resilience of computer network operations in the face of evolving cyber threats. It is an exciting field with numerous opportunities for innovation and collaboration, ultimately leading to a more secure and trusted digital landscape.

REFERENCES

[1] Prof. DUX available online: https://dux.aiiot.website/

[2] Salama, R., & Al-Turjman, F. (2022, August). AI in Blockchain towards Realizing Cyber Security. In *2022 International Conference on Artificial Intelligence in Everything (AIE)* (pp. 471–475). IEEE.

[3] Al-Turjman, F., & Salama, R. (2020). An Overview about the Cyberattacks in Grid and Like Systems. *Smart Grid in IoT-Enabled Spaces*, 233–247.

[4] Salama, R., Al-Turjman, F., & Culmone, R. (2023, March). AI-Powered Drone to Address Smart City Security Issues. In *International Conference on Advanced Information Networking and Applications* (pp. 292–300). Springer International Publishing.

[5] Salama, R., & Al-Turjman, F. (2023). Cyber-Security Countermeasures and Vulnerabilities to Prevent Social-Engineering Attacks. In *Artificial Intelligence of Health-Enabled Spaces* (pp. 133–144). CRC Press.

[6] Salama, R., Al-Turjman, F., Altrjman, C., & Bordoloi, D. (2023, April). The Ways in Which Artificial Intelligence Improves Several Facets of Cyber Security – A Survey. In *2023 International Conference on Computational Intelligence, Communication Technology and Networking (CICTN)* (pp. 825–829). IEEE.

[7] Salama, R., Al-Turjman, F., Bhatla, S., & Mishra, D. (2023, April). Mobile Edge Fog, Blockchain Networking and Computing – A Survey. In *2023 International Conference on Computational Intelligence, Communication Technology and Networking (CICTN)* (pp. 808–811). IEEE.

[8] Salama, R., Al-Turjman, F., Chaudhary, P., & Banda, L. (2023, April). Future Communication Technology Using Huge Millimeter Waves—An Overview. In *2023 International Conference on Computational Intelligence, Communication Technology and Networking (CICTN)* (pp. 785–790). IEEE.

[9] Salama, R., Al-Turjman, F., Aeri, M., & Yadav, S. P. (2023, April). Internet of Intelligent Things (IoT) – An Overview. In *2023 International Conference on Computational Intelligence, Communication Technology and Networking (CICTN)* (pp. 801–805). IEEE.

[10] Salama, R., Al-Turjman, F., Chaudhary, P., & Yadav, S. P. (2023, April). Benefits of Internet of Things (IoT) Applications in Health Care – An Overview. In *2023 International Conference on Computational Intelligence, Communication Technology and Networking (CICTN)* (pp. 778–784). IEEE.

[11] Salama, R., Al-Turjman, F., Altrjman, C., & Gupta, R. (2023, April). Machine Learning in Sustainable Development – An Overview. In *2023 International Conference on Computational Intelligence, Communication Technology and Networking (CICTN)* (pp. 806–807). IEEE.

[12] Salama, R., Al-Turjman, F., Aeri, M., & Yadav, S. P. (2023, April). Intelligent Hardware Solutions for COVID-19 and Alike Diagnosis – A Survey. In *2023 International Conference on Computational Intelligence, Communication Technology and Networking (CICTN)* (pp. 796–800). IEEE.

[13] Salama, R., Al-Turjman, F., Bhatla, S., & Gautam, D. (2023, April). Network Security, Trust & Privacy in a Wiredwireless Environments – An Overview. In *2023 International Conference on Computational Intelligence, Communication Technology and Networking (CICTN)* (pp. 812–816). IEEE.

[14] Salama, R., Al-Turjman, F., Altrjman, C., Kumar, S., & Chaudhary, P. (2023, April). A Comprehensive Survey of Blockchain-Powered Cybersecurity – A Survey. In *2023 International Conference on Computational Intelligence, Communication Technology and Networking (CICTN)* (pp. 774–777). IEEE.

[15] Salama, R., Al-Turjman, F., Bordoloi, D., & Yadav, S. P. (2023, April). Wireless Sensor Networks and Green Networking for 6G communication – An Overview. In *2023 International Conference on Computational Intelligence, Communication Technology and Networking (CICTN)* (pp. 830–834). IEEE.

[16] Salama, R., Al-Turjman, F., Bhatia, S., & Yadav, S. P. (2023, April). Social Engineering Attack Types and Prevention Techniques – A Survey. In *2023 International Conference on Computational Intelligence, Communication Technology and Networking (CICTN)* (pp. 817–820). IEEE.

[17] Salama, R., Altrjman, C., & Al-Turjman, F. (2023). Smart Grid Applications and Blockchain Technology in the AI Era. *NEU Journal for Artificial Intelligence and Internet of Things*, 1(1), 59–63.

[18] Salama, R., Alturjman, S., & Al-Turjman, F. (2023). Internet of Things and AI in Smart Grid Applications. *NEU Journal for Artificial Intelligence and Internet of Things*, 1(1), 44–58.

[19] Salama, R., Altrjman, C., & Al-Turjman, F. (2023). A Survey of Machine Learning (ML) in Sustainable Systems. *NEU Journal for Artificial Intelligence and Internet of Things*, 2(3).

[20] Ghatak, M. A., & Garg, A. (2019). Risk Management in Power Evacuation Projects–NTCP Model.

[21] Garg, A. (2022). *CoReS-Respiratory Strength Predicting Framework Using Noninvasive Technology for Remote Monitoring During Heath Disasters.* Global Healthcare Disasters: Predicting the Unpredictable with Emerging Technologies, 109–121.

[22] Garg, A., & Goyal, D. P. (Eds.). (2022). *Global Healthcare Disasters: Predicting the Unpredictable with Emerging Technologies*. CRC Press.

[23] Salama, R., Altrjman, C., & Al-Turjman, F. (2023). A Survey of Machine Learning Methods for Network Planning. *NEU Journal for Artificial Intelligence and Internet of Things*, 2(3).

[24] Salama, R., Altrjman, C., & Al-Turjman, F. (2023). A Survey of the Architectures and Protocols for Wireless Sensor Networks and Wireless Multimedia Sensor Networks. *NEU Journal for Artificial Intelligence and Internet of Things*, 2(3).

[25] Al-Turjman, F., Salama, R., & Altrjman, C. (2023). Overview of IoT Solutions for Sustainable Transportation Systems. *NEU Journal for Artificial Intelligence and Internet of Things*, 2(3).

[26] Salama, R., Altrjman, C., & Al-Turjman, F. (2023). An Overview of the Internet of Things (IoT) and Machine to Machine (M2M) Communications. *NEU Journal for Artificial Intelligence and Internet of Things*, 2(3).

Chapter 10

A study of health-care data security in smart cities and the global value chain using AI and blockchain

Ramiz Salama

Artificial Intelligence, Software, and Information Systems Engineering Departments, Research Center for AI and IoT, AI and Robotics Institute, Near East University, Nicosia, Mersin10, Turkey

Fadi Al-Turjman

Artificial Intelligence, Software, and Information Systems Engineering Departments, Research Center for AI and IoT, AI and Robotics Institute, Near East University, Nicosia, Mersin10, Turkey

INTRODUCTION

The blockchain keeps a permanent record of all transactions between two parties and is an open, decentralized ledger that does not require external authentication. When this technology, Internet of Things (IoT), and real estate are combined, we might start to see noticeable changes in how a metropolis sprawls. Parts 1 and 2 of this series on blockchain for smart cities have previously demonstrated how it may foster innovation in the IoT and real estate sectors. In this section, we'll examine the typical obstacles that arise when trying to build a smart city, as well as the dangers, benefits, and ways that blockchain technology might improve urban life [1–3]. In order to provide better services to its citizens and ensure the efficient and effective use of its resources, a smart city needs information technology for the integration and control of its social, commercial, and physical infrastructures. The IoT, also referred to as the "information of things," is a marketing strategy that promotes internet connectivity between individuals and technological gadgets. These gadgets can all communicate with one another, including intelligent homes, intelligent cars, intelligent businesses, and clever vehicles. The IoT offers many options for many businesses trying to successfully and efficiently enhance their output. The benefits of the IoT are numerous. However, it also has a number of drawbacks, including hardware limitations and issues with data security, centralization, analytics, and communication. Massive phishing and spam email campaigns compromised more than 800,000 consumer devices in 2015. According to Cui et al., a significant amount of data is being produced as the number of smart devices increases. Any IoT application must therefore solve the crucial problem of large data analytics. Numerous studies have contributed to and provided a

DOI: 10.1201/9781003461432-10

variety of solutions for this data analytics issue, employing IoT applications for technologies like artificial intelligence (AI) and deep learning. The deep learning analytical tool analyses enormous amounts of data to produce the information required for prediction, categorization, and decision-making processes. The deep learning analytics solution allows for the scaling and feature extraction of a sizeable amount of data from IoT applications. The study on the fusion of AI and IoT was presented by Osuwa et al. Their study also discusses the revenue streams, possible economic prospects, and unresolved scientific problems in various IoT applications. A user-oriented IoT system with two processes has been proposed by Misra et al. [4–6]. The first technique makes use of bidirectional processing, whereas the second makes use of uncertainty-oriented arbitration.

A distributed, secure, and decentralized network is provided by blockchain technology. Blockchain technology connects each node in a decentralized peer-to-peer network, guaranteeing that every transaction is instantly time-stamped, recorded, and shared without intervention from outside parties. Using blockchain technology, issues in a number of industries, such as banking, security, health care, and agriculture, can be resolved. Cryptographic hashing is used to better connect and secure the data that is available in blocks in chains of digital signs. Each block is linked to the one before it, making it difficult for hackers to alter transactions by inserting erroneous data into the system. A number of difficulties, including digital signature, validation, smart contracts, decentralization, secure sharing, and immutable explainable AI, have been addressed through the integration of the blockchain approach with AI for IoT frameworks. As smart IoT devices have expanded and networked in recent years, a significant amount of data has been generated centrally. As a result, concerns about privacy, security, and available space are continually raised. Building a decentralized database structure with blockchain and IoT AI will allow us to address these issues. When a transaction is exchanged with another user through a network, it should be safe, digitally signed, unchangeable, verifiable, and explicable. The majority of applications, including those in the health-care industry, smart homes, smart agriculture, smart transportation, and many others, can leverage this kind of safe transaction concept. Blockchain technology uses the concept of smart contracts to store them in a digital ledger and boost network security. To deliver highly secure and scalable data to fog intelligence in a decentralized way, Fakhri et al. developed a security architecture for IoT applications [7–10]. The architecture of an IoT framework addresses the centralization problem.

Modern technologies such as decentralized AI, blockchain, the IoT, machine automation, and many more use AI in a wide range of applications. The benefits of combining IoT with AI allow for the most comprehensive data collection and analysis. According to a study by Mohanta et al., intelligent machines can replace people in applications like medical science, automated industries, and other fields by eliminating their undesirable effects. As a result of the recent rapid growth of smart and digital technologies, IoT, blockchain, and AI have emerged as the most popular technologies, inspiring fresh research ideas across a range of disciplines. Blockchain and AI's important confluence for the IoT application is shown [11–13]. The two main contributions of this chapter are the study of AI and blockchain for IoT applications and the security of health-care data in smart cities using AI and blockchain.

Our daily lives have begun to incorporate machine learning and AI technology, which has had a tremendous impact on the IoT's explosive growth. Prof. DUX, an AI learning facilitator, is one of the pioneers in this field [14]. It is a cutting-edge AI facilitator that strives to tailor the learning experience for students and deliver the quickest and highest-quality education in a variety of subjects.

1. Challenges of transitioning from a city to a smart city
   1.1 Globally, nations are becoming more urbanized, and major cities are essential engines of economic growth because they are attracting influential individuals and businesses. However, there is a chance for worsening environmental issues and transportation congestion [15–16]. Growth in the population of cities has led to worries about rising resource demand, increased pressure on urban infrastructure, rising demand for public services, and rising environmental pressure.
   1.2 Connected technology can support the growing demand for smart cities. The economic effects of the COVID-19 epidemic highlighted the need for more reliable and efficient urban management [17–20]. Thanks to cutting-edge technology like blockchain, urban administration could be improved while also addressing these socioeconomic issues.
   1.3 To deliver effective urban services, a city must ensure that data is transferred efficiently across the numerous diverse municipal stakeholders [21–23]. Blockchain enables network users to communicate data with a high level of dependability and transparency without depending on a central administrator.
2. Blockchain applications in smart cities
   Because a smart city includes a collection of businesses and stakeholders engaging with one another, we have only selected a small number of application areas. Blockchain technology is used differently in each application area, but when put together, they can be considered the building blocks of a smart city [24].
3. Adaptive energy
   3.1 Utilizing clean, inexpensive energy efficiently is the core goal of smart energy. By promoting peer-to-peer energy generation and consumption, blockchain technology has the potential to foster an environment for the energy sector that is more robust [25].

By using blockchain to enhance energy resource management and increase energy efficiency, the city ecosystem can benefit.

3.2 Transparency of energy transactions can be improved by using blockchain to manage energy transformation and distribution. Blockchain technology can be used to speed up and secure peer-to-peer energy trade transactions and provide a reliable communication backbone for the energy network. Blockchain technology can be used to store data from energy management systems [26–27]. Decision-makers will therefore feel more comfortable utilizing this data to estimate supply and demand levels.

4. AI energy optimization in smart cities

4.1 In order to study and track how individuals and businesses use energy, smart cities may use AI. Decisions about where to use renewable energy sources are then based on this data. Additionally, this can show urban planners where and how energy is being wasted.

4.2 Data on traffic, pollution, and energy use is collected through sensors, networks, and applications. These are then used for use and pattern prediction and rectification after analysis. Open-access technologies that make that information broadly available allow people and organizations to use it in any way they see fit.

4.3 The smart energy-trading concept seeks to automate as much of the generation, usage, and distribution of clean energy from renewable energy sources as is practical.

5. Adaptive mobility

5.1 The idea of "smart mobility" makes it simpler to gain access to contemporary transportation networks that are effective for users and sustainable for the city and its surroundings. Any smart city must have this as a key element. The efficient management of a transportation network is one of the key challenges that every city must overcome. IoT systems and devices can be combined with blockchain technology to track people and cars continuously and in real time.

5.2 Transportation decision-making authority can improve schedules and routes, plan for a variety of passenger needs, and advance sustainability and the environment with the use of various blockchain applications. Regardless of the form of transportation they are utilizing, users may securely pay for transportation services across the transportation ecosystem using a dependable transportation network that utilizes blockchain technology.

5.3 Blockchain technology will enable a better understanding of commuter profiles by preserving an entire and unalterable history of commutes, driving performance, maintenance, and other elements. In mobility-as-a-service systems, which enable the delivery of a variety of extra services to citizens, such as payments, insurance, car sharing, and maintenance, blockchain can also play a significant role.

6. In smart cities, AI and safety
   6.1 Despite the fact that surveillance video is typically viewed after a crime is reported, this does not prevent the crime from occurring. Security cameras with AI capabilities can analyse video in real time to spot criminal activities so that they can be reported and stopped immediately. Thanks to the ability of these cameras to recognize people from their clothing, the technology can identify suspects more swiftly than ever.
   6.2 To monitor air pollution, global warming, and the local environment, smart cities can deploy AI.
   6.3 Governments and cities may make informed decisions that are good for the environment by using AI and machine learning to reduce energy use and pollution. In smart cities, AI is also utilized to detect CO_2, which may then affect transportation decisions.
7. Public services and administration
   7.1 The significance of effective municipal management and service delivery has increased with the growth of urbanization. Public administration needs to be reimagined if it is to operate more efficiently and offer residents value. This can be helped by decreasing dependency on centralized administration systems. Blockchain technology has raised the bar for privacy and security, and this advancement can be used to assist governments in implementing effective e-administration solutions. The smart contract feature of blockchain technology can accelerate the transition to a smart government where people can interact with public services more actively.
   7.2 Land registries, identity management and authentication, tax collection, and records administration are just a few of the services that may be automated and delivered more efficiently using smart contracts, which are made feasible by the blockchain. Blockchain can be used to guarantee openness and accountability in government. All parties involved are accountable for providing the services they have agreed to, and all transactions can be tracked.
8. Blockchain implementation risks in smart cities
   8.1 Depending on the blockchain application(s) in the city, data consolidation or transfer from several unconnected systems may be required. Existing data run the risk of being insufficient or incorrect. Additionally, under laws like the Protection of Personal Information Act (PoPIA), organizations are required to protect the personal data they have. Determining who and what data can be shared will be challenging.
   8.2 The city as a whole could become a target for cybercriminals due to the various interconnected networks and smart devices, even

though there is no direct threat from blockchain in this area. All of these networked devices and systems could act as entry points for hackers if they are not adequately protected. Any device that is internet- or smart-connected, like a smart camera or parking system, is vulnerable to attack. With just one vulnerable device, criminals can access the entire network; once, a casino was infiltrated using a smart thermometer that was placed in an aquarium! Strict controls must be implemented in order to ensure that the entire chain and network are securely protected.

9. State opportunities in the future
   9.1 One of the major opportunities for blockchain in cities is provided by cryptocurrency. In April 2021, the value of the cryptocurrency market crossed $2 trillion for the first time. As more coins are produced and significant investments are made in this industry by well-known companies like SpaceX and Tesla, the market is well-positioned to grow. This can be included in the business operations of upcoming cities. Companies might think about accepting Bitcoin payments.
   9.2 Other uses, like tokenization, might open up new revenue streams for businesses. Residents of a token village might have access to a variety of options. It is possible to pay for goods and services with tokens. Citizens may also receive incentives for their behaviour as prizes for involvement, such as tokens redeemable for health examinations. Every industry, including sustainability, health care, real estate, and education, is anticipated to have a token community.

CONCLUSION

Both smart cities and blockchain technologies are still in their infancy. Both concepts are fairly all-encompassing and can be used to describe a variety of individuals, teams, and processes. We should anticipate significant progress and breakthroughs in both fields in the near future as more technological developments are made, more people adopt the concepts of a smart city, and more people explore the potential of blockchain technology. Blockchain can drive this innovation and expand the options for applications into the many ecosystems that make up a smart city because of its broad applicability across many industries.

REFERENCES

[1] Salama, R., Al-Turjman, F., Chaudhary, P., & Yadav, S. P. (2023, April). Benefits of Internet of Things (IoT) Applications in Health care – An Overview. In *2023*

International Conference on Computational Intelligence, Communication Technology and Networking (CICTN) (pp. 778–784). IEEE.

[2] Salama, R., Al-Turjman, F., Altrjman, C., & Gupta, R. (2023, April). Machine Learning in Sustainable Development – An Overview. In *2023 International Conference on Computational Intelligence, Communication Technology and Networking (CICTN)* (pp. 806–807). IEEE.

[3] Salama, R., Al-Turjman, F., Aeri, M., & Yadav, S. P. (2023, April). Intelligent Hardware Solutions for COVID-19 and Alike Diagnosis – A survey. In *2023 International Conference on Computational Intelligence, Communication Technology and Networking (CICTN)* (pp. 796–800). IEEE.

[4] Salama, R., Al-Turjman, F., Bhatla, S., & Gautam, D. (2023, April). Network Security, Trust & Privacy in a Wiredwireless Environments – An Overview. In *2023 International Conference on Computational Intelligence, Communication Technology and Networking (CICTN)* (pp. 812–816). IEEE.

[5] Salama, R., Al-Turjman, F., Altrjman, C., Kumar, S., & Chaudhary, P. (2023, April). A Comprehensive Survey of Blockchain-Powered Cybersecurity – A Survey. In *2023 International Conference on Computational Intelligence, Communication Technology and Networking (CICTN)* (pp. 774–777). IEEE.

[6] Salama, R., Al-Turjman, F., Bordoloi, D., & Yadav, S. P. (2023, April). Wireless Sensor Networks and Green Networking for 6G communication – An Overview. In *2023 International Conference on Computational Intelligence, Communication Technology and Networking (CICTN)* (pp. 830–834). IEEE.

[7] Salama, R., Al-Turjman, F., Bhatia, S., & Yadav, S. P. (2023, April). Social Engineering Attack Types and Prevention Techniques – A Survey. In *2023 International Conference on Computational Intelligence, Communication Technology and Networking (CICTN)* (pp. 817–820). IEEE.

[8] Salama, R., Altrjman, C., & Al-Turjman, F. (2023). Smart Grid Applications and Blockchain Technology in the AI Era. *NEU Journal for Artificial Intelligence and Internet of Things*, 1(1), 59–63.

[9] Salama, R., Alturjman, S., & Al-Turjman, F. (2023). Internet of Things and AI in Smart Grid Applications. *NEU Journal for Artificial Intelligence and Internet of Things*, 1(1), 44–58.

[10] Salama, R., Altrjman, C., & Al-Turjman, F. (2023). A Survey of Machine Learning (ML) in Sustainable Systems. *NEU Journal for Artificial Intelligence and Internet of Things*, 2(3).

[11] Salama, R., Altrjman, C., & Al-Turjman, F. (2023). A Survey of Machine Learning Methods for Network Planning. *NEU Journal for Artificial Intelligence and Internet of Things*, 2(3).

[12] Salama, R., Altrjman, C., & Al-Turjman, F. (2023). A Survey of the Architectures and Protocols for Wireless Sensor Networks and Wireless Multimedia Sensor Networks. *NEU Journal for Artificial Intelligence and Internet of Things*, 2(3).

[13] Al-Turjman, F., Salama, R., & Altrjman, C. (2023). Overview of IoT Solutions for Sustainable Transportation Systems. *NEU Journal for Artificial Intelligence and Internet of Things*, 2(3).

[14] Prof. DUX available online: https://dux.aiiot.website/

[15] Salama, R., Al-Turjman, F., Altrjman, C., & Bordoloi, D. (2023, April). The Use of Machine Learning (ML) in Sustainable Systems – An Overview. In *2023 International Conference on Computational Intelligence, Communication Technology and Networking (CICTN)* (pp. 821–824). IEEE.

[16] Al-Turjman, F., & Salama, R. (2021). Cyber Security in Mobile Social Networks. In *Security in IoT Social Networks* (pp. 55–81). Academic Press.
[17] Al-Turjman, F., & Salama, R. (2021). Security in Social Networks. In *Security in IoT Social Networks* (pp. 1–27). Academic Press.
[18] Salama, R., & Al-Turjman, F. (2022, August). AI in Blockchain towards Realizing Cyber Security. In *2022 International Conference on Artificial Intelligence in Everything (AIE)* (pp. 471–475). IEEE.
[19] Al-Turjman, F., & Salama, R. (2020). An Overview about the Cyberattacks in Grid and Like Systems. *Smart Grid in IoT-Enabled Spaces*, 233–247.
[20] Salama, R., Al-Turjman, F., & Culmone, R. (2023, March). AI-Powered Drone to Address Smart City Security Issues. In *International Conference on Advanced Information Networking and Applications* (pp. 292–300). Springer International Publishing.
[21] Salama, R., & Al-Turjman, F. (2023). Cyber-Security Countermeasures and Vulnerabilities to Prevent Social-Engineering Attacks. In *Artificial Intelligence of Health-Enabled Spaces* (pp. 133–144). CRC Press.
[22] Salama, R., Al-Turjman, F., Altrjman, C., & Bordoloi, D. (2023, April). The Ways in Which Artificial Intelligence Improves Several Facets of Cyber Security – A Survey. In *2023 International Conference on Computational Intelligence, Communication Technology and Networking (CICTN)* (pp. 825–829). IEEE.
[23] Salama, R., Al-Turjman, F., Bhatla, S., & Mishra, D. (2023, April). Mobile Edge Fog, Blockchain Networking and Computing – A Survey. In *2023 International Conference on Computational Intelligence, Communication Technology and Networking (CICTN)* (pp. 808–811). IEEE.
[24] Garg, A. (2022). *CoReS-Respiratory Strength Predicting Framework Using Noninvasive Technology for Remote Monitoring During Heath Disasters.* Global Healthcare Disasters: Predicting the Unpredictable with Emerging Technologies, 109–121.
[25] Garg, A., & Goyal, D. P. (Eds.). (2022). *Global Healthcare Disasters: Predicting the Unpredictable with Emerging Technologies.* CRC Press.
[26] Salama, R., Al-Turjman, F., Chaudhary, P., & Banda, L. (2023, April). Future Communication Technology Using Huge Millimeter Waves—An Overview. In *2023 International Conference on Computational Intelligence, Communication Technology and Networking (CICTN)* (pp. 785–790). IEEE.
[27] Salama, R., Al-Turjman, F., Aeri, M., & Yadav, S. P. (2023, April). Internet of Intelligent Things (IoT) – An Overview. In *2023 International Conference on Computational Intelligence, Communication Technology and Networking (CICTN)* (pp. 801–805). IEEE.

Chapter 11

Smart global value chain

Applications across various sectors

Divya Sahu, Mahima Dogra, Veena Grover, and Manju Nandal
School of Management, NIET, Greater Noida, India

Abhijit Ganguly
Westford University College, Sharjah, UAE

INTRODUCTION

Over the past few decades, globalization has changed how countries, companies, and workers contribute to the global economy. The methods of conducting trade have also gone under subsequent changes to keep up with the trends and advancements. The introduction of technologies in this modern era is changing the face of everything as we know it. One such change has been brought into global value chains (GVCs). GVCs are the cross-border networks that bring a product or service from conception to market. Basically, instead of making the product primarily in just one country, GVCs enable multiple countries to come together to conceptualize the idea into reality with shared knowledge and technology (Garg & Ghatak, 2020). The ability to integrate know-how and key components throughout the stages of the supply chain is a key distinct feature of GVCs. With the rapid growth in the technological sector, GVCs have also adopted the technical features. The birth of digital technologies like artificial intelligence (AI), blockchain (BC), and Internet of Things (IoT) has added significant value to GVCs. They got a new identity altogether as smart global value chain (SGVC). With the help of these technologies, the value chains can function more efficiently and with transparency. They play an important role in making GVCs a totally new concept for better businesses and economic systems.

Concept of smart global value chain

The concept of SGVCs is closely tied to Industry 4.0 and the ongoing digital transformation of industries. It represents a shift toward more intelligent and interconnected supply chains that can adapt to the challenges and opportunities of a rapidly changing global marketplace. "Smart global value chain" refers to the integration of digital technologies and data-driven processes within a global supply chain network to enhance efficiency,

DOI: 10.1201/9781003461432-11

visibility, and competitiveness. It represents an evolution of traditional supply chain management by leveraging advanced technologies to optimize various aspects of the supply chain, from sourcing raw materials to delivering finished products to end consumers. It is a modern and technologically advanced approach to managing the various stages and processes involved in the production, distribution, and delivery of goods and services across a global network. It involves the integration of digital technologies, data analytics, and advanced communication systems to optimize and streamline the flow of materials, information, and products within the supply chain. In essence, SGVCs leverage the power of digitalization, data, and automation to transform traditional linear supply chains into highly interconnected, data-driven, and technologically advanced networks (Ghatak & Garg, 2022). This transformation aims to enhance efficiency, reduce costs, improve quality, and enhance competitiveness in the global marketplace.

Features of SGVCs

- **Digitalization**: The core of SGVCs is the digitalization of supply chain processes. This involves the use of technologies like the IoT, sensors, and other data-capturing devices to collect real-time data on the movement and condition of goods throughout the supply chain.
- **Data analytics**: Advanced analytics and machine learning are used to process and analyse the vast amounts of data generated by digital supply chain systems. This allows for better forecasting, demand planning, and optimization of inventory, production, and distribution.
- **Visibility and transparency**: SGVCs provide end-to-end visibility into the entire supply chain. Stakeholders can track the progress of products and materials at every stage, which improves transparency and enables faster decision-making.
- **Automation and robotics**: Automation technologies, including robotic process automation (RPA) and autonomous vehicles, are integrated into the supply chain to streamline tasks such as order picking, packing, and transportation.
- **Blockchain**: Some SGVCs incorporate blockchain technology to secure and verify transactions and data sharing among supply chain participants. This can enhance trust and reduce the risk of fraud.
- **Collaboration and integration**: Collaboration among supply chain partners is critical in SGVC. Data and information are shared seamlessly among suppliers, manufacturers, logistics providers, and customers to optimize processes and respond to changes in real time.
- **Customization and responsiveness**: With better data and analytics, SGVCs can become more agile and responsive to changes in customer demand or disruptions in the supply chain. This enables the production of customized products and quicker adaptations to market trends.

- **Sustainability**: Sustainability considerations, such as reducing carbon emissions and minimizing waste, are often integrated into SGVCs. Data analytics can help identify areas for improvement in sustainability practices.
- **Risk management**: The ability to quickly identify and mitigate risks is enhanced in SGVC. Data-driven insights help in identifying potential disruptions and developing contingency plans.
- **Customer-centricity**: Ultimately, SGVC is focused on meeting customer demands efficiently and effectively. By leveraging data and technology, it aims to provide a seamless and personalized customer experience.
- **Real-time monitoring**: Continuous monitoring and tracking of inventory levels, production processes, transportation routes, and other critical aspects of the supply chain to identify and address issues promptly.
- **Transparency**: End-to-end visibility into the supply chain, providing stakeholders with real-time access to information about the status of orders, inventory levels, and delivery schedules.
- **Responsive and agile**: The capability to quickly adapt to changes in market conditions, customer demands, or disruptions by making data-driven decisions and adjusting supply chain strategies accordingly.

Advantage of smart global value chain

SGVCs refer to the use of advanced technologies and digitalization to optimize and streamline the production and distribution of goods and services across international borders. There are several benefits associated with the adoption of SGVCs:

- **Efficiency improvement**: SGVCs leverage technology to enhance the efficiency of production processes. This can lead to reduced production costs, shorter lead times, and improved overall supply chain efficiency.
- **Cost reduction**: By using data analytics, automation, and digital platforms, companies can identify cost-saving opportunities within the supply chain. This includes minimizing waste, optimizing transportation routes, and reducing inventory holding costs.
- **Increased agility**: SGVCs enable companies to quickly adapt to changes in market demand or supply disruptions. Real-time data and analytics allow for faster decision-making and the ability to pivot production or sourcing strategies when necessary.
- **Enhanced visibility**: Digitalization provides better visibility into the entire supply chain, from raw materials to the end consumer. This transparency can help identify bottlenecks, monitor product quality, and ensure compliance with regulations.

- **Improved customer service**: SGVCs enable companies to better understand customer preferences and demands through data analytics. This information can be used to tailor products and services to meet customer needs more effectively.
- **Risk mitigation**: By diversifying suppliers and using data-driven risk assessments, companies can reduce their exposure to supply chain disruptions, such as natural disasters or geopolitical events.
- **Innovation facilitation**: Collaboration and information-sharing across GVCs can foster innovation. Companies can tap into the expertise of partners and suppliers, leading to the development of new products and processes.
- **Sustainability**: SGVCs can help reduce the environmental footprint of supply chains. By optimizing transportation routes and reducing waste, companies can lower their carbon emissions and contribute to sustainability goals.
- **Market access**: SGVCs can help companies access new markets by providing insights into local consumer preferences and regulatory requirements. This can be particularly valuable for businesses looking to expand internationally.
- **Competitive advantage**: Companies that embrace SGVCs are often better positioned to compete in the global marketplace. They can respond more effectively to changing market conditions and offer superior products and services.
- **Job creation**: While automation is a component of SGVCs, the increased efficiency and growth they can generate may lead to job creation in sectors related to technology, logistics, and innovation.
- **Global collaboration**: SGVCs promote collaboration among businesses, governments, and international organizations. This can foster economic development and improve international relations.

It is important to note that realizing these benefits often requires significant investment in technology, infrastructure, and talent. Moreover, companies must address cybersecurity concerns and data privacy issues when implementing SGVC strategies. Nonetheless, for many organizations, the advantages of adopting SGVCs can outweigh the challenges.

Disadvantage of smart global value chain

While there are numerous advantages to implementing SGVCs, there are also several disadvantages and challenges associated with this approach. It is essential for businesses and policymakers to be aware of these drawbacks and address them effectively:

- **Initial investment costs**: The initial investment required to digitize and modernize a supply chain can be substantial. Smaller organizations may face financial constraints when attempting to implement SGVC technologies and processes. Transitioning to SGVCs often requires a significant upfront investment in technology, infrastructure, and talent. Smaller businesses may struggle to afford these costs, potentially leading to increased market concentration.

- **Digital skills gap**: The adoption of SGVCs demands a workforce with digital literacy and technological skills. Many regions face a shortage of workers with these qualifications, which can hinder implementation.
- **Data security and privacy concerns**: The increased reliance on digital data and connectivity exposes businesses to greater cybersecurity risks. Cyberattacks can disrupt operations, compromise sensitive information, and damage a company's reputation.
- **Dependency on technology**: Overreliance on technology can leave companies vulnerable to disruptions caused by technical glitches, system failures, or cyberattacks. This dependence can also make it challenging to manage unexpected changes or crises.
- **Supply chain complexity**: The integration of various technologies, systems, and data sources can make supply chain management more complex. Organizations need skilled personnel and robust IT infrastructure to manage and troubleshoot these complex systems effectively. While SGVCs can optimize processes, they can also make supply chains more complex and difficult to manage. Companies may struggle to keep track of numerous interconnected suppliers and partners.
- **Job displacement**: Automation and digitalization within SGVCs can lead to job displacement in certain industries or roles. Workers with less technological expertise may find it challenging to adapt to these changes.
- **Environmental concerns**: The rapid growth of GVCs, driven in part by smart technologies, can contribute to increased carbon emissions and environmental degradation, especially if transportation and logistics are not optimized for sustainability.
- **Dependency on global partners**: Companies participating in SGVCs often rely on partners and suppliers from different countries. Political or economic instability in one of these countries can disrupt the entire value chain.
- **Intellectual property risks**: Sharing data and information across international borders can expose businesses to intellectual property theft or infringement risks, especially when dealing with partners in regions with weaker intellectual property protections.
- **Regulatory and compliance challenges**: SGVCs may involve navigating complex and evolving regulations related to data privacy, trade, and taxation, which can be particularly challenging when operating across multiple jurisdictions.
- **Loss of local jobs**: As companies optimize their supply chains globally, they may shift production and sourcing away from local communities, leading to the loss of jobs in those regions.

- **Ethical concerns**: The pursuit of cost savings and efficiency in SGVCs can sometimes lead to ethical concerns related to labour practices, human rights, and environmental sustainability.
- **Inequality and concentration of wealth**: SGVCs can contribute to income inequality if the benefits disproportionately flow to larger corporations or technologically advanced countries, leaving smaller businesses and less-developed regions behind.

It is important to note that the disadvantages of SGVCs can be mitigated with proper planning, investment, and governance. Companies should carefully assess the trade-offs and risks associated with adopting SGVCs and develop strategies to address these challenges while maximizing the benefits. Government policies and international cooperation can also play a role in addressing some of these issues, such as data security, labour practices, and environmental sustainability.

How is smart global value chain different from simple global value chain?

The concepts of SGVCs and simple GVCs pertain to distinct methodologies for the coordination and administration of the manufacturing and dissemination of commodities and services beyond national boundaries. The following are the primary distinctions between the two:

- **Technology integration**: The incorporation of technology into various aspects of education and learning processes. SGVCs are extensively exploiting sophisticated technologies, digitization, and data analytics. Organizations employ various technological technologies such as IoT, AI, blockchain, and cloud computing to optimize operational procedures, augment productivity, and improve the quality of decision-making.

  GVCs are characterized by their reliance on conventional methods and their limited use of technology. Frequently, manual procedures are employed and digital solutions for supply chain management may not be effectively utilized.
- **Complexity**: The concept of complexity refers to the level of intricacy or difficulty in a system, process. SGVCs are characterized by their heightened complexity, which arises from the integration of advanced technologies and the active participation of several stakeholders. Frequently, these entities encompass a diverse range of partners, suppliers, and service providers that are networked via digital platforms.

  GVCs are generally characterized by their reduced complexity and a smaller number of components in motion. There is a possibility that there will be a reduced number of intermediaries and partners participating in the value chain.

- **Data and analytics**: The field of data and analytics includes the collection, analysis, and interpretation of data to gain insights and inform decision-making processes. Data and analytics are key components inside SGVCs. The collection and analysis of real-time data are utilized to make educated decisions, optimize operations, and enhance the performance of supply chains. In the context of GVCs, the use of data and analytics is comparatively limited. The accessibility and utilization of information for decision-making may be limited.
- **Supply chain visibility**: The concept of supply chain visibility refers to the ability of organizations to have a clear and comprehensive understanding of the movement of goods and information throughout their supply chain network. SGVCs provide enhanced transparency into the many aspects of supply chain operations, enabling the monitoring of inventories, production advancements, and distribution in real time. Enhanced visibility facilitates the early identification and resolution of concerns.

  In the context of GVCs, it is worth noting that supply chain visibility can be constrained in simple GVCs, hence presenting heightened difficulties in effectively monitoring product movements and promptly addressing disturbances.
- **Flexibility and adaptability**: The concepts of flexibility and adaptability are crucial in several contexts. SGVCs possess enhanced adaptability to fluctuations in market demand, disruptions in supply, and other external variables owing to their advanced capabilities in real-time data collection and analytics. Organizations possess the ability to adapt and respond promptly to dynamic situations.

  GVCs exhibit a reduced level of flexibility and increased rigidity when it comes to adapting to changes. This is mostly due to their reliance on fixed processes and lengthier lead times.
- **Cost efficiency**: The concept of cost efficiency refers to the ability to achieve maximum output or desired results while minimizing the resources or costs involved. The incorporation of technology inside intelligent GVCs has the potential to generate cost reductions through enhancing resource allocation, minimizing waste, and optimizing logistics.

  GVCs: Basic GVCs may present limited possibilities for cost optimization due to their potential absence of data-driven insights and automation capabilities, which are characteristic of advanced GVCs.
- **Competitive advantage**: The concept of competitive advantage refers to the strategic advantage that a company has over its competitors in the marketplace. Companies that use SGVCs have the potential to achieve a competitive edge by providing supply chains that are more efficient and responsive. This, in turn, can result in enhanced customer satisfaction and increased market positioning.

  GVCs may encounter difficulties in maintaining competitiveness due to their limited efficiency and adaptability compared to SGVCs.

In essence, the fundamental distinction between SGVCs and simple GVCs resides in the degree of technology integration and intricacy. Intelligent GVCs employ sophisticated technology and data-centric methodologies to enhance the efficiency of supply chain operations, whereas rudimentary GVCs rely on conventional practices and may exhibit limited technological integration. The selection of these methodologies is contingent upon various aspects, including a firm's available resources, industry context, and strategic objectives.

Application of smart global value chain in different sectors

SGVCs leverage technology, data, and advanced supply chain management practices to optimize the production and distribution of goods and services across the world. They offer several benefits, including cost reduction, increased efficiency, and improved competitiveness. SGVCs can be applied across various sectors to transform traditional supply chains. There are different applications of SGVCs that can be applied in different sectors like manufacturing, agriculture, education, health-care, and hospitality sectors as shown in Figure 11.1. In each of these sectors, SGVCs can significantly improve efficiency, reduce waste, enhance quality, and create new opportunities for innovation and competitiveness. However, the successful implementation of SGVCs often requires a combination of technological investments, data management strategies, and a shift in organizational culture.

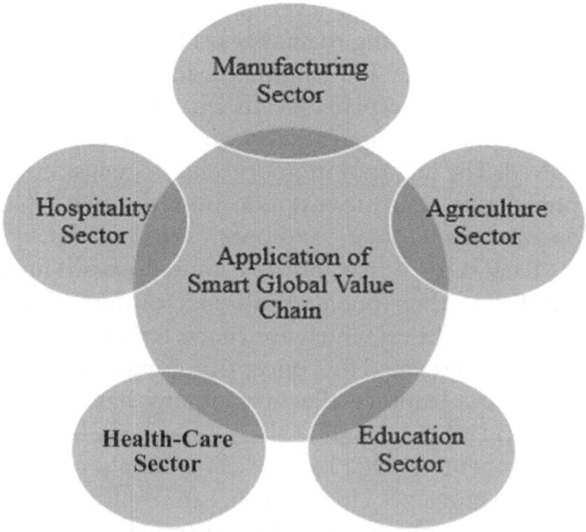

Figure 11.1 Application of SGVC in various sector.

Application of smart global value chain in the manufacturing sector

The implementation of the GVC enables companies to reduce manufacturing expenses throughout every aspect of the production system (Polloni-Silva et al., 2021). With the growing prominence of GVCs in international trade, the concept of comparative advantage in trade is observed in the different phases of production rather than in the form of bundled goods and services (Sun et al., 2019). The competitiveness of the manufacturing industry is significantly associated with sustainable manufacturing and its carbon efficiency in the supply chain (Deqiang et al., 2021). The concept of SGVCs in the manufacturing business can be categorized into three primary types – namely, technology, production, and marketing, as proposed by Galbraith (1982). Pananond (2013) conducted a study that examined the relationship between the GVC and several aspects of business operations, including research and development (R&D), manufacturing, Original Equipment Manufacturers (OEMs), as well as sales and marketing. The study specifically focused on the diffusion of information throughout the domains (Deqiang et al., 2021). In addition to the generation of value-added goods, value chains can be categorized into high value-added activities, such as technological R&D and marketing, and low value-added activities, which encompass production assembly in the context of brand marketing (Sears, 2017). Within the GVC of the manufacturing sector, numerous value-added divisions may be identified. However, it is noteworthy that most of these divisions share three fundamental activities: R&D, manufacturing, and marketing. SGVCs play a crucial role in the manufacturing sector by leveraging advanced technologies and digitalization to optimize and transform various aspects of the manufacturing process. Here are some key applications and roles of SGVC in the manufacturing sector:

- **Supply chain optimization**: SGVCs enable manufacturers to optimize their supply chains by integrating suppliers, distributors, and logistics providers. Real-time data and analytics help in demand forecasting, inventory management, and transportation optimization, reducing lead times and costs.
- **Advanced manufacturing technologies**: SGVCs facilitate the adoption of advanced manufacturing technologies such as 3D printing, robotics, and automation. These technologies improve production efficiency, precision, and flexibility while reducing labour costs.
- **Quality control and assurance**: Data analytics and sensors in SGVCs allow manufacturers to monitor and control the quality of products in real time. This reduces defects and ensures that products meet high-quality standards.

- **Digital twin technology**: Manufacturers can create digital twins of physical products and production processes, allowing for virtual testing, simulation, and optimization. Digital twins enhance product development and production efficiency.
- **Customization and personalization**: SGVCs enable mass customization and personalized manufacturing. Manufacturers can produce customized products at scale, catering to individual customer preferences.
- **Energy efficiency and sustainability**: SGVCs support energy-efficient manufacturing processes by optimizing energy usage and reducing waste. Sustainability initiatives, such as recycling and reducing carbon emissions, are facilitated through data-driven decisions.
- **Predictive maintenance**: Manufacturers can implement predictive maintenance programmes using data analytics. Sensors and machine learning algorithms predict when equipment needs maintenance, reducing downtime and maintenance costs.
- **Global collaboration and outsourcing**: SGVCs enable collaboration with global partners and suppliers. Manufacturers can source components and expertise from around the world, often at competitive prices.
- **Smart factories and IoT integration**: SGVCs support the development of smart factories where machinery, equipment, and systems are interconnected through the IoT. Manufacturers gain real-time visibility into factory operations and can make data-driven decisions for process optimization.
- **Demand-driven production**: Data analytics and market insights help manufacturers align production with actual demand, reducing excess inventory and storage costs. Just-in-time manufacturing becomes more efficient.
- **Traceability and compliance**: SGVCs enable manufacturers to track products and materials throughout the supply chain. This ensures compliance with regulations and allows for quick identification and resolution of issues such as recalls.
- **Employee training and skill development**: Manufacturing companies can use SGVCs for employee training and skill development through virtual reality (VR) and augmented reality (AR) technologies. Workers can learn and practice skills in a safe and immersive environment.
- **Data-driven decision-making**: Manufacturers can make data-driven decisions at every stage of the value chain, from design and production to distribution and customer service. This enhances operational efficiency and competitiveness.

In summary, SGVCs are transforming the manufacturing sector by improving efficiency, quality, and sustainability while enabling greater customization and global collaboration. These technologies are essential for manufacturers looking to stay competitive in a rapidly evolving market.

Application of smart global value chain in the agriculture sector

SGVC in agriculture refers to the application of advanced technologies and data-driven strategies to optimize the production, distribution, and management of agricultural products on a global scale. It involves integrating digital innovations, analytics, and automation throughout the agricultural value chain to enhance productivity, sustainability, and competitiveness. It aims to enhance agricultural productivity, reduce waste, increase food security, and promote sustainability. It contributes to more efficient resource utilization, improved crop quality, and the ability to meet the growing global demand for food in a responsible and environmentally friendly manner.

SGVC in agriculture can benefit both producers and consumers by improving agricultural productivity, reducing waste, increasing food security, and promoting sustainable farming practices. It also plays a crucial role in addressing global challenges, such as feeding a growing population and mitigating the environmental impact of agriculture. Implementing precision agriculture techniques that use sensors, GPS technology, and data analytics to optimize farming operations. This includes precision planting, irrigation, and fertilization, which reduce resource use and improve crop yields. Deploying IoT devices and sensors to monitor soil conditions, weather patterns, and crop health in real time. These sensors provide valuable data to farmers, allowing them to make data-driven decisions. Enhancing transparency and traceability in the agricultural supply chain. This includes tracking the movement of agricultural products from farm to table, which can be especially important for food safety and compliance. Using farm management software to streamline administrative tasks, track expenses, and monitor overall farm performance. This can improve decision-making and resource allocation.

Embracing sustainable agriculture practices that reduce environmental impact, such as organic farming, crop rotation, and reduced chemical pesticide use. Implementing these strategies to mitigate the impact of climate change on agriculture, such as drought-resistant crop varieties and water-efficient irrigation systems. Ensuring these agricultural practices adhere to local and international regulations related to food safety, environmental protection, and labour standards. In summary, SGVCs possess the capacity to revolutionize the agricultural industry by enhancing its efficiency, resilience, and inclusion. Additionally, they are capable of addressing urgent issues such as food security, climate change, and rural development.

Application of smart global value chain in the education sector

SGVC concepts and technologies can have several applications in the education sector, helping institutions and learners enhance the quality and accessibility of education. It can play a significant role in the education sector by leveraging technology and data to enhance various aspects of teaching, learning, and administration. Here are some key applications and roles of SGVC in the education sector:

- **Global collaboration and partnerships**: SGVCs enable educational institutions to collaborate with partners worldwide, facilitating the exchange of knowledge, resources, and expertise. This can include international research collaborations, collaborative degree programmes, and knowledge exchange initiatives, providing students with a more diverse global learning environment.
- **Online learning and e-learning**: SGVCs support the development and delivery of online courses and e-learning programmes. This allows educational institutions to reach a broader audience, including learners in remote or underserved areas, and provide flexible learning options. Institutions can offer a wide range of online courses to reach a broader audience, including students in remote or underserved areas. The technologies enable flexible and personalized learning experiences tailored to individual student needs.
- **Data analytics for personalized learning**: SGVCs utilize data analytics to track student performance and engagement. Learning analytics can help identify struggling students early, allowing for targeted interventions and personalized support. Adaptive learning systems can adjust course content and difficulty levels based on individual progress.
- **Administrative efficiency**: Educational institutions can use SGVCs to streamline administrative processes such as enrolment, scheduling, and resource allocation. Automation and data-driven decision-making can lead to cost savings and improved operational efficiency.
- **Digital content distribution**: SGVCs facilitate the distribution of digital learning materials, reducing the need for physical textbooks and printed resources. Institutions can update and distribute course materials more efficiently, keeping content up-to-date and accessible to students.
- **VR and AR**: SGVCs can incorporate VR and AR technologies to create immersive learning experiences. Students can explore historical sites, conduct virtual experiments, or engage in hands-on training in a simulated environment.
- **Global career opportunities**: Education providers can prepare students for global careers by offering courses and resources that focus on international skills and cross-cultural competencies. SGVCs can connect students with internships, job opportunities, and networking events worldwide.
- **Remote and hybrid learning models**: SGVCs support the implementation of remote and hybrid learning models, which became crucial during the COVID-19 pandemic. They enable seamless transitions between in-person and online learning as needed.

- **Lifelong learning and continuing education**: SGVCs make it easier for individuals to access continuing education and upskilling opportunities throughout their careers. Employers can offer employees access to online courses and resources to support ongoing professional development.
- **Quality assurance and accreditation**: SGVCs can aid in the accreditation and quality assurance processes by providing data and evidence of educational outcomes. Institutions can demonstrate compliance with standards and benchmarks more effectively.

In summary, SGVCs offer the education sector a range of tools and strategies to improve the quality, accessibility, and efficiency of educational services, making learning more adaptable to the needs of students and educators in a rapidly changing world.

Application of smart global value chain in the health-care sector

The concept of an "SGVC" can be particularly relevant and transformative in the health-care sector. In health care, the focus is on providing timely, efficient, and high-quality care to patients while managing costs effectively. Implementing an SGVC in the health-care sector involves leveraging advanced technologies and data-driven strategies to optimize the delivery of health-care services, streamline processes, improve patient outcomes, and enhance overall health-care system efficiency (Garg, 2022). SGVC in the health-care sector requires careful planning, investment in technology infrastructure, and collaboration among stakeholders. When successfully implemented, it can lead to improved patient outcomes, cost savings, and a more responsive and patient-centred health-care system. Expanding access to health-care services through telemedicine, enabling patients to consult with health-care providers remotely. Additionally, remote monitoring devices can collect real-time patient data, allowing for early intervention and better disease management. Using predictive analytics to identify at-risk patients and anticipate health-care needs. This can help health-care organizations allocate resources efficiently and focus on preventive care.

Implementing AI and machine learning algorithms to assist with diagnostics, drug discovery, and treatment recommendations. AI can help health-care providers make more accurate and timely decisions (Garg, 2023). Utilizing IoT devices and wearables to collect health data from patients. This data can provide insights into patient health trends and support remote monitoring. Using blockchain technology to secure patient data and ensure privacy and data integrity. This is crucial for maintaining patient trust and complying with regulations. Employing digital tools and mobile apps to engage patients in their own health care. These tools can provide health information, appointment scheduling, and medication reminders, fostering greater patient responsibility for their well-being. Ensuring that digital health solutions comply with relevant health-care regulations and standards to maintain data security and patient privacy.

Analysing health-care data to identify trends in population health, target interventions, and manage chronic diseases more effectively at the community level. Ensuring a steady and efficient supply chain for pharmaceuticals, medical equipment, and supplies. Smart supply chain management can reduce waste, lower costs, and ensure the availability of critical health-care resources.

Application of smart global value chain in the hospitality sector

SGVCs can play a significant role in the hospitality sector by leveraging technology and data to enhance various aspects of guest experiences, operations, and business management. Here are some key applications and roles of SGVC in the hospitality sector:

- **Digital reservations and booking systems**: SGVCs enable hotels, resorts, and other hospitality businesses to implement advanced reservation and booking systems. These systems can offer real-time availability, pricing optimization, and personalized booking recommendations based on guest preferences and historical data.
- **Guest data and personalization**: SGVCs utilize data analytics to capture and analyse guest information, including preferences, past stays, and feedback. Hotels can use this data to personalize the guest experience, offering tailored services, room amenities, and dining options.
- **Mobile check-in and keyless entry**: Hospitality businesses can implement mobile check-in and keyless entry systems, reducing wait times and enhancing convenience for guests. Guests can use their smartphones to check in, access their rooms, and control room features.
- **Smart room technology**: SGVCs facilitate the integration of in-room technology, such as voice-activated assistants, IoT devices, and interactive in-room tablets. Guests can control lighting, temperature, entertainment, and room service through these systems.
- **Efficient housekeeping and maintenance**: Hotel staff can use SGVCs to optimize housekeeping and maintenance operations. Sensors and data analytics can help predict when rooms need cleaning or maintenance, improving efficiency and guest satisfaction.
- **Inventory and supply chain management**: Hospitality businesses can optimize their supply chain and inventory management using SGVCs. These systems can automate the procurement of supplies and ingredients, reducing waste and ensuring timely replenishment.
- **Customer relationship management (CRM)**: SGVCs support CRM systems that allow hotels to manage guest interactions, track guest

feedback, and maintain a database of guest profiles. CRM data can inform marketing strategies and guest engagement efforts.

- **Food and beverage optimization**: Restaurants and food service establishments within the hospitality sector can use SGVCs to optimize menu offerings, pricing, and inventory. Data-driven insights can help restaurants tailor their offerings to guest preferences.
- **Sustainability and energy management**: SGVCs can assist in implementing sustainability initiatives within the hospitality sector. Hotels can monitor and reduce energy consumption, water usage, and waste through smart technologies.
- **Revenue management and pricing strategies**: Hospitality businesses can implement dynamic pricing strategies and revenue management systems. These systems use data to adjust room rates based on demand, occupancy, and market conditions.
- **Guest feedback and reputation management**: SGVCs can monitor online reviews and guest feedback across various platforms. Hotels can respond to guest reviews promptly and address concerns, enhancing their online reputation.
- **Training and workforce development**: SGVCs support e-learning and training programmes for hospitality staff. Training modules can be delivered digitally to improve employee skills and service quality.

In summary, SGVCs offer the hospitality sector a range of tools and strategies to enhance guest experiences, optimize operations, and drive business growth. These technologies enable hotels and related businesses to stay competitive, adapt to changing guest expectations, and deliver more efficient and personalized services.

Limitation of SGVCs in human life

While SGVCs offer numerous advantages and opportunities for businesses and economies, they also come with limitations and potential drawbacks that can impact human life. Here are some of the key limitations to consider:

- **Job displacement**: As automation and advanced technologies become more prevalent in SGVCs, there is a risk of job displacement, particularly in sectors that rely heavily on manual labour. This can lead to unemployment and income inequality, potentially harming individuals and communities.
- **Data privacy and security concerns**: The increased use of data in SGVCs raises concerns about data privacy and security. Mishandling or breaches of sensitive data can have serious consequences for individuals, including identity theft and financial loss.
- **Dependency on technology**: Overreliance on smart technologies can make societies vulnerable to disruptions caused by cyberattacks,

technical glitches, or natural disasters. Dependence on technology can also lead to a loss of essential skills in case of system failures.

- **Environmental impact**: While SGVCs can optimize supply chains and reduce waste, they may also contribute to environmental issues. For example, the manufacturing and disposal of electronic components and devices can lead to e-waste and environmental pollution.
- **Globalization challenges**: The globalization facilitated by GVCs can result in economic interdependence, making countries vulnerable to global economic crises and supply chain disruptions. Additionally, globalization can lead to cultural homogenization, eroding local traditions and identities.
- **Ethical concerns**: The pursuit of efficiency and profit in GVCs may sometimes lead to ethical dilemmas, such as exploitation of labour, human rights violations, or disregard for environmental sustainability.
- **Skills gap**: As GVCs become more technology-driven, there may be a growing skills gap where workers lack the necessary expertise to operate and maintain advanced systems. This can hinder employment opportunities and career development.
- **Health and well-being**: The rapid pace and demands of GVCs can contribute to stress and burnout among workers, affecting their physical and mental health. Long working hours, constant connectivity, and job insecurity are some common stressors (Garg & Singla, 2013).
- **Digital divide**: Not everyone has equal access to the benefits of SGVCs. The digital divide, driven by disparities in internet access, technology literacy, and resources, can exacerbate inequalities in education, health-care, and economic opportunities.
- **Loss of human touch**: In sectors like health care and customer service, increasing automation and reliance on technology can reduce the human touch and personalized interactions that many people value.

To address these limitations and maximize the benefits of SGVCs, it is essential for governments, businesses, and societies to adopt responsible and inclusive approaches. This may include investing in education and skills development, establishing regulations and safeguards for data privacy and security, and promoting ethical business practices that prioritize the welfare of workers and communities.

CONCLUSION

In conclusion, SGVCs represent a transformative approach to managing and optimizing supply chains across various sectors. The application of SGVCs holds significant promise in enhancing efficiency, reducing costs, and driving innovation. However, it is essential to consider both the advantages and challenges associated with their implementation. SGVCs have the potential to revolutionize industries by leveraging technologies such as IoT, data analytics, automation, and AI (Garg & Singla, 2017). This can lead to SGVCs enabling real-time monitoring, predictive maintenance, and data-driven decision-making, resulting in streamlined operations and reduced waste.

Businesses that adopt SGVC strategies can respond more quickly to market changes, offer tailored products and services, and gain a competitive edge. The use of digital twins, traceability, and data analytics can ensure higher product quality and safety standards. SGVCs can reduce environmental impact by optimizing resource utilization, reducing emissions, and supporting sustainable practices. SGVCs facilitate easier access to global markets, helping businesses reach a wider customer base and diversify their revenue streams. However, it is crucial to address the limitations and challenges of SGVCs, including potential job displacement, data privacy concerns, and environmental impacts. Ethical considerations, such as fair labour practices and responsible data handling, must be integrated into the adoption of these technologies.

In summary, the application of SGVCs has the potential to reshape industries, improve competitiveness, and enhance the quality of products and services. To fully harness their benefits while mitigating potential drawbacks, a comprehensive approach that includes regulation, workforce development, and ethical considerations is necessary. SGVCs are not a panacea, but when implemented thoughtfully and responsibly, they can contribute to economic growth and improved quality of life in a rapidly evolving global economy.

REFERENCES

Deqiang, S., Zhijun, C., Hajduk-Stelmachowicz, M., Larik, A. R., & Rafique, M. Z. (2021). The role of the global value chain in improving trade and the sustainable competitive advantage: Evidence from China's manufacturing industry. *Frontiers in Environmental Science*, 508.

Sun, C., Li, Z., Ma, T., & He, R. (2019). Carbon efficiency and international specialization position: Evidence from global value chain position index of manufacture. *Energy Policy*, 128, 235–242.

Polloni-Silva, E., Ferraz, D., Camioto, F. D. C., Rebelatto, D. A. D. N., & Moralles, H. F. (2021). Environmental Kuznets curve and the pollution-halo/haven hypotheses: An investigation in Brazilian Municipalities. *Sustainability*, 13(8), 4114.

Galbraith, J. R. (1982). Designing the innovating organization. *Organizational Dynamics*, 10(3), 5–25.

Garg, A., & Ghatak, A. (2020). An empirical study on power evacuation projects' performance: A strategic layout in the Indian context. *Asia-Pacific Journal of Management Research and Innovation*, 16(1), 31–42.

Ghatak, A., & Garg, A. (2022). Power transmission project: A framework to align project success with organization goal. *International Journal of System Assurance Engineering and Management*, 13(4), 1817–1833.

Garg, A., & Singla, N. (2017). Environment sustainability awareness model for IT SMEs. *Interdisciplinary Environmental Review*, 18(1), 1–5.

Garg, A., & Singla, N. (2013). E-waste vis-à-vis human health and environment. *Interdisciplinary Environmental Review*, 14(3–4), 187–193.

Pananond, P. (2013). Where do we go from here? Globalizing subsidiaries moving up the value chain. *Journal of International Management*, 19(3), 207–219.

Sears, J. B. (2017). When are acquired technological capabilities complements rather than substitutes? A study on value creation. *Journal of Business Research*, 78, 33–42.

Garg, A. (Ed.). (2023). *Reinventing Technological Innovations with Artificial Intelligence*. Bentham Science Publishers.

Garg, A. (2022). *CoReS-Respiratory Strength Predicting Framework Using Noninvasive Technology for Remote Monitoring During Heath Disasters*. Global Healthcare Disasters: Predicting the Unpredictable with Emerging Technologies, 109–121.

https://link.springer.com/article/10.1007/s40171-018-0186-8

https://unstats.un.org/unsd/business-stat/GVC/

https://www.adb.org/publications/global-value-chain-development-report-2021

https://www.researchgate.net/publication/265892395_Global_Value_Chain_Analysis_A_Primer

https://core.ac.uk/reader/81684630

Chapter 12

Smart global value chains in the manufacturing industry

Sumit Rastogi, Rachita Kapoor Bhasin, Priyanshi Sharma, Upesh Bhatnagar, and Tanushree Shrivastav
Asian Business School, Noida, India

INTRODUCTION

The application of smart global value chains (SGVCs) in the manufacturing industry is transforming traditional production processes and revolutionizing the way businesses operate. The application of SGVCs in the manufacturing industry is a strategic imperative for staying competitive in today's rapidly changing business environment. By embracing digital technologies and data-driven approaches, manufacturers can enhance productivity, reduce costs, improve quality, and respond more effectively to customer demands.

Here are some key applications of SGVCs in the manufacturing sector:

1. **Real-time monitoring and predictive maintenance**: SGVCs leverage IoT sensors and connected devices to monitor machinery and equipment in real time. This enables manufacturers to detect issues and anomalies before they cause downtime, reducing maintenance costs and improving overall equipment efficiency (OEE).
2. **Supply chain visibility and transparency**: SGVCs provide end-to-end visibility into the supply chain. Manufacturers can track the movement of raw materials, components, and finished products in real time. This visibility helps in identifying bottlenecks, optimizing inventory levels, and ensuring timely deliveries.
3. **Customization and personalization**: SGVCs allow for greater customization and personalization of products. With real-time data on consumer preferences and market trends, manufacturers can adjust production processes to meet individual customer needs, resulting in higher customer satisfaction and potentially premium pricing.
4. **Data-driven decision-making**: Advanced analytics and AI algorithms are used to analyse the vast amount of data generated throughout the value chain. This data-driven approach helps manufacturers make informed decisions about production scheduling, quality control, and demand forecasting.

DOI: 10.1201/9781003461432-12

5. **Collaborative robotics (cobots)**: SGVCs incorporate collaborative robots that can work alongside human workers. These cobots enhance productivity, safety, and flexibility in manufacturing operations. They can be quickly reprogrammed for different tasks, making it easier to adapt to changing production requirements.
6. **Global supplier integration**: Through digital platforms and cloud-based systems, SGVCs enable seamless integration with global suppliers. Manufacturers can collaborate with suppliers in real time, share design and production data, and ensure the timely availability of materials and components.
7. **Quality control and traceability**: SGVCs implement advanced quality control systems that use sensors and AI to monitor product quality throughout the manufacturing process. This ensures consistent quality and provides traceability for regulatory compliance.
8. **Energy efficiency**: Manufacturers can optimize energy consumption by using SGVCs to monitor and control equipment more efficiently. This not only reduces operational costs but also aligns with sustainability goals.
9. **Supply chain resilience**: SGVCs allow manufacturers to quickly adapt to disruptions in the supply chain, such as natural disasters or geopolitical events. By having real-time data and alternative sourcing options, they can mitigate risks and maintain business continuity.
10. **Market expansion**: SGVCs enable manufacturers to enter new markets more easily. They can adjust product configurations and manufacturing processes to meet specific regulatory and customer requirements in different regions.
11. **Inventory optimization**: Through data analytics and real-time tracking, SGVCs enable manufacturers to optimize inventory levels. This reduces carrying costs while ensuring that essential materials and components are always available when needed.
12. **Demand forecasting and planning**: Manufacturers can use AI and machine learning algorithms to improve demand forecasting accuracy. SGVCs analyse historical sales data, market trends, and other variables to generate more precise forecasts, reducing the risk of overstocking or stockouts.
13. **Quality assurance and compliance**: SGVCs incorporate advanced quality control measures, including automated inspections and compliance checks. This ensures that products meet industry standards and regulatory requirements, reducing the risk of recalls or fines.
14. **Sustainable manufacturing**: SGVCs play a crucial role in advancing sustainable manufacturing practices. By monitoring energy consumption, waste production, and emissions, manufacturers can reduce their environmental footprint and align with sustainability goals.
15. **E-commerce integration**: For manufacturers entering the e-commerce space, SGVCs facilitate seamless integration with online marketplaces

and order fulfilment systems. This enables efficient processing of online orders, faster delivery times, and improved customer experiences.

16. **Blockchain for supply chain transparency**: Some manufacturers use blockchain technology within their GVCs to enhance transparency and traceability. This is especially important in industries like food and pharmaceuticals, where tracking the origin and journey of products is critical for safety and authenticity.
17. **Advanced robotics and automation**: Beyond collaborative robots, SGVCs employ advanced robotics and automation solutions. These include automated guided vehicles (AGVs), autonomous drones, and robotic arms capable of complex tasks. These technologies increase productivity and reduce labour costs.
18. **3D Printing and additive manufacturing**: SGVCs can integrate 3D printing and additive manufacturing technologies, allowing for on-demand and decentralized production. This reduces lead times and enables the creation of highly customized products.
19. **Digital twins**: Manufacturers use digital twin technology to create virtual replicas of physical products and processes. These digital twins can be used for testing, simulation, and optimization before physical production, reducing the risk of errors and improving product quality.
20. **Cybersecurity and data protection**: With the increased digitalization of manufacturing processes, SGVCs prioritize cybersecurity. Robust security measures are put in place to protect sensitive data and intellectual property from cyber threats.
21. **Employee training and upskilling**: The implementation of SGVCs often necessitates a skilled workforce. Manufacturers invest in employee training and upskilling programmes to ensure that their workforce can operate and maintain the new technologies effectively.
22. **Continuous improvement**: SGVCs support a culture of continuous improvement. Manufacturers use real-time data and analytics to identify areas for enhancement, implement changes, and iterate on processes to increase efficiency and competitiveness.

REVIEW OF LITERATURE

SGVCs have emerged as a pivotal paradigm shift in the manufacturing industry, redefining how businesses operate in a hyper-connected world. This review of literature explores key studies and findings in this dynamic field, shedding light on the transformative effects of technology and data-driven approaches. Notably, Porter and Heppelmann (2014) argue that the integration of the Internet of Things (IoT) and data analytics in manufacturing processes leads to the creation of SGVCs, offering improved efficiency and competitiveness. This perspective is reinforced by Arntz et al. (2016), who emphasize that automation, driven by technologies such as robotics and artificial intelligence (AI), has significantly altered the landscape of global production networks. These developments have been accompanied by the notion of servitization, as articulated by Neely et al. (2019), where manufacturers transition from merely producing goods to providing integrated solutions and services within GVCs.

Furthermore, the role of policy and government initiatives in fostering SGVCs cannot be overlooked. Kagermann et al. (2013) introduced the concept of Industry 4.0, emphasizing the integration of digital technologies in manufacturing processes. This seminal work laid the foundation for the SGVC paradigm. Iansiti and Lakhani (2017) discuss how digital platforms, IoT, AI, and data analytics are the technological pillars driving SGVCs. These technologies enable real-time data exchange and decision-making throughout the value chain. Porter and Heppelmann (2014) highlight how SGVCs optimize supply chains, reducing lead times, improving inventory management, and enhancing overall operational efficiency. Hong et al. (2020) explore how SGVCs enable mass customization and personalization of products, meeting the diverse demands of customers while maintaining cost-effectiveness. Lee et al. (2015) investigate the use of IoT and AI for real-time quality control and traceability in SGVCs, emphasizing the importance of compliance and product quality. World Economic Forum (2020) discusses the role of SGVCs in enhancing supply chain resilience by diversifying sourcing options, mitigating risks, and enabling rapid response to disruptions. Govindan et al. (2019) analyse how SGVCs contribute to sustainability by optimizing resource use, reducing waste, and supporting circular economy principles. Ivanov (2020) explores the integration of SGVCs with e-commerce platforms, enabling manufacturers to meet the demands of online consumers efficiently. Tao et al. (2018) delve into the use of digital twins for virtual simulation and optimization of manufacturing processes within SGVCs, leading to improved product development and quality. Bian and Yan (2021) discuss the critical importance of robust cybersecurity measures within SGVCs to protect sensitive data and intellectual property. The United Nations Conference on Trade and Development (UNCTAD) (2019) emphasizes the need for international collaboration and policy frameworks to harness the potential of SGVCs while addressing global challenges.

In summary, the literature on SGVCs in the manufacturing industry underscores the transformative impact of technologies like IoT, automation, and digital platforms. These changes are redefining traditional production models and offering new opportunities for businesses to enhance their competitiveness. Moreover, the role of government policies and trade regulations is seen as instrumental in shaping the trajectory of SGVCs, emphasizing the need for adaptive strategies to harness the full potential of this evolving paradigm.

FINDINGS

SGVCs have significantly transformed the manufacturing industry in recent years. One key finding is the increased interconnectedness of global production networks. Manufacturers now rely on a web of suppliers, often spread across different countries, to source components and materials efficiently. This has led to greater flexibility in production processes and cost optimization. Moreover, the integration of advanced technologies like the IoT, AI, and big data analytics has enhanced the competitiveness of manufacturing within GVCs. These technologies enable predictive maintenance, real-time monitoring of production lines, and data-driven decision-making, thereby improving overall productivity and reducing downtime. Additionally, GVCs have enabled companies to tap into specialized skills and resources globally. This finding highlights the importance of knowledge and skill transfer across borders, facilitating the spread of best practices and innovation in manufacturing. Collaborative partnerships and information sharing have become essential for staying competitive in the SGVC landscape. Furthermore, sustainability and environmental concerns are emerging as critical considerations within GVCs. Companies are increasingly under pressure to reduce their carbon footprint and adopt eco-friendly practices. This finding underscores the need for sustainable supply chain management and the integration of green technologies throughout the manufacturing process. Following are more elaboration on the findings:

1. **Technological advancements drive transformation**: One of the central findings is that technological advancements, such as IoT, AI, and data analytics, are the primary drivers behind the transformation of global value chains in manufacturing. These technologies enable real-time data exchange, decision-making, and optimization across the entire value chain.
2. **Efficiency and cost reduction**: SGVCs significantly enhance operational efficiency. Manufacturers can optimize supply chains, reduce inventory carrying costs, and minimize production downtime through predictive maintenance. This leads to cost reduction and improved resource utilization.
3. **Customization and personalization**: SGVCs empower manufacturers to meet the growing demand for customization and personalization. Real-time data analysis allows for tailored production runs, meeting individual customer preferences while maintaining cost-effectiveness.
4. **Quality control and traceability**: The integration of IoT and AI in SGVCs enables real-time quality control and traceability. Manufacturers can ensure compliance with industry standards, reduce defects, and enhance product quality, resulting in higher customer satisfaction.

5. **Globalization and resilience**: SGVCs enable manufacturers to diversify their supplier networks across the globe, reducing dependency on a single source. This enhances supply chain resilience by mitigating risks associated with disruptions and geopolitical events.
6. **Sustainability and environmental impact**: The adoption of SGVCs supports sustainability efforts in manufacturing. These systems optimize resource utilization, reduce waste, and contribute to the circular economy, aligning with environmental goals.
7. **E-commerce integration**: Manufacturers are increasingly integrating SGVCs with e-commerce platforms, enabling efficient processing of online orders, faster delivery times, and improved customer experiences in the digital marketplace.
8. **Digital twins and simulation**: Digital twins and virtual simulations are being used to optimize manufacturing processes within SGVCs. These technologies lead to improved product development, reduced errors, and enhanced product quality.
9. **Cybersecurity and data protection**: Robust cybersecurity measures are crucial in SGVCs to safeguard sensitive data and intellectual property. Ensuring data protection is a top priority in the implementation of these systems.
10. **Global collaboration and policy frameworks**: To harness the full potential of SGVCs, global collaboration and policy frameworks are necessary. These frameworks should address challenges such as data privacy, intellectual property rights, and international standards.

CONCLUSION

In conclusion, SGVCs are redefining manufacturing by leveraging digital technologies, data analytics, and automation to enhance every aspect of the value chain. These applications are helping manufacturers become more agile, efficient, and competitive in an increasingly dynamic global marketplace. By embracing these SGVC applications, manufacturers can not only stay competitive but also contribute to sustainability, innovation, and resilience in the rapidly evolving global manufacturing landscape. It's important to continuously evaluate and adapt these technologies to stay at the forefront of the industry.

The findings demonstrate that these systems enhance efficiency, reduce costs, and improve quality while also promoting customization, sustainability, and supply chain resilience. However, challenges related to cybersecurity and the need for international collaboration and policy frameworks must be addressed. Manufacturers that embrace SGVCs are better positioned to thrive in today's competitive and rapidly evolving marketplace. As technology continues to advance, further research and innovation in this field will be crucial to unlock new opportunities and overcome emerging challenges in the manufacturing industry.

REFERENCES

Arntz, M., Gregory, T., & Zierahn, U. (2016). "The Risk of Automation for Jobs in OECD Countries: A Comparative Analysis." OECD Social, Employment and Migration Working Papers, No. 189, OECD Publishing, Paris. http://dx.doi.org/10.1787/5jlz9h56dvq7-en (1) (PDF) The Risk of Automation for Jobs in OECD Countries: A Comparative Analysis. Available from: https://www.researchgate.net/publication/303311529_The_Risk_of_Automation_for_Jobs_in_OECD_Countries_A_Comparative_Analysis [accessed October 14, 2023].

Bian, J., & Yan, Z. (2021). "Smart Manufacturing Systems Cybersecurity and Resilience: A Review." *IEEE Access*, 9, 18944–18964.

Govindan, K., et al. (2019). "Circular Economy and Industry 4.0: A Bibliometric and Systematic Review." *Journal of Cleaner Production*, 227, 992–1004.

Hong, Y., et al. (2020). "Smart Manufacturing for Mass Customization: Trends, Concepts, and Research Opportunities." *Robotics and Computer-Integrated Manufacturing*, 61, 101863.

Iansiti, M., & Lakhani, K. R. (2017). "The Truth about Blockchain." *Harvard Business Review*, 95(1), 118–127.

Ivanov, D. (2020). "Viable Supply Chain Model: Integrating Agility, Resilience and Sustainability Perspectives—Lessons from and Thinking beyond the COVID-19 Pandemic." *Annals of Operations Research*, 319, 1411–1431.

Kagermann, H., et al. (2013). "Industrie 4.0: Mit dem Internet der Dinge auf dem Weg zur 4. industriellen Revolution." *VDI nachrichten*, 13, 3–5.

Lee, J., et al. (2015). "Service Innovation and Smart Analytics for Industry 4.0 and Big Data Environment." *Procedia CIRP*, 38, 3–8.

Neely, A., et al. (2019). "Redistributed Manufacturing and the Impact of Big Data: A Consumer Goods Perspective. "*Production Planning & Control*, 30(7), 568–581.

Porter, M. E., & Heppelmann, J. E. (2014). "How Smart, Connected Products Are Transforming Competition." *Harvard Business Review*, 92(11), 64–88.

Tao, F., et al. (2018). "Digital Twin-Driven Product Design, Manufacturing and Service with Big Data." *The International Journal of Advanced Manufacturing Technology*, 94(9–12), 3563–3576.

United Nations Conference on Trade and Development (UNCTAD). (2019). "Digitalization and the New GVC Reality." Retrieved from https://unctad.org/system/files/official-document/gds2019d3_en.pdf

World Economic Forum. (2020). "Supply Chain Resilience Report: Safeguarding against the Next Disruption." Retrieved from https://www.weforum.org/reports/supply-chain-resilience-report-safeguarding-against-the-next-disruption

Chapter 13

Decentralized finance

A catalyst for smart global value chains in future financial ecosystems

Ankit Goel
Maharaja Agrasen Institute of Management Studies, New Delhi, India

Parul Garg
Amity Global Business School, Noida, India

Manjeet Kumar
GL Bajaj Institute of Technology & Management, Greater Noida, India

INTRODUCTION

The 21st century is witnessing a revolutionary shift in the financial landscape driven by the relentless tides of digital innovation. A critical part of this evolution is decentralized finance, or DeFi, the groundbreaking technology that operates on the ethos of open and permissionless networks, offering a radically different approach to traditional banking systems. This chapter delves into the exploration of DeFi and its potential to reconfigure our financial interactions, eliminating middlemen and thus democratizing financial systems globally.

DeFi represents a paradigm shift from traditional, centralized financial systems to an open, accessible, and equitable model, leveraging blockchain technology's unique capabilities. The technology embodies the principle of peer-to-peer transactions, eliminating the necessity for intermediaries such as banks, brokers, or insurance companies. DeFi puts the control of financial decisions back into the hands of individuals, instilling a sense of ownership that traditional systems often lack. At the heart of DeFi is the audacious notion that financial services—from saving and borrowing to insurance and trading—can operate on a decentralized network, free from regulatory constraints and institutional gatekeeping. This ability to establish and control financial transactions on a personal level fosters a sense of empowerment, particularly for those marginalized by the traditional financial structures.

Despite being at its nascent stage, DeFi has displayed robust potential to revolutionize the way we perceive and conduct financial transactions. As the technology matures, it is poised to tackle various issues plaguing the financial world, such as high transaction costs, slow money transfers, lack of

 DOI: 10.1201/9781003461432-13

transparency, and limited accessibility to financial services. By cutting out the middlemen, DeFi also offers a compelling solution to expedite the financial inclusion of unbanked and underbanked populations. Nonetheless, like any disruptive technology, the road to DeFi's global acceptance is paved with challenges. The ecosystem must contend with problems of security, volatility, scalability, and regulatory uncertainty. As we delve deeper into this chapter, we will confront these issues, providing a balanced perspective on the promises and perils of DeFi.

The future of finance is evolving in front of our eyes, driven by a relentless quest for transparency, inclusivity, and autonomy. As we stand on the brink of this financial revolution, the acceptance and adaptation of DeFi is not merely an option but a necessity. It's a call to break free from archaic systems, to demand more than just being a mere spectator, and to be active participants in shaping the future of finance. DeFi's transformative potential is immense, and its promise of democratized, frictionless, and open financial systems resonates with the demands of our digital age. It compels us to reconsider, reinvent, and reshape our existing financial models, challenging us to embrace the technological currents shaping our future. As we navigate through this chapter, we aim to enlighten, excite, and, most importantly, challenge the reader's perspective on what it truly means to be part of the financial revolution. This exploration of DeFi is, thus, an essential step toward understanding and embracing the paradigm shift in global financial systems.

In essence, the DeFi revolution heralds a new era of financial democracy, putting power back into the hands of the people. The journey is challenging, the path steep, but the rewards could be revolutionary. It's a future we're not just predicting but one we're actively creating.

EMPIRICAL BACKGROUND

The emergence of DeFi has sparked a surge in scholarly interest, shedding light on the revolutionary potential of this technology. This literature review synthesizes key research contributions that collectively explore DeFi's transformative impact on our everyday financial interactions.

Few researcher delved into the potential of DeFi to reshape the financial landscape. His work demonstrated how DeFi's fundamental principles—openness, transparency, and autonomy—could drive a systemic change toward more equitable financial systems. Mougayar noted that the successful integration of DeFi relies on widespread education and understanding of its underlying mechanisms. He argued that to make DeFi truly revolutionary, it must be accepted by the masses, necessitating widespread education about blockchain technology and the research offers a valuable perspective on DeFi's scalability challenges. They posit that as DeFi platforms scale, they will face challenges similar to those encountered by traditional financial systems, including transaction bottlenecks and a potential rise in costs. However, they contend that if these issues are adequately addressed, DeFi holds the promise to fundamentally alter the financial sector's dynamics.

A significant contribution comes from a researcher who examined DeFi's potential to drive financial inclusion in India. They suggested that DeFi could address the prevalent financial exclusion by providing access to financial services for the considerable population still unbanked or underbanked. DeFi, they proposed, could serve as a potent tool to minimize the dependency on informal credit sources and foster financial empowerment in rural and marginalized communities.

Zetzsche, Buckley, and Arner (2020) present a comparative analysis of DeFi and conventional finance. They argued that while DeFi holds promise for democratizing financial services, it faces regulatory and security challenges. They stressed the need for a balanced approach, combining the robustness of traditional finance and the revolutionary capabilities of DeFi to evolve into a hybrid system.

Lee and Shin (2022) further extended the analysis of DeFi's potential to spur financial inclusion. They observed that DeFi could serve as a powerful tool to reach underbanked populations by eliminating barriers to entry, thereby promoting economic equity. Their work underscored DeFi's potential as a democratizing force but emphasized the need for regulatory frameworks to ensure stability and security.

Schröder and Lodemann (2021) were among the first researchers to critically investigate the DeFi ecosystem. Their study posits that DeFi platforms' autonomy, transparency, and inclusivity could disrupt traditional finance and banking sectors. They noted that DeFi systems, anchored on the blockchain, can reduce reliance on intermediaries, significantly minimizing transaction costs and improving efficiency. However, they warned that its nascent state also brings inherent risks like technological bugs and market volatility.

Another insightful work by a researcher highlighted the potential of DeFi to disrupt India's remittance landscape. With India being the world's top receiver of remittances, DeFi can revolutionize the process by enabling faster, cheaper, and more transparent cross-border transactions. However, they also pointed out the need for an appropriate regulatory framework to address the potential misuse for money laundering and other illegal activities. Some researcher explored the potential of DeFi in transforming India's lending sector. They highlighted how DeFi could democratize lending by enabling peer-to-peer lending platforms, reducing reliance on traditional banking structures, and potentially lowering interest rates. However, they also underlined the inherent risk associated with the volatility of crypto assets and the lack of a recovery mechanism in case of defaults.

A major contribution from anonymous lies in analysing the potential challenges that DeFi poses from a regulatory perspective. The paper argues that while DeFi has significant potential, its anonymous and decentralized nature could pose challenges to the existing regulatory framework. It suggested a need for a balanced regulatory approach, one that promotes innovation while ensuring consumer protection and financial stability.

In essence, the Indian perspective recognizes the significant potential of DeFi in addressing the unique challenges of the Indian financial landscape. However, they also emphasize the need to approach this revolutionary technology with a prudent regulatory framework, balancing the need to promote innovation with the imperatives of stability and security. As DeFi continues to evolve, these considerations will be crucial in ensuring that its adoption in India aligns with the broader objectives of financial inclusion, stability, and growth.

DeFi: ADVANTAGES AND DOWNSIDES

DeFi, an emerging financial paradigm, has been hailed as the antidote to financial intermediation, promising to oust middlemen and democratize access to financial services. Powered by the robust, immutable, and transparent technology of blockchain, DeFi is reshaping our interaction with financial services by transferring control and ownership back to the individual. Yet, like any innovation, it carries a distinct set of opportunities and challenges.

Advantages of DeFi

- **Democratized access**: Traditional banking systems are often criticized for being exclusionary, requiring rigorous checks, and thus denying many individuals and businesses the opportunity to participate. DeFi, by virtue of its underlying technology, enables financial inclusivity by providing open access to financial instruments to anyone with an internet connection.
- **Financial autonomy**: DeFi places the power of managing finances into the hands of the user, eliminating the need for a centralized authority or intermediary. This new financial landscape harbours the potential for greater individual autonomy and privacy.
- **Transparency and trust**: All transactions in the DeFi ecosystem are recorded on the blockchain, which is open and transparent. This transparency fosters trust among participants, as it offers proof of all transactions and prevents tampering.
- **Interoperability and composability**: DeFi protocols are built on public blockchains like Ethereum, which are open-source, allowing other developers to build new products and services. This interoperability and the composability of protocols create a vibrant and innovative ecosystem, often referred to as "money legos."

Downsides of DeFi

- **Technological complexities and scalability**: The successful deployment of DeFi hinges on blockchain technology, which, while robust, is still maturing. It faces issues of scalability, congestion, and high transaction costs, which may hinder mass adoption.
- **Smart contract risks**: DeFi's backbone is the smart contract – self-executing contracts with the terms of agreement directly written into code. However, they are susceptible to bugs and coding errors. The immutable nature of blockchain implies that these errors cannot be rectified once the contract is executed, which could lead to substantial financial losses.
- **Regulatory uncertainties**: The regulatory landscape for DeFi is unclear, and its decentralized nature poses significant challenges for existing regulatory frameworks. These ambiguities may deter traditional institutions and risk-averse individuals from participating in the DeFi ecosystem.
- **User experience and learning curve**: DeFi applications, or DApps, often have complex interfaces that can be daunting to non-technical users. This steep learning curve may limit DeFi's broader adoption.

DeFi: OPPORTUNITIES AND THREATS

The realm of DeFi is rapidly evolving, sparking a renewed discourse on the opportunities it offers and the threats it poses. As an offshoot of blockchain technology, DeFi is set to disrupt the financial ecosystem, thereby cutting out the middlemen and empowering individuals to control their financial destiny. However, it is essential to acknowledge both the opportunities and threats of this transformative technology.

Opportunities in DeFi

Financial inclusion: The barrier to entry in the DeFi space is minimal, with a smartphone and internet connection being the primary requisites. Consequently, DeFi can serve as an instrumental force in driving financial inclusion, extending financial services to the unbanked and underbanked populations worldwide.

Yield generation: The advent of DeFi has ushered in innovative methods for users to generate high returns on their investments through yield farming, liquidity mining, staking, etc., traditionally unheard of in the centralized financial realm.

Peer-to-peer (P2P) transactions: DeFi enables P2P transactions without intermediaries, thereby fostering an ecosystem of faster and cheaper transactions. It offers the potential to lower remittance costs, improve capital efficiency, and enhance cross-border transactions.

Innovation and disruption: DeFi acts as a catalyst for innovation in the financial industry, paving the way for novel financial products and services such as stablecoins, decentralized exchanges, lending platforms, and more. These disruptions are not merely incremental but signify a potential paradigm shift in how we perceive and interact with financial systems.

Threats in DeFi

Cybersecurity threats: Despite blockchain's inherent security features, DeFi platforms are not immune to cyber threats. Smart contracts' potential vulnerabilities can be exploited by malicious actors, leading to substantial losses. Furthermore, the irreversible nature of blockchain transactions compounds the consequences of potential cyberattacks.

Market volatility and risk: Given its relative infancy and rapid growth, DeFi is highly susceptible to market volatility. Furthermore, high-yield DeFi platforms often come with high risk, and participants can face significant losses due to rapid market fluctuations or platform instability.

Regulatory hurdles: The absence of a clear regulatory framework for DeFi introduces significant uncertainty. It complicates compliance and exposes users to potential legal risks. Regulatory bodies worldwide are still grappling with how to effectively regulate this decentralized financial infrastructure.

Complexity and usability: The complexity of DeFi applications can deter widespread adoption. Managing private keys, understanding gas fees, and navigating complex DeFi platforms require a steep learning curve that might be unappealing to the average user.

DeFi DEVELOPMENTS AROUND THE WORLD: THE PRACTICAL SIDE

DeFi has become the centrifugal force within the financial landscape, promising to break free from traditional finance's constraints. By eliminating intermediaries, it is poised to democratize financial services, creating new opportunities for individuals and businesses alike. This chapter explores real-world applications and developments in DeFi around the globe, highlighting the practical side of this transformative technology.

Peer-to-peer lending and borrowing: Platforms like Aave and Compound have revolutionized lending and borrowing, eliminating the need for intermediaries. With the power of blockchain, these platforms facilitate P2P loans by using cryptocurrency as collateral. Notably, Aave, a London-based DeFi project, has over $16 billion in liquidity as of late 2023, demonstrating the immense potential of DeFi lending.

Stablecoins: Stablecoins, such as DAI, have gained popularity for their stability amidst the notoriously volatile cryptocurrency market. DAI, a project of MakerDAO, maintains a steady value pegged to the US dollar. It plays a significant role in reducing volatility risks in DeFi transactions, acting as a stable medium of exchange within the ecosystem.

Decentralized exchanges (DEXs): DEXs like Uniswap and SushiSwap have disrupted traditional exchange methods by enabling users to trade directly with each other. These DEXs offer automated liquidity provision, ensuring smooth and efficient trading operations. For instance, Uniswap, an automated liquidity protocol built on Ethereum, facilitates over $1 billion in trades daily, underscoring the potential of decentralized exchanges.

Yield farming and liquidity mining: DeFi has introduced new methods of earning returns, such as yield farming and liquidity mining. Platforms like Yearn.finance enable users to maximize their returns by automatically shifting their funds between different DeFi protocols. Yearn.finance's vaults strategy, which automates yield farming strategies, has shown how DeFi can be a game-changer in optimizing investment returns.

Cross-border transactions: Traditional cross-border payments are often slow and expensive. DeFi offers a solution through faster and more cost-effective transfers. Platforms like Ripple utilize blockchain technology to facilitate real-time cross-border transactions at a fraction of the traditional cost.

However, it's not all plain sailing. Despite the exciting developments, DeFi has also experienced growing pains. For example, the notorious "rug pulls" where developers drain the liquidity of projects, leave investors high and dry. Flash loan attacks, a form of arbitrage made possible by the uncollateralized nature of flash loans in DeFi, have led to significant losses. Regulatory uncertainties also loom, posing challenges to DeFi's growth and acceptance.

FUTURE INNOVATIONS AND THE SYMBIOSIS OF DeFi AND SMART GLOBAL VALUE CHAIN

Efficiency in cross-border transactions:
DeFi streamlines cross-border transactions by removing intermediary banks and reducing transaction times. Example: Instantaneous cross-border transfers on blockchain networks like Ripple.

Cost-effective financial interactions:
DeFi eliminates intermediary fees, reducing the overall cost of financial transactions. Example: DEXs allow users to trade assets without paying traditional brokerage fees.

Blockchain consortia for smart contracts:
Collaborative blockchain networks can be established within global value chains for secure and transparent smart contract execution. Example: A consortium of supply chain partners using blockchain for transparent and automated payment settlements.

Scalability in financial transactions:
DeFi platforms can handle a high volume of transactions simultaneously, making them scalable for large-scale global value chain operations. Example: Ethereum's DApps facilitate scalable and automated financial processes within supply chain networks.

Secure multi-party smart contracts:
Multi-party smart contracts enable secure and transparent agreements among multiple entities in a global value chain. Example: A consortium of manufacturers, distributors, and retailers utilizing blockchain for automated and secure revenue-sharing agreements.

Automated financial workflows:
Smart contracts in DeFi can automate complex financial workflows within global value chains, reducing the need for manual intervention. Example: An automated payment and invoicing system on a blockchain for seamless financial interactions between suppliers and manufacturers.

DApps: THE NEW PARADIGM IN DeFi

DApps, unlike traditional apps, run on blockchain or distributed ledger technology, eliminating the need for a central authority. They offer a democratized way of conducting transactions, providing the framework for an open, transparent, and inclusive financial system. The key characteristics of DApps – decentralized governance, censorship resistance, and borderless access – align seamlessly with DeFi's ethos of democratizing finance.

Real-world DApps and their impact

MakerDAO: One of the pioneering DeFi DApps, MakerDAO enables users to generate DAI, a stablecoin pegged to the US dollar. Through its smart contract platform, MakerDAO has successfully created a decentralized credit system, reducing reliance on traditional banking institutions.

Uniswap: As a DApp that facilitates automated transactions between cryptocurrency pairs on the Ethereum blockchain, Uniswap epitomizes DeFi's transformative potential. Uniswap's open-source liquidity protocol has eliminated the need for order books, providing a seamless platform for decentralized trading.

Compound: An algorithmically operated money market protocol on Ethereum, Compound allows users to lend and borrow cryptocurrencies. The interest rates are algorithmically determined, removing the need for negotiation or estimation and emphasizing the efficiencies DApps bring to financial transactions.

Aave: Another DeFi lending protocol, Aave has introduced innovative features like flash loans, which allow borrowers to take uncollateralized loans, provided they repay within the same block transaction. This novel feature exemplifies the innovation that DApps inject into the financial system.

Yearn.finance: This DApp aggregates the yield from various DeFi lending protocols, allowing users to optimize their earnings. It's an example of how DApps can bring sophistication to personal finance, traditionally only accessible to institutional investors.

While these DApps provide a glimpse into the potential of decentralized finance, they also bring challenges. The nascent stage of DeFi and DApps, coupled with their complex technical nature, exposes them to risks such as smart contract bugs and hacking. These underline the need for robust security measures and user education.

As we navigate the future of finance, the role of DApps becomes increasingly pivotal. Accepting and adapting to this new reality is not just beneficial – it's essential. By empowering individuals and fostering a democratized financial ecosystem, DApps are at the forefront of a financial revolution. Their adoption marks a significant stride toward a more equitable, efficient, and inclusive financial system. As we move forward, the essence of this development lies not in the technology itself but in its ability to foster economic empowerment and disrupt long-standing financial structures.

GLOBAL DeFi ADOPTION: LEADING COUNTRIES IN THE DECENTRALIZED FINANCE MOVEMENT

The DeFi movement is rapidly making its mark across the globe. With its promise to democratize finance by eliminating intermediaries, it has seen significant adoption in many countries. While the journey is still nascent, several nations stand out as frontrunners in DeFi adoption, taking the lead in shaping the future of this transformative technology.

United States: The United States, being a global tech hub, has always been at the forefront of innovative technology adoption. Many DeFi projects originate from the United States, including well-known platforms like Compound and Uniswap. Moreover, its active cryptocurrency market and robust start-up ecosystem make it a fertile ground for DeFi adoption.

China: Despite regulatory challenges, China's booming tech industry and extensive cryptocurrency market have helped foster DeFi growth. Chinese blockchain projects like NEO and VeChain are exploring DeFi applications, signalling the country's growing interest in decentralized finance.

United Kingdom: London, as a global financial hub, hosts a thriving FinTech scene and is home to prominent DeFi projects like Aave. The United Kingdom's progressive regulatory approach toward digital assets further encourages DeFi growth.

Switzerland: Known for its strong finance sector and supportive regulations, Switzerland, particularly its city Zug – known as the "Crypto Valley" – has become a nurturing environment for DeFi projects. Ethereum, which serves as the foundation for most DeFi projects, has its foundation based in Switzerland.

Singapore: With its strategic location and open regulatory environment, Singapore has become a hotspot for blockchain and DeFi projects. The Singaporean government's proactive approach to embracing digital innovation has made it an attractive hub for DeFi development.

South Korea: South Korea has one of the highest rates of crypto adoption in the world. With the government taking steps to regulate and tax cryptocurrencies, South Korea has seen a rise in DeFi adoption. Projects like Terra and Mirror Protocol have originated from this tech-savvy nation.

Germany: Home to various blockchain projects and with a solid reputation in the financial sector, Germany is actively involved in DeFi development. The country's clear legal framework for digital assets has further promoted DeFi growth.

It's important to note that while these countries are currently leading in DeFi adoption, the decentralized nature of DeFi means that its benefits can reach every corner of the world. This universality, coupled with the potential to foster financial inclusion and democratization, is what makes DeFi truly revolutionary. However, for DeFi to reach its full potential, issues around regulation, security, and scalability must be addressed. Countries leading in DeFi adoption have a crucial role to play in shaping the regulatory landscape and driving technological advancements that can address these challenges.

DeFi: the bright future of finance

Decentralized Finance, or DeFi, represents an evolutionary stride in the financial world, aiming to democratize access to financial services and eliminate the need for intermediaries. With its potential to bring about a fundamental shift in the way we manage and interact with money, the future of DeFi is not just bright; it promises to be a beacon of financial autonomy and empowerment.

DeFi: ushering in a new financial era

DeFi applications are built on blockchain technology, most notably Ethereum, providing an open-source, transparent, and permissionless financial system. In this new paradigm, individuals gain control over their financial destinies, unhindered by geographical boundaries or the need for trusted third parties.

REIMAGINING TRADITIONAL FINANCIAL SERVICES

From lending and borrowing to insurance and asset management, DeFi is steadily reimagining every facet of traditional finance. Platforms like MakerDAO and Compound have disrupted lending and borrowing, allowing for permissionless, collateralized loans. Uniswap has transformed exchange, enabling peer-to-peer trading without intermediaries. Yearn.finance has revolutionized asset management by optimizing yield farming strategies for its users. These are just the frontrunners in a burgeoning field of innovative DeFi projects.

Driving financial inclusion

Perhaps one of DeFi's most transformative aspects is its potential to drive financial inclusion. With a simple internet connection, people in underserved regions can access financial services previously out of reach. Stablecoins like DAI provide an alternative to unstable local currencies, while peer-to-peer lending platforms offer financial opportunities to those unable to access traditional banking systems.

The bright future ahead

The rise of DeFi marks a significant step toward a more inclusive and efficient financial ecosystem. As blockchain technology matures, the adoption of DeFi is expected to surge. The continuous development of Layer 2 solutions like Optimism and zkSync promises to tackle Ethereum's scalability issues, allowing DeFi to accommodate more users at lower costs.

Beyond Ethereum, other smart contract platforms like Polkadot, Cardano, and Solana are also vying for a piece of the DeFi pie. These platforms are working to improve upon Ethereum's limitations, further expanding the possibilities for DeFi.

As DeFi evolves, so too does its potential to interface with traditional finance. Institutions are increasingly interested in blockchain technology, and as regulatory clarity improves, we could see more institutional adoption of DeFi. Already, we have seen the first signs of this shift with Visa settling transactions on the Ethereum blockchain and major banks like J.P. Morgan exploring DeFi applications.

Embracing the DeFi revolution

The future of DeFi is indeed bright, but it is not without its challenges. It demands a rethinking of regulatory structures, advancements in smart contract security, and greater efforts toward user education. As we stand on the precipice of a financial revolution, embracing DeFi isn't merely an option; it's a necessity.

DeFi is a testament to the power of decentralization, demonstrating that a world where individuals have unrestricted access to financial services is not just possible; it's on the horizon. It's a world where the financial system works for all, not just a privileged few. And as we move toward this future, DeFi shines brightly, guiding the way.

The regulatory landscape of DeFi: balancing innovation with protection

DeFi has made substantial strides in redefining the financial landscape by eliminating intermediaries and creating a democratized, transparent, and permissionless financial system. However, with this innovation comes the need for adequate regulation to safeguard users and maintain market integrity. This chapter examines the regulatory challenges and initiatives in the realm of DeFi, highlighting the imperative of striking a balance between promoting innovation and ensuring consumer protection.

Regulatory challenges in DeFi

- The inherently decentralized nature of DeFi, coupled with its rapid innovation, presents unique regulatory challenges. Firstly, DeFi's permissionless and open-source characteristics create a level of anonymity that could potentially facilitate illicit activities such as money laundering and fraud.
- Secondly, the absence of intermediaries in DeFi transactions, while being a significant advantage, also raises questions about accountability and consumer protection. For instance, if a user loses their private key or falls victim to a scam, the recourse options are minimal.
- Finally, the borderless nature of DeFi transactions raises jurisdictional questions. DeFi platforms can operate anywhere globally, making it challenging to determine which jurisdiction's laws and regulations apply.

Navigating regulatory developments

Despite these challenges, some regulatory efforts are underway to address the unique aspects of DeFi.

Examples of these efforts include:

Anti-money laundering (AML) and know your customer (KYC) rules: Countries like the United States and members of the European Union have advanced efforts to bring cryptocurrencies, and by extension, DeFi transactions, under the ambit of AML and KYC rules. This approach would require DeFi platforms to verify user identities, making transactions more transparent and potentially reducing the risk of illicit activities.

Smart contract regulations: Countries like China are proposing regulations for smart contracts, a core element of DeFi platforms. Such regulations would provide clarity and legal certainty for the use of smart contracts in financial transactions.

DeFi-specific regulations: In an encouraging move, Wyoming, United States, has recently proposed the first DeFi-specific legislation. This regulation would provide a regulatory framework for Decentralized Autonomous Organizations (DAOs), a form of DeFi platform.

The path forward: striking a balance

- Regulating DeFi is a delicate balancing act. On the one hand, regulators must protect consumers and maintain market integrity. On the other hand, they must avoid stifling innovation that could benefit society at large.
- Promoting cross-border regulatory cooperation could help address the jurisdictional challenges of DeFi. A global regulatory framework, while difficult to achieve, could provide consistent rules and prevent regulatory arbitrage.
- Moreover, fostering an open dialogue between regulators, DeFi developers, and users is crucial. Such a dialogue could help regulators understand the technology's intricacies, enabling them to craft tailored regulations that protect users without stifling innovation.
- As we stand on the precipice of a financial revolution driven by DeFi, the need for a thoughtful, balanced, and coordinated regulatory approach has never been more critical. By encouraging innovation while ensuring consumer protection and market integrity, we can navigate the challenges and realize DeFi's full potential.

CONCLUSION

DeFi's impact and potential cannot be underestimated, as it promises to revolutionize the financial sector by democratizing access, enhancing transparency, and fostering innovation. However, it is essential to acknowledge and address its inherent challenges and complexities to fully reap the potential benefits. Like any transformative technology, DeFi needs time, refinement, and, perhaps most importantly, a robust regulatory framework to ensure its safe and widespread use.

By examining and understanding these facets of DeFi, we can work toward creating a more equitable and efficient financial system, embracing the power of decentralization while mitigating its associated risks. In a future shaped by technology, accepting and adapting to DeFi may not just be a choice but a necessity. Embracing this change could well mean a significant stride toward a more inclusive and transparent financial world.

Overall, we cut the middlemen and move toward decentralized financial structures; it is imperative to foster a collective understanding and informed approach toward this emerging paradigm. It is not about replacing the old with the new; it is about creating a harmonious blend where traditional and decentralized financial systems can coexist, complementing and elevating each other.

As we peel back the layers of this emergent technology, we must ensure that we harness its potential responsibly while addressing the threats it poses. Only by doing so can we create a DeFi ecosystem that's robust, inclusive, and secure, pushing the boundaries of what's possible while keeping our feet firmly grounded in the realities of today. It's a formidable task, but one that offers immeasurable rewards if achieved. Accepting and adapting to this new financial reality is not just inevitable; it's the need of the hour.

REFERENCES

DA Zetzsche, DW Arner, RP Buckley, Decentralized Finance. *Journal of Financial Regulation*, Volume 6, Issue 2, 20 September 2020, Pages 172–203. https://doi.org/10.1093/jfr/fjaa010

JH Lee, JH Shin, Effect of Chelation Therapy on a Korean Patient with Brain Manganese Deposition Resulting From a Compound Heterozygous Mutation in the SLC39A14 *Gene. Journal of Movement Disorders*, Volume 15, Issue 2, 2022 May, Pages 171–174. https://doi.org/10.14802/jmd.21143. Epub 2022 Mar 22. PMID: 35306789; PMCID: PMC9171315.

M Schröder, S Lodemann, A Systematic Investigation of the Integration of Machine Learning into Supply Chain Risk Management. *Logistics, MDPI*, Volume 5, Issue 3, 2021, Pages 1–17, September.

Chapter 14

Emerging technologies in global supply chain management (GSCM) using an automated e-audit system

Ashish Manuel and Neerja Aswale
Vishwakarma University, Pune, India

INTRODUCTION

An e-audit system, short for electronic-audit system, is a digital platform or software designed to facilitate and streamline the audit process. Auditing is a systematic examination of financial information, management processes, or other aspects of a business or organization to ensure accuracy, legality, and adherence to established policies and procedures. The transition from traditional, paper-based audit systems to electronic ones has been driven by the need for efficiency, accuracy, and improved collaboration among auditors.

E-audit, or electronic audit, in supply chain management (SCM), refers to the use of digital technologies and tools to conduct audits of various processes and activities within the supply chain. Traditional audits involve manual inspection of physical documents and processes, but e-audits leverage digital platforms to streamline and enhance the auditing process. While e-audits offer various benefits, it's essential to consider cybersecurity measures to protect sensitive supply chain data from unauthorized access and manipulation. Additionally, organizations should periodically review and update their e-audit processes to adapt to evolving technologies and industry best practices.

Global supply chain management (GSCM) refers to the oversight and coordination of the entire supply chain process on a global scale. A supply chain involves the network of organizations, individuals, activities, information, and resources involved in the creation and delivery of a product or service from the supplier to the customer. GSCM is complex and requires a strategic approach to ensure that all elements work together seamlessly. Effective management is essential for companies to remain competitive in the global marketplace and adapt to the challenges and opportunities presented by a dynamic and interconnected world economy.

GSCM is a critical aspect of business operations that involves planning, implementing, and controlling the flow of goods and services from the point of origin to the point of consumption. It encompasses a network of organizations, resources, activities, and technologies involved in the production and distribution of products on a global scale. Effective GSCM is crucial for

DOI: 10.1201/9781003461432-14

businesses to meet customer demands, optimize costs, and stay competitive in the global marketplace.

SCM technologies digitalization refers to the integration of digital technologies and solutions to enhance and optimize various aspects of supply chain processes. Digitalization in SCM involves leveraging advanced technologies to streamline operations, improve visibility, increase efficiency, and ultimately drive better business outcomes. Digitalization in SCM is an ongoing process that aims to create a more agile, responsive, and efficient supply chain ecosystem. As technology continues to advance, businesses can explore and adopt new solutions to stay competitive and address the evolving challenges of the global supply chain.

Digitalization refers to the process of using digital technologies to transform traditional analogy processes and systems into digital ones. This involves the use of digital information and technology to enhance and improve the way organizations operate and deliver value (Garg, 2022, 2023). There are numerous applications of digitalization across various industries and sectors. Digital applications play a crucial role in modern SCM, helping organizations streamline processes, improve efficiency, and enhance overall supply chain performance (Ghatak & Garg, 2022).

The Global Positioning System (GPS) is a satellite-based navigation system that allows users to determine their precise location and track movement. GPS receivers are devices that receive signals from GPS satellites and use the information to determine the device's location. These receivers are integrated into various devices, including smartphones, navigation systems, fitness trackers, and specialized GPS units. GPS technology is commonly integrated into navigation devices for various purposes, such as car navigation systems, handheld GPS units for outdoor activities, marine navigation systems, and aviation navigation equipment. GPS enhances traditional GPS by using additional data, such as cell tower information, to speed up the time it takes for a GPS receiver to obtain a satellite fix. This is especially useful in situations where GPS signals may be weak or obstructed.

Data analytics in the audit system involves using advanced analytical techniques to analyse large volumes of data to identify patterns, anomalies, and potential risks within financial and operational information. This approach allows auditors to gain deeper insights, improve audit efficiency, and enhance the overall audit process, and analytics in the audit system empower auditors to move beyond traditional methods, providing a more comprehensive and dynamic approach to identifying risks, detecting fraud, and ensuring the accuracy of financial information.

RESEARCH METHODOLOGY

Knowledge management audit is a new system that has been very well defined in many of the papers that know about a lot of audit processes in the market; however, due to a lack of knowledge about digitalization and technology, the main issue that arises is always in the knowledge management; it is difficult to understand how knowledge management is being competitive in the emerging market. Organizations are not able to earn a competitive edge in the market due to their lack of knowledge and market sentiments (Daghfocus & Khwaja, 2010).

The implementation of electronic record management will help in providing better accountability of the SCM, will ensure there is stability, and will ensure there is no risk, and there is cybersecurity, as it will majorly work with the help of the Enterprise Resource Planning software, which can easily detect the issues; it can also help with RFID tags, which can be used for authentication and fraud detections (Verma & Khan, 2015).

Management of an e-supply chain in the environment requires to analyse of the methods, techniques, and internal and external interface of any system. This e-supply chain management system will help us to check and find out the types of organizational processes that an organization is performing and how well the system is structured. Integrating this model will help the organization to adapt to a more flexible and structured process (Arsovaski, Petrovic, Rankovic, & Kalanic, 2012).

While developing a cloud-based, security-driven HRM system, various models were investigated with reference to HRM security-driven HRM model was mainly introduced to protect the scams and frauds that were going on in the current market scenario. This model helped in managing all the privacy data securely. Also, each and every data to be accessed needed permission. This means the operation of users on the system is done and executed based on permission assigned to their roles. A lot more security was implemented to make the process more protected and not disclosable readily at any point; here, the cloud helps in storing the data and then gives it the display function as and when the permissions are granted (Odun-Ayo et al., 2017).

The current management is focused only on the technical changes but is not focusing on the pure changes, as due to the technology, there are technical changes, but the industry experts do not understand the knowledge behaviour of the consumers; the audit system should be used to set a benchmark for the companies; however, there are no such accurate auditors who can do so to set the said system: that is where this is lacking; due to poor audit systems, organizations are not able to focus on the correct source (Levonic & Gerbec, 2017).

Blockchain is the new system that is helping to shape the successful career of the SCM because it is more efficient and more effective. Blockchain helps in cloud computing, which helps to make it easier for the process to run in a much more efficient manner and effective way. Blockchain allows for visualizations of huge amounts of data, makes it easy for better decision-making, and gets better accountability and creditability (Matenga & Mpofu, 2022).

OBJECTIVE OF THE STUDY

1. To design an automated electronic-audit system for the SCM.
2. To ensure resource and technology maximization with the help of new-era digitalization tools.
3. To quicken the growth of E-SCM in order to increase the knowledge within the manufacturing and logistics industries.
4. To reduce the delays in the supply of goods to the retailers from the suppliers by upgrading from a traditional method to an automated digital system that can run on Android applications.
5. To deliver an end-to-end automated system which can be tracked through the GPS and can be used for future sales and service predictions.

FUNCTIONING OF THE E-AUDIT SYSTEM WITH REFERENCE TO GSCM

The audit system will be an application which will run through software that will indicate the interface of the application, which can be accessed by both the suppliers and the manufacturer, which can help them track in real time; the system will be connected to GPS and can have a front-end operation, as well as a back-end operation. The retailer and suppliers can punch their orders in advance with the help of the audit system, which can help the company manufacturers to supply the goods within no time; in the earlier days, the traditional suppliers had to visit the retailers to check for the new stock order; now with the help of the audit application, the retailer can directly punch his order online through the application and can also have real-time GPS tracking on the services he has ordered.

EXPLANATION OF THE MODEL DIAGRAM

Electronic-audit system: This will help in giving the retailers, as well as the suppliers, a real-time audit of all the products and services procured by them during the given stipulated time; the audit system will run on a GPS chip which can track the status of each and every order; the audit system can also use a power bi tool in order to create a graphical representation of all the audits.

Data-integrated AI tool: Data is the new oil which has been tested and proven; with the help of the data, the application can provide the suppliers and the retailers with the chosen services they have used before, and a suggestion can be given about new products too.

DESIGN OF THE AUDIT SYSTEM

The retailers data services by the manufacturing companies; data can help in real-time quick decision-making, and manufacturers can plan their future process. The design of the audit system is reflected in Figure 14.1.

Big retailers: There are a lot of huge retailers who buy goods in a whole lot; however, it becomes difficult for them to set a limit to their products, as sales in the market are very volatile; however, this application can help them set a particular limit and help them to audit each and every product that is purchased by them so that they can have much better business understanding.

Suppliers: Due to the increase in demand and supply, it has become very difficult for the suppliers to keep track of the orders made by their retailers; this audit system will help them to analyse each and every order in detail and also can help them maintain E-documentations for further process.

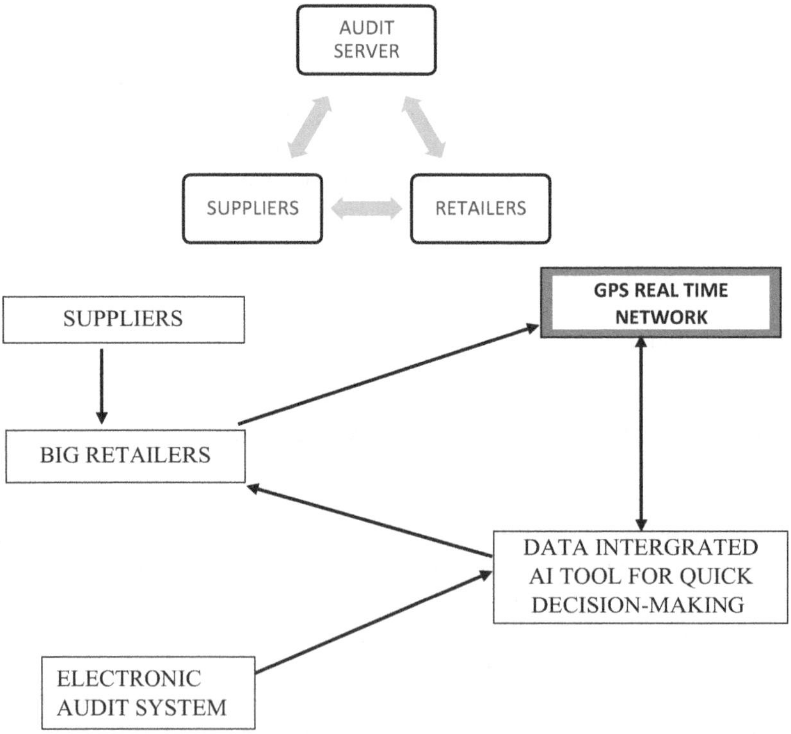

Figure 14.1 Design of the Audit System.

GPS real-time network: With the help of GPS, the orders can be tracked from both ends, from the suppliers to the retailers, and GPS can also be a helpful tool to the logistics centre of any organization. However, if this e-audit system comes into existence, it can solve a lot of delays and give much more accurate results within less time.

CORE RELATION BETWEEN THE SCM AND THE E-AUDIT SYSTEM

Let's explore the relationship between the SCM and audit system:

Compliance and risk management:

SCM perspective: SCM involves the end-to-end management of goods, services, information, and finances as they move from the supplier to the manufacturer, to the wholesaler to the retailer, and finally to the consumer. It encompasses various processes, including procurement, production, transportation, and distribution.

Audit system perspective: An audit system is designed to assess and ensure compliance with internal policies, industry regulations, and legal requirements. It helps identify and mitigate risks associated with non-compliance.

Relationship: An effective audit system within SCM ensures that the supply chain processes adhere to established standards, legal requirements, and company policies, thereby managing risks and ensuring compliance.

Quality control:

SCM perspective: Quality control is a crucial aspect of SCM to ensure that products or services meet predefined standards and specifications.

Audit system perspective: Audit systems often include quality audits to assess and verify that products or services meet the specified quality standards.

Relationship: The audit system plays a role in evaluating and validating the effectiveness of quality control measures implemented in the supply chain.

Performance monitoring:

SCM perspective: SCM involves monitoring and optimizing the performance of various supply chain processes to enhance efficiency and effectiveness.

Audit system perspective: Audit systems may include performance audits to evaluate how well the supply chain is meeting its objectives and to identify areas for improvement.

Relationship: The audit system can be used to assess the performance of SCM processes, providing insights into areas that need attention or enhancement.

Data integrity:

SCM perspective: SCM relies on accurate and timely data for effective decision-making throughout the supply chain.

Audit system perspective: Data integrity audits ensure that the information used in SCM processes is accurate, complete, and reliable.

Relationship: The audit system helps in maintaining the integrity of data within the SCM, contributing to more reliable and informed decision-making.

Continuous improvement:

SCM perspective: Continuous improvement is a key principle in SCM to enhance processes and adapt to changing business environments.

Audit system perspective: Audit systems contribute to continuous improvement by identifying areas for enhancement and assessing the effectiveness of improvement initiatives.

Relationship: The audit system supports SCM by providing feedback on the effectiveness of continuous improvement efforts and ensuring that improvements align with organizational goals and standards.

DISCUSSION

With the previous reference, we can further see how will this e-audit system benefit the industries. The main purpose is the data-integrated AI tool, which can be a very useful application for all the manufacturing and services industries. Now let's check how this model will help in all three major terms:

1. The supplier
    - It will help him keep and record of all the cost controls for the orders, and it can help him in not delaying the orders, as he has access to the GPS where he can track the orders.
    - The supplier has the right to save the documentation in a digital format so that it can be served as evidence even after a period of time.

- He can also track the logistics centre very well to easily communicate with the transporters.

2. The manufacturer
   - Can help in planning the inventory, as he will have a record of what he is going to transport over a period of time.
   - Procurement of raw materials resources utilization can be done in a much more effective manner.
   - He can easily have a record of the distribution channels through which the goods are being sold.
3. The retailer
   - He can have a systematic audit of each and every product that is being transported.
   - He can plan budgeting and warehouse planning.
   - He can use past data to make future predictions with the use of big data and data science.

CONCLUSION

In conclusion, the global landscape of SCM is undeniably crucial to the economic prosperity of nations, fostering collaboration and enhancing operational efficacy across industries. While SCM has proven to be a linchpin for gross domestic product growth in numerous countries, challenges persist in ensuring flexibility and convenience amidst burgeoning demand. This issue is particularly pronounced in India, where a lack of technological knowledge hampers SCM's potential. In the era of digitalization, this research explores the transformative potential of an electronic-audit system, leveraging GPS signals to navigate suppliers and offering real-time tracking for manufacturers. By integrating past data through big data analytics, this audit system stands poised to revolutionize order execution processes, thereby addressing the efficiency and resource utilization gaps within SCM. As India strives to embrace technological advancements, the findings of this study advocate for the adoption of innovative solutions to propel the nation's supply chain into a more streamlined and technologically advanced future.

REFERENCES

Arsovaski, Z., Petrovic, D. R., Rankovic, V., & Kalanic, Z. (2012). Integration Model of Business Processes and Interfaces in E-SCM. In *7th International Conference ICQME*.

Daghfocus, A., & Khwaja, S. (2010). Knowledge-Enabled SCM Auditing (K-SCM): A Methodology and a Case Illustration. In *2010 IEEE International Conference on Management of Innovation & Technology*. DOI: 10.1109/ICMIT.2010.5492867

Garg, A. (2022). *CoReS-Respiratory Strength Predicting Framework Using Noninvasive Technology for Remote Monitoring During Heath Disasters.* Global Healthcare Disasters: Predicting the Unpredictable with Emerging Technologies, 109–121.

Garg, A. (Ed.). (2023). *Reinventing Technological Innovations with Artificial Intelligence.* Bentham Science Publishers.

Ghatak, A., & Garg, A. (2022). Power Transmission Project: A Framework to Align Project Success with Organization Goal. *International Journal of System Assurance Engineering and Management*, 13(4), 1817–1833.

Levonic, D., & Gerbec, M. (2017). Auditing Operational Readiness of Management of Change, Safety and Reliability – Theory and Applications. ISBN 978-1-138-62937-0

Matenga, A., & Mpofu, K. (2022). Block Chain Based Computing Manufacturing SCM System. DOI: 10.3390/app12178664

Odun-Ayo, I., Misra, S., Omoregbe, N., Onibere, E., Bulama, Y., & Damasevičius, R. (2017). Cloud-Based Security Driven Human Resource Management System. In *Eighth International Conference on the Applications Digital Information and Web Technologies.* DOI:10.3233/978-1-61499-773-3-96

Verma, T. N., & Khan, D. A. (2015). Information Technology and E-risk of Supply Chain Management. *African Journal of Business Management*, 9(6). ISSN 1993-8233. DOI: 10.5897/AJBM2013.7308

Chapter 15

Decentralized finance and technology readiness

Unleashing the future of financial innovation

Channi Sachdeva and Veer P. Gangwar
Lovely Professional University, Phagwara, India

Veena Grover
Noida Institute of Engineering and Technology, Greater Noida, India

LITERATURE REVIEW

The financial industry has seen a shift in recent years thanks to decentralized finance, or DeFi. This increased accountability may make accessing banking services less convenient for certain DeFi customers (Gramlich, Guggenberger, Principato, Schellinger, & Urbach, 2023). DeFi is a decentralized and anonymous system that is based on the underlying blockchain technology and DeFi protocols. Anyone may engage and transfer assets using smart contracts as long as they abide by the unchangeable smart contract restrictions since they are publicly available and kept on the blockchain (Shah, Lathiya, Lukhi, Parmar, & Sanghvi, 2023). DeFi technology's ability to remove authorities and effective parties from the system and provide decentralized control is one of its most important achievements (Far, Rad, & Asaar, 2023). Using permissionless blockchain technology, DeFi represent a novel class of consumer-facing financial services built as smart contracts (Jensen, von Wachter, & Ross, 2021). Creativity and innovation in product development require a thorough grasp of the design and operation of various DeFi protocols. Blockchain technology and smart contracts bring a new interesting but controversial application to loans (Klagge & Martin, 2005). The whole financial system may momentarily shut down as a result of an unusual closure of one financial institution (Teng, Tian, Wang, & Yang, 2022). This technology gives novelty and awareness to the necessary community (Hosseinpouli Mamaghani, Elahi, & Hassanzadeh, 2022). The market structure is not competitive. This makes it harder for smaller competitors to enter the market, which drives up the cost of remittance services (Coutinho, Khairwal, & Wongthongtham, 2023). Identified properly, digital and electronically use of technology such as blockchain create problems in working (Srivastava, Grover, Nallakaruppan, Krishwanth & Saravanan, 2023). Further research is needed to determine whether these tokens act technically similarly and how price fluctuations relate to each other to completely classify the DeFi

DOI: 10.1201/9781003461432-15

assets as a group (Piñeiro-Chousa, Šević, & González-López, 2023). DeFi technology provides several advantages, including security, accessibility, and transparency, all on a decentralized platform. Contrarily, Metaverse is a blockchain-based take on a mirror world where users may communicate with one another in a virtual environment that replicates reality (Far, Rad, & Asaar, 2023). Because DeFi services may be combined to create new financial goods and services, the phrase "financial Lego" is occasionally used (Kitzler, Victor, Saggese, & Haslhofer, 2023). The degree of readiness for blockchain technology will depend on how well-equipped the businesses are to implement it. (Ozturan, Atasu, & Soydan, 2019). Numerous information technology (IT) apps make claims about using artificial intelligence (AI) without providing solid evidence to support such claims (Gorodetsky, 2023). The study develops tools and accelerators (layered architecture, business model, target operating model, and product mapping) that solve the managerial issues associated with redesigning decentralized business models (Saurabh, Rani, & Upadhyay, 2023). While there are many potential benefits to a geographically decentralized financial system with large, deeply ingrained regional/local clusters of agents, networks, institutions, and markets, regional/local capital markets nevertheless confront several significant obstacles (Klagge & Martin, 2005). Organizational members who feel committed to executing an organizational change and have faith in their group's ability to do so are said to be in a shared psychological state known as organizational readiness. This method of considering organizational preparedness works best when analysing organizational changes that require adjustments to collective behaviour to be implemented successfully and, in certain situations, to yield the expected advantages of the change (Ozturan, Atasu & Soydan, 2019). From algorithm machine learning model is created and effective, and can also be used in the real world (Bansal, Nallakaruppan, Mon, Grover & Balusamy, 2023).

INTRODUCTION

What is DeFi?

DeFi is a peer-to-peer financial system that is transparent, open, and decentralized. It is based on distributed ledgers, most often blockchains, and uses smart contracts to function independently of middlemen (Klagge & Martin, 2005). DeFi describes financial services that are offered on a blockchain by an algorithm without the involvement of a financial services provider (Shah, Lathiya, Lukhi, Parmar, & Sanghvi, 2023). This alternative strategy is predicated on the notion that the centralized method is ineffective and that the centralized structure and antiquated technology of the present financial systems make them particularly open to cyberattacks.

DeFi financial services companies, as opposed to conventional banks and investment businesses, offer banking and financial services such as depository services, lending, investing, and management services using digital assets rather than fiat money. Some of these services may be provided in violation of the laws as they stand.

DeFi ecosystem and architecture

Five distinct levels comprise the multi-layered architecture of DeFi (Kirvesoja, 2022).

a. **The layer of settlement**: The real DLT (Distributed Ledger Technology), in this instance, blockchain, makes up this layer. Blockchain may be thought of as the system's foundation, supporting all other levels and supplying security and trust. The settlement layer facilitates network consensus-building and securely stores transaction data. The settlement layer is exemplified by Ethereum and Bitcoin.
b. **The layer of assets**: This layer is made up of native assets from the settlement layer (the real cryptocurrency), such as Bitcoin or Ethereum, as well as extra assets that have been issued, or tokens, like Ethereum's ERC20 or ERC721.
c. **The layer of protocol**: The protocols for various DeFi use cases, including as lending, exchange, and derivatives, are covered in this layer; I will go into more detail about them later in the following subchapter.
d. **The layer of application**: This layer, often known as the UI-layer, is responsible for creating apps that enable users to connect to certain protocols.
e. **The layer of aggregation**: The aggregation layer functions as an add-on to the application layer, whose primary responsibility is to establish connections between various applications and enable the execution of various kinds of transactions (Figure 15.1).

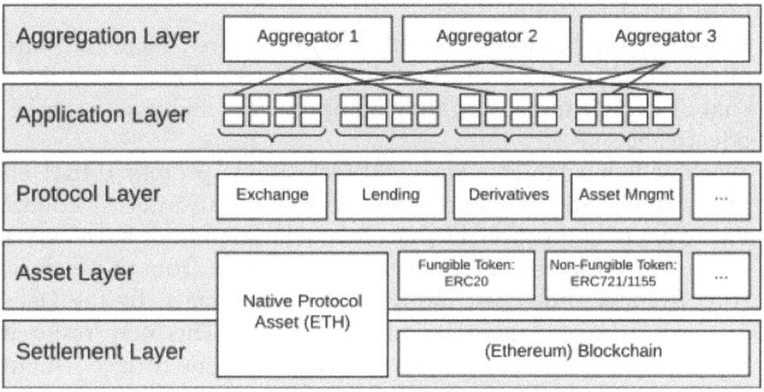

Figure 15.1 Layers of DeFi.

Source: Kirvesoja (2022)

How the DeFi architecture and ecosystem complement the smart global value chain?

There are several ways in which the architecture and ecosystem of DeFi might make the global value chain smarter:

a. **Transparent and effective transactions**: DeFi uses blockchain technology to guarantee transaction security, immutability, and transparency. In the value chain, this can lessen fraud, mistakes, and inefficiencies.
b. **DEXs, or decentralized exchanges**: DEXs, which facilitate peer-to-peer trade without middlemen, are a feature of DeFi systems. This may result in transactions that are quicker and more affordable, which would lessen friction in the global value chain.
c. **Cross-border exchanges**: DeFi is a worldwide platform that makes cross-border transactions easy to complete without the need for conventional banking middlemen. This can simplify corporate processes and international trade.
d. **Asset tokenization**: DeFi makes it feasible to represent both digital and physical assets as blockchain tokens by facilitating the tokenization of multiple assets. Tokenization has the potential to improve asset transferability along the value chain, facilitate fractional ownership, and increase liquidity.
e. **Automated contracts for smarts**: DeFi's smart contracts automate and uphold contracts, doing away with the need for middlemen and paper records. This can improve value chain transaction efficiency, cut expenses, and streamline procedures.
f. **Autonomous organizations that are decentralized (DAOs)**: DAOs are frequently used in DeFi, allowing for decentralized governance and decision-making. As a result, decision-making procedures involving several stakeholders throughout the value chain may become more open and democratic.
g. **Provision for liquidity**: Liquidity pools offered by DeFi platforms allow users to lend or borrow assets. By doing this, the value chain's capital utilization may be optimized, and assets can be used effectively.
h. **Worldwide availability**: Financial inclusion is promoted by DeFi services, which are available to anybody with an internet connection. Participants in the global value chain who might not have easy access to traditional financial services can also benefit from this inclusion.
i. **Inventiveness and trials**: Innovation is encouraged by the DeFi ecosystem's open and permissionless structure. This may result in the creation of fresh financial services and solutions to meet the unique requirements of various global value chain sectors.

Even while the DeFi ecosystem has many potential advantages, it's important to understand that there are drawbacks as well, such as unknown regulations and security threats. In order for the DeFi area to fulfil its promise and contribute to a more intelligent and effective global value chain, it will be imperative to overcome these obstacles as it develops.

Background and significance of DeFi

Using blockchain technology to revolutionize established financial institutions, DeFi is a revolutionary paradigm shift in the financial industry. Fundamentally, DeFi aims to decentralize financial services by providing a substitute framework that is open, safe, and available to a worldwide user base. This introduction gives readers a basic grasp of DeFi and lays the groundwork for further investigation into its technological readiness and potential future applications in financial innovation.

Centralized institutions have long dominated the conventional financial landscape, restricting accessibility, erecting obstacles to entrance, and frequently denying important financial services to a sizeable section of the world's population. Acknowledging these drawbacks, the decentralized alternative was paved with the introduction of blockchain technology, especially with the launch of Bitcoin and later Ethereum.

DeFi expands on the concepts of blockchain by automating and decentralizing financial operations through the use of smart contracts, which are self-executing agreements with the contents of the agreement encoded directly into the code. Individuals may now conduct financial transactions and engage in other financial activities without the assistance of conventional banks or financial organizations because of this move away from centralized middlemen.

The historical history of DeFi is examined in the background section, which traces the technology's origins from the early conception of blockchain to the creation of decentralized apps and the initial DeFi platforms. It also covers the driving forces behind the DeFi ecosystem's explosive expansion, including the need for open and permissionless systems, the need for financial inclusion, and the dissatisfaction with established financial institutions.

DeFi is ushering in a new era of financial innovation and challenging long-standing conventions as it continues to gather momentum. The goal of this chapter is to dissect DeFi by offering a thorough analysis of its technological foundations, implications for financial accessibility, and potential future developments. By doing this, it hopes to advance knowledge of the changing environment where technological readiness and DeFi meet to influence financial innovation in the future.

The significance of DeFi in the context of technological preparedness is highlighted by the following three important factors

The basis is blockchain

Decentralized ledger technology: The distributed and decentralized ledger technology used by DeFi is blockchain. Because blockchain technology is ready, financial transactions may be conducted on a transparent and safe basis, increasing confidence and decreasing the need for middlemen.

Automated systems and smart contracts

Efficiency through code: Self-executing contracts with the terms of the agreement explicitly encoded into code are known as smart contracts, and they are essential to DeFi. Financial procedures are streamlined by this automation, which lowers the need for human interaction and increases transaction efficiency.

Interoperability and scalability

Technological maturity: The scalability and interoperability of DeFi platforms are constantly being enhanced. DeFi is technologically ready thanks to developments in layer 2 solutions and blockchain protocols, which allow it to manage an expanding user base and communicate with other blockchain-based systems with ease.

Applications decentralized (DApps)

Changing ecosystem: DeFi encompasses a wider ecosystem of decentralized apps (DApps) than only financial transactions. These apps make use of blockchain and smart contract technology to provide a range of financial services, including borrowing, lending, trading, and more.

Decentralized identity and security

Enhanced security measures: DeFi explores decentralized identity solutions, enhancing the security and privacy of user data. The use of cryptographic principles and decentralized identifiers contributes to a more robust and secure financial infrastructure.

Including emerging technologies in integration

Synergies between artificial intelligence (AI) and IoT: DeFi's convergence with cutting-edge technologies like AI and IoT demonstrates its flexibility and willingness to integrate state-of-the-art solutions. While IoT devices can supply real-world data for decentralized decision-making, AI can optimize financial plans.

Integration of regulatory technology (RegTech)

Overcoming regulatory obstacles: DeFi's technological preparedness is essential for overcoming regulatory obstacles. By automating regulatory procedures and guaranteeing clear audit trails, RegTech solutions based on blockchain and smart contracts may make compliance easier.

Protocols for decentralized finance

Protocols and standards: The ecosystem's technological preparedness is enhanced by the creation and acceptance of decentralized financial protocols and standards. These protocols offer a foundation for developing financial services that are composable and interoperable across many platforms.

User-friendly interface

Intuitive interfaces: DeFi systems' user interfaces and experiences are developing to become more approachable. This technological preparedness guarantees that anybody may use and access decentralized financial services with ease, regardless of technical proficiency.

Free and open-source cooperation

Community-driven development: Open-source cooperation is frequently embraced by DeFi initiatives, which promotes a community-driven methodology for development. The DeFi ecosystem's technological advancement is accelerated by this willingness for cooperative innovation.

In conclusion, DeFi is critical to technological readiness because it leverages cutting-edge technologies like blockchain and smart contracts together with upcoming ones to build a more inclusive, safe, and effective financial system. The future of finance will be greatly influenced by DeFi's preparedness as these technologies develop and combine.

Foundations of decentralized finance

DeFi leverages DApps and smart contracts to expand upon blockchain technology. DeFi automates procedures with self-executing code, revolutionizing financial systems without the need for middlemen. Transparency, security, and open access are fundamental values that promote worldwide involvement. These foundations provide affordable, permissionless financial services, lessen counterparty risk, and enable trustless transactions. Through programmable, international, and resilient financial ecosystems,

DeFi's development challenges established banking conventions and promotes financial innovation and inclusiveness.

Definition and core principles

Decentralized protocols, smart contracts, and open-source apps provide financial services in the DeFi financial ecosystem, which is based on blockchain technology. Its fundamental ideas support the preparedness of cutting-edge technology by highlighting the following:

Blockchain establishment

- **Definition**: To ensure security and transparency, DeFi records and verifies transactions using the distributed and decentralized ledger of blockchain technology.
- **Fundamental idea**: Using blockchain as the cornerstone technology guarantees an unchangeable, impenetrable ledger, which promotes dependability and trust.

IoT-based contracts

- **Definition**: Smart contracts automate procedures without the need for middlemen by enacting self-executing code that sets the conditions of financial transactions.
- **Fundamental idea**: Smart contracts improve productivity, lower transaction costs, and automate intricate financial processes, all of which help DeFi become more technologically advanced.

Decentralized applications (DApps)

- **Definition**: DApps are blockchain-based, decentralized software programs that offer a variety of financial services.
- **Core principle**: By providing user-friendly interfaces for a range of financial operations, DApps expand the capabilities of DeFi and encourage adoption.

Unrestricted and open access

- **Definition**: DeFi systems allow worldwide participation without authorization as long as one has access to the internet.
- **Fundamental principle**: Unrestricted access improves financial services' inclusiveness and corresponds with the preparedness of permissionless, cross-border financial ecosystems.

Mutual compatibility

- **Definition:** Interoperability enables smooth communication and interaction across various blockchain networks and DeFi systems.
- **Core principle:** Interoperability among DeFi protocols improves technical preparedness overall and fosters a more flexible and linked financial environment.

Safety precautions

- **Definition:** To protect assets and transactions, DeFi uses decentralized security protocols and cryptographic techniques.
- **Core principle:** Strong security measures, such as decentralized identification solutions, strengthen DeFi's preparedness by addressing any weaknesses.

Scalability

- **Definition:** The capacity of DeFi platforms to manage an increasing number of users and transaction volume is referred to as scalability.
- **Core principle:** DeFi's scalability is facilitated by ongoing developments in layer 2 solutions and blockchain protocols, which guarantee that the technology is prepared for widespread use.

To summarize, DeFi's concept and guiding principles about technological preparedness emphasize its dependence on blockchain technology, smart contracts, DApps, open access, security protocols, and scalability. Together, these ideas support the development of a technologically resilient and flexible decentralized financial ecosystem.

What is the technology behind DeFi?

If you are conversant with cryptocurrencies, you have undoubtedly heard of blockchain, Ethereum, and Bitcoin. In a huge and constantly expanding sector, two of the most well-known cryptocurrencies are Ethereum and Bitcoin.

Built on blockchain technology, which is a decentralized digital ledger that records every transaction conducted on that blockchain, are cryptocurrencies like Ether and Bitcoin. Among other things, blockchain technology enables users to buy, trade, and invest in digital assets like cryptocurrency.

DeFi facilitates peer-to-peer financial handling by enabling users to participate in financial operations over the blockchain.

Applications known as "protocols" and "DApps," which are programmes used to manage financial transactions using Bitcoin and Ethereum and that users may access from anywhere in the world, are what power the DeFi blockchain technology (Kataria et al., 2021).

Key components of DeFi

A decentralized financial ecosystem may be established and run with the help of several essential elements that make up DeFi. Together, these elements enable open, transparent, and trustless financial services. The essential elements of DeFi consist of the following:

Technology of blockchain

- Purpose: The core mechanism that gives DeFi its immutable, decentralized ledger for transaction recording.
- Function: Promotes decentralization, security, and transparency in financial transactions.

Smart contracts

- Purpose: Financial agreements' conditions are automated and enforced by self-executing contracts with programmed rules.
- Function: Promotes trustless transaction execution, decreasing the need for middlemen and increasing productivity.

DApps

- Role: Blockchain-based apps or user interfaces providing a range of financial services.
- Function: Enables user-friendly accessibility for users to engage with DeFi protocols.

DEXs

- Platforms that let people trade Bitcoins without depending on centralized middlemen play this role.
- Peer-to-peer trading is encouraged, improving liquidity and lowering counterparty risk.

Protocols for lending and borrowing

- Platforms that let consumers lend or borrow assets directly, without the need for middlemen, play this role.
- Function: Makes it possible for decentralized lending markets to be established, which in turn makes interest-bearing loans and income opportunities easier.

Constant coins

- The role of cryptocurrencies is to provide stability in a tumultuous market by being tied to the value of traditional fiat currencies.

- Function: Within the DeFi ecosystem, it facilitates transactions and reduces exposure to volatility in Bitcoin prices.

Oracles

- The function of external data providers is to supply smart contracts with real-world data.
- Assures that smart contracts are capable of responding to actual occurrences, enabling features like asset price feeds.

Tokens for governance

- Role: Tokens that enable holders to cast ballots for the management of DeFi protocols.
- Function: Enables community members to take part in decision-making procedures about the creation and modification of the protocol.

Mining liquidity and yield farming

- Purpose: DeFi protocols' incentive systems for users to provide liquidity or stake assets.
- Function: By rewarding users with extra tokens or fees, it encourages engagement and liquidity in the ecosystem.

Interconnected platforms

- Platforms that aid in interoperability and communication across various blockchain networks play this role.
- Function: Broadens the range of decentralized financial operations and improves the connection between various DeFi protocols.

The DeFi ecosystem is growing and maturing as a result of the understanding and optimization of these essential elements, which also promotes financial inclusion, innovation, and a decentralized approach to traditional financial services.

Difficulties and hazards of DeFi about technological preparedness

Security issues

- Challenge: Code flaws, hacking attempts, and the possibility of exploits are among the ongoing security issues that DeFi platforms must deal with.
- Risk mitigation: Putting strong security mechanisms in place, auditing smart contracts regularly, and encouraging community-driven bug bounties all help to improve security in general.

Smart contract weaknesses

- Challenge: Many DeFi protocols rely on smart contracts, which are vulnerable to exploitable code faults and vulnerabilities.
- Risk mitigation: To detect and fix smart contract vulnerabilities and lower the likelihood of possible exploits, comprehensive code audits, standardized coding practices, and continuous testing are essential.

Volatility and market risks

- Problem: Because DeFi platforms frequently operate in a very volatile cryptocurrency market, customers are subject to market risks and price swings.
- Risk mitigation: Managing market-related difficulties involves putting risk management principles into practice, using stablecoins to reduce volatility, and informing users about potential hazards connected to market circumstances.

It is critical to handle these risks and problems as DeFi develops to guarantee the ecosystem's continued maturity and expansion. To improve the technical readiness of DeFi platforms and create a more robust and secure decentralized financial infrastructure, developers, auditors, and the community must work together.

CONCLUSION

The chapter concludes by outlining the direction that DeFi will take in the future and how it will affect the larger financial scene. This chapter offers a thorough overview of the DeFi space for scholars, researchers, policymakers, and business professionals. It does this by analysing the technological preparedness of DeFi platforms, analysing regulatory issues, and imagining the integration of cutting-edge technologies.

Summary of Important Points

- A fundamental change in the financial environment, DeFi is powered by cutting-edge technology that challenges established assumptions. Fundamentally, DeFi uses blockchain technology to introduce inclusion, transparency, and decentralization into financial institutions. The cornerstone of blockchain technology guarantees a tamper-resistant and secure ledger, establishing the framework for a financial ecosystem that is globally accessible and trustless.
- Smart contracts become essential elements that use code to automate and enforce financial agreements. This encourages a direct and

peer-to-peer financial experience while also improving operational efficiency and doing away with the need for middlemen. DApps function as intuitive user interfaces, opening up the intricacies of DeFi to a wider audience and enhancing the ecosystem's technological preparedness.

- Security is of utmost importance, as DeFi platforms are vulnerable to a range of threats, such as code flaws and hacker efforts. Strong security protocols, cryptographic methods, and decentralized identity management systems are used to protect resources and transactions, guaranteeing a stable environment for financial operations.
- The technological readiness of DeFi is mostly dependent on its scalability and interoperability. DeFi platforms are scalable due in part to ongoing developments in blockchain protocols and interoperability solutions, which enable them to easily manage an increasing user base. This connectivity fosters cooperative innovation by increasing the financial ecosystem's adaptability.
- Notwithstanding the encouraging developments, problems still exist. Constant attention is needed to address security issues, weaknesses in smart contracts, and vulnerability to market risks and volatility. Complete code audits, standardized coding procedures, and risk management techniques become essential for reducing these issues and bolstering DeFi's technological preparedness.
- Fostering a culture of experimentation in the spirit of invention, DeFi enables the quick development of decentralized apps and financial products. Community-driven development and open-source cooperation increase flexibility and allow for group responses to new possibilities and problems.
- DeFi's adaptability and readiness for cutting-edge solutions become clear when it connects with upcoming technologies like AI and the Internet of Things (IoT). To sum up, DeFi is a revolutionary force that will help to shape a future for global financial systems that is more robust, inclusive, and inventive when it comes to technological preparedness. Steering the further expansion and wider adoption of DeFi will need to embrace continuous technology developments and address obstacles.

IMPLICATIONS FOR THE FUTURE

In terms of technological preparedness, the future of DeFi is quite significant. The development of blockchain and smart contract technologies is anticipated to enhance the scalability and interoperability of DeFi systems, resulting in a smoother and more integrated financial environment. With its efficient, transparent, and secure solutions, DeFi's evolution presents it as a strong contender to replace established banking systems.

Moreover, the incorporation of cutting-edge technologies such as the IoT and AI is anticipated to augment the complexity of DeFi applications. Financial strategies can be optimized by AI-driven algorithms, and decentralized financial ecosystems can be strengthened by IoT devices providing real-world data for decentralized decision-making.

Still, constant innovation and cooperation are required to meet obstacles, including security flaws and legal issues. For widespread adoption, finding a balance between innovation and legal compliance will be essential. DeFi can completely change the financial landscape as it grows and evolves in response to these obstacles. It will provide people all over the world with unparalleled access to a wide range of financial services and play a major role in the overall development of the financial technology industry.

RECOMMENDATIONS FOR FURTHER RESEARCH

Research ought to concentrate on creating interoperability standards, improving security measures against vulnerabilities, and creating scalable blockchain systems. It's also critical to investigate adaptable regulatory frameworks that strike a balance between innovation and compliance. Further research is necessary to increase accessibility and comprehension of user-centric design concepts. To take advantage of improved automation and decision-making skills, the integration of AI and IoT in DeFi should be investigated. To assure the preparedness and durability of decentralized financial ecosystems, more research should comprehensively address technological scalability, security, regulatory problems, user experience, and the integration of new technologies.

REFERENCES

Bansal, A., Nallakaruppan, M. K., Mon, F. A., Grover, V., & Balusamy, B. (2023, October). Heart Disease Prediction with Hyperparameter Analysis. In *2023 International Conference on Computer Science and Emerging Technologies (CSET)* (pp. 1–6). IEEE.

Coutinho, K., Khairwal, N., & Wongthongtham, P. (2023). Towards a Truly Decentralized Blockchain Framework for Remittance. *Journal of Risk and Financial Management*, *16*(4), 240.

Far, S. B., Rad, A. I., & Asaar, M. R. (2023). Blockchain and its derived technologies shape the future generation of digital businesses: a focus on decentralized finance and the Metaverse. *Data Science and Management*, *6*(3), 183–197.

Garg, A., & Ghatak, A. (2020). An Empirical Study on Power Evacuation Projects' Performance: A Strategic Layout in the Indian Context. *Asia-Pacific Journal of Management Research and Innovation*, *16*(1), 31–42.

Gorodetsky, V. I. (2023). Basic Trends of Decentralized Artificial Intelligence. *Pattern Recognition and Image Analysis*, *33*(3), 324–333.

Gramlich, V., Guggenberger, T., Principato, M., Schellinger, B., & Urbach, N. (2023). A multivocal literature review of decentralized finance: Current knowledge and future research avenues. *Electronic Markets*, *33*(1), 11.

Srivastava, S., Grover, V., Nallakaruppan, M. K., Krishwanth, B., & Saravanan, K. (2023, December). Decentralization of Identities Using Blockchain. In *2023 10th IEEE Uttar Pradesh Section International Conference on Electrical, Electronics and Computer Engineering (UPCON)* (Vol. 10, pp. 1304–1309). IEEE.

Hosseinpouli Mamaghani, F., Elahi, S., & Hassanzadeh, A. (2022). A framework to evaluate readiness for blockchain technology implementation. *Journal of Information Technology Management*, *14*(1), 127–157.

Jensen, J. R., von Wachter, V., & Ross, O. (2021). An introduction to decentralized finance (defi). *Complex Systems Informatics and Modeling Quarterly*, (26), 46–54.

Kataria, A., Khan, F., & Garg, A. (2021). Comparative Analysis on Penetration of ATM transactions between Public Sector banks in India. *Turkish Online Journal of Qualitative Inquiry*, 12(10).

Kirvesoja, V. (2022). *Advantages and disadvantages of decentralized financial (DeFi) services* (Master's thesis).

Kitzler, S., Victor, F., Saggese, P., & Haslhofer, B. (2023). Disentangling decentralized finance (DeFi) compositions. *ACM Transactions on the Web*, *17*(2), 1–26.

Klagge, B., & Martin, R. (2005). Decentralized versus centralized financial systems: is there a case for local capital markets? *Journal of Economic Geography*, *5*(4), 387–421.

Ozturan, M., Atasu, I., & Soydan, H. (2019). Assessment of blockchain technology readiness level of banking industry: Case of Turkey. *International Journal of Business Marketing and Management (IJBMM)*, *4*(12), 01–13.

Piñeiro-Chousa, J., Šević, A., & González-López, I. (2023). Impact of social metrics in decentralized finance. *Journal of Business Research*, *158*, 113673.

Saurabh, K., Rani, N., & Upadhyay, P. (2023). Towards blockchain led decentralized autonomous organization (DAO) business model innovations. *Benchmarking: An International Journal*, *30*(2), 475–502.

Shah, Kaushal, Lathiya, Dhruvil, Lukhi, Naimish, Parmar, Keyur, and Sanghvi, Harshal. (2023). A Systematic Review of Decentralized Finance Protocols. *International Journal of Intelligent Networks*, *4*, 171–181.

Teng, H., Tian, W., Wang, H., & Yang, Z. (2022, April). Applications of the Decentralized Finance (DeFi) on the Ethereum. In *2022 IEEE Asia-Pacific Conference on Image Processing, Electronics and Computers (IPEC)* (pp. 573–578). IEEE.

Chapter 16

Entrepreneurship development within the smart global value chain and the performance of small- and medium-scale enterprises

Micro-level evidence from Nigeria

Ambrose Nnaemeka Omeje, Hannah Amarachi Uchendu, and Ravinder Rena
University of Nigeria, Nsukka, Nigeria
Durban University of Technology, Durban, Republic of South Africa

INTRODUCTION

Entrepreneurship development and the need for active performance of small- and medium-scale enterprises (SMEs) in Nigerian economic transformation and sustainable development cannot be over-emphasized. For a country to achieve inclusive economic growth, entrepreneurship development that would enhance SMEs' performance plays a vital role in encouraging people to indulge in different entrepreneurial activities, not minding the amount of resources they have already acquired (Rena, 2007; Kabuoh, 2013). The essence of entrepreneurship development rests majorly on opportunity identification and harnessing of valuable ideas and behaviours into practice (Haase, Lautenschläger, & Rena, 2011; Kabuoh, Ogbuanu, Alagbe, & Egwuonwu, 2016; Kabuoh, Ogbuanu, Chieze, & Adeoye, 2017). The key goal of entrepreneurship development could be realized either by individual or group concerted efforts that tilt towards creativity or innovation drive and the inclination of risk-taking (Rena, 2009; Kabuoh, 2012; Kabuoh et al., 2017). Strong SMEs hence encourage smart global value chains, innovation, and investment opportunities, and discourage technology challenges that could reduce performances of SMEs; this in turn helps an economy to expand sustainably and create jobs for the teaming population, especially the youths (World Bank, 2013; Jegadeshwari & Velmurugan, 2017; Ogbeide & Adeboje, 2017; Mba, Omeje, Ugwu, & Okereke, 2020; Omeje, Mba, Ugwu, Amuka, & Agamah, 2021).

Since SMEs account for the majority of enterprises worldwide, they represent the foundation of the global financial system and the first step toward industrialization for both developed and developing countries (Ikon & Chukwu, 2018). In Nigeria, for instance, SMEs account for almost 57% of the country's gross domestic product (GDP), with employment creation of

DOI: 10.1201/9781003461432-16

over 60%; hence, making them crucial elements in the advancement of the economy since they enhance poverty reduction, employment, and preservation of exchange rates (Imeokparia & Ediagbonya, 2014; World Bank, 2015). SMEs encourage trade and industrialization, as noted by Organization for Economic Co-operation and Development (OECD) (2004). With respect to the part SMEs play in an economy and the kind of deliberate policies and programmes of government agencies and/or institutions that control or regulate SMEs, different countries of the world usually lay down guiding rules or principles and definitions of what constitutes SMEs. The reason for this is that what may be seen as a small business in developed countries such as the United States or Japan may actually be seen as an average and/or even bigger enterprise in the economy of Nigeria, for instance. Even in Nigeria, what constitutes SMEs may also vary across agencies and/or institutions, depending on the focus of the policy establishing them (Etuk et al., 2014). In Nigeria, therefore, SMEDAN, which is a shorthand for Small and Medium Enterprises Development Agency of Nigeria, categorized SMEs as seen in Table 16.1.

However, from the angle of the Central Bank of Nigeria (CBN) (2005), in its asset-based criteria, an SME is seen as any business having maximum assets of about ₦200 million (land and operational capital, not included), with no range of staff bounds/limits. Not minding what SMEs may constitute or look like, they enhance the growth and development of various economies through poverty reduction, employment boost, increased productivity, rise in income levels and/or GDP, export growth, and favourable trade balance (Onugo, 2005). In fact, various Nigerian economic sectors have been affected in varying ways by SMEs, as it has hastened and progressed growth and development (Jegadeshwari & Velmurugan, 2017; Omeje, Mba, & Anyanwu, 2022a). In the words of Ogbeide and Adeboje (2017), when the number of enterprises increases in a given economy, there would be more attraction of critical facilities/infrastructure like electric power supply, roads, supply of clean water, among others, which would automatically promote citizens' living conditions and then, create room for increased saving that would be channelled to productive investment by these SMEs (Omeje, Mba, & Ugwu, 2022b).

Entrepreneurship development and SME performance have also been affected in Nigeria by some business environmental factors which have been

Table 16.1 SMEs categorization in Nigeria

S/N	*Enterprise sizes*	*Employment*	*Assets (excl. land and building)*
1	Micro	< 10	< ₦5 million
2	Small	10 – 49	₦5 million – < ₦50 million
3	Medium	50 – 199	₦50 million – < ₦500 million

Source: SMEDAN and National Bureau of Statistics (2013; 2020)

perceived by SMEs as obstacles to innovation and performance (Steven & Edith, 2012; Kabouh et al., 2017). A look at the business environment factors perceived as obstacles by SMEs would elucidate the fact. These can be shown in Figure 16.1.

Figure 16.1 reveals the top ten SME-identified business environmental obstacles and/or constraints in Nigeria, whereas Figure 16.2 identifies the top three obstacles and/or constraints to SME performance in Nigeria, fragmented into small- and medium-sized businesses. While Figure 16.1 indicates that in Nigeria, only 30.2% of SMEs were of the view that they have difficulty in obtaining financing for business development and performance purposes, 27.2% of the SMEs revealed that the erratic supply of electricity constituted a great obstacle. Corruption was shown to constitute about 14% of the business constraint of SMEs; tax rates and transportation were shown to be about 8% of obstacles; political instability and informal sector practices were shown to be about 5%; land access and customs trade regulation 4%; and tax administration was indicated to constitute about 3% of obstacles to enterprise development and SMEs' performance.

Figure 16.2 reveals that when disaggregated by small- and medium-scaled firms, the business environmental factor obstacles faced by these SMEs in Nigeria seemed to look alike, in which 30.2% of both the small and medium business firms were of the view that they have difficulty in obtaining financing for businesses development and their subsequent performances, whereas about 27.2% of both the small and medium business firms revealed that poor electricity constituted a severe obstacle. Again, while corruption was shown to constitute about 13% of the business constraint of small business enterprises, it constituted about 11% of the obstacles with respect to medium-sized firms. The grouping seen in Figure 16.2 is in respect to the World Bank's grouping of SMEs.

These business environmental factors could be internal or external to SMEs (Makinde, 2015) and may also consist of deficiency in plan sequence, improper keeping of records and/or non-existent recordkeeping, erroneous employment and placement due to corruption, over-dependent, and deliberate single-staff decision units (Onugo, 2005).

In Nigeria, SME performance has been constrained by inefficient and/or inadequate participation in the smart global value chain as a result of a lack of advanced technology, product innovation, innovation in the methods of production, and marketing innovation, among others. In fact, SMEs in Nigeria are facing technology challenges that encourage future innovations, making them drift away from the smart global value chain in this respect. This has made most Nigerian SMEs to be engaged mainly in intermediate products. However, most SMEs in Nigeria are individually making serious efforts to innovate and increase their performance. These innovations are mainly in the areas of product innovation: innovation in the methods of production and marketing, among others.

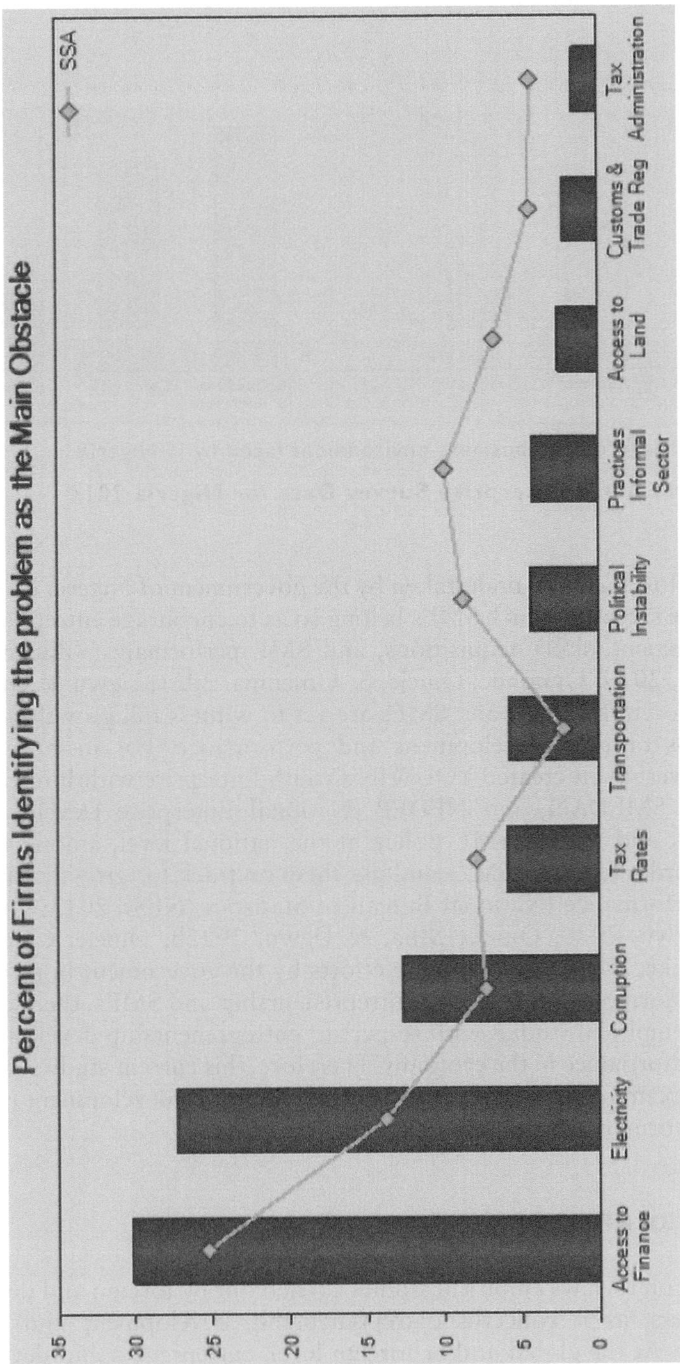

Figure 16.1 Overall business environment faced by SMEs in Nigeria.

Source: World Bank, 2014 Enterprise Survey for Nigeria

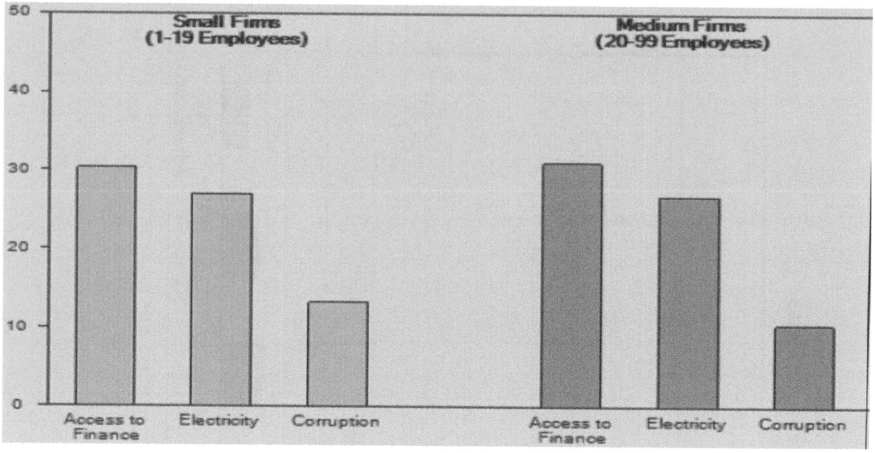

Figure 16.2 Disaggregated business environment faced by in Nigeria.

***Source:* World Bank, Enterprise Survey Data for Nigeria 2014**

A lot of effort has been undertaken by the government of Nigeria in order to reform the sector to which SMEs belong so as to encourage entrepreneurship development, skills acquisitions, and SME performance (Zachariah, Anga, & Isa, 2019; Ogbonne, Omeje, & Omenma, 2021; Ugwu & Omeje, 2021). However, the sector and SMEs are yet to witness full growth potential in terms of their development and performance. For instance, the Nigerian government created YOUWIN (Youth Enterprise with Innovation in Nigeria), SMEDAN, and NEDEP (National Enterprise Development Programme), and revised SME policy at the national level, among other policies, in order to revive SMEs and put them on track for growth innovation and performance (National Bureau of Statistics (NBS), 2013; Omeje, Mba, & Ugwu, 2020; Omeje, Mba, & Ugwu, 2022b; Omeje, Chukwu, Mba, & Okike, 2024). Despite these efforts by the government in recognition of the enormous influences of entrepreneurship and SMEs, there exists a dearth of empirical studies with respect to entrepreneurship development and SME performance in the economy. Therefore, this current study seeks to empirically examine the impact which entrepreneurship development exerts on SME performance in Nigeria.

LITERATURE REVIEW

This subsection reviews empirical studies carried out by foreign and domestic researchers, as it concerns entrepreneurship development and SME performance. At the global and/or foreign level, entrepreneurship development and SME performance have been mainly linked to economic growth.

For example, Anane, Cobbinah, and Manu (2013) investigated how microfinance institutions contribute to the viability of businesses that are small and medium in Ghana's rural areas. Survey data from 93 SME owners/heads of 9 rural areas in the District of Ghana were used for the study, and it was found SMEs were insignificantly encouraged by microfinance institutions in terms of their sustainability and, hence, economic growth. This finding is similar to that of Dogan (2015). In another study within the Mbarara Municipality of Ugaanda, Nuwagaba and Nzewi (2013) investigated the primary environmental barriers to the expansion of a subset of micro and small firms (MSEs) using survey data gotten from 60 SMEs. It was shown by the study that SMEs' growth potential was inversely and significantly influenced by inadequate access to credit and business services, high and multiple taxation, restricted market access, irregular electric supply accompanied by high cost, infrastructural decay, inadequate human capital availability, and dysfunctional competitive business imitativeness instead of innovativeness.

In yet another similar study, Quartey, Turkson, Abor, and Iddrisu (2017) studied in ECOWAS how SME growth financing could be realized and the available constraints on SMEs. Applying survey data and OLS-based multiple regressions, the study attempted to shed some light on the factors influencing SMEs' credit access at regional and national levels within the West African sub-region, with a focus on determining if there exists any commonalities or dissimilarities between them in sub-Saharan African economies. Findings indicated that a number of factors, including sizes of enterprises, possession, legally established rights, available information with regard to credit, export position, and the expertise of upper management significantly enhance credit access at the sub-regional level. Again, Surya, Menne, Sabhan, Suriani, Abubakar, and Idris (2021) studied how economic growth influences SME output, government strategies, enterprise investment, and human capital development of SMEs using sequential explanatory design. Applying the survey data, results indicated economic growth and technical innovation significantly encourage SME output and, at the same time, raise the welfare of individuals. Further, government policies, firm capital provision, and human capital positively and significantly encourage SME development to the tune of about 97.6%. It was recommended however, that there is an urgent need for implementing an economic growth mechanism geared towards technical innovation by the government if output of SMEs is to rise more in Makassar, Indonesia.

At the domestic level, Ikon and Chukwu (2018) examined the connection that exists between Nigeria's industrial progress and SME output using regression analysis and time series data for the years 2002–2016. It was discovered that a statistically significant relationship exists between Nigeria's industrial growth and SME output in Nigeria. It was recommended that SMEs should help to hasten business growth through innovation, and again, the government should mediate SMEs' situation by expediting access to finance such that it can trigger SME advancement and sustainable progress in the country. In another empirical investigation, Onwuchekwa, Emele, and Onwuchekwa (2017) used a cluster-led approach to study SMEs and their business expansion in the Onitsha metropolis of Anambra State in a bid to decipher how agglomeration of SMEs could trigger industrial progress of Nigeria. Porter's Diamond model of group contributing factors served as the study's foundation. For the investigation, a descriptive survey design was chosen. Data for the study were gathered using a questionnaire that employed a five-point Likert-type scale by Pearson: Correlation of Product and Moment. The study hypothesis was tested using the statistical tool known as the coefficient. The results showed a favourable correlation between the industrial development of SMEs in the Onitsha metropolis and strategies of government, assistance, and established information transmission to SME agglomeration.

A study on the factors influencing how Nigerian SMEs have progressed was carried out by Otalu and Keji (2015). The study evaluated the factors influencing Nigeria's industrial sector growth. The following factors were used in the study as key predictors of Nigeria's industrial growth: rate of exchange, labour (which is a proxy for total labour force in the business sector), investment, trade openness, inflation rate, capacity utilization, education (measured by number of people enrolled in school), and electricity generation. When the cointegration and error correction models were applied, the outcome demonstrated that all of the determined factors had a greater permanent impact on industrial output than a transient one. The industrial sector's growth may be hindered by currency appreciation, as seen by the positive and large impact that capital and labour have on the rates of exchange.

SMEs have also been linked to economic growth and development (Rena, 2007; Garg & Singla, 2017). For instance, Ogbuanu, Kabuoh, and Okwu (2014) examined the manufacturing SMEs' potential value in supporting Nigeria's economy. The study used a time series research design and a descriptive method of analysis to examine the role that manufacturing SMEs have played in the growth of the Nigerian economy. Relevant publications from the CBN and the NBS were used to gather information. The use of graphs enhanced the descriptive analysis of data values across time. The findings demonstrated that manufacturing SMEs contributed significantly to the GDP's continuous gains, maintained employment rates over 7% for most of the 2002–2012 period, and continued to raise their share of the GDP. In order to facilitate the development of the industries toward efficient and inclusive growth, recommendations for increasing government support of SMEs were made. In yet another study, Ilegbinosa and Jumbo (2015) looked at SMEs and Nigeria's economic growth between 1975 and 2012. The primary goal of the study was to investigate how SMEs affect Nigeria's economic expansion. Eighty-four SMEs were surveyed for primary data, and statistics records covering the years 1975–2012 were used for secondary data collecting. The data gathered throughout the study period was estimated using the cointegration, OLS multiple regressions, and ECM models. According to a study, the amount of financing accessible to SMEs positively correlated with economic progression, although the rates of interest and inflation had opposite effects. For inclusive growth, guidelines for the effective interest rate for SMEs, CBN financing, and government involvement in the industry were provided.

In their study, Taiwo, Ayodeji, and Yusuf (2012) looked at how small- and medium-sized businesses affect development and economic growth. Utilizing survey data obtained from 200 SMEs, official owners, and their managers in 5 Local Government Areas of Nigeria and applying the correlation coefficient analysis, it was found that the most frequent obstacles to the expansion of SMEs in Nigeria were inadequate funding, widespread corruption, bad administration, employment of inexperienced and well-trained persons, inadequate and sometimes infrastructural decay, low earnings, and shortfalls in demand for goods and services. To secure the survival of emerging industries, Nigerian monetary authorities were advised to urgently provide SMEs with financial support and also use import tariffs to promote locally produced items.

An inquiry into the importance of SMEs and their businesses, and how Nigeria advances its economy was conducted by Eke (2010). The study's primary focus was on financing small and medium-sized enterprises for economic development. Finding new or improved ways to finance SMEs to improve their performance and support national economic development and growth was the primary objective of the study. The two main techniques for collecting data were questionnaires with a set format and in-person interviews. The collected data were assessed using percentages and frequencies, and the results were shown as a frequency distribution in tables. The sign test and the Pearson product moment correlation coefficient were used to test the hypothesis. The study's conclusions suggested that small and medium-sized enterprises did not have enough money, and several remedies, such as direct government finance intervention, were put out to solve this problem. This stud's finding does not vary from that of Ihua (2012).

Also, a look at entrepreneurship and SMEs has shown that they are linked to poverty. For example, Johnson (2016) examined the link between poverty and unemployment as well as the entrepreneurship of SMEs in Nigeria: 326 individuals were included in the research sample, which was determined using the Taro Yamane method and based on the 1,754 study universe. A sample of 100 SMEs in Nigeria's manufacturing, services, food processing, textile, and agricultural sectors that had been in business for at least five years prior to the survey's launch provided the data for this study. During the data collection stage of this study, cluster sampling techniques were applied, and simple random sampling techniques were utilized to select the required sample size for the universe. The data were analysed using regression analysis, correlation analysis, and descriptive statistics (SPSS version 17.0). The findings indicate a high positive correlation (r = 0.746) between the degree of poverty and entrepreneurship through SMEs, as well as a notable positive relationship ($r = 0.640$) between unemployment and poverty in Nigeria. The study concludes that there are irregularities in entrepreneurial practices that need to be addressed immediately by economists. These irregularities include increased entrepreneurial activity and related rises in the variables (poverty and unemployment) in Nigeria. Because many SME owner-managers are driven more by the requirement of entrepreneurship than by a passion for it, the study recommends that the government adequately assist SMEs in order to create jobs and that their entrepreneurial methods be reviewed and adjusted. The finding of this study is in line with that of Gbemi, Bimbo, & Ekpenyong (2021), Nhuta, & Kapofu (2015), Nto & Mbanasor (2011), Suleiman (2011), Teece & Pisano (1994), and Teece, Pisano, & Shuen (1997).

Omeje, Mba, and Ugwu (2020) experimentally investigated whether youth empowerment has significantly increased entrepreneurship, which has in turn led to economic diversification in Nigeria, using data from the Nigeria Enterprise Survey (2014) and the multinomial logistic regression model. With the exception of tax rates, land access, and transportation costs when comparing micro and large enterprises to small-scale businesses, and tax rates, subsidies, and land access when comparing medium-sized businesses to small-scale businesses, almost all of the variables used to measure the growth and development of entrepreneurship in Nigeria were found to be statistically significant. It was recommended, among other things, that the World Bank, governmental organizations, private donors, and governments at all levels concentrate more effort on youth entrepreneurship training programmes. After being empowered, these entrepreneurs should get continuing training, non-financial support, and supervision of their business operations. A related study by Omeje, Mba, & Ugwu (2022b), and Wiklund (2006).

METHODOLOGY

Theoretical framework

This study adopts a model that is built on the Schumpeterian Growth Theory, which supports the premise of efficiency on the basis of innovation being the major determinant of enterprise performance. The theory postulates that efficient enterprises make up enterprises which have improved capabilities in the production of different brands of fresh goods, processes, and markets or that discover innovative raw material sources and/or reposition the market. Based on this notion, this study specifies a regression model of SME performance being a linear function of entrepreneurship development, where entrepreneurship development is defined as dummy variables with a value of 1 if the SME has (Shane, 2003; Ali et al., 2014) created a new or significantly improved product that is also brand-new in the market (Stevenson, 1990; Anane et al., 2013); introduced a new or significantly improved method of producing a product or providing services (Agwu & Emeti, 2014); introduced any new or significantly improved methods for distribution, logistics, or delivery of inputs, goods, or services (Anam & Antai, 2016); introduced a new or significantly improved organizational structure; and, finally (Drucker, 1985), introduced new or significantly improved marketing techniques. This is represented with the following linear equation:

$$\text{SME}_P = f(\text{Entd}), \tag{16.1}$$

where SME_P = SME performance, Entd = Entrepreneurship development, and f = functional notation. SME performance (SME_P) is measured here using total factor productivity (TFP), defined as SMEs annual sales shared by the aggregate number of employees (both permanent and temporary workers).

Model specification

In view of the study objectives, a linear model that captures the effect of entrepreneurship development on performance of SMEs is specified. The specification of this model comes in three forms: the model's functional shape, which is founded on well-informed economic theory and specified as:

$$\text{SME}_P = f(\text{Entd}_i, \text{X}_i) \tag{16.2}$$

Again, the mathematical form of the model which states a deterministic relationship of the model variables can be specified as given below:

$$\text{SME}_P = a_0 + b_1\text{Entd}_i + b_2\text{X}_i \tag{16.3}$$

where; SME_P = SME performance is measured by TFP, Entd = entrepreneurship development, and which represents all indicators or vector of entrepreneurship innovation such as product innovation, marketing innovation, process innovation, organizational methods, and distributional methods, while X_i represents a vector of enterprise-level factors that could affect SME performance such as their access to finance, infrastructure, labour force, among others. a_0 is the intercept term, whereas $b_{i's}$ are the parameter estimates. The econometric form of the model can therefore be specified as follows:

$$\text{SME}_P = a_0 + b_1\text{Entd}_i + b_2\text{X}_i + \mu_i, \tag{16.4}$$

where all the variables remained as already defined, but μ_i = stochastic error term.

The justification of the inclusion of these variables in the model is that, indicators of SME performance used in the study are already provided for in the World Bank Enterprise Survey for Nigeria (World Bank Enterprise Survey (WBES), 2014). The enterprise survey captured information on enterprise performance, such as SMEs' total annual sales and number of employees, thereby making it possible for the construction of the variable known as TFP, which is simply the total annual sales of the establishment divided by the number of the establishment's employees. Again, the key explanatory variables of this study are indicators of entrepreneurship development defined under the following heading: new or improved product/services, new/improved manufacturing process, new/improved delivery methods, new/improved organizational structure, and new/improved marketing methods.

In addition, several other control variables at the enterprise level are also included in the model. The rationale behind their inclusion is to mitigate the problem of endogeneity arising from a too-simple model that generates biased and inconsistent parameter estimates. Also, the general-to-specific approach is adopted in the inclusion of control variables with the aim of retaining only those variables that produce the best model. The choice of control variables is based on economic theories and empirical literature on SME performance. Table 16.2 provides a detailed description of the variables to be used in this study.

Table 16.2 Definition of variables

Variable name	*Narrative*
SME_P	SME performance is measured by TFP
Innovaton1	Assuming the value, 1 for SMEs that produce a new or significantly enhanced product, which is also new in the market, and 0 otherwise
Innovation2	Assuming the value, 1 for SMEs that have introduced a new or significantly improved method of manufacturing products or offering services, and 0 otherwise
Innovation3	Assuming the value, 1 for SMEs introducing any fresh or significantly upgraded logistics, supplies/deliveries, and/or dissemination mechanisms for inputs, goods, or services, and 0 otherwise
Innovation4	Assuming the value of 1 for SMEs that have led new or significantly enhanced organizational structure and 0 otherwise
Innovation5	Assuming the value, 1 for SMEs that have presented new or significantly upgraded marketing methods, and 0 otherwise
Domestic_Est	% of the establishment possessed by private local persons, businesses, and/or organizations
Foreign_Est	% of the establishment maintained by private overseas persons, businesses, and/or organizations
Registered_Est	Assuming the value, 1 for registered SMEs, and 0 otherwise.

(*Continued*)

Table 16.2 (Continued)

Variable name	*Narrative*
Sole_Proprietorship	dummy variable equals 1 if the establishment is owned by one individual, 0 otherwise
Working_Capital1	% of retained earnings or internal funds used to support working capital
Working_Capital2	% of bank-borrowed working capital
Finance_FixedAsset	% fixed assets funded by bank borrowing
Govt_Finance	Dummy variable equals 1 if SME receive any financing from a government in last fiscal year, 0 otherwise
Owned_Generator	% of power from the establishment's own or shared generator during the previous fiscal year
Tax_Rates	If an SME describes tax rates as a significant, severe, or extremely severe hurdle for its current operations, the dummy variable equals 1, and if it reports tax rates as a minor obstacle or not at all, it equals 0.
Workers_Edu	% of full-time employees with a high school degree
Workers_Training	The dummy variable is set to 1 if the SME offered formal training programmes to full-time, permanent employees during the previous fiscal year and to 0 otherwise
Fixed_Asset	Dummy variable equals 1 if SME purchased any fixed assets in the last fiscal year, 0 otherwise
Product_Demand	dummy variable equals 1 if SME experienced a significant increase in the demand for its products or services, 0 otherwise.
Annual_Sales	Log of SMEs total sales in past three year.

Source: Extracted from World Bank Enterprise Survey for Nigeria

Source of data

The data here was sourced from enterprise surveys steered by World Bank for Nigeria in the year 2014. This is the only latest national available data by the World Bank that captures the SMEs and their performance indicators for Nigeria private sector. It makes use of a standard questionnaire along with a common sample technique called stratified random sampling. The sample is segmented by industry, company size, and geographic region. The dataset has some characteristics that make it a suitable data for the study of how entrepreneurship development impacts SME performance in Nigeria. First, it contains information about organizational innovative activities that captures entrepreneurship development. Second, organizations that formed the population of the dataset were classified according to their sizes, further making it possible to examine factors that pertain to SMEs alone. Lastly, the enterprise survey dataset has a wealth of information on enterprise-level features that may aid in deciphering the factors that influence business performance.

RESULTS PRESENTATION AND DISCUSSIONS

Variable summary statistics

The summary statistics of the study variables are presented in Table 16.3. Information about the sample mean, standard deviation, and minimum and maximum values are provided in the table.

Table 16.3 presents summary statistics for a sample of 239 SMEs that form the study's sample. The average productivity of an SME in this sample is about ₦8,356,274. The proportion of SMEs that have produced a new product or significantly improved their product, which is new in their main market, is estimated at 71.97%. Similarly, about 86.61% have introduced or significantly improved their method of manufacturing products or offering services. The proportion of SMEs in the sample that have introduced new or significantly improved logistics, delivery, or distribution methods for inputs, products, or services is estimated at 78.66%, while the proportion of those that have significantly improved or introduced new organizational structure is given as 66.95%. About 80.75% are estimated to have introduced new or improved their marketing methods.

Table 16.3 Variable summary statistics

Variable	*Obs.*	*Mean*	*Std. Dev.*	*Min*	*Max*
SME_P	239	8356274	4.76e+07	400	5.00e+08
Innovation1	239	0.7196653	0.4501054	0	1
Innovation2	239	0.8661088	0.3412501	0	1
Innovation3	239	0.7866109	0.41056	0	1
Innovation4	239	0.6694561	0.4713962	0	1
Innovation5	239	0.8075314	0.3950664	0	1
Domestic Est.	239	80.68619	32.99946	0	100
Foreign Est.	239	3.514644	11.3755	0	100
Registered Est.	239	0.3179916	0.4666735	0	1
Sole proprietor	239	0.8033473	0.3983017	0	1
Working_Capital1	239	72.21339	33.08508	0	100
Working_Capital2	239	4.075314	11.33683	0	70
Fin. Fixed_Asset	239	2.665272	9.943374	0	100
Govt. Finance	239	0.9748954	0.1567712	0	1
Owned Generator	239	59.98326	25.09025	0	100
Tax rates	239	0.5355649	0.4997802	0	1
Workers_Edu	239	58.32636	39.88863	0	100
Workers Training	239	0.5690377	0.4962501	0	1
Fixed Asset	239	0.3430962	0.4757396	0	1
Product Demand	239	0.1380753	0.345703	0	1

Source: Author's construction from available data

The average portion of domestic ownership of establishments in this sample is estimated at 80.69%, while that of foreign ownership is estimated at only 3.51%. Only 31.80% of the SMEs in this sample were formally registered when they began operation. Over 80% of the SMEs are sole proprietors. On average, 72.21% of the working capital of a typical SME in this sample is sourced from internal funds/retained earnings, while only 4.07% is sourced by bank borrowing. The percentage of fixed assets funded by bank borrowing is estimated at 2.67% on average. Over 97% of SMEs in this sample have received financial support from the government.

The average electricity generated from the owned generator of an SME in this sample is estimated at approximately 60%. About 53.55% of the SMEs report tax rates to be major, severe, or very severe to their current operations. On average, the proportion of workers who completed high school in this sample is estimated at 58.33%. About 57% of SMEs in this sample provide formal training programmes for their permanent full-time employees. Only 34.31% of them purchased fixed assets in the last fiscal year, while just 13.81% experienced a significant increase in demand for their products or services.

Empirical results

Empirical results of this study are summarized in Table 16.4. The estimated coefficients are interpreted with respect to their signs and magnitude. References to "significant" or "insignificant" estimated coefficient values refer to the conventional 10%, 5%, and 1% levels of significance.

Table 16.4 Robust OLS regression results

Independent variables	*Coefficient*	*Robust stand. error*	*T*	*P > t*
Innovation1	1.46981	0.2467942	5.96	0.027
Innovation2	−0.5264795	0.1000878	−5.26	0.034
Innovation3	0.830541	0.4424434	1.88	0.201
Innovation4	−0.8727693	0.7290163	−1.20	0.354
Innovation5	0.4301441	0.3428051	1.25	0.336
Domestic Est.	0.0036142	0.0022557	1.60	0.250
Foreign Est.	0.0043381	0.0086994	0.50	0.667
Registered Est.	−0.0054359	0.2071685	−0.03	0.981
Sole proprietor	0.4787689	0.2872198	1.67	0.237
Working_Capital1	0.0108526	0.0052032	2.09	0.172
Working_Capital2	0.0264668	0.0009222	28.70	0.001
Fin. Fixed_Asset	0.0059741	0.0326435	0.18	0.872
Govt. Finance	1.206953	0.4065344	2.97	0.097
Owned Generator	−0.0081846	0.0004868	−16.81	0.004
Tax rates	−0.1932992	0.0203935	−9.48	0.011

(Continued)

Table 16.4 (Continued)

Independent variables	*Coefficient*	*Robust stand. error*	*T*	*P > t*
Workers_Edu	0.0096399	0.0007121	13.54	0.005
Workers Training	0.8261395	0.1841544	4.49	0.046
Fixed Asset	0.5877236	0.4149489	1.42	0.292
Product Demand	0.3957004	0.4001287	0.99	0.427
Annual Sales	0.0659672	0.0239717	2.75	0.111
_cons	7.142545	1.195894	5.97	0.027

Source: Author's construction from available data

Results obtained from the analysis show that there exist mixed findings with respect to the entrepreneurship indicators included in the study. First, the estimated coefficient of Innovation1 is given as 1.46981. This implies that SMEs that produce a new product in the market or significantly improve their product have increased their productivity by about 1.47% compared to their counterparts, which is in line with theoretical expectations. This is found to be significant at the 5% level. Similarly, Innovation3 and Innovation4 are found to have positive effects on SME productivity, meaning that SMEs that have introduced new or significantly improved methods of product or service delivery and marketing increase their total productivity compared to their counterparts. However, these effects are not significant at any of the conventional significance levels. Surprisingly, SMEs with new or improved methods of production or service delivery are found to face lower productivity than their counterparts, which is against prior expectations. In the same vein, SMEs with improved or new organizational structures were also found to have low productivity, although not significant at any conventional level.

Moving over to the controls, the first set of controls relates to SME ownership and legal status. All the variables pertaining to the first controls were found not to exert any significant impact on SMEs' productivity, though the majority were in their right signs. First, it is found that increasing the proportion of domestic and foreign ownership of SMEs is associated with higher productivity but is statistically insignificant. Against expectation, legally registered SMEs are found to have reduced productivity more than their opponents, while sole proprietors, on the other hand, are found to have better productivity levels.

The second set of controls relates to SMEs' financing. Among the variables included in this category are SMEs' sources of financing, working capital, and fixed assets. First, the study found that SMEs that finance their working capital using retained earnings (Working_Capital1) increase their total productivity by 1.09%. However, this is not significant at any of the conventional levels. On the other hand, SMEs that finance their working capital using bank borrowing (Working_Capital2) experience a significant increase in their productivity level by 2.65%. In a like manner, it is found that increasing the percentage of fixed assets financed using bank loans (Fin. Fixed_Asset) increases SMEs' productivity by 0.59%. This is also found to be statistically significant. A large positive coefficient of Govt_Finance indicates that SMEs' productivity increases with every additional financing from the government to SMEs. This effect was found to be weakly significant at the 10% significant level.

Another set of control variables included in this study aimed at capturing some of the major constraints faced by SMEs in the country. The first variable in this category is the percentage of electricity generated from owned generators (Owned_Generator). This variable captures the effect of copping cost on SMEs' productivity. As expected, this effect is negative and strongly significant at the 1% level. The value of the estimated coefficient implies that SMEs' productivity drops by 0.82% for every additional copping cost incurred in the form of electricity generation from an owned generator. This study further accounts for SMEs' perceptions of tax rates' effects on their current operations. It is found that SMEs that reported tax rates to be a major, severe, or very severe obstacle to their operations have low productivity compared to their opponents. This effect is also found to be significant at the 5% level.

The next set of controls relates to capabilities and resources that are internal to SMEs. First, it is found that SME performance increases with the percentage of its permanent workforce that completed high school (Workers_Education) and is statistically significant at the 1% level. Similarly, a significant positive relationship is established between SMEs' productivity and employees' formal training (Workers_Training). This means that SMEs' productivity increases with every additional training provided at the employee level. However, no significant relationship exists between SMEs' productivity and the acquisition of fixed assets (Fixed_Asset).

The last of set of controls captures the effect of market demand on SMEs productivity. The effects of Product_Demand – SMEs that experienced a significant increase in their product demand – and past SMEs' sales (Annual_Sales) are found to be positive but insignificant at any of the conventional levels.

CONCLUSION AND RECOMMENDATIONS

This study examined the role of entrepreneurship development on SME performance in Nigeria using enterprise data sourced from the latest World Bank Enterprise Survey for Nigeria. Entrepreneurship development is classified in the study context to include product innovation, marketing innovation, process innovation, organizational methods and distributional methods. The method of robust ordinary least squares was employed to estimate the model. The study constructed a variable defined as TFP as a proxy for SME performance. In addition, it controlled for several factors at the enterprise level that can influence SME performance.

Empirical findings from the study showed product innovation to be significantly related to SME performance with an expected positive significant impact. The effects of distribution and marketing methods were found to be positive and insignificant. On the other hand, manufacturing method was found to have a significant negative effect on SME performance, while the effect of organization was found to be negative and insignificant in the way it influenced SME performance in Nigeria.

Among the controls, the following were found to exert significant impact on SME performance: percentage of working capital financed by bank borrowing (Working_Capital2), SMEs with financing from the government (Govt_Finance), percentage of electricity generated from SMEs own generator (Owned_Generator), SMEs having tax rates as a major, severe or very severe obstacle to current operations (Tax_Rates), percentage of employees that completed high school (Workers_Edu), and SMEs providing formal training for employees (Workers_Training).

Based on the study's findings, it was recommended that the promotion of enterprise development through innovation is essential for SME performance in developing nations like Nigeria, which is characterized by a high unemployment rate. Further, in order to help improve SME performance in Nigeria, serious attention should be given to SME performance by making SMEs invest more in research and development so as to be more innovative and improve performance, encouraging increased financial credit to SMEs by the government and other stakeholders, and making relevant tax authorities review taxation policies that pertain to SMEs for tax holidays and/or concession where necessary. Again, infrastructural constraints that impose additional copping costs on SMEs should be addressed by the government; investment in human capital, especially in education, should be promoted; and, finally, SMEs should develop specific strategies such as regular workshops and in-house training for employees, in order to help enhance their capabilities, competitive positions, and performances.

REFERENCES

Agwu, M.O., & Emeti, C.I. (2014). Issues, challenges and prospects of small and medium scale enterprises (SMEs) in Port-Harcourt city. *European Journal of Sustainable Development*, 3(1), 101–101.

Ali, S., Rashid, H., & Khan, M.A. (2014). The role of small and medium enterprises and poverty in Pakistan: An empirical analysis. *Theoretical and Applied Economics*, 21(4), 67–80.

Anam, B., &Antai, A.S. (2016). Entrepreneurship and dynamic enterprise, entrepreneurship, innovation and management techniques. *African Development Charter Series* (4), 2–4.

Anane, G., Cobbinah, P., & Manu, J. (2013). Sustainability of small and medium scale enterprises in rural Ghana: The role of microfinance institutions. *Asian Economic and Financial Review*, 3(8), 1003–1017.

Central Bank of Nigeria (CBN) (2005). Guidelines for the small and medium enterprises equity investment scheme. *Central Bank of Nigeria Pubs*, 4, 1–5. Available at: cbn.gov.ng/OUT/PUBLICATIONS/GUIDELINES/DFD/2005/SMEEIS%20GUIDELINE.PDF

Dogan, N. (2015). The intersection of entrepreneurship and strategic management: Strategic entrepreneurship. *Journal of Turkey & Social Behavioral Sciences*, 195, 1288–1294.

Drucker, P. (1985). *Innovation and Entrepreneurship*. Harper and Row Publishers, New York, NY.

Eke, R. (2010).*The Relevance of Small and Medium Scale Enterprises to Nigeria's Economic Development: An Investigation*. M.Sc Thesis, Nnamdi Azikiwe University, Awka, Nigeria.

Etuk, R.U., Etuk, G.R., & Baghedo, M. (2014).Small and medium scale enterprises (SMEs) and Nigeria's economic development. *Mediterranean Journal of Social Sciences*, 5(7), 656–662.

Garg, A., & Singla, N. (2017). Environment sustainability awareness model for IT SMEs. *Interdisciplinary Environmental Review*, 18(1), 1–5.

Gbemi, O.O., Bimbo, O.A., & Ekpenyong, E.U. (2021). The gains and pains of small and medium-scale enterprises (SMEs): The way forward for entrepreneurship development in Nigeria. *Rajagiri Management Journal*, 15(1), 53–68.

Haase, H., Lautenschläger, A., & Rena, R. (2011). The entrepreneurial mind-set of university students: A cross-cultural comparison between Namibia and Germany. *International Journal of Education Economics and Development*, 2(2), 113–129.

Ihua, A. (2012). Entrepreneurial innovation: Small and medium scale enterprises health research and economic development in Nigeria. *Research on Humanities and Social Sciences*, 2(11), 49–55.

Ikon, M.A., &Chukwu A.C. (2018).Small and medium scale enterprises and industrial growth in Nigeria. *International Journal of Small Business and Entrepreneurship Research*, 6(6), 1–13.

Ilegbinosa, I., & Jumbo, E. (2015). Small and medium scale enterprises and economic growth in Nigeria: 1975-2012. *International Journal of Business and Management*, 10(3), 203–216.

Imeokparia, P., & Ediagbonya, K. (2014). Small and medium scale enterprises (SMEs): A catalyst in promoting economic development in Nigeria. *Journal of Education and Practice*, 5(33), 92–94.

Jegadeshwari, S., & Velmurugan R. (2017).Determinants of micro, small, and medium enterprises entrepreneur sustainability. *Journal of Advanced Research in Dynamic and Control System*, 10(3): 149–154.

Johnson, J.O. (2016). Poverty issue and the entrepreneurial engagement of small scale enterprises in Nigeria. *European Journal of Business and Management*, 8(19), 45–54.

Kabuoh, M.N. (2012). Branding as an enhancement to organization sustainability and profitability in five selected companies in Lagos Nigeria. *International Journal of Social Sciences*, 6(5), 12–24.

Kabuoh, M.N. (2013). Micro, small and medium scale enterprises (MSME'S) and insurance marketing in developing countries. *International Journal of Advancement in Management Science*, 3(3), 138–144.

Kabuoh, M.N., Ogbuanu, B.K., Alagbe, A., & Egwuonwu, T.K. (2016). An assessment of market performance as a dependent on market segmentation strategy in Nigerian banks. *International Journal of Advanced Studies in Business Strategies and Management*, 4(2), 1–12, ISSN: Hard Print: 2354-4236 Online: 2354-4244.

Kabuoh, M.N., Ogbuanu, B.K., Chieze, A.I., & Adeoye, I. (2017). Entreprenuerial culture and performance of small and medium enterprises (SMEs) in Nigeria. *International Journal of Operational Research in Management, Social Sciences & Education*, 3(1), 1–10.

Makinde, O.G. (2015). *Strategic Planning and Performance of Small and Medium Enterprises (SMES) in Lagos State, Nigeria*. Unpublished PhD Thesis. Babcock University, Ilishan-Remo, Ogun State.

Mba, A.J., Omeje, A.N., Ugwu, M.O., & Okereke, C.U. (2020). The effects of institution on enterprise growth in Nigeria. *The International Journal of Business & Management*, 8(1), 244–251, ISSN 2321–8916. doi: 10.24940/theijbm/2020/v8/i1/150389-371189-2-SM. Available Online at: www.theijbm.com

National Bureau of Statistics (NBS) (2013). Small and Medium Enterprises Development Agency of Nigeria (SMEDAN) and National Bureau of Statistics (NBS) Collaborative Survey: Selected Findings. Retrieved from http://www.nigerianstat.gov.ng/download/290&ved

Nhuta, S.,& Kapofu, W. (2015). Evaluation of strategic entrepreneurship approaches for sustainable growth in the commercial banking sector in Zimbabwe. *International Journal of Contemporary Applied Sciences*, 2(2), 57–83.

Nigeria Enterprise Survey (2014). World Bank, Nigeria Enterprise Survey. *World Bank Pubs*. Available at: https://microdata.worldbank.org/index.php/catalog/2361

Nto, P.O., & Mbanasor, J.A. (2011). Productivity in agribusiness firms and its determinants in Abia State. *Journal of Economic International Finance*, 3(12), 662–667.

Nuwagaba, A., & Nzewi, H. (2013). Major environmental constraints on growth of micro and small enterprises in Uganda: A survey of selected micro and small enterprises in Mbarara municipality. *International Journal of Cooperative Studies*, 2(1), 26–33.

Ogbeide, F.I., & Adeboje O.M. (2017). Financial liberalization and business entry Nexus in SSA: To what extent does resource dependence and institutional quality matter? *Development Bank of Nigeria Journal of Economics and Sustainable Growth*, 1(1), 1–18.

Ogbonne, I.P., Omeje, A.N., & Omenma, J.T. (2021). Utilisation of information and communication technology among informal traders in the local economies in Nigeria. *International Journal of Entrepreneurship and Small Business*, 44(3), 211–234

Ogbuanu, B., Kabuoh, M., & Okwu, A. (2014). Relevance of small and medium enterprises in the growth of the Nigerian economy: A study of manufacturing

SMEs. *International Journal of Advanced Research in Statistics, Management and Finance*, 2(1), 180–191.

Omeje, A.N., Chukwu, N.O., Mba, A.J., & Okike, M.U. (2024). Financial inclusion and the growth of micro, small, and medium enterprises (MSMEs) in Nigeria. *International Journal of Business Performance Management*. 25(3), 327–344. doi: 10.1504/IJBPM.2024.10052523, https://www.inderscience.com/info/ingeneral/forthcoming.php?jcode=IJBPM

Omeje, A.N., Mba, A.J., & Anyanwu, O.C. (2022a). Impact of insecurity on enterprise development in Nigeria. *Journal of Entrepreneurship in Emerging Economies*. Vol. ahead-of-print No. ahead-of-print. ISSN: 2053-4604. doi: 10.1108/JEEE-11-2021-0449

Omeje, A.N., Mba, A.J., & Ugwu, M.O. (2020). *Youth Empowerment and Entrepreneurship in Nigeria: Implication for Economic Diversification*. SAGE Open, October-December 2020: 1–12. doi: 10.1177/2158244020982996

Omeje, A.N., Mba, A.J., & Ugwu, M.O. (2022b). Electricity utilization and firm efficiency in Nigeria: Evidence from data envelopment analysis. *International Journal of Critical Infrastructures*, 18(3), 240–266. doi: 10.1504/IJCIS.2022.10041728. Available online at: https://www.inderscience.com/info/ingeneral/forthcoming.php?jcode=ijcis

Omeje, A.N., Mba, A.J., Ugwu, M.O., Amuka, J., & Agamah, P.N. (2021). Examining the penetration of financial inclusion in the agricultural sector: Evidence from small-scale farmers in Enugu State, Nigeria. *Agricultural Finance Review*, 82(1), 49–66. ISSN: 0002–1466. doi: 10.1108/AFR-05-2020-0074

Onugo, B.A. (2005). Small and medium enterprises (SMEs) in Nigeria: Problems and prospects. Unpublished. St Clements University. Retrieved on 20 July, 2021 from http://www.wasmeinfo.org/

Onwuchekwa F., Emele, E., & Onwuchekwa, J. (2017). Small and medium scale enterprises (SMES) and industrial development of Onitsha Metropolis: A cluster lead approach. *International Journal of Economics and Business Management*, 3(10), 64–77.

Organization for Economic Co-operation and Development (OECD) (2004). Promoting entrepreneurship and innovative SMEs in a Global Economy: Towards a more responsible and inclusive globalization. A Report of 2nd OECD Conference of Ministers Responsible for Small and Medium Sized Enterprise (SMEs) in Istanbul, Turkey (3–5 June, 2004).

Otalu, J., &Keji, S. (2015). An assessment of the determinants of industrial sector growth in Nigeria. *Journal of Research in Business and Management*, 3(7), 1–9.

Quartey, P., Turkson, E., Abor, J., & Iddrisu, A. (2017). Financing the growth of SMEs in Africa: What are the contraints to SME financing within ECOWAS? *Review of Development Finance*, 7, 18–28.

Rena, R. (2007). Entrepreneurship and rural development – A case of Eritrea. *The Asian Economic Review*, 49(2), 165–178.

Rena, R. (2009). Rural entrepreneurship and development – An Eritrean perspective. *Journal of Rural Development*, 28(1), 1–19.

Shane, S.A. (2003). *A General Theory of Entrepreneurship: The Individual-Opportunity Nexus*. Edward Elgar, Cheltenham.

SMEDAN and National Bureau of Statistics (2020). National survey of micro small & medium enterprises (MSMES) 2017 – 2020. *SMEDAN and National Bureau of*

Statistics Pubs, Abuja, Nigeria, 1, 1–167. Available at: https://smedan.gov.ng/images/NATIONAL%20SURVEY%20OF%20MICRO%20SMALL%20&%20MEDIUM%20ENTERPRISES%20(MSMES),%20%202017%201.pdf

SMEDAN & National Bureau of Statistics (2013). SMEDAN and National Bureau of Statistics Collaborative Survey: Selected Findings (2013). *SMEDAN & National Bureau of Statistics Pubs*, 1, 1–49, Available at: chrome-extension://efaidnbmnnnibpcajpcglclefindmkaj/https://www.smedan.gov.ng/images/PDF/2013-MSME-Survey-Summary-Report.pdf

Steven, N.M. & Edith, A.O. (2012). A study of the practice of the learning organization and its relationship to performance among Kenyan commercial banks. Problems of management in the 21th Century. *Journal of Management*, 2, 22–28.

Stevenson, L. (1990). Some methodological problems associated with researching women entrepreneurs, *Journal of Business Ethics*, 9, 439–446.

Suleiman, T. (2011). Steps up effort in SMEs, inside business, *Thursday Newspapers* published by Leaders and Company Ltd, Lagos.

Surya, B., Menne, F., Sabhan, H., Suriani, S., Abubakar, H., & Idris, M. (2021). Economic growth, increasing productivity of SMEs, and open innovation. *Journal of Open Innovation: Technology, Market, and Complexity*, 7(1), 1–20, ISSN 2199–8531. doi: 10.3390/joitmc7010020

Taiwo, M., Ayodeji, A., & Yusuf, B. (2012). Impact of small and medium enterprises on economic growth and development. *American Journal of Business and Management*, 1(1), 18–22.

Teece, D.J., & Pisano, G. (1994). The dynamic capabilities of firms: An introduction. *Industrial and Corporate Change*, 3(3), 537.

Teece, D.J., Pisano, G., & Shuen, A. (1997). Dynamic capabilities and strategic management. *Strategic Management Journal*, 18(7), 509–533.

Ugwu, M.O., & Omeje, A.N. (2021). Private ownership structure and firm productivity: A firm-level empirical evidence from Nigeria. *South Asian Journal of Social Studies and Economics*, 11(4), 9–22. doi: 10.9734/sajsse/2021/v11i430289

Wiklund, J. (2006). *The Sustainability of the Entrepreneurial Orientation-Performance Relationship*. Entrepreneurship and the Growth of FIRMs, 141–155.

World Bank (2013). *Micro, Small, and Medium Enterprises (MSMEs) Finance*. A World Bank Group Repository.

World Bank (2015). *Small and Medium Enterprises (SMEs) Finance*. A World Bank Group Repository.

World Bank Enterprise Survey (WBES) (2014). *World Bank Enterprise Survey: Understanding the Questionnaire*. Washington, DC. http://www.enterprisesurveys.org

Zachariah, E., Anga, R.A., & Isa, C.G. (2019). *The Determinants of Micro, Small and Medium Enterprises (MSMEs) Performance in Nigeria: Evidence from Business Enterprise Survey*. Munich Personal RePEc Archive.

Chapter 17

Future uses of AI and blockchain technology in the global value chain and cybersecurity

Ramiz Salama

Artificial Intelligence, Software, and Information Systems Engineering Departments, Research Center for AI and IoT, AI and Robotics Institute, Near East University, Nicosia, Mersin10, Turke

Fadi Al-Turjman

Artificial Intelligence, Software, and Information Systems Engineering Departments, Research Center for AI and IoT, AI and Robotics Institute, Near East University, Nicosia, Mersin10, Turkey

INTRODUCTION

Blockchain technology allows for reliable transactions between unreliable network participants since it is a distributed ledger based on encryption. In addition to the present fiat currencies and electronic voucher systems, a number of new blockchain systems, such as Ethereum and Hyper Ledger Fabric, have evolved since the initial Bitcoin blockchain was introduced in 2008. Blockchain technology has recently attracted the attention of an increasing number of scientific studies because of its distinct trust and security characteristics, which has sparked the curiosity of researchers, developers, and business experts. There is no denying the global adoption of blockchain technology. In addition to becoming well-known, it has had a long-lasting effect on the world. For instance, it has become monetized, impacting international financial markets and encouraging the development of dangerous dark web marketplaces. The development of financially motivated attacks on online shops and other companies, including ransomware and denial of service, has also been significantly impacted. Actually, blockchain has far more uses and applications now than when it was first introduced as the first decentralized cryptocurrency in the world. The value of a trustless, decentralized ledger with historical immutability has been acknowledged by other businesses trying to apply the underlying concepts to their current business processes [1–3]. Blockchain technology is a fascinating prospect for many industries because of its special characteristics, including banking, logistics, the pharmaceutical industry, smart contracts, and, most importantly, in the context of this study, cybersecurity. Among those moving beyond Bitcoin payments, the use of the blockchain stands out because it might enable a

DOI: 10.1201/9781003461432-17

new generation of decentralized apps without middlemen and serve as the basis for essential elements of internet security infrastructures. In order to examine how developing technologies might provide solutions to stop dangers from increasing, it is essential to discover recent research that directly relates the use of blockchain technology to the problem of cybersecurity. Knowing what research has already been done on blockchain and cybersecurity requires meticulously mapping out important publications and scholarly works. This chapter focuses on the research that has already been done on the use of blockchains as a supplemental solution for cybersecurity [4].

Artificial intelligence (AI) is a field of research that aims to create machines that are as intelligent as humans but potentially more powerful. Applications for AI span business domains like cybersecurity, data privacy, security, integrity, and accountability. Because it encourages the adoption of cutting-edge technologies in the Fourth Industrial Revolution (IR 4.0), like blockchains, cryptocurrencies, cloud computing, and the Internet of Things (IoT), AI is one of the main engines boosting industrial growth. In fact, the growth of AI has been fuelled by the enormous amount of data produced by IoT devices, social media, and online apps, which is then used to train machine learning algorithms. There are some concerns regarding AI, though. Particularly in light of recent data breaches and other instances of misuse, privacy has become a significant problem. One such instance is the Facebook incident, in which millions of users were mistakenly targeted by the political consulting firm Cambridge Analytica. Because AI cannot interact with or relate to human users, it cannot be evaluated or trusted. As a result, the ability to explain things and the reliability of technology are two additional issues that are growing in significance [5]. Future digital generations motivated by IR 4.0 will shift as AI and blockchain integration accelerates. Contrary to how AI can improve scalability and security while addressing customization and governance challenges for blockchain-based solutions, blockchain can explain the ability, privacy, and trust of AI-powered applications. Blockchain and AI may complement one another by making up for one another's shortcomings despite their stark technological contrasts. The yin and yang of digital business are thus AI and blockchain, with the former assisting in understanding, identifying, and decision-making while the latter aids in execution, verification, and recording, so reducing security breaches. If blockchain is made a payment option on such sites, the lack of security provided by AI in big businesses that use AI to study their purchasing alternatives, such as Walmart and Amazon, can be fixed. Throughout the system, secure information encryption is used to build an effective wall between hackers and user data. Through the use of encrypted data, decentralized information storage, and publicly available ledgers, a new set of cybersecurity goals may be developed. These organizations would be in a position to recognize prospective attacks and the origin of the tampered data quickly [6–8].

Our daily lives have begun to incorporate machine learning and AI technology, which has had a tremendous impact on the IoT's explosive growth. Prof. DUX, an AI learning facilitator, is one of the pioneers in this subject [9]. It is a cutting-edge AI facilitator that seeks to tailor the educational experience for students and offer the quickest and highest-quality education in a variety of subjects.

Previous work extent

Google: Gmail has been using machine learning to filter emails since it launched 18 years ago. These days, nearly all of its services employ machine learning, particularly deep learning, which enables algorithms to self-regulate and make more independent changes. Having more data used to mean encountering more challenges. More data is typically better when it comes to deep learning. Director of the Google IBM/Watson anti-abuse research group, Elie Bursztein: The IBM team is increasingly relying on its Watson cognitive learning platform for "knowledge consolidation" tasks and machine learning-based threat identification. What if some of the repetitive or routine duties now carried out in a security operation centre could be automated using machine learning? The vice president and chief technical officer of security operations and response at IBM Security is Koos Lodewijkx. The networking sector urgently needs creative answers to the problems with the current network economics, according to Juniper Networks. According to Juniper, a cost-efficient, production-ready Self-Driving NetworkTM is the answer to this problem [10, 11].

Using blockchain technologies in cybersecurity

Blockchain, a decentralized, user-operated, secure digital registration and authentication system, is now the biggest security worry. Identity theft is prevented by users' "private keys, which have state-of-the-art encryption mechanisms that ensure that the data is not claimed." The Bitcoin blockchain technology was not well-known when Satoshi Nakamoto released the article in 2008 that made the cryptocurrency public. Nakamoto's original focus on the blockchain as a Bitcoin platform has been built upon and given additional applications by many inventive minds. Data mapping may be enhanced, authentication can be raised, and edge computing can be protected. A few ways that blockchain could enhance cybersecurity are listed below: by leveraging blockchain technology, cybercrimes like identity theft, fraud, and data theft can all be prevented [12–14].

Blockchain enables security apps placed in businesses to authenticate devices and people using distributed key public infrastructure. By removing a single point of failure, the resilient Domain Name System (DNS) entry mechanism utilized by blockchains can increase security. At a single access point, such as a database, network, or data centre, it permits the resolution of single attack points against numerous targets. It enables you to simultaneously thwart single-point attacks as well as attacks with numerous targets, like a server-side attack. A few ways that blockchain could enhance cybersecurity are listed next: by leveraging blockchain technology, cybercrimes like identity theft, fraud, and data theft can all be prevented [12–14]. Blockchain enables security apps placed in businesses to authenticate devices and people using distributed key public infrastructure. By removing a single point of failure, the resilient DNS entry mechanism utilized by blockchains can increase security. At a single access point, such as a database, network, or data centre, it permits the resolution of single attack points against numerous targets. It enables you to simultaneously thwart single-point attacks as well as attacks with numerous targets, like a server-side attack.

Distributed ledger technology (DLT), a decentralized ledger technology, attempts to foster confidence in an unreliable ecosystem in a number of ways. Any encrypted transaction data in the blockchain can be seen, stored, transmitted, and recorded by participant nodes, who have transparent access to all data. Due to security, privacy, and legal issues, businesses from all over the world can connect in their cloud environments using blockchain technology without disclosing important information. A few industries have switched to cryptographic technology built on the idea of a blockchain. Some of the uses for ledger technology include identity management, smart contracts, encrypted communications, and data encryption [15, 16]. Using this technology, parties can work together to execute calculations or store data while maintaining perfect anonymity. It can cover endpoints as well as the full network, including the cloud, cloud storage, and cloud computing. To increase IT security, blockchain technology is being employed more and more in cybersecurity. Instead of creating an exact clone in the event of a breach, the blockchain can be preserved in a single location. It's important to make a distinction between the application of blockchains to cybersecurity and the primary vulnerabilities that hackers use to steal from Bitcoin exchanges. Cryptocurrency exchanges think that blockchain security is insufficient to secure transactions since data must be encrypted before processing. By combining the blockchain with a decentralized system that is immune to such attacks, this problem can be resolved. According to a recent study by the US Department of Homeland Security, fraudsters are already looking into ways to abuse the blockchain despite the fact that it is still in its infancy. Using blockchain technology might increase online security. The information in the register about earlier blocks is linked and sent to hundreds of millions of nodes when a user publishes his public key on the blockchain. This might put not only the user's private key but also the security of the entire network at risk in the case of a network attack. Blockchain technology will enable organizations, people, and governments to safeguard their data, assets, and selves. Although it primarily improves cybersecurity, innovative blockchain utilization has already had an impact on other industries, such as cryptocurrencies [17–19].

Blockchain applications in cybersecurity

1. Blockchain has developed into one of the most secure ways to carry out transactions in the world of digital networks despite the fact that it is not entirely impenetrable. The system has received praise for maintaining information integrity in line with how it was designed and constructed. If implemented properly, it has the ability to help a lot of different businesses. Because it is adaptable, blockchain technology has the potential to be helpful in many different applications. Utilizing its integrity guarantee to offer cybersecurity solutions for a variety of other technologies [20–25] would be one of the better applications. Here are a few instances of how blockchain can be used in the future to enhance cybersecurity:
2. ***Protecting private messaging***: More people are utilizing social media as the internet turns the world into a smaller, more connected village. More social media platforms exist today than ever before. More social applications are often created as conversational commerce gains popularity. These interactions lead to the gathering of a lot of metadata. To protect the platforms and their data, most social networking site users choose weak, unreliable passwords. Blockchain is evolving into a more desirable option when compared to the end-to-end encryption utilized by messaging businesses to safeguard customer data. Using blockchains, a global security protocol can be produced. A standard API architecture for supporting cross-messenger communication might be made using blockchain technology. Numerous assaults on social media sites like Twitter and Facebook have occurred recently. Millions of accounts were compromised as a result of these assaults, and user data was exposed. The use of blockchain technology in these communication systems may be able to prevent similar attacks in the future.
3. ***IoT security***: Hackers are increasingly using edge devices like routers and thermostats to access larger networks. The current infatuation with AI has made it simpler for hackers to get access to more complex systems, such as home automation, and edge devices, like "smart" switches. Most of these IoT gadgets have dubious security capabilities. By decentralizing the management of such massive systems or devices, blockchain can be utilized to secure them. The process will let the gadget choose the security measures it wants to use. Instead of relying on the central admin or authority, edge devices become more secure by recognizing and responding to suspicious requests from unidentified networks. The systems and devices are immediately taken over by the hacker when a device's central administration is breached.

By decentralizing such device authority processes, the blockchain makes sure that such assaults are more challenging to execute.

4. ***Protecting DNS and DDoS***: Users of the target resource are denied access to or service from the target resource when a distributed denial-of-service (DDoS) attacks assault is conducted against the resource, which could be a network resource, server, or website. These assaults compromise or render resource systems useless. As a result of its high degree of centralization, a healthy DNS is a prime target for cybercriminals who manage to sever the connection between an IP address and the name of a website. As a result of this attack, a website can go down, and viewers might be sent to other phony websites. Fortunately, a blockchain can lessen these attacks by decentralizing DNS entries. Hackers may have taken advantage of weaknesses that a blockchain would have prevented by using decentralized methods.
5. ***Decentralizing medium storage***: Businesses are getting more and more worried about theft and data breaches. The vast majority of companies still use centralized storage. To gain access to all of the stored data, a hacker only needs to focus on one area of vulnerability in these systems. Now, a criminal gets access to private and sensitive data, including financial data about businesses. By leveraging blockchains to allow decentralized data storage, sensitive data can be safeguarded. Using this mitigating technique, hackers would find it more challenging, if not impossible, to get access to data storage systems. A lot of storage service providers are looking into how well blockchains protect data from intruders. Blockchain technology has already been employed by the Apollo Currency Team (The Apollo Data Cloud).
6. ***The provenance of computer software***: A blockchain can be used to verify software downloads and prevent tampering with the provenance of a computer program. Similar to how MD5 hashes are used today to authenticate processes like firmware upgrades, installers, and patches, blockchain may be used in the future to stop malicious software from being installed on workstations. The identities of new software are matched against vendor website hashes in the MD5 scenario. The hashes that are accessible on the platform of the supplier might have already been altered, making this strategy insecure. But if you use blockchain technology, the hashes stay in the chain. Blockchains may be more effective in verifying the accuracy of software by comparing its hashes to those on the network because the information stored in technology is irreversible and unchangeable.
7. ***Cyber-physical infrastructure verification***: Information about cyber-physical systems has been impacted by data manipulation, improper system configuration, and component failure. However, by employing the information integrity and verification capabilities of blockchain technology, the state of any cyber-physical infrastructure may be

verified. Blockchain data generated on infrastructure parts might have a longer chain of custody and be more reliable.

8. ***Preventing unauthorized access to data while in transit***: In the future, blockchain might be used to limit access to data while it is in motion. By utilizing the technology's full encryption potential, data transfer can be made secure, prohibiting access from malicious parties, whether they be people or organizations. Data transport between blockchains would significantly increase in integrity and reliability thanks to this method. Malicious hackers seize control of data in transit and alter or delete it as a result. This leaves a significant space for inefficient forms of communication, like emails.

Loss of human safety: The negative effects of cyberattacks: As a result of recent technological advancements, both public transportation and military equipment with unmanned systems have been introduced. The internet, which enables data to go from sensors to databases used for remote control, is the only technology that makes these self-driving vehicles and weapons possible. Fraudsters have tried to access and breach networks like the Car Area Network (CAN) though. Hackers have access to these networks and can take full control of crucial auto systems. The safety of people will be directly impacted by such accidents. However, these problems might be avoided if every piece of data entering and leaving such systems is subjected to blockchain data verification.

The application of artificial intelligence technologies in cybersecurity

- Organizations have a vast attack surface that is always expanding and changing. Depending on the size of your organization, processing up to several hundred billion time-varying data points is needed to properly assess risk.
- In response to this unprecedented challenge, AI-based cybersecurity technologies have been developed to help information security teams reduce the risk of breaches and strengthen their security posture.
- Analysing and improving cybersecurity posture on a human scale is no longer a challenge.
- Because of their ability to quickly analyse millions of events and identify a wide range of threats, including malware that exploits zero-day vulnerabilities and risky behaviour that could result in phishing attacks or the download of malicious code, AI and machine learning (ML) have emerged as critical information security technologies. These algorithms analyse previous data to identify new dangers as they emerge and change over time. By creating profiles for people, resources, and networks based on their behavioural histories, AI can detect and react to deviations from the norm.

- One of the most challenging issues we face is cybersecurity, and AI is best equipped to solve it. ML and AI may be used to "keep up with the bad guys," automating threat identification and response more effectively than conventional software-driven solutions, given today's continuously evolving cyberattacks and plurality of devices.
- Despite this, cybersecurity faces a number of special challenges, such as a severe lack of qualified security professionals, a wide attack surface, tens to hundreds of thousands of devices per company, hundreds of attack vectors, and enormous amounts of data that are beyond the scope of a human problem.

A self-learning, AI-based cybersecurity posture management system should alleviate many of these difficulties. Technology can be used to create a self-learning system that gathers data continually and independently from all of your company's information systems. After data analysis, patterns from millions to billions of signals that are pertinent to the corporate attack surface are correlated. As a result, human teams are given unprecedented levels of intelligence in many cybersecurity fields, including the following:

IT asset inventory is the process of creating a complete, accurate list of every piece of hardware, piece of software, and person who has access to an information system. Inventory classification and measuring business criticality are both important.

Threat exposure: Since hackers, like everyone else, are influenced by fashion, their attire frequently changes. You may be able to prioritize important tasks based on what dangers could be used to attack your company as well as what threats are most likely to be used to attack your organization with the help of AI-based cybersecurity solutions that can give you the most recent information on regional and industry-specific risks.

Control efficacy: Maintaining a high degree of security requires an understanding of the effects of the various security tools and processes you have put in place. AI can help you pinpoint the areas where your InfoSec programme excels and where it falls short.

Breach risk prediction: Based on your IT asset inventory, threat exposure, and control effectiveness, AI-based solutions may estimate how and where you are most likely to experience a breach. This enables you to make advance plans and dedicate tools and resources to your weakest places. By creating and upgrading policies and processes based on prescriptive insights from AI analysis, you can more successfully increase your organization's cyber resilience.

Incident response: AI-powered systems could offer greater context for prioritizing and reacting to security warnings, for quick event response, and for identifying root causes to lessen vulnerabilities and prevent future problems. AI must be intelligible in order to support human InfoSec teams. Analyses and suggestions must be succinct and simple to comprehend. This is necessary for obtaining the backing of all significant internal stakeholders, understanding the ramifications of different InfoSec efforts, and delivering crucial information to all interested parties, such as end users, security operations, the CISO, auditors, CIO, CEO, and board of directors [26–30].

The benefits of AI in cybersecurity

One of the many areas where AI is useful and has applications is cybersecurity. In today's environment of quickly evolving cyberattacks and increasing electronics, AI and ML can help stay up with hackers, automate threat identification, and respond more efficiently than outmoded software-driven or manual operations [31].

Here are a few advantages and applications of AI in cybersecurity:

Identifying fresh threats: AI is capable of identifying dangers and maybe unlawful activity online. AI can be particularly useful in this situation because traditional software systems cannot handle the enormous number of new malware that is produced every week. AI systems are being trained to identify trends in malware and ransomware attacks, as well as to identify even the smallest components of these threats. By applying natural language processing, which gathers data on its own by reading news stories, publications, and cyber threat research, AI offers improved predictive intelligence. There may be information regarding brand-new oddities, cyberattacks, and defence strategies. Hackers constantly alter what is popular with them as trend-followers. You can make better decisions about what is most likely to attack your systems and how it might be done by using AI-based cybersecurity solutions, which can offer up-to-date information on threats that are both generic and industry-specific.

Bots in combat: Nowadays, a considerable amount of internet traffic is caused by malicious bots. Data fraud, creating phony accounts, and using stolen passwords to access accounts are all examples of how bots can be a severe concern. Automated threats cannot be completely defeated by manual responses. Using AI and ML, it is possible to distinguish between real people and website visitors, as well as safe and dangerous bots (such as search engine crawlers). We can analyse enormous amounts of data with the aid of AI, enabling cybersecurity teams to modify their procedures in response to a changing environment. Businesses can find out the answers to the queries, "What does an average user trip look like," and "what does a dangerous, unusual journey look like?" by looking at behavioural patterns. Mark Greenwood, chief technical architect and head of data science at Netacea, claims that moving forward, we will be able to discern the intentions of website users and outwit harmful bots.

***Prediction of breach risk*:** AI algorithms are used to produce the IT asset inventory, which is a precise and thorough list of all devices, users, and apps with various levels of access to various systems. Based on your asset inventory and threat exposure (discussed earlier), AI-based solutions may now estimate how and where you are most likely to be compromised, enabling you to plan and allocate resources to areas with the biggest risks. You may create and enhance cyber resilience policies and practices using prescriptive insights from AI-based analysis.

***Improved endpoint security*:** The protection of all endpoints used for remote work, which makes use of a rising number of devices, depends on AI. Despite the fact that VPNs and antivirus software can shield users from ransomware and other remote malware threats, these solutions mostly rely on signature-based operations. This suggests that staying current with changes to signature definitions is essential if you want to be protected from the most recent dangers. If antivirus software is not kept up to date, or if the creator of the programme is not aware that the virus definitions are outdated, this could be alarming. As a result, signature protection can become useless if a new kind of malware attack appears. A different approach is offered by AI-powered endpoint protection, which makes use of recurrent training to create an endpoint's baseline behaviour. AI is capable of seeing irregularities and, if necessary, taking the right action, such as alerting a technician or reestablishing security after a ransomware attack. Tim Brown, vice president of security architecture at Solar Winds, claims that this approach prevents assaults proactively rather than by waiting for updates to signatures.

CONCLUSION

This research demonstrates how AI has a negative impact on every area of cybersecurity. The effectiveness of CAPTCHA technology has started to decline as AI alternatives for login security progress. The enormous potential for AI-based approaches in the advancement of cybersecurity has been proved by the practical implementation of these techniques in evaluating and identifying any cyberattack on a computer system. Cyberspace breaches are thought to drastically lower the cost of detection and response. It has also been shown that integrating AI methods into the traditional detection method speeds up the process overall by more quickly identifying risks and irregularities. AI algorithms that help with input augmentation, provide a better cybersecurity approach, and other jobs improve the accuracy and spontaneity of the detecting process. Intelligence systems may be created to notify users of potential risks and attacks to which their computer system may be vulnerable, in addition to assisting in the detection process. The blockchain, however, combines scalable, trustworthy data encryption mechanisms, data integrity, and network resilience; thus, it presents numerous chances for maintaining a high level of data security. As a result, organizations in practically every industry may benefit from transitioning from a traditional system to one that is based on a blockchain. Businesses must be prepared to deal with a lot of disadvantages and difficulties when deploying a blockchain to improve the cybersecurity of their products, just like with any new technology. The main issues are dependence on private keys, difficulties adapting, and ignorance.

REFERENCES

[1] Salama, R., Al-Turjman, F., Bhatla, S., & Gautam, D. (2023, April). Network Security, Trust & Privacy in a Wiredwireless Environments–An Overview. In *2023 International Conference on Computational Intelligence, Communication Technology and Networking (CICTN)* (pp. 812–816). IEEE.

[2] Salama, R., Al-Turjman, F., Altrjman, C., Kumar, S., & Chaudhary, P. (2023, April). A Comprehensive Survey of Blockchain-Powered Cybersecurity-A Survey. In *2023 International Conference on Computational Intelligence, Communication Technology and Networking (CICTN)* (pp. 774–777). IEEE.

[3] Salama, R., Al-Turjman, F., Bordoloi, D., & Yadav, S. P. (2023, April). Wireless Sensor Networks and Green Networking for 6G Communication-An Overview. In *2023 International Conference on Computational Intelligence, Communication Technology and Networking (CICTN)* (pp. 830–834). IEEE.

[4] Salama, R., Al-Turjman, F., Bhatia, S., & Yadav, S. P. (2023, April). Social Engineering Attack Types and Prevention Techniques-A Survey. In *2023 International Conference on Computational Intelligence, Communication Technology and Networking (CICTN)* (pp. 817–820). IEEE.

[5] Salama, R., Altrjman, C., & Al-Turjman, F. (2023). Smart Grid Applications and Blockchain Technology in the AI Era. *NEU Journal for Artificial Intelligence and Internet of Things*, 1(1), 59–63.

[6] Salama, R., Alturjman, S., & Al-Turjman, F. (2023). Internet of Things and AI in Smart Grid Applications. *NEU Journal for Artificial Intelligence and Internet of Things*, 1(1), 44–58.

[7] Salama, R., Altrjman, C., & Al-Turjman, F. (2023). A Survey of Machine Learning (ML) in Sustainable Systems. *NEU Journal for Artificial Intelligence and Internet of Things*, 2(3).

[8] Salama, R., Altrjman, C., & Al-Turjman, F. (2023). A Survey of Machine Learning Methods for Network Planning. *NEU Journal for Artificial Intelligence and Internet of Things*, 2(3).

[9] Prof. DUX available online: https://dux.aiiot.website/

[10] Al-Turjman, F., Salama, R., & Altrjman, C. (2023). Overview of IoT Solutions for Sustainable Transportation Systems. *NEU Journal for Artificial Intelligence and Internet of Things*, 2(3).

[11] Salama, R., Altrjman, C., & Al-Turjman, F. (2023). An Overview of the Internet of Things (IoT) and Machine to Machine (M2M) Communications. *NEU Journal for Artificial Intelligence and Internet of Things*, 2(3).

[12] Salama, R., Al-Turjman, F., Altrjman, C., & Bordoloi, D. (2023, April). The Use of Machine Learning (ML) in Sustainable Systems-An Overview. In *2023 International Conference on Computational Intelligence, Communication Technology and Networking (CICTN)* (pp. 821–824). IEEE.

[13] Al-Turjman, F., & Salama, R. (2021). Cyber Security in Mobile Social Networks. In *Security in IoT Social Networks* (pp. 55–81). Academic Press.

[14] Al-Turjman, F., & Salama, R. (2021). Security in Social Networks. In *Security in IoT Social Networks* (pp. 1–27). Academic Press.

[15] Salama, R., & Al-Turjman, F. (2022, August). AI in Blockchain towards Realizing Cyber Security. In *2022 International Conference on Artificial Intelligence in Everything (AIE)* (pp. 471–475). IEEE.

[16] Al-Turjman, F., & Salama, R. (2020). An Overview about the Cyberattacks in Grid and Like Systems. In *Smart Grid in IoT-Enabled Spaces* (pp. 233–247). CRC Press.

[17] Salama, R., Al-Turjman, F., & Culmone, R. (2023, March). AI-Powered Drone to Address Smart City Security Issues. In *International Conference on Advanced Information Networking and Applications* (pp. 292–300). Springer International Publishing.

[18] Salama, R., & Al-Turjman, F. (2023). Cyber-Security Countermeasures and Vulnerabilities to Prevent Social-Engineering Attacks. In *Artificial Intelligence of Health-Enabled Spaces* (pp. 133–144). CRC Press.

[19] Salama, R., Al-Turjman, F., Altrjman, C., & Bordoloi, D. (2023, April). The Ways in Which Artificial Intelligence Improves Several Facets of Cyber Security-A Survey. In *2023 International Conference on Computational Intelligence, Communication Technology and Networking (CICTN)* (pp. 825–829). IEEE.

[20] Salama, R., Al-Turjman, F., Bhatla, S., & Mishra, D. (2023, April). Mobile Edge Fog, Blockchain Networking and Computing-A Survey. In *2023 International Conference on Computational Intelligence, Communication Technology and Networking (CICTN)* (pp. 808–811). IEEE.

[21] Salama, R., Al-Turjman, F., Chaudhary, P., & Banda, L. (2023, April). Future Communication Technology Using Huge Millimeter Waves—An Overview. In *2023 International Conference on Computational Intelligence, Communication Technology and Networking (CICTN)* (pp. 785–790). IEEE.

[22] Salama, R., Al-Turjman, F., Aeri, M., & Yadav, S. P. (2023, April). Internet of Intelligent Things (IoT)–An Overview. In *2023 International Conference on Computational Intelligence, Communication Technology and Networking (CICTN)* (pp. 801–805). IEEE.

[23] Salama, R., Al-Turjman, F., Chaudhary, P., & Yadav, S. P. (2023, April). Benefits of Internet of Things (IoT) Applications in Health Care-An Overview. In *2023 International Conference on Computational Intelligence, Communication Technology and Networking (CICTN)* (pp. 778–784). IEEE.

[24] Salama, R., Al-Turjman, F., Altrjman, C., & Gupta, R. (2023, April). Machine Learning in Sustainable Development–An Overview. In *2023 International Conference on Computational Intelligence, Communication Technology and Networking (CICTN)* (pp. 806–807). IEEE.

[25] Salama, R., Al-Turjman, F., Aeri, M., & Yadav, S. P. (2023, April). Intelligent Hardware Solutions for COVID-19 and Alike Diagnosis-A survey. In *2023*

International Conference on Computational Intelligence, Communication Technology and Networking (CICTN) (pp. 796–800). IEEE.
[26] Garg, A., & Ghatak, A. (2020). An Empirical Study on Power Evacuation Projects' Performance: A Strategic Layout in the Indian Context. *Asia-Pacific Journal of Management Research and Innovation*, 16(1), 31–42.
[27] Ghatak, A., & Garg, A. (2022). Power Transmission Project: A Framework to Align Project Success with Organization Goal. *International Journal of System Assurance Engineering and Management*, 13(4), 1817–1833.
[28] Garg, A., & Singla, N. (2017). Environment Sustainability Awareness Model for IT SMEs. *Interdisciplinary Environmental Review*, 18(1), 1–5.
[29] Garg, A., & Singla, N. (2013). E-Waste vis-à-vis Human Health and Environment. *Interdisciplinary Environmental Review*, 14(3–4), 187–193.
[30] Garg, A. (Ed.). (2023). *Reinventing Technological Innovations with Artificial Intelligence*. Bentham Science Publishers.
[31] Garg, A. (2022). *CoReS-Respiratory Strength Predicting Framework Using Noninvasive Technology for Remote Monitoring during Heath Disasters*. Global Healthcare Disasters: Predicting the Unpredictable with Emerging Technologies, 109–121.

For Product Safety Concerns and Information please contact our EU representative GPSR@taylorandfrancis.com Taylor & Francis Verlag GmbH, Kaufingerstraße 24, 80331 München, Germany